MADAM, HAVE YOU EVER *REALLY* BEEN HAPPY?

MADAM, HAVE YOU EVER *REALLY* BEEN HAPPY?

◆

An Intimate Journey through Africa and Asia

Meg Noble Peterson

To Caitlin,
Adventurous, imaginative,
and not afraid to seek
into the unknown. You will
go far!
Love, Meg

iUniverse, Inc.
New York Lincoln Shanghai

MADAM, HAVE YOU EVER *REALLY* BEEN HAPPY?
An Intimate Journey through Africa and Asia

iUniverse books may be ordered through booksellers or by contacting:

iUniverse
2021 Pine Lake Road, Suite 100
Lincoln, NE 68512
www.iuniverse.com
1-800-Authors (1-800-288-4677)

Qutoations from Peter Matthiessen and Rick Steves are used by permission of the authors.

Cover photo by Brandon Collins

ISBN-13: 978-0-595-34601-1 (pbk)
ISBN-13: 978-0-595-79347-1 (ebk)
ISBN-10: 0-595-34601-4 (pbk)
ISBN-10: 0-595-79347-9 (ebk)

Printed in the United States of America

I dedicate this book to my children,
Cary, Chris, Martha, Tom, and Rob,
With whom I had my first great adventure

May they never lose their sense of wonder
May they never fear walking into the unknown

The sense of having one's life needs at hand, of traveling light, brings with it intense energy and exhilaration. Simplicity is the whole secret of well-being.
　　　　　　　　　—Peter Matthiessen, *THE SNOW LEOPARD*

Solo travel is intensely personal. Without the comfortable clutch of a friend, you're more likely to know the joys of self-discovery and the pleasures found in the kindness of strangers. You will be exploring yourself as well as a new city or country.
　　　　　　　　　—Rick Steves

Contents

ACKNOWLEDGEMENTS

My heartfelt thanks go to Candy Schulman, Rich Usher, J. Carol Goodman, Peg Brown, and Suzanne Roghanchi, whose suggestions and criticism were invaluable in the crafting of this book. I also appreciate the many friends and family members who supported and encouraged me in my explorations, and urged me to tell my story: my sisters, Anne Magill and Cary Santoro; my niece, Dr. Margaret Thickstun; and my friends Jan Slepian, Carole Outwater, AmyNoel Wyman, Judy Wyman, Viola Ellenis, Jane Folger, the late Elizabeth Polk, Lynn Rubright, Karen dePlanque, Jon Pollack, Steve Herman, John Cacavas, Dr. Winston Nelson and Barry Hamilton. Special thanks go to Lee Compton, whose sharing of his travels in the Himalayas was an inspiration to me and greatly enhanced my understanding of the Sherpa people, their customs, and their religion. Of course, my children have always been my staunchest supporters, their battle cry being, "Mother, get *on* with it!"

INTRODUCTION

I wrapped my coat tightly around me, left the gym, and headed into the blustery January morning. A woman from my exercise class caught up with me. "Is it true that you took a trip around the world—alone?" she asked, breathlessly.

"Yes," I answered. "Twelve countries. I was gone almost a year."

She followed along beside me. "You mean to say that you took a whole year out of your life?"

"No, I put a whole year *into* my life!" I tightened my scarf and leaned into the wind. My thoughts turned to Africa and India—the warm beaches, tropical vegetation, endless sun.

"You went with friends, didn't you?"

"No, I went by myself."

"Was it some kind of tour?" she persisted.

"No, I went by myself."

"That's unbelievable," she said. "You actually planned the whole trip—and went all by yourself?"

"Yes." I felt as if my needle were stuck.

This wasn't the first time I'd had such an exchange. People didn't seem to care about the romance, mystery, and adventure I might have experienced during those eight months—only the fact that I had traveled alone—with no man, no advance reservations, and one backpack. At *my* age, too. Was I crazy? Women of all ages told me that they would be terrified making such a trip and I must be very courageous.

On the contrary. Far from being courageous, I was selfish. After thirty-three years of marriage, a divorce, and five grown children who returned periodically to tell me how to live my life, I was excited about being totally on my own, having no schedule, and answering to no one. I couldn't possibly foresee what would happen along the way, but I was well aware of the old saying that the only difference between a rut and a grave is the dimensions. I needed a change! Who would have thought that I would trade the comfort of my home for a bone-chilling tent in the Himalayas. And sneak out in the middle of the night, stepping into yak shit on the way to a pit toilet. No fuzzy rug there to warm my feet. But, oh, those mountains! That I would exchange gourmet dinners in my modern kitchen for hearty custom-made soups created on the spot on a street corner in old Delhi. Not something you'd find in suburban New Jersey. That I would replace my comfortable bed for Indian trains of questionable quality—cold, sooty, and crowded, with my pack chained to the upper bunk. Or that I would find turbaned old men ladling hot milk tea out of boiling cauldrons in cavernous railway stations at dawn more inviting than a Starbucks café with its foaming cappuccino. I was alone at last, facing the world as a whole person, not half a couple. And I felt good about it.

◆   ◆   ◆

My adventure began in 1986 when, after years of accumulating frequent flyer credit, I hit the 60,000 mile mark and was handed a free 'round-the-world ticket by TWA and Qantas—to be used within the year. But after the first flush of excitement at the prospect of tackling the globe single-handedly at the age of fifty-eight, I soon became overwhelmed by all the details and noticed fear creeping in around the edges.

What was I afraid of? True, I'd never been to Africa and Asia, which sounded daunting if you believed the dire warnings about the dangers facing a woman traveling alone. And I was no stranger to foreign travel, having crisscrossed Western Europe in visits to my two daughters, Cary and Martha, who'd lived and worked abroad for seven years. I'd also dipped into several Eastern bloc countries in1980 in conjunction with my work as executive director of the international organization, Music Education for the Handicapped. And in the summer of 1973 I hitchhiked through Germany and Austria with my teenage children. But this would be the first time I'd be traveling with no definite goal, no "worthy" purpose. For a preacher's kid who'd been taught that you have to be doing something worthwhile every minute of the day, just traipsing around the world for fun made me uneasy.

This surprised me, because for years I'd wanted to study the tribal music of Africa and the folksongs of the Third World. And ever since my parents took me up New Hampshire's Mt. Washington at the age of nine, I had been passionately addicted to hiking. I yearned to tackle exotic Mt. Kenya and Kilimanjaro, trek in the Himalayas, walk on the massive Khumbu ice fields, and hike into Everest base camp. These were my childhood dreams and here was my chance to realize them.

I'd taken a leave of absence from my organization. Martha had just gotten married. My mother was healthy, although a bit forgetful. My two sisters were fine. My children were all safe in the United States. Africa was still on the map, albeit in constant turmoil. And the dollar was strong. This would seem like the perfect time to disappear for a while.

The six weeks leading up to my departure were rather typical of the lifestyle I'd cultivated and honed to perfection over the past thirty years. Frantic. First, the house had to be rented. In spite of the many hours I spent talking to real estate agents, it was my second son, Tom, who located an ideal renter while having a drink at a singles bar one month after my departure. God bless Tom!

Next, my body had to be protected. I received every inoculation known to medical science in order to ward off diseases I was afraid even to contemplate. This threw my system into red alert. Upper arms became swollen pincushions, head throbbed, joints ached. I was now protected against any medical exigency.

The day before my departure, however, I received a distressing phone call from my nephew, Chip, a medical student.

"Whatever you do, Aunt Meggie, don't take Fansidar," he warned. "It killed a member of our team in Kenya last summer."

"Are you kidding, Chip? I just packed it!" Fansidar was the alternative antidote for a rare mosquito bite that can't be treated with the traditional chloroquin.

My doctor wasn't much help. "If you get falciparum malaria, the choice is between Fansidar or death. It kills some people, but not others…a little like Russian roulette."

Great! Now I had to locate the world's most powerful bug repellant if I wanted to set foot in the jungle.

The day before leaving, my eldest son, Chris, and I loaded the car with cartons of instruction tapes and music books I'd written for the Autoharp, an American folk instrument manufactured by the company my ex-husband and I owned—until it went bankrupt. We lugged the boxes up the steep stairs to a huge loft in the middle of New York City's meat packing district. This was the office of NobleWorks, Chris's greeting card company specializing in outrageous humor.

I don't know whether Chris promised to manage my small mail order business out of filial devotion, or because I loaned him my car, but I had implicit faith in his ability to keep my accounts in order. The same went for my son, Tom, a successful futures trader on Wall Street. Together, I knew that no matter what might go wrong along the way, they would keep me economically viable as I circled the globe.

I handed both sons eight pages of instructions, spelling out in meticulous detail information regarding my taxes, insurance payments, and credit card obligations. After finishing, I had the gnawing feeling that I'd left something out. Never in my wildest dreams did I imagine that my instructions wouldn't even be read! Eight months later I found a large stack of unopened mail on my kitchen table with a note in bold face: MOM, OPEN IMMEDIATELY. THEY MAY BE IMPORTANT. LOVE, TOM

My bank account was flashing red; my homeowners policy had lapsed; my car had been driven for six months without insurance; I owed hefty penalties on state, local, and federal taxes; American Express had cancelled my card; and my publisher had stopped payment on first and second quarter royalty checks. Welcome home, Mom.

◆   ◆   ◆

The day of my departure arrived—November 14—and by early afternoon I was still cleaning out bureau drawers and putting away medicines and toiletries in cardboard boxes, insulating them with enough plastic to give the mice a run for their money, and stashing them in the attic. It was so full I couldn't even walk through, single file.

For weeks I'd been collecting clothes, medicines, documents, and camera equipment. I piled everything on the double bed and started agonizing over what to take and what to leave. The essentials were no problem. It was all the elective items that gave me grief—like BandAids, small packages of Kleenex, vitamins, and "what if this should happen" stuff. What would I wear if I were invited to meet my ex-husband's friend, the ambassador to Nepal? And what if my walking shoes wore out? Could I ever find a size 10 narrow in all of Africa? Fortunately, I would avoid winter, going from west to east on the world map, so I could eliminate all heavy clothing, renting a down jacket and sleeping bag in Kathmandu for my journey into the Himalayas.

I made my selection, then cut it in half. I looked down at the small pile on the bed. How could someone who had just filled the attic to overflowing live for eight months with so little? My journals weighed more than my clothes. But once the decisions were made, I felt as if I'd extricated myself from a spider web of possessions that had held me prisoner for years.

Aside from my open ticket and passport, the most important item I carried was a pocket-sized leather loose-leaf notebook. It was my very own travel guide. I had organized major geographical areas by color, slipping the names of the African countries into yellow index tabs; India and Nepal, blue; Thailand, Hong Kong, and China, green; and Australia, New Zealand, Fiji, and Hawaii, red. I wrote a tentative timetable at the beginning of every section and listed places I absolutely must not miss. I pasted a small map on the first page of each country category, since my sense of direction is so bad that I don't know where I am even when I'm there. Then came the addresses of people to look up, special notes about hostels or hotels, and the location of the American consulate and American Express offices in each country I planned to visit.

Taped under "expenditures" was a guide to the money exchange, which, along with a tiny hand calculator, gave me some idea of the value of each currency in relation to the dollar. And under "miscellaneous" were extra passport pictures and the addresses of eighty-five friends and relatives who had received my itinerary and promised to write, care of American Express. I promised to answer every letter I received, and I did.

It was two hours before I was to leave, but the phone would not stop ringing. It's great to have friends, but not when you're trying to make a plane. Everyone had advice, or wanted to sell me something, like a last minute limited partnership or a thief-proof money belt. Fortunately, my mother is not long-winded. Nor does she worry. But my ex-husband is another story. He was sure I was throwing my life away by not writing articles for the local newspaper—single woman encounters lions in Africa—that sort of thing.

"I really can't talk now, Glen, I'm in a screaming hurry."

"You're always in a hurry," he said. "Here I am giving you a wonderful opportunity to make some money and Nick says you haven't even called, yet. He's a crackerjack editor. And a friend. Why are you being so antagonistic?"

"Glen, we're divorced. Remember? You don't need to help me anymore. I can help myself. But thanks, anyway. On this trip I just want to absorb life for a change, not write about it. I also don't want to miss my plane." Why did he get to me so? Always leaving me with feelings of sadness and guilt.

I was grateful for 'call waiting.' It was Chris. "Where are you, Mother?"

"Where do you think I am? You just called me, didn't you?"

"Very funny. You're an hour late, and Robert is here in the office, waiting to say goodbye, and waiting for the typewriter." Robert, my youngest son, was being given custody of the typewriter while I was gone. Computers had not yet taken over our lives.

"Did you read my list?" I asked.

"No, but we can discuss all that on the way to the airport. Now get going this minute!" He hung up.

Sit down. Breathe deeply. Then slowly go from room to room and take stock....How bare the refrigerator door looked with all the children's photos gone. *Don't think about the refrigerator, or the leaves still on the lawn, or the hanging plants that will be dead in a month. Just don't forget your backpack.*

It was less than three hours to plane time when I roared out of the driveway. A money belt was fastened securely around my waist. My blue pack sat majestically in the back seat alongside the camera bag, which housed my new camera and enormous telephoto lens. It also doubled as a purse and survival kit (comb, collapsible toothbrush, small flashlight, vitamin C, emergency toiletries).

Stashed in one pocket of the bag were single-edged razor blades and a thick guide to Africa. Everything had been carefully planned, down to the amount of weight I'd save if I sliced out all the pages of the countries I wouldn't be visiting. But first I was going to read about them on the way over. I certainly couldn't sleep fourteen straight hours on the plane.

Five o'clock traffic was building up as I reached Chris's office. He came running out. "Forget the typewriter. Robert couldn't wait," he said, jumping into the car and slamming the door. "Gee, Mom, couldn't you have cut it a little closer?"

I jammed the car into first, did a U-turn and headed for the highway. The ride to the airport was probably the most dangerous part of my trip. I almost missed the turn-off. Chris dived to the floor as I cut in front of a tractor trailer truck to reach the small, hardly-visible exit off the Van Wyck Expressway leading into Kennedy Airport.

"How about that?" I shouted gleefully. "One hour from Midtown to Kennedy…during peak traffic. That's some kind of record!"

When I reached customs, Chris hugged me, then held me at arm's length as if to get one last look before letting me loose. He had a sober, yet slightly quizzical expression on his face.

"Listen, Mom," he said. "Have a great time and try not to take life so seriously. For once, just enjoy yourself. You'll see so many new places, meet so many people, have so many adventures. You'll be a completely different person when you return."

"Oh, Chris, do you really think so?" I asked.

"Well," he said. "We all have our fingers crossed!"

1

CAIRO

The lights of New York City disappeared. Suddenly I felt the loss of this connection as never before. I was totally on my own. Now only the moon relieved the blackness, which surrounded and held me as the plane headed out over the north Atlantic.

I lay back, trying to quiet my swirling emotions. Suddenly, from a place within me a little voice cried out, "O.K., lady, you've got what you wanted. Now what are you going to do with it?" True. I craved adventure. I wanted to test the limits of my endurance. Discover exotic places. Flirt with danger. Meet new people. But I was cutting myself loose from everything I knew, every support I had. My entire family. I was fed up with the monotonous daily responsibilities. The broken shingles, the wet basement, the lawn maintenance. I needed a new challenge. And I needed to get away from the still-present conflict with my ex-husband. From my dependency on men.

I also needed time to think. Alone. My son, Chris, said I'd be a totally different person when I returned. What did he mean? More content, less driven? Sorted out? Slowly my worries were swallowed by the soporific roar of the engines. Excitement and anticipation battled with apprehension. In the end excitement won.

Fourteen hours later we began our descent into Cairo. I looked out the window. The great Giza plateau was spread out beneath me. Highlighted in the late afternoon sun were Egypt's most famous pyramids—Cheops, Chephren, and Mykerinos—until now only storybook giants, relics of an ancient civilization.

I walked off the plane into a shiny new airport. Marble stairs led to the customs office. Already the contrast between the old and the new was enormous. I got a glimpse of myself in a mirrored corridor. My money belt had worked its way northward, making a sizeable lump just below my sternum. My two-piece cotton outfit clung to my body, limp and rumpled. In such a state of disarray and fatigue, it's no wonder that I forgot the warning of my travel agent, Carmela.

"Whatever you do," she had said, "never change more money than is absolutely necessary when you arrive in a foreign country."

Her words, unfortunately, remained buried in my subconscious until it was too late.

"Give me $300 worth of pounds," I said to the cashier. This was twice the required minimum. I figured that I could always change the extra pounds back into dollars when I left the country. I didn't know, as I accepted the small pink slip, my "proof of exchange," that there was a thriving black market in dollars in Egypt, which the government was trying desperately to eradicate by requiring proof of exchange for all major transactions—like hotel bills, tours, and airline tickets.

A fellow American, standing in front of me in line, changed the minimum amount, and stopped to watch as I signed over my traveler's checks.

"You mean you didn't bring dollars?" he asked.

"No," I replied. "Only the fifty my son slipped me at the airport—for emergencies."

"Too bad. You can get a helluva lot more for your dollars on the street than in here."

Just before I left home I called my old friends, Hamal and Judy Wasim. I knew they lived in Dokki, a residential area of Cairo and I wanted to be sure to see them. I had no intention of barging in, since I'd proclaimed to all and sundry that I wanted to be totally on my own. But they insisted that I come. Inwardly I was overjoyed not to have to find a hostel on my first night in Egypt. "Go to the Dokki-Sheraton," they said, "and we'll pick you up." I decided, instead, to surprise them.

Once through customs, I stepped outside the terminal. "Limousines," which looked like little black cabs, were lined up at the curb, spewing forth exhaust fumes of a magnitude far in excess of their size. The drivers were waving their arms and shouting. I walked over to one and asked the price to Dokki.

"Six Egyptian pounds, about four U.S. dollars," replied the pudgy, smiling driver, bowing courteously. "Don't worry. Cab fares are regulated by the government."

My mistake was to believe him. In Egypt you bargain for everything, and when you've agreed on a price, you stick to it. It's a game that everybody plays. It's half the fun of doing business. On this first night, however, I was innocent—a perfect touch for my affable driver.

"Do you know, Madam, you are lucky. There are 650 cabbies in Cairo and I am one of two who speak English." I believed that, too, and considered myself blessed.

"On the right is the famous statue of Ramses II," he said, launching into an unsolicited tour of Cairo by sunset. "And on the left is the stadium where Sadat was assassinated and later buried." I felt a chill go through me, remembering the day it happened.

We roared down a wide boulevard lined with palm and eucalyptus trees, past American College and Cairo University—their modern buildings in marked contrast to the proud obelisks that cut into the orange sky along the route.

"You have picked a good time to come," he continued. "It is big holiday—the First Day of Mohammed—and traffic is not much."

I shuddered to think how I'd have fared had traffic been normal, for this mild-mannered fellow was a wild man behind the wheel. He never hesitated at stop signs. And traffic lights were obeyed only if a policeman was in sight.

It was completely dark by the time we reached Dokki. The heat poured in through my open window and the car bounced unmercifully over the cobblestones as we inched our way up and down the side streets, searching for a readable street sign. Shops, cafés, and outdoor markets were open for the holiday and jammed with people.

"Just take me to the Sheraton," I said, at last. I could not bear to hear this paunchy little fellow complain about his back one more time as he laboriously got out of the cab to ask directions.

"That would cost an extra three pounds, Madam," he said. I should have paid it.

In an effort to show renewed vigor in the search, my driver gunned the motor and swung around a corner, going full blast. As he did, a skinny dog followed by several noisy boys brandishing sticks, scooted in front of him. "Watch out," I screamed.

Too late. There was an awful thud as the driver hit the brakes and swerved, pitching me to the other side of the seat. Before I could recover we had come to an abrupt stop astride the midsection of a well-stocked vegetable stand. The dog and the boys had vanished.

The little man shot out of the car, not even stopping to turn it off. Everybody was shouting, but nobody seemed to be hurt. The vendor and driver were nose to nose. Oranges, melons, and lemons, thrown onto the hood in the crash, were dancing haphazardly to the vibration of the motor.

"The dog," I hollered, when I had gotten my bearings. "What about the dog?" I scrambled out of the car and headed for the place where I had last seen him. Tears started. I was remembering my little black cocker spaniel that had been killed by a hit-and-run driver when I was ten years old.

I pushed my way through the crowd. "Excuse me, I'm looking for a dog. Please, he must be here somewhere." I fully expected to see a bleeding carcass. Instead, people were looking at me as if I were crazy. Why make such a fuss over a stray dog? They didn't know that I came from a society that pampered dogs, treating them like a member of the family…and sometimes better.

The driver was at my side. "Who cares about a dog?" he bellowed. "Look at my cab. I could *kill* that dog!" I walked back to the cab in disbelief.

Fifteen minutes later the driver hobbled back, wiping his brow with an old kerchief and muttering to himself. We said nothing until we'd reached the Wasim's.

Judy ran out to open the gate. She gasped when she heard the driver's price.

"Twenty pounds? That's outrageous! Meg, my dear, you should pay no more than half."

"Madam," began the driver, "Do you know how many times I had to stop and ask for directions, and how difficult it is to get around Cairo at night, and…." There was a sigh, a rolling of the eyes, a sad look. I put my hand on his shoulder to silence him.

"You were wonderful and very helpful," I said. "You gave me such a great tour of Cairo. It was worth every pound. And I'm very sorry about the accident." He grinned, and nearly shook my hand off my arm before departing.

Judy and Hamal Wasim live half a year in London and the other half in Cairo. I met them in Denmark when I was running an international symposium on music and medicine, and decided right then that if I ever married again, they would be my model. Hamal, an Egyptian, is a prominent medical doctor, author, and composer—the kind of Renaissance man women die for. Judy is English and was a concert pianist before she settled down to teaching. She met Hamal—ten years her junior—after having given up all hope of ever finding a man she'd want to live with the rest of her life. Twenty years later the two of them still behaved like young lovers.

I stepped into a large foyer—dark paneling, ornamental brass fixtures, heavy carpets. The downstairs rooms were occupied by Hamal's mother, who had already retired for the night. Hamal and Judy lived upstairs. Judy looked radiant, her stylishly cut salt and pepper hair complementing her gray wool sweater. We hugged like a couple of old school chums. The two years since our last meeting evaporated.

She grabbed me by the hand and rushed me up the back stairs to greet Hamal. He seemed thinner, more angular, his pale olive skin in marked contrast to the thick black hair and full moustache. But I could feel the same old magnetism as he spoke.

"So here's our crazy Meg at last. I never thought you'd do it. You actually left everybody to fend for themselves, and now you plan to disappear into Africa."

"As much of Africa as I have time for," I said. "Kenya, Tanzania, Zimbabwe, South Africa, maybe Zambia, you name it. Then it's on to India and Nepal...and then...but first I'm hoping to disappear into the Sinai. And when I return, I'll sail up the Nile in a *felucca*—to test the waters."

"Whoa, lady. I can tell you without even testing, that they're frightfully polluted," said Judy. "And if you go by *felucca* you'll end up adding to the pollution. Ever seen one of those old scows up close? They don't come with beds, just hard wooden benches. Or toilets. There's just the good old Nile. The trick is to hang your bum overboard without falling in. If you're a contortionist, it's easy...but even as adventurous as you are, Meg, I can't picture you mooning the Nile."

"That's something I hadn't thought of," I said. "But I've always wanted to ride in a *felucca* and I'll be damned if I'll leave Egypt until I do. Besides, how else will I go up the Nile? I certainly won't take a commercial tour."

"Don't worry. We'll figure it out. We'll go to the Sheraton tomorrow. They have all kinds of alternatives." She put her arm around me. "Come on, let's have some tea."

Judy scurried around the small kitchen, preparing tea while Hamal and I moved into the sitting room. It was like an inviting salon—pillows on low couches, French doors opening onto a long balcony, floor-to-ceiling bookshelves, woven carpets in muted tones. We sat around an oval table in one corner of the room, talking late into the night, drinking tea, and eating grainy whole wheat pita bread, cream cheese, honey, and tiny green bananas.

In the middle of the night I was aware of dogs barking and angry shouts. I awoke in a cold sweat, shaken by vivid images of the dog we had hit and of my own dead puppy. Where *was* I? I switched on the light. Then slowly I sank back into unconsciousness.

It was 11 A.M. before I shook off my stupor, opened the heavy shutters, and ventured onto the balcony. I looked down at an old stone courtyard rimmed with shrubbery and flowers. Sun sifted through the thick leaves of a jacaranda tree.

The street was quiet, but in the distance jackhammers chattered and dust swirled around half-built structures that looked like bombed-out buildings after a war.

I soon discovered that nobody escaped the continual construction going on in Cairo. Down the street from these solid old stucco houses was an empty lot, and next to that a demolition crew at work, and next to that the rising girders of a new building. All of Cairo was in flux, a swarming, churning anthill of never-ending activity.

"How did you like the barking dogs last night?" asked Hamal, his dark eyes peering out from under finely arched brows. An impish smile on his face. We were sitting at the table eating a traditional Egyptian breakfast of brown beans, cooked overnight, then dowsed in heavy oil and sprinkled with cumin.

"So it was real after all. I thought maybe I was having nightmares because of the cab hitting that dog."

"Yes, it was real all right. Moslems don't believe in keeping dogs as pets, and they're not very sympathetic about the ones that roam wild in the streets. This is a sound you'll have to get used to as you travel in this part of the world."

"You'll also have to get used to the soldiers," he continued. "We're living in a police state, contrary to what anybody says, and it's very sad."

"Better not start on politics now, Hamal. Meg has to get to the Registry *tout de suite* and show her passport to the police. After all, they have to know she's here…officially." She gave an exaggerated salute.

"That's exactly what I mean," said Hamal. "Putting Meg through a labyrinth of bureaucratic nonsense. For what? A census of all tourists? Ridiculous. Egypt is already drowning in paper. What are they going to do, throw her in jail if she fails to register?"

"You may have noticed that Hamal is not too happy with the government," Judy said as we hopped into her new Russian Niva, a jeep-like four-wheel drive vehicle outfitted for desert travel.

We arrived at the Registry. It was drab and uninviting. "This is one ugly building," said Judy, vehemently. "I wish they'd demolish it, since they seem to be tearing down all of Cairo, block by block."

There were no legal parking spaces left, so Judy stayed with the car and I entered the huge building alone. I felt small and somewhat intimidated. I knew this was a routine procedure, normally handled by the hotels, but since I was staying in a private home, I had to make a personal visit to the local authorities.

A wide circular staircase led to the fourth floor landing. I peered over the railing and down to the entrance far below. It was like so many of those old-fashioned government buildings—the kind that dare you to jump into the hole and see if you can land safely on the marble floor. It reminded me of the rotunda in the Richmond, Virginia, city hall where my husband, Glen, had been an assistant city manager in 1953, a year after our first child was born. We lived in a tiny apartment and paid $75 a month for rent. Our one appliance was an old Bendix washer with a clothesline for a dryer. We drove a 1949 Volkswagen beetle—rather unconventional in those days. But who cared? We were happy, looking forward to the time when he would be a city manager in his own right. There were no storm clouds, yet, in our future.

I turned and walked through a maze of corridors, noticing the water stains on the once grand ceilings and the paint flaking off the walls. Barefoot children played tag. Young women, holding their babies, sat on the floor amidst piles of plaster. Everyone was waiting. And everyone was smoking. They stopped talking and stared at me as I walked by. Or were they glaring? Angry or just curious? I felt uncomfortable, a little threatened.

Policemen and soldiers gave me directions. They seemed well meaning, but each one contradicted the other. Soon I was totally lost. Now I felt stupid.

Each time I stuck my head into one of the stuffy, cage-like offices to ask a question, there would be tittering and embarrassment, and "the one who speaks English" would be pointed out. I was an oddity—a lone tourist fending for herself, without even a hotel manager to run interference.

By the time I reached "cage" 44, my feet were burning and perspiration had soaked my hair and clothes. Would I ever find my way out?

A man was stamping each page of a very fat ledger book with such ferocity that his moustache trembled, while another man, standing next to him at the high, barred window, hurriedly turned the pages, wetting his forefinger now and then to expedite the process. Neither man looked at the list of names on each page. They worked like machines, expressionless. Stamp. Turn. Stamp. Turn.

After waiting for the entire book to be stamped, I stated my business and was handed a card—exactly like the one I filled out at the airport. Without even examining what I'd written, the man stamped the card, and I was free to leave.

Miraculously, I found my way back down the hall past the staring women, negotiated the circular staircase at a gallop, and fled the dreary building. Judy was parked in a cluster of cars, each one facing in a different direction.

"You were right," I said as I jumped in. "This place is crumbling and should definitely be demolished. But crazy as it is, everyone tried to be helpful. I think they sympathized with me."

I sat back, exhilarated at having come through my initial encounter with Egyptian bureaucracy unscathed. I'm glad I didn't know what lay ahead.

2

INTO THE SINAI

It's—how do you say it, refreshing?—to meet someone who really wants to see my country and not just its monuments," said Umar, the young man who ran the travel desk at the Sheraton-Dokki.

It was late afternoon. Judy had just driven me to the Sheraton. I still hadn't firmed up my plans when I stumbled upon Umar and convinced him that I didn't want the usual tourist fare.

"There's a luxury bus trip to the little town of St. Catherine in the Sinai and an overnight stay at the Greek orthodox monastery located there—in the shadow of Mt. Moses," he suggested. "You know. Mt. Moses, the former sacred Mt. Horab."

"Of burning bush and Ten Commandments fame?" I asked.

"That's the one," he replied.

How perfect! I was afraid the Sinai might be off limits because of Arab-Israeli disputes. "And Mt. Moses. Are we allowed to climb it?"

"Every morning before dawn pilgrims gather to climb up and watch the sunrise," he said. "You may join them if you wish. It's very beautiful...sunrise in the Sinai." I was hooked.

"But why the luxury bus?" I asked, fearing that it would come with loud music and an even louder tour guide.

"It's air-conditioned. Have you ever been on the desert in this heat? For a Westerner, it is not an adventure. It is a disaster." That's all he had to say. I'd do anything to escape the heat. That's why I head out of New Jersey for the mountains every summer.

He started writing out a ticket for a bus leaving at 7 A.M. "Oh, no," I cried. "I'm still in the throes of jet lag. Please, don't you have a later one?"

"Yes, but you'll have to buy that ticket yourself at the bus station—tonight."

This seemed strange, but I set out, immediately, to find the station. Umar had written the address in Arabic on a slip of paper. I handed it to a cabbie and asked the price. He whistled, then rolled his head from side to side. "Oooh, long way," he said. "Ten pounds."

Having been initiated into the art of bargaining the night before, I was prepared. "Ten pounds is too much," I said, and started to get out of the cab.

"Wait, Madam," said the driver, putting up his hand and smiling. "Eight?"

I continued to get out of the cab.

"No problem," he said. "O.K. Five."

I smiled and got back into the cab. I had passed the test.

It was late by the time I arrived back at the Sheraton to begin my walk home. The streets were dark and I was apprehensive about being alone. There were few unaccompanied women, and even fewer streetlights. So I decided to behave as if I were in New York City and walk with authority—long strides, head held high, no looking around, no gawking.

Twice, young men came alongside and started talking, asking where I was from and whether I liked Cairo and if I was lost. I quickened my step, becoming increasingly nervous. They fell in alongside me, matching my step. I looked at their faces, their sleek, slender bodies. Dark hair carefully combed, a thick black moustache, long aquiline nose, olive skin. Certainly not sinister.

"There's no problem," I said, trying not to show my rising panic. "I'm fine. I know where I'm going." Was my predicament so obvious? I thought I was walking with authority….

All of a sudden I became suspicious of this solicitude. A new ingredient had been slipped into the conversation. "Madam, since you are a stranger to our city," it began, in precise English, "let me call my sister. She would love to meet you. She has a perfume factory. Sadly, it is going out of business. Perhaps you would like to visit it…a lovely lady like you uses perfume, yes?"

Now I understood. This friendliness was only part of a sales pitch—not a prelude to robbery or seduction. I felt a little ashamed, but was very glad when I reached my street and could gracefully bid my pursuers good evening.

Early the next morning, after promising Judy I'd return in two days, I stuffed my provisions into an old cloth sack, slung a canteen of boiled water over my shoulder, and made my way through the sprawling city to the Sheraton. Swirling sand nipped at my ankles as I strode past a hodgepodge of coffee houses, gardens, mosques, and shops. Colorful vendors selling fabric, rugs, and fresh vegetables hawked their wares loudly in tuneful chants. When I closed my eyes it took on the quality of a Middle Eastern Beggar's Opera, a Kurt Weill fugue for the common man. One-story cubicles with no windows and flat metal roofs, the entire front open, lined the streets and unpaved alleys. I peered through the openings and could see the actual work being done—repairing cars, mending upholstery, sewing clothes, cooking. Prosperous establishments abutted hovels. One merchant swept the hard mud walkway in front of his store, while his neighbor hosed down a fancy tiled sidewalk. A donkey eating out of a bucket stood in the gutter in front of a parked Mercedes. A young woman dressed in rags sat dejectedly on the curb between two cars, a baby in her arms.

In the midst of these contradictions, chaos ruled the road. Horns beeped constantly, and a free-for-all at intersections kept the pedestrians agile. I had become a skillful jaywalker by the time I reached the Sheraton. I found a cab, handed the driver Umar's slip of paper from the previous day, and gambled. "Three pounds," I said.

He looked at the paper, then at me, and nodded.

So, I *had* been taken last night after all.

The iron gates of the bus station were opened for me by a wooden-faced soldier. A motley crowd was already milling around the dirt courtyard: a barefooted old man with a droopy gray moustache and soiled turban; young men wearing *gallakas*, the ankle-length dress of the Arab; four western students with backpacks; and soldiers in faded khaki uniforms. I was the only woman. Buses came and went, emptying their foul exhaust into the air, which encircled the customers who sat on wooden benches, waiting. I decided to go inside to change my film and get away from the stink. As I opened my camera, a soldier came rushing over and wagged his index finger at me. He looked very fierce, not the kind to be swayed by charm.

"But I'm just loading it," I protested.

He shook his head and reached for the camera. I pulled away, slammed it shut, and fled out the door to join the safety of the lengthening line of passengers.

My bus finally arrived. Was this Umar's idea of luxury? It made the Toonerville Trolley look like the Orient Express. The sides and fenders were badly dented, and graffiti-like bright aqua Arabic lettering wrapped around the body.

We filed in and I found a seat by the window. Everyone lit up! So this was a smoker, too. Through the haze I could barely see the curious mementos plastered all over the windshield. A scalloped fringe, white to simulate clouds, and bordered in Kelly green, hung across the top with a horseshoe tacked to the midpoint. A large picture of Nasser was pasted on the right side. Above it glowed a decal of a curvaceous blonde whose full red lips were clearly visible under a thin veil. Bright-colored trinkets hung from the dashboard and rear view mirror. This was, indeed, an imaginative driver.

The bus departed on Egyptian time—90 minutes late—got as far as the corner, and rattled to a standstill. Several men jumped out and pushed it into what looked like a bus graveyard—a dusty, garbage-littered lot strewn with old metal carcasses. More men piled out of a nearby tin shack, and together they formed a semicircle around the driver, listening intently. The men prodded, the bus coughed. The rest of us hung out of the windows, watching.

By the time we chugged out onto the bumpy roads of the outskirts of Cairo, my confidence in the vehicle's safety was completely shattered. It was then that the driver decided to check the horn. There was little traffic, but he honked anyway. A grizzled man sitting in front of me turned on his radio, blasting us with the plaintive wail of Arabian music. Mixed with the clanking of the bus and the honking of the horn, the resulting sound mimicked a convention of yowling cats at midnight. As for air-conditioning, if opening the windows and letting the hot desert air mingle with the thick smoke of pipes and unfiltered Turkish cigarettes defines air-conditioning, we had it!

I sat next to a personable young Egyptian engineer named Isham, who was going a few towns beyond Suez. The seats were so narrow that we were practically in each other's lap. Suddenly the bus lurched and I spilled my canteen while trying to juggle my sandwich and keep my camera bag off the floor. I shrieked, inadvertently dumping the rest of the water on the floor and soaking Isham's pack and newspaper. The cheese, melted by the heat, oozed out of my sandwich onto his neatly pressed pants.

"No problem, no problem," he assured me, but I was mortified.

Only after I'd cleaned up the mess did I dare ask him to teach me a few words of Arabic. He agreed, and I filled several pages of my journal before succumbing to severe mental fatigue. I tried taping his voice on my pocket-sized recorder, but it was impossible, because of the roar of the engine and the whining Arabian rock. The music seemed to have no beginning and no end. After two hours I leaned forward and asked the man to turn it down. Please. He looked crestfallen.

"It is love song," he said. "You not like?"

"Yes, but it is too much love song for me," I replied.

The land was flat as we drove toward the canal. Lone sentry boxes stood guard over long stretches of empty desert. Tire tracks in the sand mysteriously appeared and disappeared as if leading to invisible army camps. I longed for a rest stop. I'd run out of water. Sweat matted my hair. My clothes were stuck to the seat. And all I could see for miles was desolation.

A rest stop at last! A sign hung by the road—"6 October, 1973"—commemorating the war between Egypt and Israel. Men milled about in a thatched hut in which cooked beans, bread, fruit juice, and soft drinks were served. I drank a can of mango juice, my first introduction to the thick, sweet liquid. It was heavenly!

Near a barbed wire fence, where the wind had piled up broken glass and paper, I caught sight of several Bedouins in flowing desert garb kneeling in the sand, facing Mecca. I watched, fascinated, as they went through their ritual prayers, bowing low and resting their heads and arms on the ground. How hot they must be, I thought.

"Why are we stopping again?" I asked Isham. I had been dozing, drugged by the heat, and feeling a little queasy from all the smoke.

"It's the Suez Canal. We're at the tunnel. It has only one lane, so we'll have to wait." Grass-covered mounds, like green velvet tombs, led to a square tunnel. Palm trees lined the route. Soldiers stood at attention. My heart leapt when I saw the tall black letters: **SINAI**.

"Oh, Isham, please ask the driver if we can get out," I begged. "I want to see the canal.

He shook his head. "We are only allowed to go underneath it. Look at all the guards." I craned my neck to get a glimpse of this historic place, the site of so much romance and so much international turmoil. I remembered studying about it in grade school. And swooning over Tyrone Power who played the dashing industrialist Ferdinand deLesseps in the 1938 movie, "Suez," with Loretta Young and Annabella.

A blur of sky and grass filtered through the dusty windows as we entered the gleaming tunnel. On the other side ships of many sizes were lined up in the Gulf of Suez waiting to enter the locks, while the sun—almost blinding—danced on the water.

As we headed down the coast, the landscape changed dramatically. There were no more palm trees. Instead, distant plateaus and buttes appeared on the horizon, out of which arose dramatic pillar-like formations. They reminded me of Arizona, Utah, the Bad Lands of South Dakota—all places I'd visited eighteen years earlier on a trailer trip across the United States with my children.

The mountains, with rivers of sand cascading down their sides, seemed to grow before my eyes. I could see where the earth had heaved up huge rock masses, and bands of different colored layers swirled around them, like giant ribbons entwined in a thick braid of rusts, yellows, browns, and midnight black. I felt very much a part of this undulating landscape—traveling in the old bus, without air-conditioning to insulate me.

We stopped in a small town. Isham jumped up and offered his hand. "I leave here," he said. "I go to my new job." He had taken a job with a company that generated electricity for the many small communities in the Sinai. He was very excited…and a little scared. "Good luck, Isham," I said, giving him an impulsive hug. "Have a happy life." I followed his powerful stride as he walked off the bus. Just as the bus jerked forward, he turned around, grinned at me, and waved. Then he was gone.

The water of the Gulf was still very blue in the waning light, and the mountains had taken on that picture book look of the craggy pink peaks of the Sinai. I was a little girl, again, sitting on my grandfather's lap, looking at his old bible—faded pastel pictures of the Holy Land that he, an old-time preacher, never got to see. A feeling of contentment washed over me.

I thought of Catherine, the martyred saint who was tortured and beheaded in 300 AD because of her Christian faith. The monastery I would visit a few hours from now was built in the era of Justinian, 527-565 AD, in her honor. The suffering she must have endured at the hands of her captors was sobering.

Before leaving the Gulf, we passed several grim shantytowns and small inland settlements, oases where the scant vegetation was surrounded by rock walls. Soon a few spindly pines began to appear. Sand no longer encircled the rocks. We were almost out of the desert and the stifling heat was behind us. Way in the distance I could see another range of mountains stretching in purple layers toward the horizon.

At six o'clock, as darkness fell, the old bus rattled to a stop. We had arrived at St. Catherine's—a mere two hours late.

3

SUNRISE ON MT. MOSES

The four young men with backpacks hopped off the bus at a small café.

I hesitated. This looked like the middle of nowhere. But I got off, anyway, and followed them down the unpaved road.

A pickup truck started out of the parking lot behind me and I waved for it to stop. "Going to the monastery?" I asked the driver.

"No, but I'll drop you at the hotel. It's only a short walk up the hill from there." It was getting darker and I had no idea how far the monastery was. "I can take your friends, too," he added.

They're not my friends, yet, I thought, but they will be soon, if I get them a ride. I motioned to them. "Going to the monastery?" I asked. They nodded. "Then hop in." We squeezed into the open back.

"Thanks," said a tall, sandy-haired man. "I'm David. I'm on my way to Zaire—that is, after I climb Kilimanjaro. And this is my buddy Tray." My eyes took in a dark-haired fellow, lean and handsome. Made me think of my son, Tom.

"Aren't you headed in the wrong direction?" I asked.

"Yeah, looks like it," David answered. "I have a grant to do anthropological research for a year, but I don't start until January. So I'm going to cover as much of Africa as I can before that. Tray, here, is just going along for the ride. A Louisiana boy with nothing better to do." We laughed as Tray threw a mock punch. David was Canadian, but had just graduated from Wesleyan University in Connecticut.

I turned to a plump blond fellow sitting next to David. "Nigel, a renegade banker, that's me." he said. "Been living on a kibbutz for the better part of a year. Jolly good, actually."

"What's a banker doing on a kibbutz?" I asked.

"Well, one day I came to work, looked at all the bored faces I'd been looking at for eight years, turned right around and walked out—just buggered off.

Thought I'd get as far from London as I could, and try a completely different life-style. And I did." He introduced his traveling companion, Greg, a skinny Australian spray painter turned teacher of disabled people in Melbourne. They'd met while living in Israel. Greg—funny, the clown, and Nigel—reserved, and droll. Perfect foils.

What a varied lot we were—two Americans, one Canadian, one Englishman, and an Australian, bumping along a lonely road in the Sinai in a pickup truck driven by an Egyptian. And I was old enough to be the mother of them all.

None of the four had heard of the traditional climb up Mt. Moses, so I spent the rest of the ride persuading them to join me. All but Tray seemed willing. "Sounds like a lot of work," he said. "And I hate to get up early. Besides, I've got the runs."

"You'd better hurry," yelled the driver when he dropped us off at the cross-roads near a seedy imitation of a Swiss chalet. "Those monks are strict about closing time."

We walked silently and rapidly up the hill. The rocky terrain was forbidding in the white glow of the moon. Half-an-hour later we arrived at the monastery and circled the high wall, trying to find an opening. Luckily, a young monk heard our shouts and opened the heavy iron gates leading into a cobbled courtyard. He graciously ushered us down some worn stone steps into a bare room where a stocky, thickly-bearded monk was registering visitors. Of the small group that lived at the monastery, he was the only one from the United States—a Greek Orthodox from Utah.

By seven o'clock we were famished, but there was no place to buy food at the monastery, and only one restaurant and one grocery store in town. In spite of the solemn warning that the gates would be locked at nine, we turned around and raced back down the hill. We *had* to buy food for the next day.

The road was a booby trap of sharp rocks and treacherous holes waiting to devour us. This was no five-minute walk! It was a two-mile round trip. Fortunately, we found the market—a small tin shack with the hand-printed sign "Super Market" above the entrance—just as the owner was turning off the string of lights adorning the front. After loading up on canned fish, fig jam, corned beef, and French cheese, we looked around for bread.

"There's a bakery down the road," said the owner. "And a restaurant. But you'd better hurry." Hurry we did, like nomads in the wilderness, scrounging for any morsel of food.

In the distance we could see the outline of a rectangular stone building. As we approached, a thin shaft of light reached across the empty yard, and muted laughter filtered through the air. A low wooden door opened into a small cheery room with four tables and benches. The smell of food was intoxicating.

A diminutive Arab greeted us and motioned us to a table. We sat down opposite two couples, one French and one English. The Arab returned to his tiny kitchen. Barefooted, he paddled around, going from one vat to another, stirring and tasting the contents, which bubbled on an old gas range. After peering into his pot of stewing chicken, he announced: "There is enough for one dinner each."

"I could sure use a beer," said David, forgetting that Moslems never drink or serve alcoholic beverages. The owner looked shocked. He brought Pepsi, tea, and canned juices, and—in answer to our request for bread—advised us to hurry to the bakery before it closed. "Hurry" seemed to be the operative word that evening.

Tray and I ran down the path to a barn-like building where stacks of pita bread, still steaming, were piled two feet high on a stone counter. We grabbed about thirty at three *piasters* each (three cents), and headed back to the restaurant.

The bread tasted marvelous, but later—when we were less hungry and more discriminating—we agreed that it had almost as much sand in it as flour, and could be used in a pinch for emery boards. Dinner arrived: one stringy chicken leg, baked beans, macaroni salad with canned sauce, and thin soup. It was divine and it was awful. But the price was right—about $1.50.

As we headed back up the hill Nigel burst into an English dance hall ballad. He was immediately eclipsed by the bawdy offerings of Greg. I was debating whether to contribute one of my tame folk songs when a German-Egyptian couple stopped and offered us a ride in their dilapidated Niva. I'll never know how we all piled into the back seat, but if they hadn't come along we'd never have made our deadline.

"Aren't you sleeping at the monastery," I asked as we got out.

"There were no rooms left," they answered ruefully. "We'll have to sleep in the car." My heart went out to them for it was already getting cold.

Tray was the first to reach the gate. The monk from Utah had waited for us, and as we entered, put his finger to his lips. He hurried us to the lower courtyard and showed us our rooms. My bunkmate was an English woman who taught school in Cairo. She'd brought some of her students with her, and was all excited about giving them a first-hand glimpse of biblical history.

"I've set my alarm for 3 A.M. How's that for you?" she asked.

"Perfect," I answered and ran to tell my companions. They groaned. "If you don't get up, I'll leave without you," I warned.

I lingered for a while in the yard, which was paved with blocks of stone, fitted into an irregular pattern and imbedded in sand. There was a shallow wall of the same stone along the back, wide enough for sitting. I peered over the top into the monks' sparse garden below—four olive trees, a row of limp vegetables, a faded scarecrow. Just beyond the hostel you could see the silhouette of the ancient towers and massive wall surrounding the monastery. Several stray cats darted around, leaping onto the stone picnic tables that glistened in the moonlight. Otherwise, all was silent.

Later I lay on my bunk, contented and warm under two wool blankets. The wind began to stir, increasing in volume as it blew off the mountain and leaned into the trees, causing them to bend and hum. How sweet the air was, probably no different than it had been in the 13th century B.C. when Moses crossed the Sinai, leading his people out of Egypt and into Canaan, the Promised Land.

The next thing I heard was the alarm. I dressed quickly and ran to wake the others. David came out, shivering in his thin flannel shirt. "I can't believe it," he said. "We're practically in the desert and it's freezing!"

I doubled back and found my wool turtleneck. "Come on, take it," I said over his protestations. "My polypropalene shirt is fine, and I also have a windbreaker." But I had failed to pack a wool hat and mittens. My body was warm, but my head and hands were frigid.

Tray was having severe stomach problems, but after the camaraderie of the previous night he didn't want to be left behind. So we waited while he spent the next hour in the unisex bathroom, which, in retrospect, was rather grand compared to others I would encounter. It was divided into four doorless stalls, each with a hole in the stone floor and indentations for the feet. A can of water resided on the left and sinks with cold water spigots lined the wall.

At 4 A.M., the exact moment we finally started, bells began tolling to wake up the monks—bells of such depth and power that their dissonant tones could be heard echoing back from the mountain like a melancholy refrain long after the initial sound ended. As we reached the edge of the grounds David suddenly fell on his knees, raised his head to the sky and pleaded: "It's gawdawful cold down here. If anyone important is listening up there, we could sure use a burning bush right now!" We had to laugh in spite of our discomfort. He spoke for all of us.

There were two routes up the 7500 ft. "Holy Peak." One was very steep and short—3750 stone steps built by hundreds of pious monks. The other—carved in the 19th century by the Egyptians—was a longer, more indirect route which could be traversed on foot or on the back of an animal. This was the one we took.

The trail was a series of switchbacks that were clearly visible in the moonlight, except when they disappeared into a cavernous pass between cliffs so high that the light was obliterated. Then we had to use my feeble flashlight.

The climb was slow and the cold night air seared our lungs. Whenever we looked up we saw a thin line of flickering lights on the sections that were shielded from moonlight. Then darkness. Then another line of lights higher up. It reminded me of those old newsreels of Tibet that showed an endless pilgrimage of the faithful, winding upward around sacred Mt. Kailash like an illuminated snake. But today the faithful used flashlights, not torches. Exhilarated, I concentrated on each step, acutely aware of my steady breathing and the little clouds of vapor my breath formed in front of me. We hardly talked, except when one of my companions came back to ask if he could carry my camera bag. I knew that each one was afraid I'd collapse on the trail. David finally admitted it. "Are you sure you're O.K., Meg? My mother won't even walk up a hill…."

"David, if I die you'll be the first to know. But thanks for your concern." My mind wandered back to when my children were teenagers and I had wrenched my knee on the Tuckerman Ravine trail of Mt. Washington. It was son Tom who hovered just behind me as I inched my way down. He tried not to let me notice, but I did…and I was grateful.

We each went our own way at the first glow of light on the horizon. There was an unspoken desire to experience the sunrise alone. David found a giant outcropping of rock and started setting up his camera. I climbed off the trail until I found a ledge almost as high as the summit, with a sheer drop to the valley below. I lay on my stomach, a little squeamish, hugging the flat rock. Way in the distance the mist slowly lifted. It looked as if there was a great ocean between the ranges, with hundreds of sharp peaks rising out of it like islands. Soon the "ocean" disappeared and in its place were rows of black mountains—layer upon layer of differing intensities—which turned to deep purple against the reddening sky. The moon was still bright as I watched these first stirrings of daybreak, and it hung in the sky even after the rocks around me had begun to turn a pinkish hue. The colors changed, moment by moment, as the sun moved higher. Deep shadows gave way to shades of clay, salmon, and amber, until, finally, the hollow crevasses of rock were bathed in yellow sunlight—pockets of gold eating away at the gray fabric of the night.

We climbed to the summit and walked its perimeter, viewing the awakening earth from every angle. Then we sat for a long time in the shelter of an overhanging rock, huddled against the cold wind, and savoring the special bond created by this extraordinary experience. People from all around the world had gathered near a small stone chapel dedicated to the Holy Trinity. The chapel was locked, but not far to the north was a cave where tradition holds that God put Moses, covering the opening with His hand so that Moses would not see His face while He passed by (Exodus 33:22). There we found the couple who had given us a ride the night before, and had slept outside the monastery wall. They looked miserable. It had been too cold in the car, so they'd started climbing at 2 A.M., reaching the summit by 4. Two hours of bitter cold had preceded the sunrise.

At 7 A.M we started down the steep trail built by the faithful old monks. Halfway down we stopped on a small grassy knoll to rest our knees and to eat our pita bread, jam, and cheese. The rocks surrounding us, deeply etched, told of a time when swirling water and ice had covered the land. No signs of water today. Only miles of parched landscape, blending with the towering sand-colored mountains.

"Get a load of this bush," said Tray, jumping up to photograph the charred remains of a small scrub pine. "You don't suppose…."

"I suppose you're a sacrilegious clown," said David, who'd been sitting, serenely looking into the distance. "I also suppose that if Moses could see what people have done to his mountain he would add an 11th commandment: *Thou shalt not litter.*"

We all agreed. The trail, which had looked so pristine at night, was a promenade of paper and trash in the daylight.

As we descended the ancient stone steps the distant monastery lay before us, framed by a natural archway. At the bottom we passed an ornate well near the north wall. It was here that Moses—after escaping from Egypt—found Jethro's seven daughters gathering water. As the story goes, he married one and lived for forty years at the home of his father-in-law, tending his flocks and cleansing his soul in the solitude of the Sinai desert. It wasn't until then that he felt prepared to return to Egypt and free his people from slavery.

Four hundred years later another great prophet, Elijah, came to this same area seeking refuge from the rage of Queen Jezebel. A room in the small chapel on the summit of Mt. Moses is dedicated to him.

So many stories, so many legends, and so many diverse traditions came together for me that day, as I completed my own private pilgrimage into the past.

"Ciao, David," I said, as he and Tray left for the 9:30 bus. "I'll try to meet you at Kilimanjaro. I'll save the sweater for you."

We hugged. I lay my wool sweater out in the sun. It was wringing wet. What did I care? I wouldn't need it again until Tanzania.

4

FRIENDS AND PYRAMIDS

Judy was teaching piano in her ground floor studio when I returned, and Hamal was immersed in his latest play. I walked out onto my balcony and looked up and down the deserted street. The moon poked feebly out from under its veil of dust and filtered through the leaves of the jacaranda, casting lacy shadows on the stone floor. How different from the crystal clarity of the Sinai.

Hamal's 80-year-old mother called me from the backstairs. "Come on down, Meg, and tell me about your trip. I've hardly seen you since you arrived. This is our chance to be alone."

I grabbed my camera—hers was a face I wanted to remember—and followed her into a spacious living room.

Memories of the old parsonages I'd lived in during my childhood came to life. High ceilings, dark wood, ponderous furniture, the kind that was bequeathed to the church by a wealthy parishioner and came to rest in the minister's home. Brocaded draperies, flowered wallpaper, faded oriental rugs. Pictures—religious or family—hanging over the flowers.

How I had hated the heaviness of those houses! They seemed spooky and sinister. Whenever my sisters and I were left alone, we'd creep up the wide front staircase, fighting over who would lead and who would bring up the rear. I usually maneuvered the middle slot, having persuaded my older sister to be the adventurous one and my younger sister to be the brave one. Slowly we would advance until something creaked in the upper hallway and we'd turn tail, squealing and bumping into the high banister as we tumbled back down the stairs and took refuge in the kitchen. Strange that when I grew older I eschewed the modern split-level dwellings to return to the same high-ceilinged old houses that I had disdained as a child.

"The room is a little crowded," said Mrs. Wasim, rousing me from my reverie. "But I couldn't bear to part with my favorite pieces when I moved into this apartment. When Hamal's father was alive we had the whole house."

"It's warm—it's wonderful," I said, pulling up a footstool for her feet, and moving into a small carved chair next to her.

She was a handsome woman, with dark, deeply lined skin and satiny white hair pulled severely into a bun. Penetrating eyes were the focal point of a strong, authoritative face, and held me captive for the next hour. Intermittently she would run her hands over her full black skirt as if to smooth out every tiny wrinkle, and then adjust the delicate embroidered shawl that hugged her plain cotton blouse. I rested the camera in my lap and waited for just the right angle before snapping the shutter.

"Never mind an old lady's face," she protested. "You are not looking at Nefertiti."

"Nefertiti would not be as interesting," I assured her.

I listened as she told of her work as a chemist in producing an anti-cholera vaccine with her biologist husband in the '40's, her leadership in the educating of females in both the Sudan and Egypt, and her support of strict child labor laws, which were so desperately needed in Egypt.

"You're an inspiration to women," I said, reaching over and squeezing her hand. She smiled, and then her face darkened.

"Life is difficult in Egypt," she continued, in her cultivated British accent. "You can see that just in our house. Judy has to boil all the drinking water, wash the vegetables for half-an-hour, and constantly fight with dust and pollution. Most of the good artisans, plumbers, and carpenters left when Nasser arrived, so we put up with poor workmanship and leaking roofs and plugged drains. And everyday appliances, which you take for granted, are out of the reach of the ordinary citizen." She sighed and smoothed her skirt once again. "We are a developing country with many problems. We are half in and half out of the technological age. There is a saying: Egypt dances in the middle of the stairs, and nobody looks up or down."

After a long silence, she spoke again. "There are a lot of good things about Mohammedanism. And it's tragic the way it's being presented by the zealots of Iran and Saudi Arabia. They do not live by the true spirit of the Koran." There was great sadness in her eyes.

"Perhaps you can tell me what all the howling was two nights ago when I was trying to sleep," I said. "I don't mean the dogs. I mean the people." We laughed, for we both knew that there were no immediate answers to the problems we'd been discussing, and this was as good a way as any to change the subject.

"Oh, that…it's really against the law, for it disturbs others," she began, "but people do it anyway. That howling, as you call it, is mourning relatives chanting for their dead loved ones."

"I think it's a great idea," I said. "How often during those last years of marriage I felt like howling to the heavens. I couldn't believe what was happening to me…to us. I felt powerless. I was distraught. A part of me had died and I was mourning. That's worth howling about."

Judy came bursting into the room. "So, Meg, you have sneaked back from the Holy Mountain and are now sitting at the foot of the Wise One. And that she is." Jane leaned over and kissed her mother-in-law.

That night I slept fitfully, dreaming of the house I'd lived in just before my divorce—seven bedrooms, six fireplaces, two sun porches, a solarium, an elevator, formal gardens. It had been cheap in the 1960's—nobody wanted that much work—but in the 1980's, taxes and heating expenses had made it impossible for us to maintain. In my dream, the new owners were renovating the third floor, and I kept following the architect around, protesting each change. They had also built a fancy swimming pool in the backyard, shaped like Venetian Pool, a place I'd taken my young children when we lived in Miami, during happier times. As I walked to the edge of the pool, there, floating face down in the water was John, the best man at my wedding. I awoke feeling bereft.

Friday in Egypt is like Sunday back home—a day of rest. I tried to relax, but I was haunted by the symbolism of my dream. On the surface I appeared excited and happy, but, deep down, the failure of my marriage and the loss of my house were still very painful. And here I was with two people whose very happiness highlighted my own failure. Doting on each other. Hugging and kissing. They reminded me of my parents, who often locked themselves in the bedroom in mid-afternoon, leaving us children to wonder why they took so many naps. I expected my own marriage to be like theirs—idyllic. But I was not quiet and circumspect like my mother and Glen was not idealistic and accepting like my father. Both men were charismatic, but Glen had a tyrannical, controlling streak.

"Do you want to marry again?" Judy asked, after I'd shared my dream with her.

"No," I said without hesitation. "Men wipe me out. I want to see what I can do completely on my own. When I have a man I think of his needs first and somehow I get lost in the shuffle."

"Is it men you're talking about, or just Glen?" she asked.

"I don't know. I was a helpmate for so many years—the woman behind the dynamic man dedicated to a cause—that it became a habit. And then when we owned a company I worked alongside him, a sinecure without pay. Still the help-mate. That's undoubtedly why I feel incomplete without a man, as much as I hate to admit it. But I intend to change that pattern. It's the curse of my generation. And it's especially wrong for me."

"There's nothing wrong with being a nurturing woman, Meg…if the man appreciates you. It's a wonderful thing and you don't have to deny yourself while you're doing it. I happen to love it."

"I'll be the first to admit that I'm the one who lets men wipe me out," I said. "Even when you know divorce is the best alternative, it still leaves an emptiness in the heart. And the temptation to fill that void and find a companion is very strong. But I don't want to repeat the pattern of emotional dependency. I just need to be alone for awhile and become comfortable with who I am."

"Great," said Judy. "I'm all for that. And try letting go of all the old preconceptions while you're at it. You only find what you want by letting go. This trip will be good for you."

That afternoon I went back to the Sheraton to enlist Umar's help in a one-day attack on Cairo. He was delighted to see me, and guffawed when I described my ride on the broken-down "luxury" bus to St. Catherine.

"There are many definitions of luxury," he said, shrugging. "But now you are a real Egyptian." He booked me on two half-day tours of the major historical sites of Cairo and then offered a special deal on a luxury trip up the Nile from Aswan to Luxor.

"No more luxury deals from you, Umar," I said. "I don't mind dirt blowing into the windows of a bus, but I don't want to find myself becalmed in the middle of the Nile without a paddle."

He laughed. "See these people walking around the lobby? They're paying $1,500 for one week on the Anni, one of the Sheraton's most luxurious cruise ships. I will give you a private room exactly like theirs for only $460. And the air-fare to Abu Simbel, returning from Luxor is included."

"What's the catch?" I asked. "Do I give you a pint of blood and my first born?" What happened to my vow to avoid all commercial tours?

"No, no. You just pay in dollars. We have a few extra spaces we need to fill on the cruise leaving day after tomorrow."

Reluctantly, I handed him my Visa card. Here's where I should have used up some of the Egyptian money I acquired at the airport when I arrived. But everyone, even Umar, wanted dollars. It looked as if I'd never unload my pounds.

The next morning, on my way to the tour, I was struck by how much Cairo seemed like a collection of small towns. No skyscrapers walled the streets or shaded the sun. It was just one continuous community.

I arrived at 9 A.M., starting time. The bus was ready to roll by 10:30.

"My ladies and gentlemens," began the tour guide. "Cairo has twelve million people, 400 mosques, and 1,000 minarets. From his balcony in the minaret, the *muezzin* faces east five times a day and calls the faithful to prayer. And to your left we have a botanical garden and zoo with most of the animals in Africa." A ripple of laughter ran through the bus. Sounded like a lot of animals!

As we drove out into the country, I noticed donkeys laden with saddlebags, women washing clothes in filthy canals, and barefoot children playing on parched land next to mud dwellings. Women swept the dirt courtyards with homemade brooms. Some were dressed in bright-colored wraps, while others wore the traditional black *chador*, the lower half of their face covered by a veil. Many carried baskets or bundles of sticks on their head.

A fellow tourist leaned over and whispered to me as I gaped at the misery all around. "I understand that if a child can live in this squalor for seven years it can live to be one hundred."

"I'm not at all sure I'd want to live to be one hundred under these circumstances," I responded.

Forty minutes later we reached Memphis, once one of the most renowned cities of the ancient world—the site of the first medieval university, and the first capital of a united Egypt. Now all that was left were the ruins of the Temple of Ptah. Lying on the ground, but still a commanding figure, was the colossal fallen statue of Ramses II. Nearby, a perfect sphinx shone alabaster in the sun.

A few miles from Memphis we entered Sakkara, which means graveyard. First we explored the *mastaba* of Idout (5th dynasty, 2630 B.C.), an oblong tomb with sloping sides and a flat roof. Crouching, I worked my way down a slim passage, whose walls were transcribed with the pyramid texts, a collection of skills to help the deceased king on his journey to the netherworld.

Next we visited an imposing step pyramid, the tomb of King Zoser, who reigned for ninety years in the 3rd dynasty (2800 B.C.), and lived to be 120 years old. He was reputed to have run around the sizeable square courtyard in front of the pyramid every thirty years to prove to his subjects that he was fit to reign. Now there's a worthy platform for physical fitness advocates!

I started to scramble up the crumbling steps, which resembled five banks of tapered bleachers forming a giant cone of light brown stone. But halfway up I looked down and froze. It was so steep I thought I might faint. One false move and….Embarrassed, I sat and slowly bumped on my bottom all the way back down.

After lunch we drove along tree-lined boulevards and across Gesera Island in the middle of Cairo to the great Giza plateau, built in 2700 B.C. Photographs of President Hosni Mubarek smiled at us from lampposts, public buildings, and park benches. He was everywhere.

We spent the afternoon wandering around the sandy plateau dominated by the three biggest pyramids, Cheops, Chephren, and Mykerinos—the ones I'd viewed from the plane a few days earlier.

Our guide was a cheery, roly-poly young Egyptian who also doubled as the driver. "There are only eighty-two pyramids left in all of Egypt," he began. "Many more have been destroyed, and many have not yet been uncovered. And very sad to say, most of them were robbed long ago by the priests—the only people who knew how to gain access to their hidden treasure."

Groups of Arabs with white headdresses clustered around the bus. They sat astride their camels, which were adorned with tiny copper bells and multi-colored, tassled saddle blankets.

"Camel rides, five pounds. Jade necklaces, only ten pounds. Metal scarabs…." they chanted.

The driver, blunt and outspoken, warned us all. "It's junk," he said. "Genuine junk. Only a fool would buy." This caused a heated argument between the driver and the merchants, and provided the tourists with authentic drama to photograph.

I walked into the tomb of Cheops, the largest of the pyramids (450 ft.), and made my way, stooping, down the long tunnel to the king's final resting place. Completely solid inside, except for the elaborately decorated burial chamber, it had taken thirty years to build and ten years to carve. More than two million blocks of limestone had covered the outside surface. Now, almost all were gone.

We walked a few yards and the guide grinned triumphantly. "Here, my friends, is the famous sphinx. Just like the Hollywood movies, yes?" He paused. "Of course, it is being repaired."

Here was the mammoth head of King Chephren and the muscular body of a lion carved out of a single hunk of stone. The paws had been damaged and the nose and beard were missing. Instead of standing alone in its majesty, it was surrounded by a barbed wire fence. But in my mind Anthony and Cleopatra were still alive and cavorting outrageously around the great stone beast.

I lingered for a long time at our last stop, the Valley Temple. Here I had a very real sense of the grandeur that was Egypt as well as the blood and suffering that had made it all possible. The temple had sixteen stately pillars, each made from one seamless block weighing five tons. These blocks had been brought 1500 miles from the quarries of Aswan, in the south.

I stood in the ruins of the mummification rooms, the first important step in the burial process of a ruler. It took seventy days for the mummification to be complete and each king had his own priest, who, alone, knew the process. To keep his secret safe, he had to die with the king.

Pictures of pharaohs, their rectangular beards in place, filled my mind. I imagined I saw thousands of slaves, like swarming locusts, pulling on ropes to produce these grandiose feats of engineering that even today confound the experts. I couldn't begin to understand the life these people had led. But it was with great respect that I looked, in silence, upon their creations.

I walked down the causeway to the funerary temple, where the last prayers were said over the body. High walls kept the service private—for the immediate family. From here the king's body would be carried down another causeway for burial in the pyramid. I lingered in awe, running my hands over the smooth stone and contemplating the mystery of these ancient rituals.

"Come, Madam," shouted the driver with irritation. I turned, abruptly, and snapped a picture of him waving his arms frantically, like an umpire in a ball game. He smiled and softened. "We will feed you to the sphinx if you keep us waiting any longer."

I raced to the bus.

The sun was setting as we left the plateau. For an instant the tops of the pyramids were bathed in gold. Wind had picked up the sand and was tumbling it in little circles along the ground. A few wispy clouds peeked out from behind the famous triumvirate. A lone camel driver, outlined against the white fringes of the deepening sky, headed home.

5

WAY DOWN IN UPPER EGYPT

The plane was flying south, tracing the Nile from lower Egypt, where it emptied into the Mediterranean Sea, to Aswan, the location of its first cataract in upper Egypt. From my window I looked down on the river, a mighty snake that slithered eight hundred miles through the desert, isolating its narrow green valley from the vast expanse of arid land. To the east I could see the Red Sea. To the west the Sahara.

Excitement coursed through me when I caught sight of Lake Nasser and Abu Simbel. We circled, getting a perfect view of the transplanted statues and temples of Ramses II and his favorite wife Nefertari. It was exactly one week since I'd left New York and I was about to visit the heart of an ancient culture that had flourished on the fertile banks of the Nile long before biblical times. Before Athens or Rome. Before Socrates, Alexander the Great, Jesus, or Mohammed. This was a culture that had helped shape the history of civilization, as we know it. I felt a calmness and a freedom. I'd moved into another dimension, another time. Recent worries and obligations faded into the past.

Upon arriving, my bag was thoroughly inspected for the fourth time that day by soldiers dressed in faded yellow-khaki uniforms, which looked hot and uncomfortable. Their leather holsters were worn and shiny, and their carbines hung loosely over their shoulders.

I found all this snooping invasive, and muttered under my breath to one customs policeman as he rummaged through my underwear, "What's the problem? Do you have a *thing* for ladies panties?"

My fellow tourists laughed, and, fortunately, the officer didn't understand me. I soon realized that this was not a time for jokes. These guys—who looked no older than high school kids—were deadly serious. You could see it in their faces as they stood guard outside the plane.

I was boiling hot by the time the bus pulled up to Abu Simbel. How I wished I'd packed some shorts and sleeveless shirts. I had been warned, however, to dress conservatively, so as not to be pegged as a vulgar American in this strict Arab country. How wrong I was! There were plenty of tourists around me who put forth that image. I needn't have worried. At least I'd gotten rid of the money belt, which had become a binding albatross, adding to my discomfort. My money now resided, happily, in my camera bag.

No photograph could capture the enormity of the statues I faced that afternoon. I stood beneath the giant feet and looked up at figures that had been sculpted out of a mountain—four colossal seated likenesses—one of Nefertari and three of Ramses II—with life-sized replicas of several other wives and miscellaneous relatives standing, dwarfed, on the pedestals under their feet. These statues and the two temples had been moved when the construction of the second Aswan dam threatened to cover them with water. They'd been cut up into blocks, numbered, and reassembled. Even the huge fallen head and arms of one of the figures lay on the ground just as it had been found at the previous site. The move had cost thirty-six million dollars and required prodigious knowledge of astronomy and architecture to place the rooms in just the right position to receive the first rays of the morning sun.

The dome constructed to house these giants was 110 ft. high with a depth that stretched as far as two football fields. Imagine! Its solid concrete walls were seven feet thick. From the outside it looked just like a real mountain, but on the inside it was an enormous hollow vault. Nervously, I inched my way along a catwalk, clinging to the railings as I looked down on the flat roofs of the temples far below.

The thirty-two dynasties of Egypt covered 4,000 years. Ramses II dominated the 19th (1300 B.C.), and had an ego to eclipse all the rest. He had one hundred children and 68 wives. No wonder he was so big on fertility!

We entered the temple through a dark, high-ceilinged corridor, along which stood immense statues at even intervals. It was like being in a gigantic tomb. Ceremonial rooms branched off from the three main chambers. Faded paintings covered the walls: a slender boat taking a dead pharoah to the after-life; a woman holding the explicit symbols of fertility in her hand, indicating the continuation of life; a warrior sporting a large black erect penis. There was a hush as we walked through the chambers. They were lined on two sides with stone ledges, and adorned with elaborate carvings. Each room was smaller than the previous one. At the end of the corridor was the last and smallest—the holy of holies. A large stone block rested in the middle, on which the first rays of the morning sun shone twice a year for twenty minutes—on October 21st and February 21st. The statues were situated so that the god of sun, god of fertility, and god of the wind would be bathed in the light, but the god of the underworld would remain in the dark.

Back in Aswan, I hailed a cab to take me to the Anni, the Sheraton cruise ship that would be my home for the next week. A striking young man, not more than sixteen, bowed as I entered the car. He was dressed in a simple gray *gallaka*, which reached to his ankles. I found the garment very attractive and very elegant. I wondered what my sons would think if I presented each of them with one—upon my return. The thought amused me.

The back seat of the taxi was covered in fake leopard skin and the front in a black and white striped fabric. Shimmery purple fringe fluttered from the dashboard, and imitation oriental rugs lay on the floor. The driver sat on a patterned, throne-like elevated cushion. His driving matched the interior design—exuberant and jarring.

In record time we reached the banks of the Nile, where the Anni was anchored. For the first time the tab was so low that I felt obliged to tip. The driver bounded out of the car, opened my door with a flourish, and grinned boyishly.

"Many thanks, dear Madam. Welcome to the most beautiful Nile."

I stood for a moment looking at the expanse of blue water, its calm interrupted now and then by the playful antics of two sailboats. A perfect reflection of the far bank—sand-colored rocks, high grasses, and low, dense trees—greeted me. What a change from the chaos of Cairo.

The Anni—named after a very wise teacher who had lived in 1300 B.C.—was, as Umar had promised, luxurious. I walked down a long gangplank and checked in at the purser's office.

"We have been waiting for you, Madam," the crisply-attired officer said. "The captain will have lunch with you and then you will join the others. They are at the tomb of the Aga Khan."

After a sumptuous lunch the captain announced: "Now I will take you by motor launch to meet the tour. If we hurry you can see the famous botanical gardens."

"No, no. That's not what I want to take," I said, pointing to an old *felucca* hovering in the shadow of the Anni. "That boat over there is what I want." I was determined to get my *felucca* ride.

"Madam," he countered. "They are very rustic. They are not for ladies. You would be more comfortable, and we would get you there sooner, if…."

I shook my head. "Sir, if I changed my clothes and put on jeans you wouldn't think I was so fragile. That *felucca*. That's what I want," I said, putting my hand resolutely on his arm.

He threw up his hands and motioned to the skipper of the boat. "Whatever Madam wishes," he said.

The *felucca* is like an overgrown dory with sails, an old fishing boat with flair. I settled myself on a long narrow brocaded cushion while the skipper scurried about, putting up the sails. I was thrilled when he motioned for me to hold the heavy rudder in place as he sorted out the rigging. We tacked back and forth from one bank to the other, squinting into the afternoon sun. It was exhilarating to feel the power of the wind grabbing the sails, and the boat tilting and shifting in graceful response.

Squatting on his haunches, the sturdy little man deftly maneuvered the heavy boat. He held several lines in one hand and guided the rudder with the other. He had the face of a Nubian—very dark, delicately sculpted, with aquiline nose and thick black eyebrows that came together in a near-satanic V whenever he smiled. A flat, light-green knitted cap covered his curly hair. I sat snapping pictures and moving from one side to the other whenever the boom shifted.

The felucca skipper.

The sky had turned amber by the time we reached the tour. Reluctantly I left the quiet of the *felucca* and stepped into a motor launch full of noisy tourists. The change was jarring. I wasn't ready for their boisterousness. I was still wrapped in the glow of my *felucca* ride.

Out of the corner of my eye I caught a glimpse of the skipper as he turned his little boat northward. He nodded and, removing his green knitted cap, waved a silent farewell. I felt a sadness as I waved back in response.

6

JERRY

I was thrilled! This was my first day exploring the ruins along the Nile. I had read guidebooks late into the night until my brain ached, but nothing could have prepared me for the grandeur that lay ahead. We had already met our guide, Sayed, a professor of hieroglyphics at Cairo University. His knowledge of history and mythology was phenomenal. And his patience, too. There was never a question too trivial for Sayed. He loved his subject.

We were a congenial group on the Anni—Canadians, Germans, and several American families on vacation from their jobs in Saudi Arabia. The Americans had entertained us at dinner the first night with bizarre tales of life in an Arab country, much of which was distressing and not altogether believable when told from the vantage point of affluent Americans. But I was getting a kick out of the fancy meals and luxurious cabin, knowing that they would soon be replaced by the more humble mode of travel I had chosen for my trip.

From a ledge high above the Aswan quarry I looked down at the great obelisk—1,200 tons of solid limestone lying on its side, held captive by a membrane of uncarved rock. People, antlike, swarmed over its broad side, walking from the massive base to the conical top and peering cautiously over the sides into the deep unfinished ditch, a chasm separating the chiseled surface from the rock face, begun and abandoned thirteen centuries ago.

"Imagine putting mud on the face of that huge rock, heating it, and then running cold water over it until the surface cracked—just where you wanted it to," said Sayed. "That's a pretty powerful mud pack, isn't it, ladies? I wouldn't suggest trying it."

The ladies laughed, and one of the men in our group moved in closer with a video camera to record Sayed's explanation. Behind the man stood his wife, loaded down with a battery of lights and the latest home video equipment.

"Yes, that's how the ancient Egyptians started their cutting," continued Sayed, a little unnerved by the constant blinking of the camera. "After that they placed cedar wedges into the cracks and wet them. These expanded and further cracked the rock." With a dramatic flourish, he took a sharp wooden wedge out of his pocket and passed it to the crowd.

Unfinished obelisk.

"Once they'd cut the obelisk out of the mountain, they built a canal large enough to float it to the Nile. Then they waited for the annual flooding and, with the help of twenty-seven boats, guided the giant stone to its permanent location, and put it in place."

"How did they ever pick it up?" I asked impulsively, as if I were talking about a tinker toy.

"They didn't pick it up," answered Sayed. "They placed it in a bed of sand and slowly drained the sand from one end, while pulling it with ropes from the other, until it was standing erect. The entire process took seven months. Not bad, when you consider that it took the French nine years, with all their engineering skill, to transfer one obelisk—a gift from the Egyptian government—from the Temple of Luxor to the Place de la Concorde in Paris."

The heat was unbearable by the time we reached our next stop, the Aswan dam, a structure seventeen times bigger than the great pyramid at Giza. I struggled with my camera, still a neophyte when it came to angles and focusing and lenses.

"Perhaps I could be of help. I've photographed this country from one end to the other."

I wheeled around to face a tall, blond man in his early fifties. He wore thin khaki pants, a red checked shirt, and a white sailing hat with the brim turned down against the sun. He had craggy good looks—a trim, athletic body and a face that gave the impression of controlled amusement.

"Jerry Blum," he said, smiling at me as if reading my frustration. "I've been watching you. Are you a stenographer? I never saw anybody take so many notes so fast."

"Hi. Meg Peterson," I said, thrusting out my hand. "No, I'm not a stenographer, and I'm certainly not much of a photographer. I don't want to settle for the tourist shots, but I feel that if I blink I'll miss several dynasties."

"It's a lot to absorb all right. I'm an archaeologist, Canadian, actually, and even after five trips I'm still uncovering new facts. This guy is great. He really knows his history. But as far as I'm concerned, we can skip the dam. I hate what it's done to Egypt!"

"I thought it was one of the seven wonders. At least that's what the guide books say."

"What they don't say is what's happening to people's lives as a result of this ill-conceived exercise in national ego gratification. No more annual floods. Goodbye fertile farmland. And on top of that the humidity from the evaporation of Lake Nassar causes increased rainfall. You know what that's doing to the old temples, don't you?"

"Actually, I don't," I said. "I'd think it would give them a good washing."

"On the contrary. The reason they've lasted so long is because of the dry, hot climate. And now, with the rise in the water table, moisture is seeping into the foundations, causing them to crumble. Not a pretty prospect for the treasures of antiquity—or tourism."

"I'm glad I decided to visit now—before it's too late," I said, attempting humor.

Jerry wasn't listening. "The real heartbreaker is what the building of the dam did to the Nubians. Completely wiped out their culture. Flooded their land—it's now at the bottom of Lake Nassar. Relocated them in government housing—a far cry from their old homes built right into the hillsides. And promised them government grants and employment. Know what they're doing now? Menial jobs, like waiting on table at the Anni. You've seen them. A beautiful people. They look like the prototype of the ancient, pure Egyptian—dark skin, aquiline nose, muscular body. And they had one of the most honest, most cohesive communities in all of Egypt."

Back on the bus, I left the problems of present-day Egypt and immersed myself in the carnival atmosphere surrounding Sayed's presentation: "Next stop, folks, Temple of Philae, first of the Greco-Roman ruins, built in the second century A.D."

Jerry and I climbed to the knoll alongside Sayed, and stood for a moment looking up at the sky through the open columns, which were bound by a simple layered cornice.

"Ten years ago the colors on these columns were brilliant," he said, "but they were almost completely covered by water after the Aswan dam was built. By the time they were transported to higher ground most of the color had washed away. A real shame."

Sayed waited until the last straggler reached the temple before continuing. "Now you're going to meet King Osiris," he announced. "He was very important in the everyday lives of the ancient Egyptians centuries before the great prophets visited the earth. Here he is with his wife, Isis, who was also his twin sister—having fallen in love with him in the womb. And the baby beside them is their son Horus, who soon became a big cheese in Egyptian mythology."

"This man is a real showman," I whispered to Jerry. He smiled.

"Generous, trusting Osiris had a brother named Set, who was very jealous of him. At a birthday feast Set tricked Osiris into lying in an ornate box, then clamped the lid on it. Later he hacked the body into pieces and scattered the remains throughout the land. Nice guy, eh? Isis, heartbroken, collected all the pieces with the help of Horus, buried them, and took revenge on Set. Osiris, not to be upstaged, was resurrected and reincarnated in the bull Apis, becoming the god of the dead and the source of new life through his son."

I never tire of this myth and its many versions. In fact, my children gave me a small sculpture of Isis in all her regalia nursing the baby Horus. It sits in the middle of my dining room table. How wonderful to see the original story depicted on these ancient walls.

I strolled in the open space, surrounded by columns, some plain and unfinished, others decorated with hieroglyphics and pictures. The perfectly proportioned, unroofed temple stood alone on a hill overlooking Lake Nasser. I felt very tiny and very insignificant, my head barely reaching the slender feet of the giant paintings.

"Take a look at these figures," said Sayed, pointing to a heavily pockmarked relief. "This was done by Egyptians who converted to Christianity. It took a lot of energy to deface these walls with a stone chisel, so they had to be selective. Only hacked out the left leg and the left side of the body—the seat of the living heart."

"But here are some clusters that survived the vandals." He pointed to a group of guitar players, a harpist, a drummer, a flutist, and several pygmy dancers. "These are Somali dancers. Somaliland was as holy for ancient Egyptians as Mecca is for Moslems. Dwarfs, or pygmies, were protected, since one of them was thought to be the god of music. When a king died, he had to answer many questions to prove that he had been a good man on earth. One of the questions was: 'Have you ever harmed a dwarf?' The answer had better be negative if he wanted a smooth journey into the afterlife."

Jerry couldn't wait to elaborate on Sayed's tales. "See this scarab?" He pulled a small polished beetle out of his pocket. "I found it on my first dig. It's become my favorite talisman." He pointed out several places where the insect had been etched into the stone columns. "This little critter was very important to the ancient Egyptians. After a person died, his heart was removed, and scarabs were placed in the cavity. There they laid eggs, which hatched, and symbolized resurrection and new life. Pretty neat, eh?"

"Pretty creepy," I replied. "I prefer the cobra. Look at the drawing over there." I walked to a nearby corner. "He's shedding his skin—dying. Same symbolism. Now here he is, getting a new skin—rebirth. I can relate to that. And it's better than a lot of insects crawling around inside my body. Yuk." I shivered. Jerry put his arm around my shoulder. There was that amused look again.

We returned to the Anni and ate lunch while slowly cruising down the river. Jerry introduced me to his two children, David and Marcia, both in their twenties. He seemed very close to them. Every year since his wife had died, he'd taken them to a different place, many of them sites of past excavations in which he'd participated. His enthusiasm for Africa and the Middle East was shared by his son, who talked avidly about the political and economic problems facing the region. I watched them relate, listening to one another, agreeing, disagreeing. How I ached when I thought of what it would have meant to my three boys had they been able to share a trip like this with their father. But he could never have listened the way Jerry did, or let them come up with their own theories. Glen always had to be right.

By mid-afternoon we'd reached Kom Ombo, a majestic temple which had been completely buried in sand until 1893. Digging it out had taken a team of archaeologists twenty-five years.

"This temple is the best example of the cult of the crocodile," announced Sayed. "Here's a whole room of them—mummified." There they were, piled to the ceiling, dark leathery green, teeth bared. "They were deified because the people were terrified of them. But that's no longer a problem. There hasn't been a crocodile in the Nile for twenty-seven years—not since they were trapped by the Aswan dam."

"Well, that's a relief," I said. "I can take my early morning swim tomorrow."

The guy with the video guffawed, never moving the camera from his eye. I felt sorry for his wife. Why did she keep lugging all those lights, when the sun was so bright that it quivered?

We wandered down the long passageways, through a series of rectangular openings into stone courtyards, and past banks of immense columns, each group with a different base and capital, uniquely ornamented. I never knew there were so many different designs for a column of stone.

Take a look at the way these blocks are put together," said Jerry, who had been photographing me next to the columns, in order to get their size in perspective. "No mortar—just sand, bronze, cedar, or ebony to dovetail the joints. It's amazing!"

My head was full of pictures as I started back down the hill to the boat: seven muscular gods with the faces of falcons; complicated solar calculations on calendars denoting rituals, feasts, and festivals; carvings of medical tools from early transplant operations, using real and artificial body parts. And all of this before computers, anesthesia, antiseptics, and flush toilets.

"Forty pounds, Madam, only forty pounds." The twentieth century returned, abruptly. A heavy-set man in a *gallaka* walked beside me, holding several dresses over his arm. I remembered Sayed's warning, that all souvenirs were "genuine junk," and never worth more than ten pounds. I decided to try my hand at purchasing a spangled dress for the traditional costume party to be held on the Anni that night.

"Too much," I retorted.

"How much you pay?" he asked.

"Ten pounds," I replied.

"Oh, Madam. Thirty pounds, no less."

"Too much," I said again, walking more briskly toward the boat.

"I give you this one, too," said the man, thrusting a bright aqua cotton shift into my hand.

"I don't want two."

"You can have both for twenty pounds," he said, undaunted.

"No."

"Both for nineteen. Look here." He fingered the material, lovingly. I walked away.

"O.K. Ten pounds," he said, with a grin.

I called to Jerry. "Loan me ten pounds?"

"You're crazy, Meg," he said, as he took out his wallet.

"O.K. Twelve," said the man. Again, I walked away.

He finally gave in, but I heard him shout, "It is worth eleven, Madam!" as I disappeared into the Anni.

I sat on the deck enjoying the sharp, sweet air as evening approached. The waning sun cloaked the passing scene in reds and pinks. The Nile was smooth, the reflections along the bank flawless. In the stillness, the fertile stretch of land on either side of the river seemed abandoned, except for a solitary camel or a few children playing in the shallow water of a marshy side stream. Patches of farms created a quilt of greens, rusts, and yellows. Sand-covered hills rose beyond the narrow plain and irregular rock formations pierced the darkening sky far in the distance. Palm trees clustered at the flood line and dense, willowy rushes lined the banks. A *felucca* was lowering its sails for the night as we passed.

I felt someone move up behind me. Startled, I turned around. It was the video man without his camera.

"Party time!" he crowed, lifting his glass and swirling the ice. I pulled back as part of the drink spilled on the deck.

"Well, you're rather good looking, now that I can see both eyes," I said, keeping a careful watch on his drinking arm.

He laughed. "Eric Jameson," he said with a bow. "I'm in charge of this crazy party. How about being one of my concubines? I'm playing the dirty old pharaoh, Ram Sex II."

"You certainly have a way with words. But how about your wife?"

"Oh, she'll be handling the video. Can't miss my first big stage role…ha, ha."

So, his mouth was as big as his bulk. Yes, now I remembered him from the Sheraton-Dokki, glass in hand, arguing with his wife. He couldn't see any reason to leave the nightclubs of Cairo for a few dingy tombs. But now he was in his element. Cock of the walk.

"How many concubines do you need?" I asked, playing along.

"As many as I can get. Ha ha. I thought you could be Lux-hor. Get it? For Luxor?"

"Yes, I get it. Very original. Do I have to do a soft shoe, or just look radiantly beautiful? Of course, for a fee I might write the screenplay."

"Hey, you're pretty funny," he said, motioning to his wife, who was tangled up in lights and wires in her effort to tape the last rays of the sun. I could see that this was going to be too precious for words.

It took me an hour to put on my Cleopatra eyes, fashion a headdress, and locate a body stocking to make my spangled dress presentable—not that any of us was really presentable.

After about two hours of New York on the Nile, cabaret style, Jerry and I settled down to serious disco dancing. He was a fabulous dancer. I closed my eyes and moved to the music. I was transported back to my twenty-fifth wedding anniversary. In Vienna Glen and I had booked an evening excursion down the Danube so we could waltz, not knowing that it was disco night. How we had laughed at our folly! But it didn't matter. That night the Danube belonged to us.

"I'm exhausted. Let's sit down for awhile," Jerry said, leading me to a table. We ordered two beers and sat watching the dancers.

"Will you look at David and Marcia? Tireless…like whirling dervishes. Makes me feel old."

"They're a handsome pair," I said, "And I thoroughly enjoyed them this afternoon. In my opinion, you're a wonderful father."

"Thanks, but they make it easy. I've been very close to them since my wife died. Much more than before. I guess we've managed pretty well." He reached over and put his hand on my arm. "Hey, don't look so sad, Meg. I'm going to survive."

"Yes, I'm sure you will. You're too upbeat not to. Actually, I'd say you're doing better than I am. But there are times when I think a divorce is worse than a death. There's always that connection, that reminder of your failure just around the corner, ready and waiting to haunt you."

Jerry took me by the hand. "Let's go up on deck, away from the crowd. I'll tell you the story of Ra-Atum, the creator of earth and sky, and my special version of the story behind the murder of Osiris…while you count the stars. No notebook. All you have to do is listen. This is my favorite myth, and Sayed will be right back in the middle of it tomorrow."

He bounded up the stairs, pulling me after him. Once more I was with Glen, rushing up the four flights to our tiny loft in Vienna.

7

TEMPLES AND TOMBS

The insistent pounding on my door jolted me awake. "Are you there, Meg? We're leaving in half-an-hour." It was Jerry's voice.

"What time is it?" I asked, suddenly aware that the sun was streaming in my window.

"Seven-thirty. And the carriages are waiting. We'll save you a seat. But hurry!" I heard his footsteps recede down the hall.

Just before eight I rushed down the gangplank to a waiting caravan of old-fashioned horse-drawn buggies, complete with tattered black "bonnets." Touristy, but a good way to get through the narrow, cobbled streets of the old town of Edfu.

En route Temple of Horus.

Dingy cafés were already filled with men smoking long-hosed water pipes. Children in soiled and ragged clothes played on hardened clay stoops. Goats and sheep sprawled inside the dusty courtyards.

The carriages stopped at a large empty square. I walked across the weathered stones toward two immense sandstone pylons, which were guarded by a polished granite falcon. The walls slanted inward and housed three rooms, one of which contained a double row of towering columns. Heavy doors of ornately carved cedar, originally covered with gold, graced the entrance.

"This is the Temple of Horus" said Sayed, with great reverence. "It took forty years to excavate and forty-nine houses had to be removed in the process. It was begun during the reign of Ptolemy II (237 B.C.) and completed during the reign of Ptolemy XII (57 B.C.) Notice that the roof is made of huge stone slabs, put in place by mud ramps. The reason it's so black is because the Christians used the halls for their cooking."

"Why did the Egyptians allow this?" I asked.

"I don't think they even knew. They considered it the house of the gods and were sure it was haunted. And the stories painted on the walls were far too scary for them. So the buildings fell into disuse for centuries and were eventually covered up by sand and earth."

I looked up at the black ceiling and surveyed the cavernous space. How could anything so big be swallowed by earth and sand? And such beautiful paintings! Weren't these people proud of their artistry? Didn't they want to preserve it? Or maybe they felt it was just for the ruling class and had nothing to do with them.

Jerry pointed out the empty oblong *cartouches* etched in the stone, waiting to receive the name of each king as he died. This would assure the ruler of an afterlife and the clever priests of a good source of extra income. But the priests didn't stop there. When the kings came into the dark temple to ask questions of the god-statues, the priests manipulated the statues by strings attached through small holes in the wall. If the god moved to the left, the answer was "yes." If it moved to the right, the answer was "no." The answer often depended on the amount of money involved.

"Looks as if corruption has been around a long time," I said to Jerry. He nodded and walked up to the wall to read the hieroglyphics.

"Look here," he said, pointing to a young man on horseback. "Egypt was ruled from Alexandria in those days, so the king had to come once a year for his re-coronation. Here he is, heading for the ceremony, with a series of lotus leaves in a perpendicular line behind him, denoting the number of concubines he had. You can see what the favorite form of recreation was."

Sayed motioned us to the opposite wall. "Here's a story for all you romantics." It was dark inside the room, but Eric's wife had the floods fully operating and the simple reliefs stood out clearly. "Once there were several brothers—all gods. When they had to go to Syria to fight, one brother refused. So they left him in charge of the home front. Upon their return they discovered that all the women were pregnant. As punishment they cut off one of his arms."

This seems to have proved ineffective, since the next relief was a drawing of him with the arm missing and a large, erect penis preceding him into the bedroom of one of the women. Eric leaned over and whispered, "I'd say somebody cut off the wrong appendage."

Just before leaving Edfu I climbed up onto the high, half-destroyed mud wall built so long ago to keep the common people out of the temple. The view of the complex was outstanding. I turned around and called to Marcia and David.

"Hey, you guys, come on up. It's the best view in...."

A large chunk of dry mud broke away and I started to fall. As I did I was aware of Eric's video grinding away. I landed spread-eagle in the arms of three men who were about to follow me up the wall.

"Thanks for saving my life," I said, clearly shaken. I brushed myself off and attempted to regain my dignity.

"Thanks for saving ours," one of them countered. "We'd have been next, and nobody could have caught us!"

After lunch we set off by foot to visit our last Greco-Roman site, the Temple of Esna, thirty feet lower than the rest of the village. It was uncovered in the fifteenth century by Mohammed Ali-Pasha, who wanted a place to store his gun powder. Three rows of columns, decorated in blazing reds, yellows, blues, and greens, stood in the main hall, which was painted to represent the entire universe—sky, earth, and all the flowers and creatures inhabiting it.

The rest of the temple is still underground. The people living in the old houses over the probable ruins are forbidden by law to improve their property, since the site will be excavated, eventually. How strange it must feel to be living on top of another civilization.

Leaving the temple, we threaded our way through the bazaar. Men grabbed my arm, throwing dresses and scarves at me, and bargaining loudly. Children, dirty and bedraggled, begged to have their pictures taken for money. Artisans worked in tumbledown shacks, and goats ate from the ubiquitous piles of garbage. Everything stank! I couldn't wait to return to the Anni and the pastoral beauty of the river.

The depressing pollution and poverty nagged at me as we sat having Turkish coffee on deck. The boat passed through a series of narrow locks. Distracted, I watched the water rushing through the holes in the dam. It was hypnotic. Children, standing in the reeds by the river's edge called out, "Pens! Fountain pens! Mister and Missus!" Rows of swaying sugar cane dwarfed a cluster of low mud huts on a distant hillside. I leaned back and watched an evening traffic jam on top of the dam. It was all part of Egypt's incongruous mosaic.

◆   ◆   ◆

The next morning we worked our way to the Valley of the Kings in the Luxor area (land of women), passing many caves nestled in the limestone cliffs. These caves had been used as homes by the Egyptian grave diggers and later became Christian catacombs.

The valley was a series of rolling hills, which formed natural step pyramids. Swirling winds had subdued all but the most stubborn outcroppings. It was strangely beautiful. Desolate, hot, silent. Walkways connected the sixty-two known tombs, but new ones were being unearthed every year. It would have taken weeks to cover the whole area.

I walked slowly, feeling as if I'd entered another world. I was acutely aware of the contrast between the magnificent tombs carved out of the mountains, with sumptuous treasures filling their underground rooms, and the stucco hovels where the people of the adjacent village lived. I couldn't help comparing the elegant life depicted in these tombs with the unshaven ferry boat captain who took us across the Nile early that morning, dressed in a ragged *gallaka*, heavy western shoes, dirty red and white striped socks, and a seedy leather cap with ear flaps. Two worlds. Light-years apart.

Jerry and I wandered off on our own, poking into numerous tombs—Ramses II, Amen Khophef, son of Ramses III, Ramses VI, Ramses XII—and inching our way down narrow passageways to the burial chambers.

"Look at that wall," said Jerry. "You can't imagine how complicated they made the journey to the afterlife. These pictures are supposed to help each pharaoh overcome the difficulties he'll encounter. There are the enemies he has to slay to get through the underworld. And over here are the monsters and serpents that will attack him, and a list of the spells he'll need to know to keep from losing his heart, or being forced to walk upside-down, decapitated."

"Dying is scary enough for most of us without all this," I said, turning away.

I was getting claustrophobic. I had to get some fresh air. All of this gave me the creeps. But first Jerry insisted that I see the only mummy, other than King Tut, remaining in these tombs—that of an embryo, thought to be the aborted baby of one of the workers. I looked with awe at the small, perfectly formed fetus. Then I fled.

The sun was merciless by the time we gathered at the tomb of King Tut Ankh Amun (1350 B.C.) "Can you imagine the surprise on the face of Howard Carter in 1922 when he poked a hole in the thick walls housing the sealed burial chamber of this sixteen-year-old king?" asked Sayed, his eyes gleaming. "What a find! The first thing he saw was the gold filigree of the outer case, into which three more had been fitted. Inside the smallest box was the gold case you see in front of you, with the gilded body of the king."

Later that week I was to see the outer cases in the National Museum in Cairo and wonder how they ever could have fit into such a small room. Obviously, they'd been built inside the room.

The heavy limestone slab, which had covered the sarcophagus, was resting in a corner of the small room. There was absolute silence as we all leaned over the coffin to view the slender body wrapped in golden armor.

"Since King Tut died so young, his tomb was unfinished," said Sayed. "The treasures escaped the grave-robbers because he was a forgotten pharaoh, buried in a small, insignificant place."

I started to move from the close, damp room. I was ready to leave the tombs of Egypt.

8

THE SPLENDOR OF LUXOR AND KARNAK

"Don't be such a chicken, Meg. Everybody does it!" chided Bob Andrews, as he handed two crisp ten dollar bills to a young Egyptian running alongside our carriage. The man counted out a fistful of paper money and shoved it into Bob's waiting hand.

"How do you think I finance my getaways from Saudi Arabia?" Bob said, stuffing the money into his pocket. "With good old greenbacks, that's how."

"Aren't you afraid these guys'll cheat you?" I asked.

"The rate's so good, a little skimming wouldn't even matter," he replied. "Double what you can get at a bank." I remembered the American at the airport chiding me for not having dollars. So this is why the government is so fussy about its pink slip—its hallowed "proof of exchange."

I huddled in the back with Marilyn Andrews as the rickety carriage dived in and out of each waiting pothole. Bartering was going on all up and down the street. I hadn't realized how many people traded openly on the black market.

"Perhaps I'm a fool, but I'm terrified of getting caught," I said. "I was the kind of kid who couldn't even sneak into a movie when nobody was looking."

"The black market keeps the bureaucrats busy, gives the hustlers a little extra income, and makes the tourists happy," Bob said, patting my arm like a Dutch uncle. "It's good for the economy, so what could be so awful?"

Judy, their daughter, oblivious to the financial maneuvering going on around her, was sitting beside the driver, holding the reins, and behaving like any normal ten-year-old who suddenly finds herself guiding a horse-drawn carriage. Excited and proud.

"Mommy, look. The horse likes me," she squealed. "He puts his ears back when I talk to him." Her grin was matched by that of the driver, whose thin shoulders seemed even more stooped next to the straight, energetic little girl.

The carriages pulled into a barren, dusty field. An old thatched shed, leaning at an angle, stood at the far end near a cluster of palms. Painted on one side was a large ad for Pepsi Cola.

Sayed was jollier than ever as he gathered us around him. Folding his arms across his chest, he smiled beatifically as Eric's wife steadied the lights. "For 1,000 years Luxor was the greatest city in the world—the much fabled Thebes of Mediterranean history. It was the center of all politics, art, and religion under the protection of the fertility god Amon, creator of the universe. His most enthusiastic follower was Ramses II. Here on the east bank are the mighty temples of Luxor and Karnach, and across the river are the parched valleys where the kings and queens hid their tombs—the tombs we visited this afternoon." He waited while Eric took a long shot.

"You are about to see the most spectacular ruins known to man. It took 2,000 years—from 2200 B.C. to 300 B.C.—to build twenty-nine temples on sixty-one acres of land. On the horizon you can see the remains of the mud walls that once completely surrounded the area."

The night air was cool. I drew in my breath as much in anticipation as to savor the perfume of pink and white oleander. My feet crunched monotonously on the gravel as I walked down a broad avenue flanked with sphinxes. The rows of identical ram's heads, perched on sinewy lion-bodies, glowed eerily in the spotlight.

Avenue of Sphinxes, Karnach.

Through the main entrance stretched a double row of columns which led into a courtyard to another row of columns, and another, until the stone giants—134 in all—faded from sight, a duplication repeated to infinity. But each image was slightly different; a fluted frieze, a flat slab cornice, a bowed shaft, a flared top. Designer columns imaginatively carved and placed to please the eyes of the gods. And rising from among the shadowy shapes, two slender obelisks pierced the sky.

Jerry and I meandered among the dark columns, stopping to feel the cold, rough stone, and trying to encircle their enormous bulk with our arms. But all we did was cover our clothes with dust as fine as talcum powder. It was like standing in a forest of colossal redwoods—like the ones I'd seen in California twenty years ago—only made of stone. My children and I had tried to link hands around one of the huge trunks, but we were unable to encompass its girth.

The colossal columns of Karnach.

Suddenly the lights came on and we were dwarfed by these giants, whose pedestals, alone, extended to the tops of our legs. The crowd gasped. For one long moment nobody moved. Then music and voice blended in a poetic litany of history and mythology as the light shifted slowly from one temple to the next.

"Just think, Meg," Jerry whispered. "We're standing in the empty houses of the king-gods. Can you imagine that there was once a roof way up there covering these columns? Do you realize what single-minded ferocity it took to conceive and build them?"

"I know, I know, Jerry, and a lot of people died in the process. But I still can't help feeling awed. It's a religious experience for me. Allow me that. And…and all the talk about Akhenaten, the heretic king. It's fascinating to me. How he worshipped Re, the sun disc. How he used simple open shrines instead of elaborate temples. How he tried to be monotheistic. And he believed all people were equal, too. What a dynamo! And look what they did to him for his new ideas. Damned him as a rebel, destroyed his writings, and made him an historical 'non-person.'" I was almost sputtering.

"Hey, wait a minute," Jerry admonished me. The main show was over and we were moving to bleachers high above a large rectangular pool—the sacred underground lake of Karnak. The main temple, which looked like a Roman fortress, was perfectly reflected in the water.

"Forget the romanticized version of this maverick," he said, "and listen to some of the facts. The guy was a real weak sister and a slipshod ruler. Nearly lost Egypt's empire. He was a notorious glutton who sat around all day at the groaning table, being fawned over by sniveling court sycophants. If it hadn't been for his wife, Nefertiti, nothing would have been accomplished. Let me give you a couple of books on Akhenaten, and you may change your mind."

"I've read quite a bit about him already," I said, trying to keep calm. "And I relate to iconoclasts, even if they fail. Maybe he was an effete slob, but he was also sensitive, and encouraged the arts. Wrote music. And poetry. You can't take that away from him.

For the first time Jerry's encyclopedic knowledge seemed inappropriate. It brought back unpleasant memories of Glen, always ready to burst my bubble, dispute my facts, and prove how smart he was. On this evening I didn't want stark reality. Or smart. I wanted wonder.

Much later I lay in bed, soothed by the gentle roll of the Anni, and thought about Akhenaten—controversial, cloaked in mystery, accused of being more interested in the arts than in law and order. I decided to read his poetry and forget about his bad habits.

As I fell asleep, his simple words filled my being: "Your love is in my heart like the reed is held by the wind."

◆   ◆   ◆

"The first Europeans to see the ruins of Luxor and Karnak were Napoleon's soldiers. They threw down their weapons, broke into spontaneous applause, and saluted," said Sayed. "How ironic!. The heroes of a people's revolution paying homage to the greatest autocracy the world has ever seen." We were standing, once again, on a section of the two-mile-long Avenue of Sphinxes. But this time it was the morning sun that illuminated the rows of dull-eyed ram's heads.

I walked beneath the pillars in the hall of Khonsu Temple, which lay within the great Temple of Amon, and tried to grasp the enormity of Karnak by day. The ruins stretched as far as I could see. They had lost none of the wonder of the night before. In front of me was the 320 ton obelisk to Queen Hatshepsut—the memorial her enemies hadn't dared destroy—a stark reminder of one woman's power in the middle of the ornate heaviness of the ruling pharaohs.

As we left Karnak, Sayed stopped and pointed to a balcony hanging precariously from the top of one of the columns. "Here's proof that all of this was once completely buried," he said. We all craned our necks and Eric adjusted his camera skyward. "That balcony is all that's left of a mosque, built on what was ground level before the excavations began." I found this amazing.

We continued down the avenue toward the Temple of Luxor, an imposing structure 330 feet long and 170 feet high. As we approached, Sayed went over to one of the sphinxes.

"Notice anything different?" he asked.

"No more ram's heads," answered Marcia, without hesitation.

"Smart lady," said Sayed. "It's now the head of a pharaoh, signifying intelligence instead of fertility. But notice something else. They all look the same, because Ramses II, in his megalomania, destroyed the faces of his predecessors and substituted his own. He also removed their names and replaced them with...guess whose?"

Jerry was on his knees, lining up the sphinxes and the temple entrance for a perfect shot. He looked up at me. "He's right about Ramses. He obliterated your buddy Akhenaten in short order."

"Now he's my buddy?" I said. "You never quit." I strode into the temple.

Jerry came running after me. "Just kidding, Meg. They were all a bunch of bastards. If I were a woman, I wouldn't give any of them the time of day." He pulled me over to a statue of Ramses and his wife, sitting side by side.

"Look. In all these statues the woman is portrayed much smaller than the man. In this one 'little' Nefertari's arm is reaching around 'big' Ramses's back." Jerry motioned to me from behind the statue.

"See her hand, perfectly carved and resting on his shoulder? Do you know why that was done?"

I was thanking God I hadn't lived in the time of the pharaohs. "I give up."

"Because the Egyptians must always show every limb, to make sure the king or queen comes back in the next life as a whole person. And they depict that person as between twenty and twenty-seven years old, considered the optimum age at which to go through eternity."

"I'll settle for that," I said, "but do you realize, Jerry, that this is exactly the opposite of the Christian view of death and resurrection—that the physical presence of the body is not necessary to the continuation of the spirit?"

"Hey, not a bad analysis from a preacher's kid."

"Stop patronizing me, Jerry," I said, punching him playfully. "Let's go back for lunch." We walked lazily along the Nile to the Anni, savoring the midday sun.

Our final excursion took us to the west bank, beyond the cultivated land of the Nile. There on a rocky hillside stood the terraced Temple of Hatshepsut, the only queen to rule in ancient Egypt. She dominated the 18th dynasty, from 1479 to 1458 B.C. "Here lived a powerful woman—not somebody you'd want for an enemy," began Sayed. We entered a three-tiered structure of simple doric columns—one tier cut right out of the mountainside.

"This temple—Deir el-Bahari, meaning northern monastery—was built for Queen Hatshepsut by her lover, an architect for whom she built a tomb—an act frowned on by royalty, and especially by her stepson, Thutmose, who hated her intensely. There was much speculation about how she died, because her body was never found, and Thutmose had her statues defaced and her name removed from all buildings. But he couldn't touch that powerful obelisk at Karnak."

Sayed paused, letting the full weight of his words sink in.

"Queen Hatshepsut demanded all the rights and privileges of a king. She even wore the artificial beard and clothes of a man."

What an adventurous lady, I thought, examining the pictorial record covering one whole wall. There were the boats used to cross the Red Sea for her pilgrimage to the holy land of Somalia. And the special fish, unlike those found in the Nile. And the Somali houses built on stilts.

"Can you imagine that this exquisite home had been completely buried until the early 1900's? It took twenty-seven years to uncover." Sayed gestured dramatically. "See those fragments of statues and columns lying on the hillside in those roped-off areas? Well, teams of archaeologists still live close by, working each day to piece them together, like a gigantic jigsaw puzzle."

We walked around the grounds, glancing back at the symmetrical colonnades and the tree-lined forecourt, while Jerry explained to me the numbering system used to reassemble the ancient stones.

On the trip back we stopped for a moment at the great Colossus of Memnon, two 38-foot seated stone figures erected by Amenhotep III. It was called the singing monument, because it emitted a sound like a lyre when struck by the rays of the rising sun—that is, until the cracks in the stone were repaired. Now it no longer sings.

Everyone returned to the boat, but I wanted to explore the back streets of Luxor alone. I had a lot to digest. Buoyed by the images of the past two days, my spirits soared.

I stepped carefully around the stones that pushed up through the muddy street. Donkeys, tethered so they had to face crumbling stone walls, turned their heads as I passed, lifting heavy lids to observe me curiously. Bicycles wove in and out among the dusty, ill-clothed people. Men sat together, cross-legged at the edge of the street, smoking pipes. There were no mixed groups of men and women. And no women alone. Donkeys pulled loaded carts of produce. Old men, feet nearly touching the ground, rode astride the sad-looking animals. Little boys used switches to force the poor sagging creatures into a trot. I saw one car and a couple of buses. They honked vigorously. Pedestrians, without looking up, moved slowly out of their path.

My mood plummeted. I put my camera away. How could I photograph such misery? But even without my camera I was pegged as a tourist.

"I know what you want, lady. Come here and smell my perfume. It's the essence." A ragged, dark-toothed Arab touched my sleeve.

"What you give me for this beautiful, genuine, hand-carved scarab?" This time the man was young, ingratiating.

I was a disappointment to the eager merchants, for all I wanted was pens. I pulled away and ducked into a nearby stationery shop. The owner, a thin, clean-shaven, middle-aged man in a western suit, parted a fringed curtain and stepped into the room.

"Good morning, Lady," he said.

"Good afternoon," I said automatically, not meaning to correct him. We both laughed.

He showed me several pens. The price stayed the same. Good. No bargaining. I didn't have enough change so I asked if he minded taking all the ragged small notes I'd collected in my bag.

"Give them all to me," he said. "I'll give you new pounds for them. It's all right. It's still our money—old, but good." There was something very proud in that simple statement. My mood brightened.

After a lavish farewell dinner aboard the Anni, several of the guests left for Cairo. Eric was one. Still taping, he backed off the gangplank amid cheers and waves. He didn't put his camera down until his wife turned off the lights. Then he opened his hands in a futile gesture of resignation and got into the cab. Applause rang out.

I turned to Jerry and whispered, "He's going home to see his vacation on video."

"I think you're right," he said.

I started to leave. Jerry grabbed my arm. "What do you say we hire a carriage and see Luxor by night? Not the ruins or the tourist spots, just the back alleys."

Surprised, I looked at him. He was smiling. All of a sudden he looked boyish, carefree—not the serious academe I had become acquainted with over the past week. I was pleased. A real date on my last night in Luxor!

"Great idea," I said. "Let me get a sweater and I'll be right back." I ran to my cabin, strangely excited.

Jerry hired a carriage driven by a young man in a striped *gallaka*. The air was so still that the pinpricks of light from the Anni seemed to puncture the clear water. We cut through town to the back streets. The horse trotted slowly, his hooves a staccato counterpoint to the steady grind of the wheels. The streets were deserted, except for an occasional yowling dog, and the donkeys standing patiently, face to the wall. It was far more charming than it had seemed that afternoon. Now and then I caught a glimpse of a courtyard and a family sitting around a fire, eating. Men, like shadowy forms gathered in a conspiracy, sat in the doorways, smoking.

Suddenly Jerry told the driver to stop. We were in front of a small, brightly lit café. Loud music spilled from the open door.

"Stay here," he said as he hopped from the carriage. "I have a surprise."

In five minutes he was back, holding two beers.

"Whew, talk about smoke!" he said, handing me an open bottle. "I could hardly see my way to the bar."

I held up my bottle. "Here's to you, me, Akhenaten, and Hatshepsut. May our spirits thrive forever." We clicked bottles and drank thirstily.

Just as we reached the Nile, Jerry started whistling.

"What's that, an Irish jig?" I asked.

"That's one of your good old Appalachian folk songs," he replied. "Thought you were a country musician."

"I am, but don't stray too far from 'Aunt Rhody' and 'Turkey in the Straw,' or I'll get lost." I giggled. I felt contented and a little light-headed.

"I never told you, Meg, but I'm crazy about folk dancing. Square, contra…all kinds. Can't get enough of it! How about you?"

I looked into Jerry's eyes—so kind, so clear—and felt a rush of affection. "Oh, yes, Jerry. I love square dancing." He put his arm around me. I liked it. "Say, this ride was wonderful. What a great idea!"

"I have an even better idea," he said. "I'm going to promenade you right back to the Anni." He motioned the driver to stop, and jumped down, pulling me after him.

"Now, for a little *dos-a-dos* and swing your partner." I started to laugh as Jerry's powerful hands encircled my waist, twirling me around and around in the street, finally lifting me until my legs splayed out and I was red-faced with laughter and embarrassment.

It was late by the time we reached the Anni. It seemed abandoned. Jerry walked me to my room. Neither of us talked. When we reached my door he put both hands on my shoulders and drew me close to him.

"Meg, you've become very special to me these last few days. Please…." He leaned down and gently kissed me. Unexpectedly, I found myself pulling away. He held me closer.

"I'm sorry, Jerry. Truly sorry. I'm not ready yet. I didn't know how much pain I was still carrying around."

My excuses tumbled out. I grabbed for the doorknob and disappeared into the darkened stateroom, where I stood, numbly, looking out the picture window. Traces of moon glanced on the water. Delicate rushes swayed lightly on the opposite bank. Deep, searing loneliness enveloped me, and filled me, as Glen's love once had. For the first time since I left home, I wept.

9

MONEY-CHANGERS, BEWARE!

When I flew into the old Cairo air terminal from Luxor, it seemed like the perfect time to buy my ticket to Nairobi. I still had two hundred and fifty dollars in Egyptian pounds left from my initial exchange, and I planned to use all of it toward the purchase of the ticket, paying the rest by Visa. I could then leave the country with no extra currency. It was always a challenge to make everything come out even. But I hadn't figured on Egyptian bureaucracy.

"A one-way ticket to Nairobi," I said to the glum clerk at the Egypt air office, handing him a stack of Egyptian pounds and the small pink bank slip, my original proof of exchange.

He counted the money slowly. "Sorry, but we can only accept one hundred and fifty dollars in pounds with this proof of exchange. You must pay the rest in dollars. Even this is not strictly legal. You exchanged three hundred dollars and have been in Egypt two weeks, no? After ten days—at the legal minimum expenditure of thirty dollars a day—this was no longer a valid proof of exchange." Menacingly, he waved the pink slip in front of me.

"But I've been staying with friends," I protested. "I've had very few expenses. And I've paid for my tours by Visa. And I didn't know about the thirty dollar daily minimum....You *must* believe me." How I wished I'd heeded Carmela's advice and only exchanged the one hundred and fifty dollar minimum when I'd arrived. What would I do with all those extra pounds?

The clerk's eyes narrowed and his lips curled in a wordless, self-satisfied smirk as he pushed the pile of money and the pink bank slip toward me. I grabbed them and stormed out. That was my second mistake. My first mistake was to assume that I could buy airline tickets easier and cheaper in Africa than in the United States.

Early the next morning I started out for the Hilton Hotel office of Egypt Air, eager to get my ticket and spend the rest of the day museum hopping. I was beginning to feel at home in Cairo. Noisy, dirty, and disorganized, it was still very much alive—so different from the poor rural areas I had just left. I hurried along the street, blending with the crowds that surged across the main square at the railroad station almost toppling the policeman, who stood in the middle of the intersection against a backdrop of gaudy billboards, his frantic gestures a meaningless charade.

Unsuccessful at the Hilton, I went on to the Sheraton office.

"Madam, I can't accept *any* of your Egyptian pounds from the original proof of exchange," said the clerk, shaking his head vigorously. "You must pay the entire ticket in U.S. dollars."

"What are you saying? That I've been dealing in illegal currency?" I asked, abandoning any attempt at friendly persuasion. "Are you accusing me of being a black marketeer?"

"I am accusing you of nothing, Madam. I am simply telling you the rules." He shoved the pink slip across the counter at me.

Refusing to give up, I looked around for a tourist agency and finally found a sympathetic friend at Abercrombie and Kent. She accepted $150 in Egyptian pounds, the original offer at the old terminal, in exchange for the precious bank slip. But first we had to walk down the block to the Egypt Air office to get it okayed. I despaired. They had just turned me down an hour ago.

At the office we were shuffled from one agent to the next, each one examining the pink slip before announcing that it was against the law to accept my pounds. The A & K agent stood her ground and demanded to be taken upstairs to the big boss. There he sat—a portly man with a wispy moustache and a nervous squint—looking out from behind a desk, which was covered with mountains of paper and rolls of tickets wrapped in rubber bands. It reminded me of the cluttered government office in Dokki, where I had gone to get "registered" on my first morning in Egypt.

The boss thumbed absentmindedly through a roll of tickets. We waited. He was enjoying his power. We pleaded: he explained. We argued: he shouted. Finally, he took the pink slip, stamped it, signed it, and accepted my Visa for the remainder of the payment.

Ecstatic, ticket in hand, I ran down the street to the American Express office. By now there would certainly be mail for me. I showed my identification and was handed a small bundle of letters. One letter, scribbled hurriedly by Cary, my eldest daughter, 34, tickled me.

Dear Mom,

I'm poring over a map of the world, which I've nailed to the wall above my desk. I bought a red marker so I can keep track of your journey. I'm writing now, hoping to catch you in Cairo before you head into the bush. I bet I'm as excited about this trip as you are—and a lot more worried.Yes, worried. I never thought I'd be writing such a "motherly" note, but, for the first time, I realize what you must have gone through with Martha and me roaming around Europe all those years, and during my Wind-cheetah* trip around the U.S., peddling in a near-horizontal position, a sitting duck. Lucky no trucks rolled over me. Right? That's what it looks like to me five years later. And I remember nothing but encouragement from you. Perhaps it's time to thank you for not scaring me...but, hell, I'm scared about you now, and I'll admit it! Please keep the hitch-hiking down to a minimum and don't have any blood transfusions—if you get hurt, that is, which I don't expect. And WRITE. And CALL.

Love, Cary

*A seven foot, three-wheeled recumbent human-powered vehicle designed by Mike Burrows in Norwich, England. Cary went 10,000 miles around the U.S.—up the west coast and across the continent to New England.

For Cary, life was one long exciting paragraph. I pictured her sailing down the hills of Seattle on her racing bike, long hair flying, no helmet, strong, confident.

When I returned to Dokki, Hamal and Judy were preparing for an overnight trip to their orange grove on the Isle of Dingway in the middle of the Nile, and invited me to go along. Sounded great to me, since my plane didn't leave until 12:30 the next night.

"We're bringing Mother along as a tour guide," said Hamal, as Mrs. Wasim wrapped her shawl around her shoulders and settled into the front seat of the tiny sedan. "She can give you more facts than the official government travel bureau...with about as much accuracy."

His mother poked him playfully and said something in Arabic.

For the first half hour we wound through tangled traffic, trying to get out of town. Cars slipped through red lights like ballplayers stealing bases. Pedestrians ran for their life.

"Let me tell you," said Hamal as we reached open country and headed north toward Mansoura and Sherbin in the heart of the Nile Delta. "People wouldn't dare drive on the open road the way they do in Cairo. The highway police are much stricter. If you get a speeding ticket you lose your license on the spot. And you have to go through an almost impossible process to get it back." (I had begun to understand what *that* could involve.)

We traveled through small villages and fertile fields. Large eucalyptus trees hugged the narrow two-lane road. Canal-like ditches ran on either side, overhung with willows and a high, reedy, fake bamboo whose furry tassels waved gracefully in the wind. Donkeys, water buffalo, and camels were a common sight.

I learned a lot about the Egyptian mentality that day, and about their struggle to understand new technology while still retaining the quality of their own culture. "All kinds of home industries could be introduced," said Hamal. "But dependency on outside technology is killing their spirit and their basic feeling of self worth."

"And our women! There's a neglected resource. More and more they're trying to speak...."

"Yes, Hamal," Judy interrupted. "But they have so little power! They can't even persuade their husbands to use birth control."

"Some women are beginning to be heard," he said. "And raising their consciousness is our only hope. The men simply don't understand. Like so many poor people in Africa, they stay frightened all their lives. They have almost no human rights and they defy their real or imagined 'oppressors,' perhaps unconsciously, by having children. They feel abused if alone. Weak. They think children will take care of them in their old age. Hah! In the meantime, nobody gets ahead."

"Well," said Mrs. Wasim, "things are not as bad as you paint them. Look at all those school children we just saw in Mahala. Education is the answer." She turned to me and started quoting statistics. I listened intently, and deluged her with questions.

"Mother," said Hamal, chuckling. "You sound like a government mouthpiece and Meg like a typical eager tourist. She even gets excited over a dirty canal!"

By 4 P.M. we had arrived at the riverbank opposite the Isle of Dingway. We parked beside a rudimentary stone house occupied by the squatter family who tended the Wasim's orchards. The family came out in force to greet us—eleven children, two wives, and the beaming farmer who would ferry us across the Nile. Three cows grazed lazily on a knoll next to the river. Papyrus, like the biblical bulrush, hung in a delicate arch from the bank, rising and falling in the wind.

The women stood holding heaping platters of warm baked bread, rice, beans, and fresh tomatoes. One wife was careworn and bent, a black shawl tied around her graying head, several bottom teeth missing. The other was young and round, a colorful bandana holding back chestnut hair, a full skirt covering her swollen belly.

We loaded everything into a large dory and set forth, letting the farmer, with his sturdy bamboo pole, push us to the other side, aided by the gentle current. I imagined myself Cleopatra, sitting in the bow of my barge, hair blowing in the cool afternoon breeze.

I stepped out of the boat onto a grassy bank. In front of me stretched rows and rows of fruit trees—pear, fig, lemon, orange. "How's this for a tangerine?" shouted Hamal. He cupped his hand around a great orange sphere attached to a branch bursting with fruit.

I peeled the fruit, devouring each succulent slice as I walked down a palm-lined path to a rambling stucco house with ornate wooden doors and colorful tiled floors. Judy, shouting and laughing, raced upstairs to throw open the shutters. We stood together, silently, as the sun, now a fiery ball, slowly disappeared behind the trees.

Dinner was lavish—mountains of rice, fresh baked bread, homemade cheeses, stuffed peppers, fresh garden vegetables, roasted chicken, and a special bean dish with spicy sauce that left me breathless.

As darkness set in we pulled the shutters and sat talking until after midnight. Don Giovanni played in the background. "I've never known such peacefulness," I said as Judy was preparing my bed on the brocaded sofa. "I feel enveloped in a quiet that I can almost touch."

"You're lucky there hasn't been a wedding, a birth, or a death," she said. "The first two bring singing and dancing all night, and the other brings chanting and lamenting—enhanced by the loudspeaker from the minaret on the mainland. It's enough to drive you crazy."

I lay on the couch mulling over our evening of conversation, and fighting a giant mosquito.

"The sale of military weapons is the new slave trade in Africa," Hamal had said. "This is how the petty dictators keep their people subjugated. And it's the U.S., Western Europe, Russia, and Israel who are the biggest offenders. If this madness isn't stopped, there'll be no hope for freedom or democracy in the Third World." I didn't know that I was to come face-to-face with this reality wherever I went in Africa.

I would miss Judy and Hamal. They had a closeness that I envied. I wondered if I'd ever again know such a relationship. "I really do want to let go of huge chunks of the past," I had said during the evening. "Sure, I'm at a turning point, but sometimes I feel paralyzed, unable to change, unable to let anyone or anything in."

"But you *have* changed, Meg," Judy interjected. "I can see it in the past two years. You no longer seem to be wound up like one of those rubber band toys—just waiting to be released so you can spin in circles. You're much more relaxed. Give yourself a break!"

We started back to Cairo early the next afternoon so I could catch my late evening flight. Just before I was to leave the house in Dokki, Hamal insisted on calling Egypt Air to make sure I had the right airport. I did, but the plane had left at 12:30 A.M. that morning. I'd gotten the date right, but I'd failed to realize that the new day started at midnight. I was a day late.

There's nothing worse than an anticlimax when you're primed to leave. Egypt Air would not have another flight to Nairobi for two days, so I was determined to switch my ticket to Kenya Airways, which had a flight the very next evening. Luckily, they had space available, but said I would have to get a refund and buy the ticket all over again. They would also need an MCO (Miscellaneous Charge Order, whatever that means) from Egypt Air and, of course, the pink bank slip. Help from Abercrombie and Kent was out of the question. I should have quit at this point. But no. I was in too deep.

Since nothing is negotiated by phone in Cairo, I raced back and forth between the Kenya Airways office in the Hilton and the Egypt Air office. I could soon navigate the route with my eyes closed. I sneaked upstairs and tackled the same man who had sold me my ticket two days earlier. He shook his head in disbelief as he slipped the elastic band from a bundle of tickets and handed me the pink slip and Visa receipt. Just as he was getting ready to tear up my ticket, I shouted, "Wait—give me half-an-hour to make sure I can do this!" and headed off to the Hilton again.

When I arrived at Kenya Airways with the pink slip, I suddenly realized that I had not gotten my Egyptian pounds back. On top of this I was told that my Visa card would not be accepted for the remainder of the ticket price, since the transaction had to be either all in cash or all by credit card. That would mean going to a bank and cashing more travelers checks. And I'd still be stuck with the extra hundred dollars in pounds. Oh, my God! I was right back where I started.

Once again at Egypt Air, I faced the big boss. "I cannot give you the three hundred and twenty-three pounds," he said, smiling triumphantly. "You'll have to get it from Abercrombie and Kent."

Tears of frustration started down my cheeks. I took back my original, updated ticket, surrendered the precious pink slip, and retreated to old Cairo. A sudden shower sent me running for shelter into Ibn Tulin Mosque. After removing my wet shoes at the entrance, I wandered past rows of columns that ringed the large open courtyard, then stood, quietly, lost in the soothing chanting and bowing of the faithful.

Just before leaving, I climbed to the top of the tower overlooking the city. Spread out in front of me was Cairo—a mosaic of muted colors—the mingling, once more, of the ancient and the modern. I remembered the words of Mrs. Wasim: Egypt dances in the middle of the stairs, and nobody looks up or down. Like Jerry, I knew I'd be coming back.

The next evening, as I buckled up for my flight to Nairobi, I started chatting with the man sitting next to me. He looked exhausted—said he had spent the previous night in the airport.

"Why?" I asked.

"I was ticketed on the Kenya Airways flight last night to Nairobi," he replied. "It was cancelled at 2:30 A.M. without explanation. I'm lucky I could get a seat on *this* flight. I've never experienced anything like Egyptian bureaucracy! I spent the whole day shuttling from one airline office to the next. You can't imagine...."

"Oh, can't I?" I said.

10

NAIROBI

It was 6:15 A.M. A pink glow still hovered around the edges of the earth as the plane landed in Kenya and I caught my first glimpse of the Ngong hills, made famous by Isak Dinesen's <u>Out</u> <u>of</u> <u>Africa</u>.

"When you get off the plane in Nairobi, Meg, breathe deeply," Allen Tinker, my minister, had said, shortly before I left home. "There's a special quality, a perfume in the air. I don't know what it is, but you won't find it anywhere else in the world." It would be four days before I experienced the truth of these words. I had caught a cold and it was all I could do just to breathe. Smelling was out of the question.

I'd been awake most of the night, anticipating my arrival in the heart of Africa and being verbally bombarded by my seatmate, Benjamin Hall, a medical student from South Carolina. He filled me with dread about what could happen to a lone female backpacker, what transpired in African hostels, and the number of locks needed to protect my belongings. He insinuated that even the guards at the YMCA tip the thieves off as to which guests look prosperous and what rooms they occupy.

"I don't believe that," I said. "But it wouldn't affect me, anyway. I don't look prosperous—wrinkled black skirt, Minnie Mouse clodhoppers...."

"Camera bag. New backpack," he countered. "You look prosperous. Trust me."

But Benjamin damaged his credibility when he started bragging about how he'd defrauded Egyptian vendors and cabbies, passing himself off as a Canadian so they wouldn't think him a rich American, and showing an empty wallet to prove that he had no money for fares. I was wondering whom I should fear the most—him or his horror stories.

The bus rattled toward Nairobi. Posters of President Daniel arap Moi grinned down from high poles along the highway. I didn't want to admit that Benjamin's negative comments had influenced me, but I decided to treat myself to a room in the Ambassadeur, a modest hotel in the middle of town…just in case. There'd be plenty of time to look into hostels and buy locks.

The first thing I noticed when I stepped into my room was a sign: *Water from the tap is safe to drink.* Eureka! I soon discovered that this only meant in Nairobi, but at that moment all I wanted to do was crash.

Three hours later I threw open the front windows and looked down into a sea of black faces. What a strange feeling. For the first time in my life I was in the minority. It was lunch hour and scores of people milled about the square. There was lots of shouting and waving. Everyone seemed to be having a wonderful time.

I stepped outside into the bright sunshine. Nairobi reminded me more of a sprawling frontier town than a former English colonial capitol. Except for government offices and swanky hotels, most buildings were only a few stories high, and many had overhangs supported by square wooden pillars that made a canopy over the sidewalk. Modern parking meters lined the streets. Department stores, curio shops, and electronic outlets—invariably run by go-getting Indian merchants—crowded the bustling commercial district. For an hour I shopped, and was overjoyed to find emery boards at a chemist's—something I'd forgotten to pack and had tried to buy in Egypt.

At the Hilton I came upon just the right safari hat—a true <u>Out</u> <u>of</u> <u>Africa</u> replica for four dollars, complete with leather chinstrap. How splendid! How British! It bonded to my head, instantly, and remained there for the next eight months.

My last chore of the day was to find the post office and call home, something I'd promised to do every two weeks. I was late and this made me nervous. Suppose my mother had died. Suppose one of my children had been hit by a car. Suppose my house had burned down.

Despite a detailed map, I managed to get lost, so I resorted to asking directions—a great way to meet people when you're in a strange place. In Nairobi it was especially rewarding. Nobody seemed to be annoyed or in a hurry. The answer always came in a soft sing-songy cadence punctuated by a rolling "r"—as in one and thrrrre ninety, meaning 193—a courteous bow, and a radiant smile. The kind of smile that makes you feel good all day.

It was almost closing time when I walked into the post office at 193 Kenyatta Avenue. I placed an overseas call to my eldest son and entered a small cubicle to wait for him to answer. "Nairobi to Jersey City, come in please." What could be taking so long?

A sleepy voice answered. "Good heavens, Chris, did I wake you up?" I asked.

"Of course not. I always stay up until 3 A.M., just in case you call." He sounded next door.

"Oh, I'm sorry. How's everything and everybody?"

"Fine, fine. No major accidents or deaths. Have you fallen in love, yet?"

"Chris, give me a break. I'm soaking up culture."

"Mom, we're all afraid you'll run off with some Arab, and they don't treat their women well...."

"Unlike the non-Arab I was married to for thirty-three years?"

"You're right. You're right. I take it all back."

"Hey, buddy, I'm headed for the African bush. No more Arabs. Just spear carrying lion-killers...." I paused, aware of the incessant ticking off of message units. "I have to go, now. I'll write. And I'll call in two weeks. Friday night, before midnight. I promise. Love to everybody."

This was probably the shortest phone call of my life.

I suddenly felt very much alone. I had no friends to return to and no idea what I'd do. My cold was debilitating. And it was the 3rd of December and hardly a Christmas decoration was in sight. But why would that bother me? I'd always hated the commercialization of Christmas. Could I be just a little bit homesick?

Sleep was impossible. The streets were hopping with boisterous, laughing people, reminiscent of New Orleans at Mardi Gras. At 10 o'clock I gave up and went downstairs to an Indian restaurant for a bite to eat. The turbaned waiter seemed very excited when I told him that I planned to visit Bombay.

"My friend runs a hotel in Bombay. He's *Sikh*, like me."

"Oh," I said. "You don't look sick."

"But I am."

"So am I. In fact, I feel miserable. What seems to be your problem?" I asked.

"Oh, no, Madam," he replied. "I mean *SIKH*, not sick."

"Oh, of course," I murmured, embarrassed. I never did become an expert in deciphering the Indian-English accent.

◆   ◆   ◆

"Nobody is climbing Mt. Kenya at this time, because the rainy season is late, and the summit is very dangerous," said the clerk at the fifth mountaineering agency to turn me down. "So it's best you stop searching." He looked at me consolingly.

For two days I'd tramped around Nairobi looking for a way to get to Mt. Kenya. It was at the top of my wish list as a result of my nephew, Chip, whose glowing report of his ascent put it right up there with Kilimanjaro and Everest base camp.

I finally gave up and turned my efforts toward finding a safari. This sent me into a frenzy of indecision. Safaris came in all shapes and sizes, from tent camping to unabashed luxury. And prices were negotiable. I wasn't prepared, physically or mentally, for the kind of comparison-shopping it required. Exhausted after three hours, I retreated to my hotel to nurse a pounding headache.

By the fourth day I had to get out of town. I booked an afternoon tour to a *Masai* village in the legendary Rift Valley, which cuts through the heart of Africa from north to south.

Tums aids upset stomachs read the banner on the back of a dirt-encrusted bus. As it passed, a new Mercedes rolled out of the driveway of a colonial mansion—the kind you see in the movies, with a high stone wall, filigreed iron gates, orange tiled roof, and elegant carved shrubbery.

I hung onto my seat. This was my first exposure to Kenyan roads. Our small van bumped along, swerving to miss the largest potholes, and coming dangerously close to the edge, where the pavement dropped off into a narrow bed of red clay. No shoulders, no center lines, no guardrails.

Neat little farms laced with dirt footpaths crisscrossed the countryside. Barefoot children played in small pools of mud, and waved as we passed. Vendors stood by the side of the road selling basketsful of small red plums, luxurious sheepskins, and native crafts.

Thirty miles out of Nairobi we turned off the main road and started down into the valley. A picture book Africa unfolded—the silent, unspoiled world of umbrella acacia trees, flat-topped and lacey, flowering jacaranda heavy with purple blossoms, and candelabra cacti reaching their prickly arms to the sun. Above it all, rolling clouds cut through a sky of intense blue. Only the thump-thump of the van going in and out of dirt ruts broke the stillness.

Our first stop was Mayers' Ranch, a 6,000-acre estate boasting one of the most exquisite gardens in Kenya. The indigenous *Masai* live on the ranch property by special arrangement. They are a pastoral, semi-nomadic tribe of about 115,000 people inhabiting lands as far south as northern Tanzania. They're very tall and slender, with narrow heads and lithe, muscular bodies. Since their diet is predominantly milk, cow's blood, and meat, they keep large herds of beef cattle. For me they became the most easily recognized ethnic group in Kenya, because of the male attire—a flowing piece of material attached at one shoulder—and the large, elongated holes in their ear lobes. Stretched since childhood, the lobes become thick loops of hanging skin. The women shave their heads—a sign of beauty—and adorn themselves with masses of beaded ornaments: elaborate, heavy headdresses; necklaces; and wide collars in vibrant primary colors. Eager to sell their handwork, they swarmed around us. I yearned to buy one of the collars, but settled for a simple necklace of flat beads, silver, red, and black. There was no room in my pack for extra weight.

Young Masai woman.

I wandered around the tiny village, talking to young girls, many with babies strapped to their backs. One took me by the hand and pulled me into her home, a hut made of dung, aromatic leaves, and wooden supports. Inside was one large room. Straw mats covered the hard mud floor. I pondered this simple life as I watched a spirited dance program put on by the men in the village.

As we left the ranch we came to a *manyatta,* a semi-circle of low dung-plastered huts surrounded by a thorn bush barrier. This was an army barracks, one of hundreds scattered throughout the valley. It housed eighteen *moran,* or junior warriors, and was the center for the various stages in the life of the young male, culminating in a proscribed act of bravery and his circumcision. (I tended to think of the two as synonymous.) Their skin and hair were dyed tile-red by applying a mixture of pulverized earth and animal fat. Patterns were drawn on their faces and bodies and wild sisal fibers twisted into their long hair to protect the back of the neck during a fight. What a contrast to the shaved heads of the women.

The drive home gave me my first glimpse of the patience of the African—something I could well imitate. Large buses and tractor trailer trucks wound slowly around the hills, taking up the entire road. Passing would have been suicidal. But the driver never complained about the delay, and continued chatting pleasantly with his passengers. I spent the time reading signs: *Caltex*, written in large red letters over a Texas star; *Kobil*, with the Mobil oil insignia; and *Esso*, a familiar trademark I hadn't seen in years.

Sitting next to me was a Swedish forester. "Will you look at these specimens!" he exclaimed as he pointed out trees I'd never seen before. "*Kepchestnut, gravillia*, and the familiar eucalyptus. Thank God Kenya is still relatively unspoiled." Then he added, "Have you ever noticed an unusual, sweet smell in the air?"

I nodded.

"Well, that's a combination of cedar and eucalyptus. I've never encountered anything quite like it."

I couldn't wait to tell Allen Tinker.

The following morning I called Mwangi Maine, a friend of Allen's. Now that my cold was gone I felt like being sociable. Mwangi is an import-export broker and proud member of the *Kikuyu* tribe, the largest, most highly educated ethnic group in Kenya. He has three children studying in New Jersey colleges, three in Kenya, and a large extended family. He drives a gleaming white Mercedes, and lives in a large colonial home with a guard at the gate.

At noon I walked up the three flights to Mwangi's office in the center of Nairobi, a modest room with a large window and plaster peeling off one wall. As I entered, he rose from behind an imposing desk and reached out a beefy hand. He was striking, square-jawed, and very black.

"So this is the lady from New Jersey?" he said in a booming baritone. "I see you have a *Masai* necklace. Lovely. We must get you *Kikuyu* earrings to go with it."

I stammered something about my visit to the Rift Valley.

He tilted his head slightly, amused. "Here's my daughter, Njeri—we call her Jerry—and her sister Njambi, and their friend Amina. They'll join us for lunch."

He introduced me to several associates. Among them was Clive Nderi, the only member of the staff who used an English first name. "Clive will show you the sights around Nairobi—anything you wish—for as long as you stay."

Clive, like Mwangi, was very dark, but had a short, wiry build. And an impish grin.

After a photo session—during which I made a big hit by taking everybody's picture individually and in groups, we headed for a grand *Kikuyu* buffet at the New Stanley Hotel.

The food was beautifully laid out, but everything tasted like potatoes to me. I tried *ilio* and *irio*, and finally settled for *ungari*, made with maize meal, flour, vegetables, and meat. Even mixing beans and *mieli* (maize) into the various roots didn't help, because there wasn't any butter or sauce to counteract the dryness. It became a challenge just to swallow. And I had to taste every dish or risk insulting my host. By the time I got to the meat specialties and desserts, I was full to the brim.

The conversation at dinner was lively, however, and made me forget the food. "College in the United States is costing me a lot of money," Mwangi said, with a heavy sigh. "But it's worth it. Children and family are very important to me. I think we have a slightly different concept of what constitutes a family here in Africa. Nobody gets left out. If an aunt is in trouble or needs money we all help. If a cousin has a baby and no husband, that baby is welcomed by all of us. Right now I have two cousins and an elderly uncle living with me…and my mother, and a younger brother, and Njeri's baby. Next year it may all change. Who knows?"

After lunch, in a quiet corner of the lobby, Mwangi talked into my small tape recorder. He sent lengthy messages to his children—in English, and in *Kikuyu*.

"I'm really impressed with all the languages I hear in Kenya," I commented, after he'd finished. "And it makes me feel awfully provincial."

"Most people don't realize how diverse our culture is," he said. "Imagine if America had thirty tribes—with separate languages—all of them vying for power. That causes big, big problems. That's why we feel we must speak at least three languages. *Swahili* and English, the official ones, as well as our own tribal tongue." Before I left Kenya I had met members of six of these tribes—the *Kikuyu, Masai, Kamba, Luo, Boran,* and *Somali.*

"But let's not talk any more about problems. They're always with us. You're not." He put a powerful arm around my shoulder. "Here's my plan. Njeri will take you to the bazaar to buy earrings, or whatever you want, and then get some ice cream. After that Clive will take all of you to the *Bomas* dancers and maybe Karen Blixen's plantation. Do you like that idea, Meg?"

"Sounds marvelous, although a bit exhausting," I replied.

"That's why we *Kikuyus* eat *ungari.*" He laughed, handed Njeri some money, and shook my hand. "Tomorrow you must come to my home for dinner. Perhaps we can help you plan your safari. You can make arrangements with Clive." He turned and strode down the stairs, leaving me with the three smiling girls.

Typical teenagers, they had giggled at most everything I said at lunch and now were eager to find just the right gift for me. Arm-in-arm we walked down a back ally into one of the bazaars.

A man brushed by me. "Watch out," yelled Njeri. She grabbed my arm and pulled me toward her. "That man tried to unhook the straps on your camera bag just now. You must be careful," she warned.

"I never even noticed," I said, feeling foolish. Clutching the bag to my chest I continued looking, until I found some red and white heart-shaped dangling earrings to match my necklace.

We wandered back up the alley and into Slush, a Baskin-Robbins look-alike, complete with striped uniforms and countless flavors. I was overjoyed! Being an ice cream addict, I decided that this was a good time to begin my search for the greatest chocolate ice cream on earth. Slush lived up to its slogan: *Nobody does it better!*

I was hungry, again, by the time we left the *Bomas* dancers, who performed a variety of tribal dances in a large indoor amphitheater. Clive dropped the girls off in town, then stopped at a tiny shop to buy me a spicy meat pie, before driving to Karen, the town named after Baroness Karen von Blixen.

"Nobody in Kenya ever thinks of her as Isak Dinesen," he said. "She was quite a celebrity, and very much loved long before the world discovered Out of Africa.

We drove on tree-lined roads and through dense forests, which were once part of her 600-acre coffee plantation. We passed the country club, church, and street named after her. A haunting feeling of long ago came over me, of a richly creative life punctuated by sadness and searing disappointment. It was hard not to let the drama of her heartbreaking love affair overshadow her success as a writer and storyteller.

The house was smaller than I had expected. Flowering shrubs lined the pebbled driveway. The ceilings were low and the library dark-paneled. It was at the small desk by the window in this room that Karen wrote her letters from Africa. There was a gun rack in front of the fireplace.

"You can see it in the movie, Out of Africa," said Clive, proudly.

A single lantern—which Karen had used to signal to Denys Finch-Hatton that she was home—hung outside the front door.

We left as the sun was sinking behind the Ngong Hills, silhouetting the tall grave marker where Karen's lover is buried.

11

THE FUNERAL

On our return through town we spotted Mwangi and his friends hanging out in front of his office, leaning against the parking meters, laughing and joking. It reminded me of the male gatherings thirty years ago in front of the Stonewall Jackson Bar in Clarksburg, West Virginia, where my husband had been the city manager. Even then I suspected that parking meters were really designed to give men something to hang onto while they talked.

Mwangi flagged us down. "I just left a message at your hotel, Meg, inviting you to dinner tonight at my home."

"But I promised Richard we'd eat at his place," said Clive.

"Bring him, too. In fact, everybody come. Tomorrow is my stepmother's funeral. Tonight we'll honor her with a party." He slapped the fender of his Mercedes, motioning the men to get in.

Clive drove down a side street to the warehouse section where Richard Mburu, an old schoolmate, owned an Indian restaurant. We entered through a beaded curtain and into the warm smell of curry and incense. A string of colored lights flickered over the bar.

Richard embraced us both. "O.K., I'll go to Mwangi's, but first we'll have tea." He ushered us to a wobbly table in the back. "Nobody goes anywhere in Kenya without first having tea."

We also had to have hot, spicy Indian appetizers. The kind that bring tears to your eyes.

"I've been around the world twice and spent six months in your country," said Richard, as he drew up a metal chair and started pouring from a decorative clay teapot. "I loved it—especially New York City—and plan to return as soon as I sell this restaurant." He was tall, light-skinned, and immaculate in pressed jeans and a tan linen shirt. His speech was reserved and straightforward, quite different from Clive's rapid staccato.

"My sister wasn't as crazy as you about the U.S.," Clive countered. "She just returned and thinks you romanticize it."

"Yeah, but where did she go?" asked Richard. He smiled, knowingly, deep grooves forming on either side of his strong face.

"Well, mostly West Virginia—to visit a girl friend. But the people were not very friendly. For example, she was the only black person in a bar one night and said she could feel everyone staring at her as if she were some kind of freak. Felt it so strongly it scared her. So she left."

"That doesn't surprise me," I said, not wanting to minimize his sister's experience. "West Virginians aren't overly friendly to strangers, regardless of color. They have to get to know you first. This would not have happened to her in New York City. At any rate, she wouldn't have felt so outnumbered." I remembered when Glen became the city manager of a small city in West Virginia. It took them a long time to accept us, because we were "Yankees."

"You can find prejudice anywhere," said Richard. "For example, if you were British, Meg, I wouldn't be sitting here having tea with you. That's something I have to get over."

We headed for the suburbs west of Nairobi. As the neighborhood became more affluent, the roads became worse. I complained to Clive as he swerved from side to side to avoid the deep ruts.

"You can blame it on the colonialists," he said. "They didn't trust the black drivers not to kill their precious white children, so they left the potholes to slow down the cars."

"Oh, come on, Clive. You blame everything on the colonialists and they've been gone for years!"

"Well," he said, sheepishly, "*we* also feel that it keeps the cars from speeding. The British had a few good ideas."

"Hell, the kids who live inside these walled mansions don't play in the road, anyway. That's just an excuse for doing nothing," I said. "Is that how you explain the lousy highways?"

Clive chuckled. He knew I'd caught him. "We're a poor country, Meg," he answered.

We drove through an iron gate and up a long circular drive. Mwangi was standing in his front yard, examining a large acacia tree that had fallen on one of the family cars. If it had been *my* car I'd have been desolated, but he found it amusing. The tree had sliced the car right down the middle. "Amazing," was all he said, scratching his head, and shaking it slowly from side to side.

An old lady appeared in the yard, holding a baby in her arms. "Meet Grandma, my natural mother," Mwangi said, bowing. "She doesn't speak English, but she welcomes you....And this is Njeri's baby. Bless her. She's given the old woman a reason to live."

Grandma smiled and motioned us into the house. She was bent and thin. A colorful kerchief held back her gray hair, accentuating the prominent earlobes of the *Masai*. I wanted desperately to reach over and stick a finger through one of the large loops of skin.

Photographs of Mwangi and his family hung on all the walls. Every inch of space was crammed with knick knacks and heavy stuffed furniture, each piece covered in a different floral material. More flowers adorned the curtains and fought with the flowers smiling up from the oriental rugs, making the room into a stylized still life of the Garden of Eden. A table heaped with cooked, mashed vegetables stood at one end of the dining room. Mrs. Maine, a handsome, robust woman, presided over the festivities. She looked elegant in a black silk dress.

Two teenagers jumped up and turned off the television when we entered. Their attitude was pleasant and respectful. They seemed to fit in with the adults, not dominate, as so often happens in the U.S.

The men sat in groups talking. They did not defer to the women. It was a man's world and they were the leaders.

"You must leave for the funeral early in the morning," said Mwangi. "It's a long way to Gilgil, and the roads are bad. Take the pickup, Richard."

"Why are you burying your stepmother so far away?" I blurted out. "I mean...didn't she live in Nairobi?"

"It's part of our tradition, Meg. To a Kenyan, and especially a *Kikuyu*, the plot of land where he was born is his real home, no matter where he's living at the time of death. Part of the reason we fought so hard with the British is that they tried to take our land from us. Without land you have no identity, no roots, no wealth...and no future. Nothing to pass on to your children."

I felt uncomfortable. What could I say? I knew nothing about living under tyranny.

Fortunately, Mrs. Maine changed the mood, entering the room with a heaping plate of what looked like dessert. Tired of vegetables, I inquired about it. She smiled and offered me hers. I dived into it eagerly, only to discover that it was sweet potatoes.

Exhausted, my stomach feeling like lead, I motioned to Clive to leave. "Wait a minute," he admonished me. "Richard is having his coffee." The minute stretched into half-an-hour. And I waited, and waited. Nobody did anything in a hurry in this country.

By the time we left, the night watchman had taken his place inside a small sentinel box next to the imposing gate.

"In the U.S. most of us can't afford servants," I said to Clive, teasing. "Aren't you acting a little like the hated colonialists? I mean, how do you explain a cook, a gardener, a maid, and even a night watchman?"

"Who says they're servants? We're just giving people jobs."

I smiled. "Oh, Clive, you have an answer for everything!"

We dropped Richard at his restaurant before going to my hotel.

"Come on up to my room, Clive, and I'll give you the photographs." He'd promised to send a package home for me—pictures I'd had developed (I would keep the negatives to guard against loss), and the musical instrument I'd bought at the *Bomas* concert that afternoon.

I realized right away that I'd made a big mistake. As Clive entered the room, he kicked off his shoes and sat down on the bed. I handed him the photographs and sat in a chair across the room. He came over and sat on the arm of my chair to ask about various pictures. I moved to another chair. He moved, too. I got up and thumbed through my papers, nervously, coming across a recent Time magazine with a lead story about disease in Africa.

I thrust the magazine at him and said, "There's a story here that may interest you." How ridiculous! Nothing could have been further from the truth.

"Let's go dancing," he said, ignoring the magazine, and moving closer. "You're a beautiful, charming woman."

"Thank you, Clive, but it's after midnight. I'm very sleepy." I raced to the door and opened it wide.

He shrugged and began putting on his shoes. "I'll pick you up at eight A.M.," he said, giving me a quizzical look as he departed.

After he left I remembered the trouble I'd had the night before with the room clerk. He'd called several times, asking if my room was single or double. He wanted to make sure the bill was correct, and suggested that he come up to check it. No, thanks, that won't be necessary, I'd said. It hadn't occurred to me until now how my traveling alone was interpreted by a lot of men—that I was "available." Maybe if I'd known that, I would have been scared. I promised myself to be more circumspect in the future.

At eight A.M. I was standing in front of the hotel. Swarms of people were already queued up for the buses that rolled into the semicircle in front of the

Ambassadeur. Brakes screeched and engines rattled, coughing up black smoke. I was not as patient as the Kenyans, and moved inside where I could breathe.

Clive finally came by at 9:00, shouting and waving his red baseball hat as if he were going to the World Series, not a funeral. He whisked me and my camera bag into a white pickup.

"We're meeting Richard at his new cappuccino café. You'll love it," he said, as he pulled out of a one-way street the wrong way.

"You're really crazy, Clive," I said. "Some day you'll get caught." He grinned like a naughty boy. "And why are we starting so late? We'll miss the funeral and Mwangi will be furious."

"Don't worry, I drive fast. But we have to have tea, first." Of course.

The café was on a cobbled side street. It was right out of Paris, and bursting with people.

"*Jambon*, Meg," said Richard, extricating himself from a crowd of friends to give me the traditional *Swahili* greeting. Palms together, head bowed. "Cappuccino? Espresso? Tea?" His grin was irresistible.

Richard's café was as bright and clean as his Indian restaurant had been dark and grungy. Clusters of smartly groomed professional women sat at polished tables, and exuberant men stood in the aisles, obstructing all those entering or leaving. But nobody seemed to mind. The ritual of hellos and goodbyes reminded me of my experience in Germany in 1951, where everyone had to shake hands around the circle, even if it meant missing a train and being late for work.

Clive plunked me at a small table by the window and brought me coffee and a *maandasi*, a triangular, deep-fried bread made with flour, coconut juice, milk, and sugar. He poured himself tea, and proceeded to load it with sugar. I watched, fascinated, as the men stood by the tables, talking while stirring their tea—an incessant, unconscious motion that accelerated until the liquid slopped over the sides and into the saucer. By the time they drank it, the tea was worn out and cold.

It was warm and sunny as we headed out of town. Traders stood beside the road, waving and shouting for us to stop. I couldn't believe how many hub caps were for sale, all shiny, hanging on racks. Where did they come from? Who bought them? I'd never thought of hubcaps as a popular item, but maybe the bumpy roads jolted the old ones loose. And therein was the supply—and the demand.

Sheepskins, large and small, were draped over cars or lying on the ground. I was dying to get one. Clive tried to negotiate for me, but every time the vendor saw my face the price went up.

"I won't stop again unless you crouch down in the cab," he said. "You're white. Therefore, you're rich."

I gave up. There was hardly enough room in the cab for the three of us to sit. Crouching was out of the question.

We drove for miles past the Aberdare Mountains, which framed fields of towering maize. The summit of Mt. Kenya, barely visible, played hide-and-seek with the distant clouds. Flowering gum trees, purple jacaranda, and richly scented bougainvillia lined the road.

"How do you feel about being called a member of a tribe?" I asked Clive. "I know that the Blacks in South Africa resent it, so I was surprised to hear you use the word."

"Everybody in Kenya is in a tribe," he answered. "That's how we identify ourselves…and we're proud of it. But tribes can also cause dissension. That's the excuse our leaders give us for one-party rule. They say we'd be too fragmented otherwise. Some democracy! One party and one candidate with an unlimited term."

I had heard very few compliments about the autocratic government of Daniel arap Moi.

"But don't ever call us 'natives,'" Richard added, emphatically. "*That* is an insult. To the British we all had bones through our noses and spears in our hands. They could never accept the richness of our diversity. Tribal chiefs had many wives to show their status, and females used to be circumcised, but that's mostly over, thank God. So it's time to get rid of the stereotypes."

"No, I think that was a great idea. Me big chief, have many wives. Very important honcho," said Clive, grimacing fiercely.

Richard scowled at his friend and turned to me. "Kenya has always had an oral tradition, and Clive is what's left of it. He can't stop talking even though he doesn't have anything to say."

Clive wiggled his eyebrows comically.

"I have to laugh when I think of how old Jomo Kenyatta drove the British crazy with his riddles—that's how *Kikuyus* talk—and they could never figure him out," Richard said. "He was brilliant!"

Suddenly the conversation grew serious, the two men swapping stories about their life during the time of British concentration camps and *Mau Mau* guerrillas.

I was very quiet. I had never heard, first-hand, the other side of the dispute—the suffering of the villagers as the English tried to starve them out.

"I was just a boy," said Richard. "My family sent me through the lines to find bread, because I was small and could sneak through. Do you know how many of us died? Eleven thousand *Mau Maus*. Compare that to thirty-two Europeans, and a thousand African collaborators." There was a long, uncomfortable silence.

"I can understand your hating the British, but why, then, have you taken such English names?" I asked.

"It's business, and a little politics," replied Clive. "I haven't reached Mwangi's position, yet. But it's too complicated to explain. And you colonialists wouldn't understand, anyway."

"Cut that out!" I shouted. "For the last time, I am *not* a colonialist. I'm an innocent, peace-loving American."

Clive burst into laughter. "I like your honesty, Meg. In fact, you're the first white woman I've ever talked so freely with. And the first white woman I've sat so close to and not felt sexually aroused." He looked sheepish. Richard gasped.

"Maybe you're over the hill, now that you're almost forty," I quipped, trying to hide my surprise.

He smiled. "No, Meg, I guess I'm beginning to see white women as equals and as people to communicate with, not enemies to be conquered. And I'm really glad for the change. Does that sound strange—or offensive—to you?

"No, not really. I appreciate your frankness. But what took you so long to make this discovery? Kenya's been free since 1963."

"Perhaps it's more than color. And perhaps it's that I'm growing up in my attitude toward women—*all* women. I'm realizing that the sex organs are really in the brain, after all, and only I control my brain."

Now it was my turn to laugh.

Richard was mortified. "We're almost at Lake Naivasha Safari Club," he announced, hurrying to change the subject. "You'll love this place, Meg. It was the pride of British society. Gorgeous grounds, thousands of pelicans and flamingoes...." He flashed a disapproving glance at Clive, who was looking straight ahead, enjoying Richard's discomfort.

We turned into the entrance and stopped beside a bank of flowering hibiscus. The men huddled at the rear of the truck for a moment, talking, heatedly, in *Swahili*. Suddenly Richard strode by, and, without a word, he headed down the stone path toward the clubhouse. Clive sauntered over to where I was taking pictures.

"Richard is a prude. Let him go. He'll cool off." Clive watched me with amusement. "Are you really that excited about the flowers?" he asked.

"I don't see beauty like this every day. Back home I grow these flowers in pots. If I'm lucky, they blossom twice a year."

"Tell me, Meg, why did you come to Africa?" he asked, looking me straight in the eye.

"You can't be serious, Clive. I've already told you."

"You only started to. So tell me again." He stood with his arms folded across his chest, as if to say *I dare you.*

"O.K. Ever since I can remember I've wanted to come here. When I was a young woman Africa was the continent of the future—full of turmoil and change. It had everything. Wide-open spaces with unspoiled, uncharted terrain, wild animals I'd only read about in books or seen in zoos, and cultures vastly different from anything I'd ever known. It was mysterious, exotic—the Dark Continent—and I wanted to explore it on my own. Now, are you satisfied?"

"I don't believe you for a minute, Meg," Clive said. "I think you came to Africa for the same reason most American women do—for the great big ebony stick!" On the last word he thrust up his right arm, made a fist, and slapped his left hand across his forearm, making the classic obscene gesture.

I moved closer, almost nose-to-nose, looked Clive directly in the eye, and said very slowly, "B u l l s h i t."

He stepped back, as surprised as I was at my reaction.

"Listen to me carefully, Clive," I continued. "If that's what I had wanted, I could have gotten plenty back in my own United States of America." I stood for several moments to let my words sink in.

For the first time Clive looked subdued.

"Hell, Clive, for all your talk, you haven't changed a bit."

He smiled ruefully and offered an apology. Maybe now real communication could begin. We walked silently to a table on the spacious lawn where Richard was waiting. And sat down. After a moment Clive lifted his head, flashed a killer smile, leaned back in his chair and crossed both legs on top of the table, shocking Richard. "Damn it Meg," he said. "You are *some* woman."

After tea, we strolled down a narrow boardwalk through a tropical swamp, its stalks and spires a gauzy imprint against the sapphire sky. A thin breeze parted the reeds, opening up a panorama of Lake Naivasha covered with a pink blanket of flamingoes perfectly reflected in the still water. The delicate birds stood as one solitary body, their individuality betrayed only by an occasional flutter of wings. Pale mountains hung in layers behind the blue-green lake.

Lake Naivasha, Kenya.

It was eleven o'clock by the time we left. The funeral had already started. We turned off the main route into a maze of narrow country roads. Dense cedars loomed dangerously close to the shoulders. My head hit the roof twice as we bounced from one rut to another.

"Now do you understand why we're driving the pickup, Meg?"

"Yes, Richard. But it would be nice if someone introduced seatbelts into Kenya," I said, rubbing my head. "It could prove a very lucrative business."

At noon we arrived at a huge clearing. Cars were parked haphazardly in the ditches and along the road. Dozens of people milled about.

Mwangi greeted us warmly, too gracious to show his displeasure at our lateness. The casket had already been lowered into the grave and covered with dirt, as each person took a turn throwing a shovelful on top. A large mound of earth was forming, while various ministers, relatives, and friends made impassioned speeches.

"Brothers, sisters, we do lament the passing of this dear lady—only sixty years old—cut down in the prime of life by that most diabolical of all diseases: cancer. We thank God her suffering is over. We pray for her peaceful journey to the other side...."

The speakers droned on. A giant picture of the deceased, attached to a long wooden pole, was rotated slowly above the crowd. In a thin, reedy timbre the women sang "God Be With You 'Til We Meet Again." It was repeated over and over in the *Kikuyu* language. The singers swooped to a crescendo in the middle, and ended in a sad, plaintive whisper. I slipped my small tape recorder out and tried, unobtrusively, to record the sea of voices.

Unobtrusive is the last thing I was! I was the only white person. I was wearing my long black skirt, a bright aqua t-shirt, *Masai* beads, *Kikuyu* earrings, and a safari hat. And my camera with its conspicuous lens was hanging from my neck. Clive had dropped me off in the middle of the gathering and promptly disappeared. Being a head taller than most of the people, I stood out like Meryl Streep at a pygmy wedding. I was stared at—everything from a sidelong glance to an open-mouthed gape—as each person moved by to place cut flowers on the grave.

I looked over the crowd. Most women wore the traditional tribal costume—colorful long dresses and shawls, with bright kerchiefs or turbans covering their heads. Children darted around, and babies, secured by towels or blankets, clung to their mothers' backs. Other women wore short, thin Sunday-Go-To-Meeting dresses, but Grandma Maine had on a stunning gray winter coat with a fur collar. And I was sweltering! The men appeared in everything from formal black suits to sport shirts, jeans, and baseball caps.

I felt overwhelmed by the tidal wave of humanity. People were moving everywhere—some crying, some hugging, some just standing in the open field and listening. And with each moment I felt more and more conspicuous. I wanted to run and hide behind the thorn trees near the grave, but I couldn't get through the mob. Finally, Clive bounded back, clutching his Instamatic.

I glared at him. "You know, Clive, I feel exactly like your sister in a bar in West Virginia. And I'm most uncomfortable."

He apologized. "I'm sorry, Meg. I see what you mean."

Mwangi appeared and grabbed me. "Please take some pictures," he begged.

Now I felt like Margaret Bourke-White, Time-Life photographer. By now I managed my telephoto lens like a pro, and everyone stepped aside to listen to my instructions. I took group after group of smiling relatives as they placed wreaths on the grave. Mwangi had removed his suit coat. He was stunning in a smart leather jacket as he stood at the graveside helping me direct the photo session. When I ran out of film I sat down on a log near the woods to change the role. I looked up to see a dozen silent, smiling faces—little children encircling me with their wonder.

"Here, let me show you," I said, pulling one child onto the log next to me. Giggles of delight. I was now fully accepted.

A tent materialized at one end of the field, and women began walking around with tea kettles, pouring warm water over eager, outstretched hands. I was sure this was some kind of cleansing ritual, symbolic of entering the hereafter. Instead, it was preparation for eating. The vegetable dishes were to be eaten with the fingers! I was already familiar with *irio*, a green mixture of vegetables and beans, and *githeri*, a mush of potatoes, red kidney beans, and maize, but I had not discovered *hatha*, a type of cooked cabbage, which slithered and slipped through my fingers.

After all the tears had been spent and the goodbyes said, we piled into Richard's pickup, having added about five more people—neighbors to be dropped off along the way and wives returning to Nairobi. They squeezed, good-naturedly, into the back of the truck.

In a small town not far from the Nakuru game reserve we stopped for tea. As I walked into a combination cafeteria, market, and video/record shop, I was startled by a familiar voice. Could it be? Yes. It was the unmistakable, growling bass of the old-time country singer, Ernest Tubbs.

"I'll Have A Ba-luuu-e Christmas Without You,
I'll be so ba-luuu-e thinking about you.
Decorations of red on a green Christmas tree,
Won't be the same, dear, if you're not here with me...."

It was Christmas, 1949. I was in college. Glen had given me this record, the current country hit out of Nashville. He was trying to broaden my musical repertoire, feeling that I was hopelessly stuck in the classical mode. Six months later he asked me to marry him. Now, almost forty years had passed, and I was in Kenya, drinking tea and eating fried meat pies with a laughing throng of *Kikuyus*. I looked out the window at the palm trees and *agapanthus* that grow like weeds by the side of the road. "I'm Dreaming of a White Christmas" sang Bing Crosby. The sun beat down. The years dropped away.

Mwangi jolted me from my trance. "Come on, Meg, we're taking you to Lake Nakuru. You'll get your first glimpse of wild animals." We all transferred to his car.

The shadows were long by the time we reached the sand flats leading to the lake. I walked very slowly, not wanting to disturb the flamingoes and waterbuck. I recorded the chattering of the birds and got as close to the hippos as I could, before sinking into the soft sand. Graceful impala skittered away. The only sounds were those of the wind and the wild creatures.

It was time to head back to Nairobi. Jagged mountains sliced into the setting sun. Acacia trees stood out on nearby ridges like filigreed umbrellas. I felt so at home, squashed in the back seat, whizzing down the highway, listening to American Country and Western music on Radio Zimbabwe.

I recognized a recording from the "Live Aid" concert. "We are the ones. We are the people." Everyone started humming. When it was over, Grandma Maine spoke in *Swahili* to Clive. He turned to me.

"This old lady has lived a long time and suffered a lot," he said, "but she is full of love and forgiveness. She said she hoped you would go back home and tell your people that we are human beings here in Kenya, just like them."

12

SAFARI FEVER

Something inexplicable drew me to Badru House on Moi Avenue. I had been wandering around Nairobi for days, agonizing over which safari to take, when I saw the small green letters out of the corner of my eye: *Safaris, from Camping to Luxury, at Affordable Prices.* I walked up the wide, dusty stairs and down a dark, dreary hall. A crack of light drew me to the end of the corridor and into the office of Sunita Ruzaik, an Indian woman in her early thirties, dressed in a stunning silk *sari*. An hour later I walked out with a package of safaris that started with camping in the *Masai Mara*—no toilets, no mosquito netting—and ended one week later with luxury in the *Amboseli National Park* and *Tsavo West.*

"This will be the adventure of your life, Madam," she said, rolling her r's and flashing a captivating smile. "You will not forrr…get Sunita."

Full of anticipation, I left her tiny office and headed for the Ambassadeur. Better tell Mwangi of my plans. Better give Clive my latest pictures to send home.

Halfway to the hotel I bumped into Benjamin Hall having lunch at a stand-up eatery. "Guess what, Benjamin? Tomorrow night I'll be sitting by the fire under a starry African sky, watching monkeys frolic around the campsite, and sleeping in a tent beside a wild river. That's what I call class!"

"A camping safari? You're crazy," he said. "I heard of one guy who got mauled by a lion just as he was…."

"Never mind," I interrupted. "You're taking your life in your hands eating that hot dog wrapped in greasy dough. It's probably dog guts." I decided that Benjamin was a coward as well as an alarmist.

"I'm headed for the *Masai Mara* game reserve tomorrow morning," I continued, enjoying his disapproval. "Three days and two nights of camping, complete with cook, guide, my own tent and sleeping bag, three meals a day, and *Masai* warriors with long spears to stand watch at night—all for $130. Can you beat that?"

"Jesus, you *are* in trouble!" he exclaimed, surreptitiously pushing the hot dog aside.

"Look at it this way. After lions and cape buffalo, those hostels you've described won't seem half so scary, will they?

That was the last time I saw Benjamin Hall, Spoilsport. I'm sorry, for he'll never know whether I survived.

◆   ◆   ◆

Moffat Wachera, our guide and driver, was a *Kikuyu*, but had quite a different face from the square-jawed, jet-black Mawangi Maine. He was brown-skinned and oval-faced, forty-five years old, and about to become a father for the eighth time. His body was stocky and powerful, and his wide eyes narrowed expressively when he was pleased, as if to say "the joke's on you."

"When will we get there, Moffat?" I asked.

"Lunchtime," he answered.

"But it's already one o'clock! When is lunchtime?"

"When we get there."

I finally gave up, ignoring my growling stomach. I didn't want to antagonize him. I wanted him to concentrate on the road. I hung onto the sides of my seat as he swerved almost sideways over the tops of ruts and down into worn gullies, decelerating going into the holes and gunning the motor on the way out. Moffat's powerful arms moved constantly. Riding his minibus like a wild horse, he leaned into each curve, lifting his body off the seat, posting with accelerator and gearshift. I was glad I was sitting in front and could hold onto the door strap.

"Does Kenya have a big military budget, Moffat?" I asked.

"We have no enemies. We are not the Ugandans." A diplomatic non-answer.

"How do the Kenyans feel about Daniel arap Moi?"

"The Kenyans loved Jomo Kenyatta."

"Are we near the game reserve, Moffat?"

"Just down the hill, through the gate, you'll see, Mama." Mama was Moffat's term for "Mrs."

After getting a good dose of Kenyan humor I stopped asking questions and feasted on the changing landscape. The flat-topped plateaus and 8,000 ft. mountains were covered with cyprus, eucalyptus, junipers, and a variety of cacti. My favorite was the *yuphobia*, which came in small, medium, and large, its curved and jagged stipules reaching skyward against the horizon. Next we passed flat maize fields and oceans of low yellow grass until, abruptly, the land filled with spiny thorn bushes and a sea of mahogany trees, their fluttery, light green leaves invoking a misty fairyland.

When we climbed out of the valley we said goodbye to any semblance of highway and continued on hard-packed dirt roads. God help us if we'd broken down. There wasn't a car in sight. I hung on for dear life as we sped wildly through miles of uninhabited land.

"Take only ten minutes, folks. We have to hurry. I smell rain," announced Moffat, when we stopped in Larok, a small town with one store and a scattering of thatched huts. So what's the big deal about a little rain, I thought, as I stepped out of the van, the ground still moving under my feet.

During our roller coaster ride, we had become one big family. The Willises were from Australia—Mike, Lorraine, and their teenage children, Cathy and Robert. And Orjan and Lena were from Sweden. They'd taken the Orient express from Russia, planning to end up in China. Even with my limited knowledge of geography, Kenya seemed a little out of the way. But they didn't care. The purpose of the trip was to test their ability to live together under any condition. If it worked out, they'd marry. After six months I'd say it looked pretty promising. They were still smiling.

Lena and Orjan had meat pies. The Willises bought some dreadful looking hot dogs on a stick. But I was cautious and, thus, remained famished. All I had were half a dozen almonds left in my camera bag. If only I'd bought a candy bar! But hadn't Moffat assured me that the camp was just down the hill and through the gate?

As long as I didn't ask questions, Moffat talked. He described the landmarks of various tribes, and pointed out acres of wheat fields owned by large companies or the government. And when we passed a mission, he talked bitterly about the support the Roman Catholic Church had given to the British during his country's struggle for independence.

"These people became the interrogators," he said, "and undermined the *Mau Maus*."

"Then the Protestants must have an advantage in Kenya," I said.

"No, they're too disorganized and always fighting among themselves. This makes them ineffective. Western religion is not doing well here." This corroborated what Clive had told me.

Animals began to appear. Zebras, topi, Thompson gazelles, wildebeests. The road had become gravelly and the soil red, as in Nairobi. High escarpments with exposed rock layers and dense vegetation replaced the level terrain.

We rounded a corner and started down a hill. A shout went up. There was the sign we'd been waiting for: FIG TREE 5 km. Now all we had left was the gate."

Fig Tree was a luxurious safari lodge with a central dining and sitting room area and large walk-in shelters with twin beds and attached baths. Grass and bamboo roofs covered all the buildings. It was like a miniature native village. We dropped off the Willises, with the promise to return for a late afternoon game ride.

Right outside the game park, next to a roaring river, we pitched our small tents. Sunita was right. This was as close to nature as you could get. The *real* Africa. In spite of my hunger I had never felt so energized. I thought I might explode.

"Can you believe it, Mama?" exclaimed Moffat. "Last week this great muddy river was dry. Not even a trickle. Just a huge gully you could walk through. And after two days of rain...this." With a dramatic flourish he pointed to the churning water. "I hope you brought your bathing costume, just in case we get more rain and your tent floats away."

Oh, great. That's what I needed...to drown in my sleep. I never could tell if Moffat was kidding. Exaggeration was his forte. But I knew that the rainy season was late this year, causing a great deal of trouble in the safari business.

"Well, what'll we do?" I asked.

"Pray, Mama, pray!" The eyes narrowed mischievously.

"But before I can pray, I have to eat, or I shall die," I retorted. It was now seven hours since we'd left Nairobi—the longest 170 miles I'd ever traveled—and the cook bringing the supplies still hadn't arrived.

"Never mind. I'll find some food," said Orjan, who had spotted a kingsize fig tree that formed a long arc over the river. He shimmied up the sturdy trunk, much to Lena's chagrin, until he was hanging precariously over the angry water. My hands began to sweat as I watched him tentatively perched on the highest limb, holding on with one hand and reaching for the fruit with the other. He began throwing it down. What a disappointment. It was dry and tasteless, not at all what I'd expected from such a majestic tree.

Lena yelled at him in Swedish.

Orjan turned to answer and missed his footing. Clumps of fruit and leaves came off in his hand and he started to fall. Lena screamed. I was transfixed. Down through the branches he spiraled. The instant before he would have hit the water, he latched onto a thick vine, which was tangled around the upper branches. A miracle.

"Swing," yelled Moffat. "Kick your feet and swing. I'll grab you."

Frantically, Moffat climbed up a smaller tree and skillfully worked his way along a branch not far from where Orjan was dangling. He locked his legs tightly around the branch and as the vine swung by, grabbed Orjan with his powerful arms. He lifted him down and laid him on the bank, pale and frightened. Lena knelt beside him.

"My young friend," said Moffat, clearly shaken. "You are a very lucky man. You would be far away by now if the river had swallowed you. O.K. O.K. so your arms will be sore, but we shall let you lead us against the lions tomorrow. You are strong and you have courage. And you are also a little foolish."

He made a feeble attempt to regain his customary good humor. "So, now that the excitement is over, let's finish making camp."

At 3:30 the cook and his helper arrived. Since they had not had time to scavenge for wood—a rare commodity in these parts—we settled for a cold meal. It didn't matter. After Orjan's close call, none of us was very hungry.

At last we were ready for our first game ride. I could hardly contain my emotions as we headed for Fig Tree to pick up the Willises. Here I was in the *Masai Mara* (5,210 ft.), Kenya's leading game reserve, experiencing the Africa that I had only read about in books. And now it was real, and even more vast. It covered 100 square miles to the border of Tanzania, and another 4,900 as it moved, uninterrupted, into the great Serengeti. There were no roads, just a few muddy ruts made by other vans. Moffat took off over the expanse of gently rolling grassland. He knew just where to find the animals—giraffes eating berries from treetops while their young played in a stream, stolid elephants that scarcely blinked as we drove right up to them, hoards of shaggy wildebeests migrating from Tanzania, and black vultures fighting over bloody carrion. The zebras roamed as a group, seemingly unaware of other species, as did the Thompson gazelles, the topi, and the cape buffalo. Each one had its separate domain.

"Folks, this cape buffalo is the meanest animal in Africa," announced Moffat. "Weighs 1500 pounds, and will even attack humans. It's a grazer, but will viciously kill and maim its enemy just for sport. And if you climb a tree to get away, it'll stand at the foot for hours until you give up. It has a tongue like sandpaper and can rip the skin right off your face. Stay out of its way!"

Did Moffat think that any of us needed such a warning?

Now and then we came upon a clump of bushes where the male lions hung out in small groups. Since the females did the "food shopping," all these lazy creatures did was lie around, yawning and relaxing after their meal had been served.

After dinner nap.

I never realized how docile lions can look. And not at all frightening, at least not from the bubble top of the van. It was too early in the year for cubs, and it was too late in the day for a chase. Tomorrow morning. Moffat promised.

But I didn't really care if I saw a chase or took more pictures. Just riding out in these wide-open spaces was exhilarating. Just breathing the clear fresh air with its shared scent of grass and trees and earth was enough. I felt so free, so unencumbered, so much a part of the land.

On the way back to camp, we came upon a young gazelle lying in a shallow hole, unable to stand. Moffat got out of the van and tried to help, but it was obviously too sick to respond. I was petrified. We were near the bushes that housed the lions. Suppose they attacked Moffat? While the injured creature struggled, dozens of older gazelles gathered in a semi-circle several feet from us. They made a continuous angry, hissing noise, but never moved, like soldiers standing at attention.

Moffat returned to the van. "Look over there," he said, pointing to an ugly hyena skirting the field. "He senses that an animal is in trouble, and he's coming to investigate."

Slowly and deliberately the hyena walked around the hissing gazelles and toward the baby. As he went in for the kill, the entire pack stopped hissing, turned, and, in perfect formation, walked silently away.

I cannot erase the awful whine the baby made, or the picture of its twitching body hanging from the hyena's mouth. I know it's the law of nature, but I can't get used to the killing.

The search for wood was still going on when we reached our campsite and unloaded some large branches, resembling driftwood, which we'd picked up during the afternoon. Added to the cook's collection, the pile was worthy of Georgia O'Keefe. Pale gray, gnarled, parched. And oh, what a fire it made!

Dinner was a feast—green salad with a spicy dressing, special stew with lots of meat and fresh vegetables, and a tropical fruit compote for dessert. The cook, a small man with an ebony face, was a member of the *Kamba* tribe. He wore a flat-topped white hat and a long apron, and had everything organized in tin boxes. He cooked over an open fire, and as soon as one meal was finished he started on the next, setting out meticulously washed plates, mugs, and silverware.

Halfway through the meal Lena dropped her plate, gave a shriek, and threw herself into Orjan's arms. I spun around, expecting to be attacked by a cape buffalo. Instead, I saw two tall figures walking stealthily toward us through the mist—two elongated shadows, barely visible, each one carrying an impressive spear.

"Lena, it's the *Masai*," said Moffat, turning in alarm when he heard her cries. "Don't be afraid. They're gentle people. They'll stand guard all night against the animals."

The two warriors walked into the circle of light. They bowed, first to me, then to Lena. The fire shown through their ear loops and danced on the colorful fabric draped over their shoulders. Moving to the other campfire, they arranged themselves next to Moffat and the cook, and began talking, hurriedly, in *Swahili*.

"What's the reason for separate campfires?" I asked Lena and Orjan. "Is there some sort of unwritten rule? The Whites can't sit with the Blacks?"

"Seems crazy to me," replied Orjan. "We're short of wood and might as well consolidate."

I walked over to Moffat. "We'd like to join you, if you don't mind. And maybe swap some stories. You know, one from Africa, one from Sweden, one from the United States."

"Splendid," he said, and began rearranging the seating logs so we could move into the circle. The *Masai* looked uncomfortable and started fidgeting with their costumes, draping them more tightly around their bodies, which exposed their skinny legs. Silently they leaned forward and stared into the fire.

"Since you're our leader, Moffat, you begin."

He nodded, resting his chin on his hands. "Once upon a time there was a little boy who lived in a small village in Kenya. He was a member of the *Kikuyu* tribe. He tried to get food for his parents and relatives, who were members of the *Mau Mau*, and were surrounded by the colonialists, who were trying to starve them." It was Richard's story all over again. When he'd finished he said, "And now, Mama, do you see why we are proud to have been *Mau Maus*? And why we are so happy to be free?"

There was a hush around the fire, as Moffat stared at the three of us.

During the story a light rain had begun to fall. Now it was coming down hard and the wind had picked up. A hundred yards from us two vans were unloading. People were running around, trying, frantically, to set up tents. One of the drivers walked toward us.

"We lost four vans coming from Nairobi," he said, slapping the arms of his rain-soaked jacket to keep warm. "Stopped for lunch and it started to rain. The roads became rivers of mud. I'm lucky two of us got through. Do you have any dry wood? It must be ten o'clock and we haven't had dinner."

Poor fellow. So this was why Moffat wouldn't stop for lunch.

Hours later I lay in my sleeping bag listening to the rain. I was carried back to my honeymoon when I went climbing up King's Ravine in the White Mountains. I wanted to introduce my new husband to the wilds of New Hampshire. He had never climbed anything higher than the hills of New Jersey. How I longed for him now...the man that used to be. His voice crept into my consciousness: "Only half a mile to the summit? And straight up? How I hate those signs. I'd rather not know. Christ, I'll be dead! Did you ever see such rain?" His foot dislodged a pile of loose stones. When he regained his balance he turned to me, shaking his head. "Are you out of your mind? Is this your idea of fun? Four years in the army were easier than this!"

"Be quiet and stop complaining or I'll push you over the cliff!" I spun around and put my hands on his chest. He laughed, and grabbed me around the waist. His curly hair was matted. His face glistened.

"You're wonderful, do you know that?" he said, kissing me lightly, "I don't know any other woman who has your energy, your adventurousness...and is quite so mad." Wrenching free, I took off, scrambling over the slippery rocks, the freezing wind and rain forcing me on.

Once inside the cabin, we took off our sopping clothes and snuggled into down sleeping bags. All night long we held each other. And we listened to the rain.

Through the mist of my sleep I heard Moffat shouting. "Get out, Mama, we have to leave this moment, before the roads get worse." My tent was saturated, water dripping from its seams.

I threw on my clothes, but in the rush, forgot my sweater. Damn! Why hadn't I brought a windbreaker? I was soaked by the time I reached the van.

The wheel spun in Moffat's hands. We fishtailed and zigzagged, turning around full circle as if on ice. Nobody spoke. Perspiration covered Moffat's face. The rain was a solid sheet, but, miraculously, we made it to the lodge.

In Kenya they don't provide for emergencies. If it rains for days and you can't go anywhere, that's your problem, not the tour company's. When we walked in, two Lufthansa stewardesses were trying, unsuccessfully, to charter a plane to get them to Nairobi for a late afternoon flight to Johannesburg. Equally frantic were two Dutch photographers, who were doing a documentary on the handicapped in the Third World, and had been forced to leave their equipment in the car, which they'd abandoned a few miles away. They had walked to Fig Tree, up to their shins in mud.

For the next six hours we were marooned. The only happy person was an Englishman who sold balloon rides at $300.00 an hour. He said the animals would die if they didn't get rain. They got it! By nine o'clock we "campers" were ready to eat the table legs. There was no way we could get back to camp, and Moffat made it clear that Star Tours would not pay extra for our breakfast.

Orjan, who was on a strict budget, was adamant. "We paid for three meals a day, and this is one of them. It's not our fault that it rained."

Moffat shrugged and walked outside to avoid a confrontation. So we ate, and ate. When the waiter presented the bill Orjan said, "Star Tours will pay." Moffat shook his head.

The assistant manager was awakened. He, in turn, awoke the manager. I could see that a Third World War was in the making. Orjan and Lena refused to discuss the matter before talking with the tour company. But there was no phone and only one CB call a day was made to Nairobi. My God, I thought, suppose somebody got sick.

Moffat was enjoying the debate, especially when the manager threatened to have the police lock us in his office until we paid, or, if that didn't work, throw us in jail. And where were they going to find a policeman? Such a ruckus over a breakfast bill.

Mike Willis, who had remained neutral during the argument, now became incensed. "You can't do that. This is a democracy. You've gone too far."

Democracy, I thought. Who says?

The manager turned on Mike. "Shut up, it's not your business." Then to me. "And you, Madam, will never leave here until you pay for your terrible abusiveness."

"Abusiveness? Who's being abusive?" I shouted.

Orjan was doubling his fists and the entire dining room seemed ready to explode.

Moffat walked quickly over to the manager, unfolded several bills, handed him 180 shillings, and left the room.

As the manager passed by me, stuffing the money into his pocket, he smiled triumphantly and said, "No problem."

Suddenly, I became enraged. I had lived for years with a man who caused huge crises, stirred everyone up, and, after the drama was over, acted as if nothing had happened.

"Who says there's no problem?" I screamed.

Mike Willis turned pale.

"You've been insulting to me and my friends…even threatened us with jail. That's a problem. I want you to know that I'm angry and think you owe *me* an apology." And I stormed out.

Moffat was leaning against a railing, holding his head. I didn't know if he was laughing or crying. "I've never liked that man, Mama," he said. "He's not nice. You were right."

"Yes, Moffat, but you were enjoying the battle or you would have paid sooner. Shame on you!" This time I got a full-fledged smile.

At two o'clock a German pilot, driving a jeep, offered to drop us at our campsite. The rain was abating, but the ride through mountains of mud was so frightening that both Lena and I felt sick to our stomachs. The driver could get no closer than 200 yards from the camp, so we walked from there—mud curling over our ankles, arms akimbo for balance—fearing each moment that we'd fall and be permanently sucked into the mire. But despite the discomfort, we laughed all the way.

"Great training for foot soldiers, Moffat. You should put that in your publicity," said Orjan, attempting to click his heels together.

By four o'clock, after we'd eaten lunch and moved our tents to higher ground, the cook volunteered to drive us to the van. Would we never learn? Just before we entered the gate we had a flat tire. Half-an-hour later, back in our van, we stopped to rescue another vehicle. The two men had been stuck for four hours. They'd dug into the earth under the wheels with their bare hands, terrified that they might have to remain in the park all night. You can imagine their joy at seeing us. In our attempt to free them, we sank down to our axles, once again.

Two male lions watched from a hill as we struggled to extricate ourselves. This *really* made me nervous! I stayed close to the door while the men pushed and the mud splashed. It was worse than getting out of snow. A shovel was useless. The more we dug, the deeper we sank. And the dirtier we got. You can forget about fashion on safari.

The sun was setting when we returned to camp—muddy, but ready for a dinner of fried chicken, cauliflower, ginger cabbage, mashed potatoes, and onions. This time, when the *Masai* appeared, they were far less threatening. They moved even more slowly, their spears and cadaverous bodies highlighted by a half moon.

But instead of two there were three. I think last night's guards had told a friend about this curious little gathering—where the white people sat around the fire with the black people and chatted and laughed—and he wanted to see for himself.

When the three men reached the camp, Moffat had just sung a typically sad *Kikuyu* song into my tape recorder—a ballad about a little girl who was dying, her pleas for help unheeded. I played it back for the *Masai*, which intrigued them. They agreed to sing one of their own.

How different their music was. They used vocal noises—often a repetitive guttural or tongue-clicking ostinato—as accompaniments. Rhythmic breaks occurred between each verse. And the verses went on and on, each member taking a turn, perhaps making the story up as he went along. The songs dealt with the simple themes of their daily life—tending cattle, stealing cattle, spending nights alone on a hillside, killing their first lion, and, most of all, bravery.

While singing they moved their heads forward and backward, getting so excited I thought they'd break into dance. I also thought they'd never stop singing, once they heard themselves on tape. After it was over they stood around looking awkward and embarrassed. And pleased.

"The *Masai* are a funny lot," Moffat said. "Very smart, but they don't believe in formal education. And many of their babies become blind because of the minute flies that infect their eyes. They wail about it, yet they won't see a doctor. They seem to live in another era, but their feet are really in both worlds."

"It's your turn, now," I said, pointing to the cook. Each time I'd ask him, he'd disappear into his domain of pots and pans set up on the back of the supply truck, and start rattling the dishes.

I finally gave up and went to bed. Black-faced velvet monkeys scampered in the trees just as Sunita had described them, and perched, saucily, on my tent, their young clinging to their mother's stomach. The female cuddled her baby much like a human mother.

I couldn't sleep, so I returned to the campfire where the cook was stirring flour into boiling water and working it until it formed a thick, spongy cake called *ugali*. I was just in time to see him cut it into slabs and serve it with sweetened sour milk.

"You can eat it with meat and gravy, too, if you want," he said. "Here, try some."

I'll try almost anything...once.

It was still dark the next morning when Moffat shook my tent. "*Jambon*, Mama, it's six o'clock. Coffee time." We sat around the fire, warming our hands on the steaming mugs, and filling up on pancakes and sausages. The air was crisp. The river had gone down considerably, and it looked like a perfect morning for our early game ride. A lion chase at last. Was it, finally, to be?

This time the van broke down within sight of a *Masai* village. All of us pushed and got completely covered with mud. At one point I steered as the two men rocked the van. No use. Off Moffat trudged to get help.

"I don't understand these people," said Orjan, disgusted. "In Sweden we'd never go on a trip like this without the proper equipment. A shovel, ropes, sand."

"Yes, but in Sweden you don't have elephants and giraffes and lions. Or killer hyenas. This kind of excitement would never occur in Sweden."

We all laughed.

The wait seemed interminable, but Moffat finally returned with a shovel and two *Masai*. In the meantime, two others had ambled by and stayed to help. Everyone was relaxed and amiable.

Lena and I watched with amusement as one of the *Masai* took his long ear loop—the one on the side where he was pushing—and wrapped it around the upper ear so it wouldn't get in the way. He looked so funny—one loop up and one loop down. After he left, we realized that he'd forgotten to unloop it.

"Do you suppose we should have told him?" asked Lena.

"Don't worry. His wife will," I replied.

"Meg, do you think we'll ever make it back to Nairobi?"

"Lena," I said, "I'm just hoping we make it to the lodge before lunch."

13

WILD CREATURES

The day after I returned to Nairobi, I walked to the outskirts and poked around the back streets. There, just as the Dutch photographer had said, were the makeshift shelters of the disabled.

"Of course you haven't seen any handicapped people in Kenya," he had declared on the day of the big breakfast battle at Fig Tree. "In Kenya, they hide their handicapped. Some of them even live in dirt holes. And when it rains, they just cover the hole with plastic."

Having run an organization centering on the needs of disabled people, I was appalled. I'd heard that a country has to be wealthy before it pays attention to its severely handicapped population. Now I knew it, firsthand.

"But don't be depressed. We're making progress," he'd assured me. "And you can be certain we give nothing to this corrupt government. If a person needs an artificial limb, we give it to him personally. Our organization works with hundreds of disabled people all over Africa. And we know our aid is getting to the individuals who need it. Just wait. When our film is finished, more eyes will be opened, more help will come."

I returned to the Ambassadeur and stood on my balcony watching the crowded streets and observing a living, breathing montage. Veiled Moslem women all in black, businessmen in western suits, Indian girls in colorful *saris*, and stylish ladies hurrying in and out of the shops. All Kenyans. All different.

The next day was the beginning of the luxurious leg of my safari. I felt very self-contained as I took down my clothesline, packed my newly washed clothes, and carried everything to the lobby. My bill for five nights, breakfast included, was $157.97.

Clive and Richard surprised me as I was standing in front of the hotel waiting for the minibus.

"How did you ever get going so early?" I asked.

"We didn't go to bed," Clive answered. Richard shook his head. He'd never get used to Clive's outrageous sense of humor.

"Hey, are you really going to live out of that pack for eight months?" he asked, skeptically.

"I already told you, Clive. My motto is: If you can't stand the clutter, get out of town. So here I am."

"That's pretty drastic, don't you think?" Richard said.

"Not really. It'll all be there when I return, but by then I won't be so attached to it."

There was a three-way hug. No final farewells. "See you when I come through on my way to Bombay," I shouted, as we drove away.

George was the driver of the new safari. Being half *Kikuyu* and half *Masai*, he spoke four languages. He wasn't as colorful or as talkative as Moffat, but he knew his history and his animals.

We headed south through verdant *Masai* country. They didn't own the land, but it was theirs to use. How strange to see ordinary farm animals being herded by the tall, skinny warriors. Now and then we spotted an elegant blue Somalia ostrich in a forest of acacia trees, or a stray giraffe that had stepped over the fence and was obstructing traffic. What they stepped over most mortals would have needed a ladder to negotiate.

"A giraffe is a strange creature," volunteered George, as we sat, waiting for this one to move out of the road. "It weighs about 2,000 pounds, has a gestation period of eighteen months, and gives birth standing up. We say it drops its young like a stone."

Ouch. And I thought nine months was interminable.

"If attacked, it swings its neck back and forth, violently. Or a group will get in a circle with their heads together and kick any predator that tries to harm them. Not even a lion can penetrate that circle." So much for the gentle storybook giraffe.

Once off the main highway we sped over miles of dirt roads, plagued by enormous potholes still full of water. In the distance mountains rose in layers—light green mottled by dark green cloud shadows. On either side were yellow fields dotted with cone-shaped red clay anthills the size of hay stacks. The kind you'd imagine belonging to the killer ants of science fiction.

Three hours later we entered Amboseli Game Park (3500 ft.) and drove up to the Kilimanjaro Safari Lodge. Narrow boards had been placed, precariously, over logs along the flooded paths. I slogged across a field to a cluster of cabins, each with a thick overhanging thatched roof. My room was large, and the walls were made of wide, hand-hewn logs. Faded curtains hung over the entrance to the bath and the dressing room. A tiny afterthought of a shower poked out from the back wall. Mosquito netting hung in readiness over the bed and oil lamps stood on the tables. The ample front porch faced the game park and Mt. Kilimanjaro with its snowy summit. I felt as if I'd stepped into a movie set. Stanley, Livingstone, von Blixen...just around the corner.

Lunch was a sumptuous buffet of tropical fruits, vegetables, and sliced meats, served in a cavernous room with windows along one side and a huge fireplace on the other. Katie Malloy from Toronto, the Scheidle family, returning to France after a year in Nigeria, and the Tippets from California made up our group.

Katie's husband was a geographer working closely with the government on natural resources mapping. "You can't believe the corruption he's seen!" she said. "Daniel Moi pockets about fifty percent of all foreign aid, and sends it to Swiss banks. Naturally, the economy's slipping, so Kenya is becoming more and more dependent on this aid. But you might as well pour money into a bottomless hole."

"Why doesn't the West fund projects directly, as the Dutch are doing in their handicapped program?" I asked.

"That's much too logical. I don't know about the Dutch program, but if it's successful it's one of the few. Moi manages to keep down any opposition, so he can do pretty much what he wants. And the West has never been very careful about who it supports."

"If you want frustration," interjected Bernard Scheidle, "go to Nigeria. I tried to set up a plant to make disinfectants, but after a year I could see it was hopeless. And I'm not the only one who feels this way. Westerners are leaving in droves because of government red tape. As a result there's rampant inflation, and a dictator kept in power by western arms. Who can operate under these conditions? The people have lost heart. They feel they have no control over their destiny."

Hamal's prophetic words, spoken on the Isle of Dingway, came back to me. "The sale of military weapons is the new slave trade in Africa."

After this depressing conversation, it was a relief to get into the van and do nothing more taxing than look at wild animals.

Elephants were everywhere. Once we stopped they surrounded us, pulling on the windshield wipers with their trunks and gently nudging the front wheels. Oh, God, if they should decide to turn us over and look underneath, just for the exercise....One old female stood directly in front of us and drank water from a muddy pothole. She slurped and sucked and, when she'd emptied the pool, picked up trunkfuls of dirt and dusted herself—and the van—all over.

"That keeps the bugs away," said George, who was looking a little nervous, himself, until the old girl finally moved out of our way in order to scratch her rear end on a nearby tree. The tree swayed, cracked, and groaned. Bark flew in every direction.

Watching the elephants eat gave me severe indigestion. After pulling the leaves off the trees, they started in on the tall grass, ripping up huge chunks and stuffing it into their mouths. There didn't seem to be any swallowing, just more stuffing, letting the excess hang out as they chewed. Made me think of some of the people I'd seen at Wendy's all-you-can-eat salad bar.

The elephants at a distance were more palatable—twenty in a row, tail to trunk—miniature cutouts against the horizon. They marched slowly, a line of orderly soldiers, the babies in the middle and the biggest daddy bringing up the rear. If any of the little ones strayed, the adults trumpeted loudly, and they scampered back in line, like kids who'd been given a sharp spank.

The sky was turning pink as George halted near a large watering hole. One elegant umbrella acacia stood out near the edge. The water was churning, and a circle of thick, gray bodies watched the commotion taking place in the center.

"Here's something you seldom see, even in Africa." George couldn't disguise a smile as we squinted to see what all the excitement was about.

An enormous body thrust itself out of the water, then under—lurching, twisting—like a fat man performing a water ballet.

"He's going to drown...uh...one of them is going to drown," I shouted. "They must be having a terrible fight."

George broke into laughter.

"Well, I'll be," said Jamie. "Hippos humping...with the whole family watching."

"Mating, Jamie," admonished Helen, hoping nobody was offended.

I was embarrassed by my ignorance, but having never witnessed such a spectacle, how could I know? It seemed to go on for an eternity, ending happily, with lots of snorting and the male leaping as high out of the water as such an immense creature could, turning his head, abruptly—as if to check audience reaction—and swimming away. The released female just stood there, blinking.

"Isn't that just like a male," said Katie. "Gets what he wants and leaves."

"*Absolutement non...mais non*," said Bernard, adamantly.

Katie patted him on the shoulder. "Oh, come on, Bernard. Not all of life is as romantic as you French would like us to believe."

That night a wind came up, and I was glad for the extra sweater I'd packed. The trees bent low under its force, and the thick reeds in the marshes surround-

ing the lodge whispered a soothing cadence. Maybe this would blow the mosquitoes away. In the moonlight, as I made my way to my cabin, I could see the
outline of pelicans standing motionless in the tall grass.

Once in my bed I snuggled under the blankets and looked up at my mosquito
netting canopy, a little girl, again, secure in my camp tent. I imagined a gentle
wind blowing across the lake and waves splashing rhythmically against the shore.
I knew that nothing would harm me. But this was not that world of childhood. It
was unlike any place I'd ever been. The night sounds were different—not the
chirping of crickets, but the chatter of tropical birds and monkeys. The smells of
the damp marsh and the fresh grasses were different—sweeter, more pungent
than the odor of warm rain on pine needles. And I was isolated, not surrounded
by a loving family ready to support me at every turn. Yes, I'd been lucky. I hadn't
known much disappointment or pain as a child. And that was both my strength
and my weakness. I wasn't prepared for what happened when I grew up, but,
somehow, I was able to survive it. And here I was alone—after all the pain and all
the joy and all the struggle—wondering what my next step would be. A feeling of
renewed strength fought its way into my aloneness. And it was the greater feeling
as I lay there through the night.

I awoke before sunrise and stumbled, half asleep, across the soggy field to the
lodge. As I was surveying a full layout of breakfast goodies, I heard someone call
from across the room.

"Hey, Meg…aren't you Meg Peterson?"

I wheeled around to see a young woman dressed in high boots, climbing
pants, and a woven poncho, ropes of *Masai* beads around her neck. She walked
toward me, hand outstretched.

"Oh, I'm so excited. I've always wanted to meet you. I saw you at the Winfield
folk festival. Maggie Finch. You didn't see me, but you were judging my Autoharp playing. I lost, of course, but I didn't blame you." She stopped for a breath.

"Why do you say 'of course?'" I asked. "You had pretty stiff competition. Try
again. You must be dedicated if you came all the way to the *Amboseli* to meet
me."

She threw her head back and laughed, then grabbed me, impulsively, and gave
me a real bear hug. Winfield, Kansas, how far away that seemed. And we finally
meet in Africa.

"Did you bring your Autoharp with you?" I asked.

"No," she said. "I left it in Nairobi. I'll be teaching in Kenya for a year, and I
wouldn't be without it."

"I'd sure like to hear how you'll combine it with drums, and a whole lot of other native instruments I can't even pronounce."

She surprised me. "Maybe I will and maybe I won't. I'd rather spread the country sound, and authentic folk songs. I'm sick of nothing but loud popular music saying 'America' to Africans."

"Six-thirty and the sun is up. Everyone into the van." George's voice filled the room.

We finished our breakfast and exchanged addresses. Africa was lucky to meet Maggie. So was I.

It was cold on the ride. We huddled together to keep from freezing. The terrain was totally different from the *Masai Mara*—flat, and full of lakes and marshes. How peaceful the reflection of the grass in the still water, the rising of the morning mist, the clouds moving across Kilimanjaro.

But would I never see a lion chase? George said we took too long at breakfast and missed the action. All we saw were four female lions lolling in the sun. Probably digesting.

At 8:45 we left the game park. The roads were worse than ever, with rocky depressions as deep as *arroyas*. We got stuck so many times that, after awhile, I didn't even bother taking pictures. Once there were as many as four vans that had to be pushed—one at a time—through a mammoth mudhole. This became a game to the drivers, punctuated by laughter and camaraderie.

Shortly before we reached a ridge of volcanic mountains, we had a flat tire. The minibus behind us stopped to help. In the midst of all the excitement, several *Masais* came by. At that moment a gust of wind lifted the scanty material that covered their bodies. So that's what they wear under those bright wraps—nothing! I resisted the impulse to run for my camera. Those long spears had a way of intimidating.

A group of women and children joined the men. One young woman, holding her baby, came up to me. The baby hung in the usual cloth sling, this time pulled around to the front, so he rested on his mother's chest. The woman pointed to the baby's feet, which were swollen, encrusted, and shiny. It looked like some dreadful disease.

"Please, Madam, medicine," she pleaded.

I asked what was wrong, but she didn't speak English. "Fire burn," volunteered another woman.

I went through both buses and asked if anybody had ointment or salve, explaining the situation. Everyone looked the other way. I had one tube of first aid cream, but wasn't sure whether it would do more harm than good. There were other sores on the child's body. Perhaps this was more than a burn. The sores were festering and needed to be cleaned before applying medicine. And what about the insects and dirt that might cling to the cream?

"A doctor. You *must* see a doctor," I said to the young woman.

I turned to George. "Don't the *Masai* have some sort of herbal medicine—some sort of tribal anecdote for infection?"

"They have customs and beliefs and old, old traditions," he explained. "Don't interfere."

Everyone was looking at me as if I were the sick one.

"To hell with tradition," I blurted out. "This baby will die if he doesn't get help." I looked at the infant's wide black eyes. Miniscule flies were lining the lids and crawling on his face. But he just lay there, passively. This was what Moffat had talked about—the flies that cause blindness.

The woman's eyes were pleading. "Please, Madam, medicine," she repeated over and over, following me to the van.

Depressed, I stared out of the window as the van rolled away. I will never forget that beautiful, anguished face. And my own feeling of helplessness.

In an hour we had passed the Shetani lava flow—black pockmarked rock that stretched for miles on both sides of the road—and arrived at Tsavo West Game Reserve. We drove through the Chyulu Gate and up to Kiliguni Lodge where the grasses seemed as tall as the bushes. Gardens bursting with color crisscrossed the velvet lawn and hugged the paths leading to the neat white cottages.

How different from last night's humble cabin. Polished tile floors, modern bath, overstuffed furniture. I walked onto the screened-in front porch, situated at the very edge of the reserve. A black weaver bird peered out of its nest, hidden in an old fig tree. The nests looked like woven purses. Some had fallen on the ground with their parcel of tiny eggs still inside.

The main lodge was just as luxurious. Windows stretched across the entire front, looking out at the mountains and a clear, spring-fed pond. Impala and waterbuck grazed by the water.

During lunch we watched the activities of a host of wild creatures—lizards with bright blue bodies and yellow heads, translucent blue-green starlings, ostrich, mongoose, and Malibu storks that stood around in groups, like skinny old men hovering over the poker table.

In the afternoon we hiked to a river deep in the jungle. Languid hippos bobbed up and down in the sparkling water, while an occasional crocodile slithered by. Date palms and outsized tropical vegetation lined the banks. Multicolored birds and gray, velvet monkeys kept us company.

On the way back we passed piles of elephant bones resting on the floor of the tangled wilderness. A gentle rain had started, releasing the wet, cleansing smells of the forest.

That evening, in the middle of dinner, the waiter scurried over to our table and exclaimed, excitedly, "Ladies and gentlemen, there are two lions out by the water."

We scrambled to the window in time to see a mama and a papa lion walk around the pond, linger a moment, then disappear into the bush. The impala rimming the pond stood stark still, making no attempt to run away. Four of them faced the pond, four of them faced the bush, and the rest faced the lodge—as if guarding against an attack from every angle. The air was alive with tension. For one hour the impala stood, not moving. Then, slowly, they dispersed into the night.

The air was balmy, so I sat on my porch and listened to the interwoven harmonies of frog, insect, and bird. The sound would last about ten minutes, reaching a deafening crescendo. Then it would stop abruptly. Utter silence. Minutes later the chorus would begin again, louder than ever. Then more silence. This pattern was repeated over and over throughout the night.

At six A.M. I was awakened by shouts from Helen Tippet.

"A lion, Meg. Lock your screen door," she yelled.

Did she think a lion could enter by turning the door handle?

I rushed onto the porch. A wildebeest thundered by, pursued by a lion two feet from where I stood. Smaller animals were running in every direction. Hooray—a lion chase, at last! But I'm glad I didn't see the kill. It happened way out in the field.

There was no sleeping after all the excitement. Everyone wanted to sit on the veranda in front of the lodge and lion watch. But all we saw were birds. The Malibu storks were taking their morning constitutional, delicately high-stepping, while keeping an eye out for nuts. Stooping down, cracking them open, and spitting out the shells. The egrets, white as chalk, flew round and round in formation, occasionally fluttering to a halt by the pond, like pieces of tissue paper falling gracefully to earth. I floated with them. And dominating the scene was Kilimanjaro, its summit gleaming in the morning sun. I'm going to climb you, I vowed. Once I get to Tanzania nothing will stop me.

At eight o'clock sharp we started for Mombasa. Right outside the gate I noticed a large alabaster mosque with nine towers. "Why is there so little Moslem influence in Kenya?" I asked George. "Somebody must go to this impressive mosque."

"Wait and see," he answered. "When you get to the coast it will be different. Especially if you visit Lamu."

The roads began to improve as we drove east, and the scenery changed drastically. Large plantations growing vegetables, sisal, and fruit stretched for acres on either side of the road. The palm trees were bigger. And there were no high mountains, no wild animals, no *Masais*.

It was common to see men, standing with their backsides to the road, urinating. They turned their heads and smiled as we passed. No ceremony, no apologies. After having been cooped up in the van for four hours, I envied them. Men had it made!

It wasn't long before we came up over a small knoll and were greeted by a dazzling panorama. The hot afternoon sun illumined an array of stately mosques and reflected off the choppy water of the harbor, creating a perfect semicircle of light. Flags were flying. One or two freighters lay offshore.

"There she is, folks," exclaimed George. "The great harbor of Mombasa on the Indian Ocean."

14

MOMBASA

Snuggled next to the harbor I found the elegant Oceanic Hotel with its wide veranda and reasonable rates. I had given myself one day to explore this ancient city, so headed for town without delay. Hell could not have been hotter! Thank God for the sleeveless T-shirt I'd packed at the last minute. Fortunately, there seemed to be no dress code. Most people wore scanty summer clothing, and even though the city was predominantly Moslem, I saw very few *chadors*.

Mombasa is an island, bordered on three sides by small inlets and swampy areas, and on the fourth by a natural harbor. I reached the old port and strolled way out near the retaining wall to watch the boats come and go. How peaceful the harbor was, belying the many battles fought over its possession. In the distance was Fort Jesus, which dated from the late 16th century, when the port was taken by the Portuguese in their quest to destroy the Arab grip on maritime trade in the Indian Ocean. One hundred years later the *Omani* Arabs threw out the Portuguese and held on to Mombasa until the arrival of the British at the end of the 19th century. Add to these cultures the Africans who originally populated the area and you can imagine the mixture of people I saw as I walked around.

I reached the middle of town. How run-down and crowded it was compared to the lovely, tree-lined walkway around the harbor. Shops were tacky and disorganized, with everything piled on tables. Only the pharmacies had neat, attractive displays.

My feet were burning! The high socks and leather shoes had to go. One of the many Indian shopkeepers finally found me a large pair of rubber thongs for one dollar.

Shadows were lengthening by the time I arrived at American Express and picked up my mail. A letter from Chris and one from Carol.

December 14th

Dear Mom,

I hope you get this letter before you call, because I'm afraid you'll panic if I tell you on the phone about Tom's operation.

First of all, there's no crisis. Last Wednesday he had an emergency appendectomy here in Hoboken. He's now recuperating at Robert's apartment and we're all taking turns playing nursemaid. I think Tom likes the attention! He made me promise not to tell you unless he died—overly dramatic in true Peterson style—but I now see no reason to keep you in the dark. He should be back on Wall Street next week, ready for his next illness, probably a nervous breakdown this time. What's left?

Everyone asks about you. They whisper, in conspiratorial fashion, "Is your mother all right? I hear she's in Africa all by herself." That sort of thing. I tell them you've disappeared into the bush and we figure you've either found a lover or are getting a face lift.

Seriously, everything is fine here, except that it's cold and dreary as only New Jersey can be in December. Robert is heavily involved in some kind of self-awareness seminar and trying to change everybody's life. Martha has a surprise for you, which means I can't say a word. And I, of course, am continuing to produce cards that you can't show to your respectable friends. At the same time, I'm handling your business, which is more complicated than I'd anticipated. What a bunch of long-winded customers! I've had to devise a form letter to keep up with the correspondence.

Carol and Jan called, and Mimi and Lisa say letters are on the way. You'd better take care of yourself. I could never find time to answer the sympathy cards from all the friends who seem to be coming out of the woodwork.

I guess you know we all miss you. The office seems dull without your weekly interruptions.

Much love, Chris

I felt good that my children cared so much for each other, even though I felt bad not being there for Tom. Bless Chris. He was a great "action central" in my absence.

I lay in the hotel pool all by myself, luxuriating in a late afternoon swim—floating, and watching the palms sway. Some were short and squatty and others reached their feathery branches high into the sky, bright green against deep blue. The hibiscus bushes lining the patio were heavy with blossoms, their faces closing as the birds loudly heralded the coming of evening.

I thought about Tom. First the stabbing two years ago, then the auto crash, then the broken shoulder, and now an appendectomy. Was he accident prone or just unlucky? At almost thirty years of age, he could certainly take care of himself. And what good was worrying? My grandmother specialized in that—a Protestant catalog of worst-case scenarios—and drove the family crazy.

I wondered what Martha's secret was. Could she be pregnant? I remembered her words shortly after the wedding: "You keep talking about wanting grandchildren, Mom, but I think you'll freak, especially when they start calling you 'Grandma.'"

"Wait and see!" I'd said. "I'll fool everybody." I was eager to be a grandmother. I just never thought I'd be that old.

I returned to my room, showered, and stood on the balcony watching the sun go down. A slight wind stirred the air. My body shivered, momentarily, under the wet towel. The birds were chirping vociferously and flying wildly in and out of the palm trees, which seemed even taller from this vantage point than from below. One-by-one the freighters turned on their lights and the harbor reflected each tiny glowing point. It was hard to distinguish them from the stars. When I looked up I could see every constellation. When I looked down I could see one spindly acacia tree with a few twinkling Christmas bulbs. The delicate perfume of bougainvillea still hung in the air. My heart was full.

A loud knock on the door shattered the silence. "Who is it?" I called, moving into the room, cautiously.

A key turned in the lock. I froze.

A tall dark man in a turban faced me. "I am Aman, Madam. I have come to prepare your mosquito netting."

A netting-preparer, how romantic! I stood in the corner of the room, wrapped precariously in the skimpy towel, while this Arab-looking man undid the cords and let the net fall. He made quite a ceremony out of what looked like a relatively simple task—checking the material for holes, tugging on the ceiling connection, and, finally, tying the strings to the four corners of the bed and tucking the netting in all around.

When he finished he gestured toward the bed. "Would you like to try it?" he asked, bowing graciously. I stood paralyzed as he moved slowly toward me. I tried to speak, but my mouth just flapped inaudibly. I must have looked like a simpleton, standing there, wrapped in a towel, making no move to excuse myself.

"No, no, no," I stammered, finding my voice at last. "I'm familiar with mosquito nets. I...I used them in the *Amboseli*. Now I must get ready for dinner." I backed away and, when I reached the bathroom, I slammed the door shut and locked it.

"All right, Madam." He stood by the door. "I shall leave you now. But I will give you a card with my number. If you have any problems with the netting, call me. I am available all night." He thrust the card under the door and left as abruptly as he had come.

I stayed in my room a long time, fearful of bumping into this presumptuous man, wondering if he was standing outside in the hall waiting to capture me. I was imagining everything from the white slave trade to a simple mugging. Was there a signal that went out to all hotel personnel in Africa when a single lady came to town?

That night I bolted the door. I didn't trust all those keys floating around. A wedding celebration was in progress down below and a ferocious drumming invaded the night, drowning out the music of the birds and the wind. I slid under the gauzy canopy to get away from the jarring rhythms. At least I wouldn't have to worry about that special brand of malaria mosquito famous in these parts, for I was protected by my "prepared" netting.

When I awoke the sun was streaming into the room. It was hot and sticky for the beginning of the big Independence Day celebration in Kenya. Parades, dancing, speeches, feasting. I started my feasting at breakfast, and, when no one was looking, loaded my ziplock bags with enough goodies to last 'til dinner. It was all part of the price.

At noon I hired a taxi. I was going to Lamu, a village on the coast recommended by my nephew, Chip. Halfway to the airport I wondered if we could make it. The windshield on my side was shattered in three places and taped together. The side window had to be pulled up, manually, to be closed and pushed down to be opened. Missing handle. Shock absorbers and seat belts were nonexistent, and the wheels seemed to be going in four different directions at once.

"These roads are terrible, Madam," said the driver as my head hit the roof. "But don't worry about the car. I have it inspected once a year."

"You mean all this happened in less than a year?" I asked.

"We are not a capitalist country like America," he replied, still smiling and full of good humor. "We are very young and just getting started."

All along the route immense arches emblazoned with slogans—Love, Peace, Unity—were ready for President Moi's arrival. Flags lined the road and pictures of the president smiled down from every pole.

Orange blossomed gum trees decorated the spacious entrance to Mombasa Airport. The waiting room—blinding white stone with a flat roof—was open on all sides, attesting to the reliability of the weather. I bought a ticket on Pioneer Airlines, Ltd. and checked my pack. Good Lord! Forty pounds and climbing. Each passenger was allowed only twenty-five pounds. After paying for the extra weight I noticed an ample German who had four times too much and was shouting and waving his arms, insisting that not one bag be excluded. The steward stood firm.

"This is a small plane, Sir," he said, pointing to the one-engine Cherokee sitting on the runway. "It has only six seats and we cannot give three of them to your baggage."

One hour later the little plane lifted off, minus the German and his beloved baggage, and circled low over Mombasa. Spread before me was the "other" part of town—mansions and villas nestled luxuriously along the serpentine coastline with its beaches and multi-colored reefs. The water rimming the coral was an intense aquamarine that followed us all the way to Lamu.

The first thing I saw when I stepped off the plane onto the tiny airstrip was a group of smiling black men. Was this the welcoming committee, or were they selling something? One of them spotted me—noticing, perhaps, that I was alone and struggling with my pack—and came toward me with arms outstretched. He was tall and muscular, dressed in khaki shorts, an open-necked cotton shirt, and a colorful turban.

"Lovely lady," he said, grabbing both of my hands in his, "I am Ali Swaleh and this is my friend Kassim Nikuru." He gestured toward a teenager dressed in warm-ups and running shoes. "We are both Moslems, very honest and very reliable. Together we can take you everywhere in Lamu."

"But...but," I stammered, as Ali swooped up my pack and hoisted it onto his head. "What is your fee? Wait a minute. I'm perfectly capable of...."

"Trust me," said Ali, grinning. He had won an easy victory. "I know everything about Lamu. We can work out a price. No problem."

How did these phrases circle the globe so fast? *Trust me. No problem....*

Ali and Kassim started off with my belongings. Half running to keep up, I followed them through a thatched shed, which served as the terminal, and along a narrow wooden walkway to a small dock where a motor skiff was waiting. Across the inlet I could see the dark outline of a thick forest of mangrove trees.

"Our city is hidden just beyond the grove." Ali said. "You will love it. Everyone loves Lamu."

15

LAMU

Ali, Kassim, and I squeezed into the small boat and rode across to the main island. Single file, we took another walkway through a dense, swampy forest of mangrove trees to the edge of town. Ahead on the right was a wide deserted beach. Following its curve, I spotted two old-fashioned *dhows*, lateen-rigged and reminiscent of the *feluccas* of the Nile. They seemed to be hurrying in our direction, their sails puffed out and straining. Everybody, except me, was headed for Peponi's, a fancy resort at the end of the beach, half-an-hour by foot. That explained the hurrying *dhows*. When I saw how the boats tilted, their sails grazing the water, I was glad to stay firmly planted on the shore and follow Ali along the wide dirt path into town.

We walked beside a six-foot retaining wall, sending small puffs of fine dust into the air with each step. Fishing boats were unloading the day's catch. Children—squealing and jumping with pleasure—gathered on the docks, eager for a look. Next to the wall, clumps of wooden stanchions, exposed by the receding tide, leaned toward the ocean. Donkeys—their coarsely woven saddlebags heavy with produce—stood beside piles of overflowing feed sacks. And age-old trees, laden with moss, hung lazily over the stone walls surrounding elegant waterfront homes.

"That's Petley's Inn," said Ali as we walked by an impressive structure with cement columns, arches, and dark wooden balconies. Across the front was a terrace where smartly-dressed couples were being served by waiters in starched white uniforms.

"It's the only hotel in town—500 shillings a night. But I'll take you to a better place. A nice guest house, excellent, bath, and everything. Very safe, Madam, very quiet. It is in the old part of town. The real Lamu. And only 150 shillings."

That was less than nine dollars. "How far is it?" I asked.

"Nothing is far in Lamu."

We turned away from the water and headed down an alley barely wide enough for two. It was like entering the 15th century. Stone houses with slanting walls rose on either side of us, jammed together, some two, some three stories high. The pavement was a mixture of stone and dirt. Shallow grooves—formed by years of rainwater—ran alongside the buildings. I peered through rustic wooden gates into courtyards, where women cooked over an open fire and babies crawled on the clay floor. A cat scurried past. A donkey stood passively underneath a crooked stairway, untethered. Rows of windows, cut into the stone, seemed to be watching me, like eyes with no lids.

We wound through a maze of side streets, past furniture stores, craft shops, and bakeries, each with its small oblong sign hung over the door. Striped banners and colorful bunting stretched above the road between the buildings. But the feeling of antiquity remained. It was as if the shops were built right into the solid stone, a part of the earth, not a flimsy facade to be replaced in a few years. Women in *chadors* walked in twos and threes through the streets, their eyes averted, their heads lowered. Men sat on cement steps talking and laughing. Nobody seemed to be in a hurry.

"This is a happy, friendly town," said Kassim, as he waved to a friend. "We are all brothers and sisters. It's safe, too. No crime. No violence. You can walk anywhere at any time without fear. And you won't be run over by a car, either. Only the police chief is allowed to have one."

We came around a corner and stopped abruptly in front of a crumbling wall. A brightly painted sign announced: YUMBE GUEST HOUSE. "Here we are," said Kassim. "I must leave, now. My friend will take care of you. I'll stop by tomorrow."

He bowed and was off down the street. How different these two men looked. Ali—dark-skinned, with strong Arab features. Kassim—light-skinned, with a round face and negroid features.

"Kassim is a very devout Moslem. I'm not as good," said Ali, with an apologetic smile. "He prays five times a day and still manages to hold a part-time job and be on the winning high school soccer team."

We started up a freshly cemented, curved stone staircase, which led to a balcony overlooking a courtyard. I gasped. Below me were trees, flowers, and green grass like velvet. A small fountain bubbled in the center. Each part of the building was separately thatched, in long shaggy layers, including a small tower where you could look out over the town. Ali summoned a stunning young caretaker who bounded up the stairs to greet us. He looked like a well-tanned California beachcomber, wearing a sarong of red cotton tucked around the waist and hanging at an angle just below the calf. And that was all! Very sensible in this steamy weather. I'd gladly have traded my heavy black outfit for a length of cool cotton cloth.

My room had two simple beds—delicate mahogany frames with skinny legs that flared at the bottom like horses' hooves, and webbing instead of springs under the thin foam mattresses (The only place I'd seen such a bed was at the Cairo Museum). Everything in the room blended harmoniously—the blue-green woven spreads, the scenic batiks, the wooden shutters, the netting hanging from hand-hewn rafters. Unfortunately, the shower had only one faucet—cold—but it was far too hot a day to complain about that.

I reached into my wallet and handed the caretaker 150 shillings. Could it be—only one hundred shillings left? I'd completely forgotten about the bill at the Oceanic Hotel.

"Ali, I have a big problem," I said.

"No big problems in Lamu, Madam."

"Oh, yes. I need to change money, immediately!"

"Hmmm. You *do* have a problem," Ali admitted. "The Yumbe is too small a place to change traveler's checks, and it's after four o'clock on Friday. All banks are closed until Monday, except for the first and last Saturday in the month, and that's not tomorrow. Maybe we can cash a check at Petley's. It's worth trying."

We walked back through town and into Petley's. The lobby looked like a posh living room with its heavy carved furniture, oriental rugs, and old lamps. But the desk clerk was unsympathetic. "We cannot give you money, Madam, only vouchers on your Visa. And only if you stay at our hotel. You can eat in our dining room, of course."

I wouldn't dream of trading my little thatched hut for one of their rooms, no matter how grand. I was disconsolate.

Ali and I went out and sat on the retaining wall in front of the hotel. We watched the *dhows* tack back and forth in the harbor.

"Lovely lady," he began, "It pains me to see you so sad. I think I may have a solution, but you must never speak a word of it to anyone, especially Kassim."

"Oh, God, Ali, what are you suggesting…that we rob a bank?"

"Nothing so bad—just a little bad. And only if we get caught. But, first, tell me, do you have any dollars? Cash, I mean."

Should I tell him about the fifty dollars Chris gave me on the way to the airport, saying that it might come in handy in a pinch? I'd just told him that I had only travelers checks. Now I must admit that I lied. Well, not really. I was just withholding information.

"Yes, Ali, I do have a few dollars put away for an emergency. And I'd say this qualifies as an emergency. So, since I'm already a total wreck, what do you propose we do?"

"I have a friend—an Indian—who runs a dry goods store. He needs dollars for his business. I think he can help you."

"Please be careful," I pleaded. "Make sure nobody sees us." I couldn't believe that this fine, upstanding Moslem was about to involve me in a black market transaction, even though it would be at the legal rate of exchange. I was almost as amused as I was scared.

We ducked down a number of back alleys and into a gray, musty showroom. A huge Sikh, dark except for his white turban, arose from behind a glass display case. Ali quickly took him aside and they began whispering. I poked around in the corner, nonchalantly fingering material and trying to be as inconspicuous as possible.

"Come with me, Madam," said the Sikh, motioning with a snap of the head. I was sure all the people in the room were staring. My skin was clammy, my mouth dry. I followed him into a small back room.

"So you have fifty dollars," he said, much too loudly. "And you would like shillings."

I nodded.

"I can only give you 800. That is the legal exchange."

"Oh, Sir," I responded, handing him the fifty dollar bill. "That's fine. That's all I want. I assure you I would *not* do this if it were not a dire emergency. You do understand, don't you?"

He seemed to be holding back a smile. Was I making a fool of myself over nothing? Just as I was about to take the money, a tall thin man in a dark brown uniform strode into the room.

"Mr. Khalil?" he asked. The Indian nodded, and skillfully shoved the money from the counter into a drawer. "I was told I could find you here. Can I have a word with you?"

The two men left the room.

The police. I knew it was the police by the official-looking hat he was wearing. Did he have a gun? Now I didn't have my fifty dollars *or* the shillings. And I'd left my passport at the guest house. Nobody knew who I was and I might never be seen again.

"Oh, Ali, let's get out of here. Is there a back door?"

"You are a nervous woman, Madam. Khalil will be back. There is no problem."

"No problem?" I said. "The police are here. I don't have my money. And you say no problem! What is a problem to you, Ali?"

"That was not the police," he said.

"How do *I* know? They've been gone a long time." An old clock at the end of the counter ticked off the minutes—two, three, four. I decided to make a run for it. With sweating hands, I reached over the counter, opened the drawer, grabbed the faded bills, and thrust them into my camera bag. Ali looked at me, horrified.

"I'll meet you in the street—somewhere," I said, hurrying down the hallway, just as the big man was returning. I squeezed by him, almost knocking him over.

"Madam, where are you going?" he shouted. "Your money…."

I didn't answer, but fled out the door, past the uniformed man who was standing on a ladder adjusting a light fixture. The showroom was dark and empty.

Once outside, my breathing returned to normal. This was worse than seeing a lion run in front of my cabin at *Tsavo West*.

A few minutes later Ali caught up with me. "Madam, my friend thinks you're crazy. He wonders why an electrician should scare you so much. So do I."

"I know, Ali. I'm sorry. I freaked. But that is the last illegal act of my life. I swear to it."

"You are too serious," he said, "but I wish you luck in your resolution. Now let me buy you a cup of tea."

"No, no. It's my treat," I insisted. "We're going to Kenya Cold Drinks. I read about it in my guidebook. Supposed to have great shakes. And I'm doing a world survey of chocolate ice cream."

He looked at me strangely. "I know where it is. Let's go."

Ali stopped in a market along the way and bought what looked like a bunch of tea leaves. We sat outside under a grass canopy and drank two very disappointing milk shakes. The chocolate ice cream would definitely not make the top ten.

Afterwards, as we talked, Ali started chewing the leaves. I watched him. He was twenty-seven, the age of my youngest son. But he seemed wise beyond his years. He looked Egyptian—aquiline nose, delicate features—and was very proud of his ancestry. "I'm a mixture of Arab and Black," he said, "and a member of the *Bajun* tribe. We are only 13,000 people—an honest, hard working, religious community. But President Moi is now trying to force us to integrate with Blacks from the mainland, especially Nairobi. They want us to give them jobs, and accept socialistic land reform. If we allow these foreign elements to come, they'll destroy the good life we have and bring crime and unhappiness to our community."

This lament had a familiar ring to it. I'd heard it all before from the tourists on the plane.

"Ali, what is it you're chewing?" I asked, noticing that he now had what looked like a wad of tobacco in his cheek.

"It's *miraa*—comes from the town of Meru, near Nairobi. It makes you feel good. Everyone chews it, even women after their day's work is done. Here, try some." He thrust some leaves at me.

"No, no. I don't need any more stimulation for today," I said, pushing the leaves away. "Say, do you have a wife, Ali—or wives?"

He laughed. "No, not yet, but I will. And only one. I couldn't possibly cope with more. Women are difficult."

"Will you insist that she wear the *chador*?"

"Oh, yes, the *chador*. And a veil, too. She would want to, or her mother and my mother would be very angry. It would be her choice, you see."

Her choice? I couldn't imagine being a woman in such a strict Moslem community. True, it was safe, but there was no freedom. Perhaps, secretly, the women would welcome a little assimilation into the rest of Kenyan society.

That night I ate dinner with Margaret, a young Kenyan woman, whom I had met at the guest house. She was short and round, with closely cropped black hair and smooth, cocoa-brown skin. We talked over fruit shakes and lamb kebobs at another tourist attraction, The Yoghurt Inn.

"I'm one of eleven children," she said, "and we're all well-educated and scattered around the globe. We love one another, but hate the idea of the large extended family that's common here in Kenya. It's stifling. And we don't want to be categorized as a member of any tribe, either. My parents live alone, are well-off, and don't interfere in our lives."

"Sounds like a most unusual family," I said.

"It is," she agreed. "For example, my folks encouraged me to join Outward Bound several years ago, and I climbed Kilimanjaro with a group of students, from the Kenyan side...with ropes. It was real scary. Later that year I climbed up the other side on a regular trail with a group of blind students who were raising money for their school in Nairobi. Many parents wouldn't allow their children to do this. Mine thought it was great!"

"What brings you to Lamu?" I asked.

"I love old towns," she said. "I'd like to see them preserved. Modernized, without changing their character. And I think Lamu is the most beautiful place in Kenya. I got involved with a Dutch company that plans to restore the center of the town, without destroying its ancient beauty."

She was the kind of modern woman who would have appalled Ali.

After dinner we walked through the abandoned streets, past hidden entryways and dark corners. Any minute I expected someone to jump out at me. There wasn't another woman around.

Margaret must have sensed my nervousness. "Don't be so afraid," she said, putting her arm around me. "Nobody would ever hurt you in Lamu."

I was awakened at 5 A.M. by repetitive chanting in Arabic, an insistent cock crowing, high soprano singing, and a radio blaring the news in *Swahili*. I had little choice but to start my day. I tried to record the sounds, but there were too many. It was total cacophony.

I shuffled down to the open kitchen where the caretaker was making coffee. He handed me boiled water from a Gilby's Gin bottle.

"What are those women singing?" I asked. "It's lovely."

"Prayers. They are *Moisini*—Moslems. Madam, do you wish to stay another night?"

"Oh, yes. I feel as if I've just stepped into the bible."

"Well, we're old, but not *that* old," he said, chuckling.

I knew that Lamu had been an important trading center in the 14th and 15th centuries—one of many *Omani* Arab ports along the east African coast. But it still looked biblical to me.

The streets were deserted when I started for Petley's. My guidebook had touted their breakfasts, and said they started early—for those who wanted to go fishing. That's the last thing I wanted to do, after years of getting seasick while dutifully fishing with my husband off the New Jersey shore. But I did want an early breakfast.

At breakfast I met newlyweds, Annette and Emile Dearborn, stock brokers from New York. Together, we enjoyed a lavish buffet.

"We're moving to Peponi's for the next two days, and then back to New York City and the grind," Emile said. "Would you like us to call your family when we get home?"

"Wonderful!" I said, and wrote down Chris's number. "Say, would you feel it an imposition if I gave you some letters to mail for me in the States? It's so much quicker and more reliable."

"Not at all," he replied. "Just get them to us before Monday."

This was the push I needed to answer the letters that had piled up over the past four weeks.

I took one more spin around the buffet table before ordering a cup of thick Turkish coffee. In the harbor fishermen were rigging their sails for the day. Two women scurried by with large baskets of laundry on their heads. All around me was the fragrance of flowers and bushes. Suddenly I jumped up and started photographing the bougainvillia. It clung to the archway and spilled over the walk. I tried to capture the pattern of the shadows on the terra cotta floor. At that moment a middle-aged, sandy-haired man passed my table. He hesitated, and turned around.

"Do you mind if I join you?" he asked, putting his coffee and fruit on my table. "I've been watching you take pictures and I'm the same way about this place. It's a photographer's dream! Say, didn't I see you and Margaret Magobe at the Yoghurt Inn last night? She's a bright girl—a good friend of mine."

I recognized a Dutch accent. For seven years Cary, my eldest daughter, had lived in Holland.

"You must be the architect in charge of reclaiming the center of Lamu," I said.

"Yes, I am—Hans Van Kleist," he answered, reaching to shake my hand. "And you are…?"

"Meg Peterson," I replied. "Do join me. I'd like to hear more about Lamu from an expert."

He sat down opposite me. His eyes were a clear blue. Penetrating. "One more year to go and we'll be finished with the project. I'm amazed at how cooperative the people have been. And it wasn't as difficult as I'd expected, because it's such a well-built and well-engineered town." His enthusiasm was infectious.

"Lamu has an excellent drainage system—centuries old—and each home has its own septic plan. The water comes from the outlying sand dunes and has to be boiled, but there are still two large wells in town that are used daily by the inhabitants."

"Yes, I've seen women with long poles over their shoulders, a bucket of water at each end," I said. "It's a real balancing act. I tried to photograph one, but she put her hand over her face…."

Hans interrupted. "And don't try to photograph the fishermen."

"I know. Believe me, I know. I was shouted and waved at until some woman pointed to my camera and shook her head violently. I was so embarrassed. I wanted to dissolve into the vapors."

I helped myself to more mango juice and watched the inch-wide strips of woven matting, which hung from all the doorways, part and quiver as people flowed in and out soundlessly. I liked the hum of the simple white ceiling fans.

"This is a tropical paradise," I said, dreamily.

"Yes, it is."

There was a long silence as we looked at each other. I felt my cheeks turning warm. Hans picked up the conversation and was going on about the rainy season and the water supply. But I was only half-listening. I was looking at his naked forearms, his expressive hands gracefully punctuating every sentence. They were like Glen's. Strong. Nails perfectly oval. I was drawn to hands. By now I must have been beet-red. Why could I never hide my feelings?

He leaned forward. "Meg, let me show you some of the sights this morning before it gets too hot to breathe. We could start with the mosques. There are twenty-five, all of them unique."

I wondered how such a small town could have so many mosques.

"Or maybe you'd like to see the National Museum of Kenya. It's quite famous—full of tribal crafts, native houses, furniture, and unusual musical instruments."

"Now that appeals to me," I said. "But I only have 'til noon."

I thought I might change my mind during the morning, but by twelve I was ready to be alone. We had had a wonderful time—talking, laughing, roaming around the beautifully appointed museum. Hans seemed certain that I'd spend the afternoon with him. He said he'd planned to take the day off as soon as he met me. That was a bit presumptuous, I thought, but flattering. And I had to admit that I was very attracted to him. Was this Jerry all over again? Or was I so scared, so skeptical of relationships that I didn't feel like being with any man, not even an interesting, decent fellow like Hans? He must have sensed my ambivalence, and, in some measure, understood it.

"Perhaps we can meet later, for dinner…or for breakfast tomorrow," he said, taking my hand.

Without hesitation. "Yes, Hans. Breakfast. That would be fun."

I hurried back to the Yumbe, hoping I wouldn't bump into Ali or Kassim. Sightseeing was the last thing on my mind. I wanted to close the shutters against the sun, turn on the fan, and spend the afternoon writing. But I couldn't shake the lingering feeling that I was closing down, becoming an emotional hermit. And that was not how I wanted my life to be.

When I reached my room there was Kassim, sitting on the stairs, looking crestfallen. "Oh, Madam," he said, "I'm so sorry to be late."

"You're not late," I said. "I've had a fine time at the museum and now I'm going to rest."

"You don't want to see sights?" he asked, disappointed.

"No, I don't want to sightsee anymore, Kassim."

"And your bag. Do you want me to help you go to the airport?"

"Oh, yes, that'd be wonderful. Can you come to the Pioneer office tomorrow morning at nine o'clock?" I didn't think I needed him, but I felt guilty not giving him some work after he'd found me such a terrific guest house.

"O. K. I'll be there. Ali will, too. We like you, Madam."

"I like you, too," I said. He grinned and shook my hand.

I caught up on my journal before tackling the unanswered letters. Much to my chagrin I discovered, after three hours of writing, that I had reached the end of my third journal and had only one pen left. My first task, when I reached Tanzania, would be to stock up on pens and spiral notebooks…if I could find them.

I shoved the packet of letters into my camera bag and proceeded to work my way back to the harbor. The streets were crowded. Groups of shiny-faced children played in the dust around the racks of clothing in front of the shops. It was Africa's own version of New York City's 14th Street. *Mohamed Ali Mohamed Ladies' Wear. Abdullah's Men's Furnishing.*

Just as I reached the center of town I heard what sounded like bagpipe music. People were standing in a circle around two men, who were sparring with long staves, jumping back, doing a step and a shuffle, locking sticks, and starting all over again. I sidled up to one of the spectators. "Is this a dance of some sort?" I asked.

"No, it's a *Kirumbesi*," he replied, "a *Swahili* drama celebrating a wedding. In just a few minutes the bride and her entourage will be here. She'll have perfume and jasmin in her hair. It's beautiful, don't you think?"

"Yes, very graceful…almost like a dance," I said. But the sparring and the sticks. What did that bode for a marriage?

A little girl in a party dress reached over and took my hand. "Dance, Missus?" she asked, pulling me into a newly formed circle. Several of her friends stood around, clapping and stamping as the dance gained momentum. Other children joined the celebration, selecting an adult partner from outside the circle. Round and round we went, encouraged by the whining bagpipes. A drum had been added, giving the music a repetitive, hypnotic quality. We became one all-consuming, whirling motion, like interlocking gears. I felt totally free and with this freedom came pure elation.

I regretted not waiting for the bride to appear, but it would be late by the time I reached the waterfront and it was a long walk to Peponi's. When I left, a small group of children followed me. I wondered where their parents were. But nobody seemed to worry about lost children in Lamu.

As I started down the beach a man with a limp came toward me.

"Would you like a ride to Peponi's, Madam?" he asked.

"How much?" I asked.

Fifty shillings."

Not bad. It was almost sundown and I was anxious to get those letters to the Dearborns.

"Suppose I want to return…then how much?" I asked.

"One hundred and twenty," he replied.

"One way fifty shillings, round trip one hundred and twenty. How do you figure that?"

"We have to wait for you."

"Fair enough," I said. I was escorted to a pair of decrepit stone stairs and inched my way down a thin plank from the top step to the bow of the boat. It had one large sail, a hand-made rudder, and sturdy thwarts for seats. A narrow replica of the Egyptian *felucca*. Six other people were already aboard—young men in western business suits returning from work. This struck me as an unusual form of commuter transportation.

Everybody cheered as I teetered on the plank, righted myself, and entered the boat safely. I sat down on the middle thwart and secured my camera bag on the floor between my legs. All around me were burlap sacks full of rocks for ballast.

The sun was now a bright orange disk lighting up the tips of the waves as we cut through them. We were flying! Wind blew my hair and skirt. But I didn't care. I joked along with everyone else—mainly to keep up my courage. Most of the men sat on the gunwales, as if daring the boat to capsize. And each time it tilted almost horizontal to the water, everyone quickly moved to the other side. It was terrifying…and exciting. I'd grab the rough gunwales and lean away from the water, inadvertently yelling, "Jesus," until one of the men asked me whether Jesus was my husband. I was certain I would go into the sea, camera bag, letters, and all.

"Not to worry, Mama," said one of the men. "He's a good captain." A smiling, brown-toothed Arab sat on his haunches in the stern, watching each gust of wind and each movement of the *dhow*, one hand on the rudder and the other adjusting the sail.

"See, he's not worried. He's having as much fun as we are."

When we arrived at Peponi's, the men rolled up their pant legs and stepped into the water.

Were they crazy? While I was debating what to do, one of the men swooped me up and carried me to the beach. Big thrill of the day. What am I saying? Big thrill of the month!

After delivering my mail, I returned to the beach with the Dearborns. They looked at the weathered old *dhow* skeptically.

"Are you sure it's safe?" asked Annette.

"Well, so far so good," I replied. "I was a little windblown, and more than a little scared. But we made it."

The Dearborns gave me the thumbs up signal as I was carried on board. No more treacherous gangplank. The wind had died down so I was able to record the captain. He was pleased to be the center of attention and smiled more than ever. After reciting a Moslem poem, he sang a song in Arabic. Everyone, in turn, said something into the tape recorder. It was a time of closeness and beauty—the moon on the sea, the lights in the windows of a distant Mosque, and the rhythmic lapping of the water against the shore.

The Equator Restaurant was not far from the beach. It was built in a circular design with a domed roof and a stick frame—all thatched. I sat on a carved bench and surveyed a cozy combination of Moorish, oriental, and African decor. Large patterned porcelain bowls hung between pictures of the sea and President Moi.

"What a sour look your president has on his face," I said when the waiter came over to take my order. I'd been wanting to say that for some time.

"Oh, he's just starting to smile, can't you tell?" he said.

"You mean he's trying and not succeeding," I countered.

We both laughed. The ambiance was now complete. A chivalrous waiter in a flowing *gallaka*...and with a sense of humor.

He began. "Today we have three seafood specialties—lobster for forty-eight shillings...."

"Sorry," I interrupted. "The price is right, but I'm allergic to all seafood."

"That's not possible, Madam, not in Lamu."

I settled for steak au poivre—which I feared was donkey—garnished with stuffed vegetables, rice, and salad. After dinner, the ample maitre d'—a bearded man wearing what looked like a bed sheet imprinted with hieroglyphics—insisted that I try a glass of his special wine. It was so good that I tried another. By the time the bill arrived I was glowing. I asked the waiter for directions to the Yumbe Guest House, and he drew me a meticulous map. Then he wanted to know my name. I thought he was just curious about names, so I told him. He couldn't pronounce it, and asked me to write it down. What a foolish thing to do! But I forgot about it when I went by Petley's and the waiter, who was standing out front, suggested that I come in and try the papaya wine. No charge. He even showed me the bush it had come from. Three glasses of wine in one evening? I hadn't felt this good since my trip up the Nile.

I walked home past the docks and along the sea wall. I longed to stay a few more days, get to know these people, visit their homes. If ever I had another honeymoon, I'd spend it here.

The next morning the chanting began even earlier—4 A.M. This time I was able to get it on tape, for it was louder and clearer, and unencumbered by other sounds.

After I paid my bill and was about to leave, the caretaker stopped me. "Oh, I hope you don't mind, Madam, but a gentleman came here late last night asking for you. He had your name on a piece of paper. I knew you were leaving early in the morning, and I didn't want to disturb you. So I didn't give him your room number."

"I appreciate that," I said. "You were right. I wasn't expecting anybody."

I really did have a guardian angel!

At the bottom of the steps I was greeted by a throng of children. One little boy pointed to my tan safari hat and insisted on wearing it while I took his picture. He was carrying his breakfast—a plate of fried mashed peas.

I felt like the Pied Piper as I made my way to Petley's through the streets and alleys, lugging my heavy pack and being followed by an enthusiastic band of little friends.

Hans greeted me warmly at breakfast. It was fun watching the early morning activities together from the airy terrace. Neither of us said a word about yesterday. We exchanged addresses, but it was just a formality.

When I arrived at Pioneer Airlines Kassim was already there. Was I glad to see him!

"Ali sends his regrets, and wishes you a safe journey," he said, bowing. I guess I was a big disappointment to Ali.

"We'd better hurry," he added. "The boat's almost loaded."

He lifted my bag onto his head and started off.

How thankful I was that it was Kassim, and not I, who carried that pack over the wobbly plank into the motor skiff, saving us both—the bag and me—from toppling into the bay.

This was a larger boat than before, full of workmen, tourists, and women with babies. I marveled that the infants didn't suffocate, pressed so tightly into their mother's backs each time the women leaned against the seats. I looked around at the people—black workmen in drab clothes and baseball caps, Indian women in diaphanous *saris*, Indian men draped in white, Arabs with pillbox hats on their heads, and sunburned western tourists in sleeveless dresses or shorts. It amused me to see several serene-looking young Moslem women open their *chadors* after leaving shore to reveal low-cut, seductive dresses. I wondered if their men knew about this. It was probably the only way to keep from getting sunstroke. Or maybe it was a subtle form of rebellion.

I felt sad as we disembarked and started the long walk to the terminal. I hated to leave. But I couldn't stay sad for long. Kassim was too full of excitement over his plans for the day.

"I'll be going to the beach with my school football team this afternoon—I guess you call it soccer. We won the championship and this is our celebration," he told me with great pride.

"You seem very fond of your school," I said, caught up in the enthusiasm of this eager young man with the contagious smile.

"Yes, it's wonderful. I plan to be an engineer when I finish. That will mean college. My parents believe in education. They think I should get out of Lamu."

"Have you always been so religious, Kassim?" I asked, after he'd told me about his daily regimen of prayers.

"Oh, yes," he said, "it's a family tradition. My brothers are the same. I want to be a good person. That's more important than anything else."

The plane was late, so we sought refuge in the rustic terminal. A hand-printed sign hanging at one end of the open room proclaimed: DUTY FREE SHOP. There were warm soft drinks for sale, shells, and local crafts. A smaller hand-written sign stated: "If you don't have money, we will take anything in exchange you may wish to give. e.g. watch, bags, skirts, shirts, ties, trousers." I saw absolutely nothing in that room that would warrant sacrificing any part of my wardrobe.

Kassim hugged me and asked me to write. He refused to accept any money for his help.

As the plane circled, I looked down at the grassy field around the terminal. There stood Kassim, with both arms stretched high above his head, waving.

16

HIDDEN DANGER

I had grabbed one of the back seats to get away from the smell of two heavily robed men, who had stood too long in the sun. It didn't work, but it gave me a good view of the ground as the little plane followed the checkerboard of islands, marsh, and sea, its propellers whining and groaning like a giant eggbeater in heavy batter. As we approached Malindi I noticed large squares of cream-colored soil—salt drying on the flats—bisected by the best roads I'd seen in Kenya. We followed the coastline—its untouched beaches, its layers of waves—all the way to Mombasa, where the wildness yielded to large villas and summer homes. Countless manicured rows of sisal began to appear. Beyond them, green rolling hills.

I staggered off the plane, my clothes sticking to me like moist seaweed, my head still full of the roar of the engine.

A young man walked up to me. "Would you like help with your pack? Americans find the heat of Kenya difficult."

"How did you know I was American?" I asked, very glad to accept his offer.

"The monster pack, the new camera bag, the way you hugged your porter at the Lamu airport. Your openness." His manner and his accent told me he was English.

"How long have you been watching me?" I asked. "And what are you? Some kind of social scientist, or anthropologist?"

"A little bit of both, I guess." He hoisted my pack over his shoulder. "You get like this after you've been here awhile."

"He's also an adventurer who won't come home. So his family has to come to Africa if they want to see him," said a bubbly young woman walking beside him.

"Hello," she said, extending her hand. She had freckles, red hair, and a beguiling smile. "I'm Kathy Richards and this is my intractable brother Ian." Ian nodded.

"Actually," he continued, "I'm a businessman. For six years I've run safaris throughout Africa—three to four months long—and a coffee plantation here in

Kenya." He turned as we entered the terminal and walked toward the refreshment counter. "Come on. Let's have a couple of meat pies and a beer. I'm dying to find out where you're going with all this paraphernalia."

"What do you mean? I thought I was traveling light."

"Light, my ass," he said. "If you were traveling with me I'd have you down to one skirt, one blouse, and a couple of knickers."

"I packed for one year, not three months," I said defensively. "I tried to keep things down and so far my judgment has been right on. Not a single unnecessary item."

"O.K., I'm wrong. You win," he said, and went off to check my bag.

I hated it when anyone said that to me. It was such a cop out. And it reminded me of Glen. Everything with him became a battle. Not a desire to communicate. If he didn't agree, or felt he'd been proven wrong, he'd throw up his hands and say, "There I go, wrong again—you win."

Kathy and I located a secluded table on the second floor, with a view of the runway. And a breeze.

"Bum news," Ian related, when he rejoined us. "Meg's flight on Air Tanzania won't leave for Dar es Salaam until six. And it's only noon. It looks like we'll have plenty of time to chat."

Damn! I could have stayed an extra day in Lamu.

"Didn't mean to taunt you back there," Ian said. "But I'm used to rugged, bare-bones camping in places like Zambia and Botswana…you know, where the little bushmen live. I take my truck anywhere, but I wouldn't advise a white woman to go it alone in most African countries."

"What makes you think I don't have a tour all planned?" I asked uneasily.

"Just a hunch, that's all. Where are you staying in Dar?"

"I have the names of some hotels," I answered tenuously.

"Just what I thought. No reservation. That's crazy! Tanzania is not tourist friendly. They're still smarting from the war with Idi Amin and are plenty angry about the little help they received, especially from their neighbors. Right now they're big on black freedom and suspicious of white visitors. They make it as difficult as possible to get there…and to get around after you arrive. You'll see. No reservation, no bed."

"You sure are a cheerful fellow," I said, wondering just how much to believe. "But I'm not really worried. If I can't find a hotel room, there's always the ANC school outside Dar."

"What do you know about the ANC in Tanzania?" Ian asked, looking at me suspiciously.

"Oh, nothing much. I have the school's phone number and the name of the director." I took out my small loose-leaf notebook and showed him the list of African National Congress members I had for Tanzania, Zimbabwe, and South Africa. I'd gotten them from Dr. George Manwe, a professor of African history at Queens College, who had escaped from a South African prison ten years ago, but remained in close touch with friends in the anti-apartheid movement. I met him through my brother-in-law, who'd been a medical missionary in Durban in the 1960's.

"Dr. Manwe advised me to write the school before calling," I said, "but there wasn't time. He also gave me some confidential letters to hand-deliver in Durban." I hadn't seen the danger before. Now it looked as if I had no sense at all.

Ian started reading the names out loud. "Winnie Mandela, Jonathan Paton....You could have gotten into a lot of trouble, Meg. Do you realize what this would look like to someone who didn't know you or your professor? A hit list, that's what. ANC members are very suspicious people, and they have every reason to be. Get rid of this list right away. And don't call the ANC school."

"Boy, you sure know how to burst my bubble and make me feel like a fool at the same time," I said.

"Don't mean to. How could you know it was dangerous? Things have really heated up in the last few months, especially in the countries bordering South Africa. I never expected one of my clients to be hauled off at gunpoint in Lusaka last summer just for writing a post card to her boy friend in France. The police couldn't read French, so they accused her of being a South African spy, sending subversive messages. We had to wait in a crumby dump next to the post office until she was released. Can you believe it? Four hours of interrogation for writing one bloody post card!"

"And the road blocks. Tell her about those," said Kathy.

"Hell, those are routine. Every teenage guy in Zaire seems to have a gun. After-school sport is to stop foreigners and search them. Happened to me four times on my last safari. Talk about scared! Here's a guy twice your size holding a loaded automatic to your head, behaving as if he's half in the bag. You don't move. You just sweat...buckets. Fortunately, I had a cache of rock tapes and western magazines. I doled them out—very judiciously—and we got home. At this point, Zimbabwe, Botswana, and Kenya are the only places where I feel safe."

While Ian was telling his horror stories, my mind was frantically reviewing past conversations with Mwesa Mapoma, the Zambian ethnomusicologist who had invited me to Lusaka. I'd met him at an international music conference in Warsaw eight years ago and we'd carried on a lively correspondence until last year. Why hadn't he answered my letters? Was he trying to tell me something? Could he be in trouble because of his frequent visits to the West? Would I cause a problem if I visited him?

"Time to go," announced Ian. It was six o'clock and there was no sign that my plane would leave any time soon. We'd gone through three meat pies each and the same number of beers. "Hope I haven't depressed you, Meg. You'll discover that Africa is a fantastic place, even with all its problems. That's why I can't see going back to merry old, dull old England. Don't say it. I know I'm talking out of both sides of my mouth. But what the hell....Cheerio."

I hated to see them go. I watched as they walked out the door, arms locked, delighting in each other. Just like my own kids.

I took Dr. Manwe's letters and the controversial pages from my notebook and hid them in the secret compartment of my camera bag next to my South African loose-leaf visa. I didn't destroy them in case Ian had been exaggerating. But I did resolve not to call the ANC school in Dar es Salaam and to skip my visit to Lusaka. For the first time, deep in my gut, I was scared.

"We have very few planes, Madam," said the pleasant Air Tanzania flight manager when I asked why it was taking the "Pride of Africa" so long to fly from Dar to Mombasa. "When one plane breaks down, every one is late in turn."

I looked around. There were no computers in sight. I didn't dare ask how many planes they had. Instead I asked, with instant regret, "Are the planes safe?"

There was a hint of a smile. "When they're finally fixed, they're perfect. Must be some small thing—a minor mechanical problem," he answered.

"Some small thing?" I said. "Eight hours to fix some small thing? Like, maybe, a wing falling off?"

"No, the wings are fine." Now there was a full smile. I think he liked me because I was one of the few who still had a sense of humor after eight hours of waiting.

"Say, why don't you have some tea and cakes with me?" he said. "You must be very hungry." He motioned me into his office and poured two cups of lukewarm tea from a tan thermos.

"Tell me, if the plane doesn't leave will Air Tanzania get me a hotel room?" I asked.

"Oh, yes," he said, with a comical grin, "your hotel room is right here." He slapped his molded plastic chair. What did it matter? My clothes were already welded to the seat.

"Why do you want to go to Tanzania in the first place?" he asked, offering me a cake. "Things are bad there. Sometimes there's no water and sometimes no light. The economy is very poor."

"I've booked a climb up Mt. Kilimanjaro…plan to meet a group in Moshi and be on the summit Christmas morning." I was a little disconcerted by his negative attitude.

"I hope you don't expect to take a bus from Dar to Moshi," he continued. He took a bite of the very dry cake. I watched the crumbs gather on one shiny pant leg. "It's impossible this time of year. The roads are treacherous, and if you do get a bus it might break down and take two or three days—with nowhere along the way to buy food, or to sleep."

"I plan to take a plane. It's quicker," I said.

"Oh, that's even more difficult." He shook his head slowly, giving me the feeling that I was doomed. "The planes are unreliable and overbooked. And the weather is unpredictable. You should have taken a bus from Nairobi. That's the way most people do it."

I gulped the rest of my tea. So why didn't someone tell me…like the tourist bureau where I booked my climb?

For the next few hours I wandered around the airport, talking with anyone who could speak English. Nobody was very communicative. Everybody just hung in the seats limply. I moved on to the tiny bookstore and started browsing.

"Really interested in the old romance, aren't you?"

I wheeled around. A tall man with graying hair smiled down at me. "You tourists are fascinated with Karen von Blixen," he said. I was leafing through a book about her and Denys Finch-Hatton. "She's a legend in Kenya. When I first came to Africa I lived in one of the houses on her former coffee plantation."

"You knew her?" I asked. He looked too young.

"No, not quite," he said, chuckling. "But my uncle did. He told me a lot about her. Knew Finch-Hatton, too. Evidently he was just the way Redford played him in the movie, Out of Africa. Independent, charming, aloof."

I interrupted. "Do you think he ever loved her?"

"Oh yes," he replied, "and many others. He was quite a ladies' man. But he was a sportsman first. Loved the out-of-doors and flying over the parks in search of big game. I think Beryl Markham—you know, the one who wrote West With The Night—was more his type. Fiercely independent. Excellent pilot. He had asked her to go with him the night of the crash. They don't tell you that in the movie."

"Karen seemed like a loner, too," I said.

"Maybe. But she didn't want to be. She longed to be accepted by English society in Nairobi, but she was Danish, and never quite made it. And never understood why. I find it a sad story."

Tony Rowland, who reminded me of Jacques Tati in <u>Mr. Hulot's Holiday</u>, owned a construction company in Dar, and was on his way to Zanzibar for a meeting. He grumbled about the African mentality, but loved his life as an ex-colonial living like a colonial. His attitude added to my lack of enthusiasm for going to Tanzania. Or maybe it was just my regret at leaving Kenya.

At 11 P.M. we began our march through customs. I stood very quietly, remembering what Ian had said. I must have looked innocent because I breezed through the line without unzipping so much as one pocket, while the Indians and Kenyans had their suitcases open, everything spilling out onto the floor.

This was my first time on a Fokker Cherokee Friendship turbo-prop, and I loved it. I also loved getting away from the humid airport and being able to breathe again. Fortunately, I sat between two progressive Tanzanians who helped counteract the negative publicity I'd been getting all day. They agreed, however, that although tourists were not particularly welcomed in Tanzania, I'd find a big difference in Moshi…if I managed to get there.

We flew over Zanzibar because the pilot didn't feel like landing. It was too late, he said. That was where Tony was supposed to get off. I hadn't noticed his presence until my turn came to go through customs in Dar. I was the last passenger of the evening. The official—a huge ink-black man with a stomach straining to escape his shirt and eyes that rolled up almost out of sight when he looked at me—was very drunk. He reared back at a forty-five degree angle, jaw jutting forward, arms flapping, and bellowed: "Laaa-dy, open it all up."

His fist slammed the counter. I jumped, inadvertently, and let out a small cry.

At this point Tony stepped forward, grabbed my closed bag, and pointed his finger at the official. It almost touched his thick chest. "Don't you ever shout at a lady like that again, or I'll report you. And go get a cup of coffee. You're stinking drunk."

The official swayed widely, but caught himself just before he would have hit the counter.

"Come on," said Tony, "let's get some money changed and get out of here. I hung around because I knew this guy was trouble. Hope you don't mind."

"Mind?" I said. "I feel as if God sent you to watch over me. This has never happened before in all my travels. I don't know if I'd have dared do what you did."

"These guys are mostly bluster, especially when they're drunk. You just have to act as if you're the boss. Actually, I was a little nervous, myself."

As we drove into town Tony began to tell me about the currency problems in Tanzania, the total inefficiency of services, the breakdown of power lines and telephone equipment, and how I probably wouldn't get a plane to Moshi, or even find a hotel for the night. All of this when I was hot, hungry, and tired.

There wasn't another car on the road. The cab driver sped through every red light without even hesitating. I finally asked him if the system of lights was different in Tanzania—that is, did red mean go and green mean stop?

"Oh, no," he said. "The traffic lights are for the tourists."

Tony guffawed. "Now, that's a new one."

I didn't think it was funny and held tightly onto my seat, ready to throw myself on the floor if necessary.

We stopped at four hotels, all of them seedy, with sad-looking palms drooping over dirt courtyards. Tony was dead right. Ian was dead right. There wasn't a vacant hotel room in town. What was I to do?

Tony seemed to read my thoughts. "Meg, we can't just ride around all night. You're welcome to stay at my place. It's protected by a night watchman. And my new manager and his girl friend also live there. You have nothing to worry about."

It was either Tony's or the park bench. For one long moment I hesitated, then slumped back into the seat as I heard him say, "Driver, take us to the compound on Ocean Drive and Macauley."

17

GET ME OUT OF HERE!

Jim Henderson and his girl friend, Andrea, lived in Tony's spacious modern pad next door to the famous chimpanzee woman, Jane Goodall. The one-story house came with a gatekeeper, houseboy, gardener, four dogs, and a diminutive night watchman who sat on the stone patio until dawn—bow and arrow at the ready. Tony was true to his word. I had nothing to worry about.

I was given a large, air-conditioned bedroom and would probably not have emerged before noon if I hadn't needed a ticket to Moshi. I stepped onto the sun porch where breakfast was waiting, and Andrea—looking like a cover girl for *Mademoiselle*, her long blond hair resting on delicate, bare shoulders—smiled a greeting. How could she look so cool while perspiration was already creeping over my body, promising to keep me uncomfortable the rest of the day? I knew right then that I could never live in the tropics, for all I wanted to do was sit around and be fanned. Instead, I faced an ordeal that rivaled, in its frustration, the Egypt Air episode of a month ago.

Andrea McCurdy was sweet, willowy, and twenty-six. Eight weeks ago she had left her husband and moved in with Jim. I was just the person she was looking for—a mother figure to whom she could tell her story, a listener who would not judge but would also not hesitate to give an opinion when asked. And I, in turn, had found a patient companion willing to endure long hours of waiting as I searched for a plane, bus, or automobile to take me to Moshi, the starting point for my anticipated climb up Kilimanjaro.

We headed for town in a Toyota that had no muffler and only one fender.

"You can't buy such things in Dar," complained Andrea, her lilting Scottish accent making the situation seem less serious. "Jim had his windscreen and headlights ripped off last month. That's why the clamps and screening over the headlights. Nothing is safe, but I guess I should be glad just to have a car to drive because there's such a shortage of petrol. We can only buy it Monday through Wednesday."

And I thought we had it bad in 1973. At least there was gas if we were willing to wait in line for it.

Kearsley, Limited, the only tourist agency in town, was our first stop. It was packed. Impatient travelers crowded around one small desk, waving their arms, shouting out their names, and demanding attention from the lone clerk on duty. It took me an hour to jockey my way to the front of the lines. It was much like reaching the hub of a wheel.

After joining a tour which connected with my scheduled climb up Kilimanjaro, I was informed that no buses or private cars were going to Moshi—the road had been closed due to flooding—and there was a three day wait for plane reservations.

"Come back in three days and we can let you know if there's a seat," said the clerk. "Just leave a deposit and we'll hold your reservation at the Marangu Hotel in Moshi."

"Why didn't you tell me this before I planned the tour?" I asked, incensed.

"One can never be sure about the weather," he replied, smiling fatuously. "And, in addition, we have a serious petrol shortage."

"Are three days going to make a difference in the petrol shortage? And would I get my deposit back if I couldn't get a seat?

"Madam, shall I put you on the list?" he asked impatiently.

"I...I don't know," I stammered. "I'll have to get back to you." To wait so long and maybe not even get on the plane...then what would I do? Impose on my friends for another three days?

The clerk pressed his lips together. "I have no control over the future. And I cannot decide for you....Next!" He turned away.

So I wasn't going to climb Mt. Kilimanjaro after all. Or meet up with David and Tray. Or stand on the rim of the Ngorongoro Crater and view the trapped animals milling below. Or witness the Serengeti's annual migration of wild creatures.

I fled the crowded, steamy room, Andrea trailing behind. Disappointment enveloped me as I walked through the run-down city with its pot-holed streets, its cracked, curbless sidewalks, its noise and pollution. Dar wasn't quite as dirty as Cairo, but it had none of Egypt's charm. Ugly square columns buttressed the overhanging second stories of drab office buildings. And a total disregard for traffic regulations made walking perilous. My only thought was "Get me out of here!"

"Come on, let's buy that journal you keep talking about. It'll cheer you up," suggested Andrea, pulling me into a shabby stationery store. The stale odor of glue and mold emanated from dark corners and packed shelves. I eagerly looked through a collection of bound journals with narrow lines and extra long pages, and picked a thick book covered in a faded paisley print. My mood changed. If I couldn't get out of Dar, at least I could sit in my air-conditioned room and write about it in style.

After lunch we went directly to Air Tanzania. The office looked like an old-fashioned high-ceilinged railroad station. Stony-faced customers sat on leather couches and the unfortunate overflow, like us, stood leaning against the cement wall. There was only one slot for international travel. And reams of handwritten lists were piled on the desk.

An hour passed. Still no movement at the international desk. I finally button-holed the duty officer and asked if there was some other way to get tickets to Moshi or Harare.

"Oh, don't bother waiting," he said. "All flights to the mountains have been cancelled indefinitely due to the petrol shortage. As for Harare, they're fully booked for the rest of the week."

"You've got to be kidding!" I said. "Then I'm going back to Nairobi and start over."

"All those flights are booked, too. But come back tomorrow," he added, with a touch of sympathy. "I'll talk with our international office and see what we can do for you."

It was a terrible feeling to be at the mercy of bureaucrats. I felt as if I were back in Poland in July, 1980—during the birth of Solidarity—where I'd stood in line at the Warsaw railroad station, waiting for an ancient teletype machine to slowly grind out one reservation at a time.

The next day at Air Tanzania was a repeat of the previous one. The duty officer recognized me. "Come back at two," he suggested. "We're checking to see if there are duplicate bookings."

By four o'clock, after much paper shuffling and conferring, one lone tourist class ticket—for two days hence—was located. I was ecstatic, and, in my enthusiasm, embraced the surprised clerk.

"Let's celebrate," said Andrea, almost as happy as I that the ordeal was over. "I'll take you on a drive around the coast and show you the bright side of Dar before you leave."

We talked and laughed as we wound around the sharp embankments from whose rocky surfaces large palms hung precariously over the ocean. We stopped at the highest point and looked down at the busy panorama: freighters and sailing ships struggling to right themselves on the incoming tide; fishermen folding their nets, their catch squirming on the wharf; and naked bathers darting into the water from the grassy spits of land.

But there were other not so pleasant sights. People living by the side of the road in tin shacks that must have been boiling hot, washing clothes in muddy streams, and tending skimpy gardens which wilted before my eyes in the hot sun. And children, so many ragged children.

I was glad to get back to Tony's house. It was like an oasis in the midst of an urban desert. I walked around the manicured grounds, relishing the onset of dusk. A large *frangipani* bush outside the front door delighted me, its delicate pink-rimmed white flowers hanging tenuously from fragile maroon stems, filling the courtyard with heavy perfume. Dark green clumps of spiked cactus stood in the garden like feisty armadillos guarding the fort. In one corner the gardener, a slight man with close-cropped white hair, was lovingly working the soil. One flame tree with its tiers of bright orange blossoms graced the far end of a carpet of grass, which was bordered by a tightly woven thicket of hedge clipped to perfection. At the other end a lofty acacia tree reached up, its crooked branches fanning out to provide all comers with relief from the unforgiving sun.

How I could have used some of Tony's help—a maid, a cook, a gardener—while my children were growing up. I pictured the elegant English Tudor Glen and I had bought in the early sixties when large houses were out of fashion and yours for the remodeling. And heating oil was cheap. The grounds were reminiscent of Tony's but the house was quite different. At first the children were sure it was haunted, with its imposing staircase, high ceilings, elevator, dark paneling, and labyrinthian basement. The seven bedrooms and six fireplaces, porches, solarium, and gardens were perfect for a large family, but a tremendous burden for the maid...me.

Of course, there were five children to help with lawn work and cleaning—under duress—but the supervisor, laundress, chief cook, and top sergeant always ended up being me. Top sergeant...that's the part I didn't like. That was Glen's idea of how to run a large family. "You're a pushover," he'd say. "If you don't exert more control, before you know it, the kids will take over."

In those days most fathers had little to do with child rearing. That was the mother's job. When they came home from work they wanted a stiff drink, a good meal, and a couple of hours on the couch with the newspaper. They let you know they were too exhausted to help. And since you didn't expect it, you seldom asked, even though you were every bit as exhausted.

I had no idea that Glen felt cheated by all the time I spent with the children. After all, they were *his* children, too. Wouldn't he want me to do the best possible job? But once he did say, as I was putting the last one to bed, "Is this ever going to end? When will we get a little time together?" It didn't occur to him that if he'd give me a hand it wouldn't take so long. I remember, with great emotional pain, sitting at my kitchen table signing our divorce papers twenty-five years later. "I think it might have gone better for us," he'd said, "if we hadn't had so many children."

"What are you doing, Meg?" shouted Andrea, who was now standing on the patio, her slender body draped in a long silk caftan. "The men will be home soon. And the evening creatures will eat you alive if you don't come in."

"Don't worry about me," I said. "I'm too tough for your creatures."

I spent my last evening in Dar es Salaam at a fancy English yacht club. We sat on the patio overlooking the ocean. A full moon shone above. It was hard to imagine the poverty and squalor I'd seen at the old market that day and on the road leading out of Dar.

"I'm really discouraged," Jim said. He did site analysis for construction projects, most of which were funded by foreign grants. "I'm trying to encourage my staff to take more responsibility, but instead of working harder to improve themselves and their country, they ask for more perks and continue in the same old easygoing way. Maybe their way is better, but they can't expect the world to support them if they don't even try to make the country work."

"This is the result of Nyere's disastrous economic policies," added Tony. "There's no incentive for a person to try if he feels, deep down, that there's no hope. I think we're nuts to keep shoveling in aid when it only goes to line the pockets of greedy politicians. And the people end up hating us in the bargain."

Andrea looked uncomfortable. The conversation had been as depressing as it was long. She reached over and lightly touched Jim's arm. There was such tenderness in that motion. "Have you men nothing cheerful to tell Meg before she leaves us?" she asked.

Jim, the prototype of a young, self-assured entrepreneur, turned to me. "Don't despair, Meg," he said impishly. "Four years ago you couldn't even buy toilet paper in Dar."

"Well, that's certainly a measure of progress," I said.

"And maybe in a year or two we might even get a phone in the house," said Tony.

Late that night we all sat in the living room having a nightcap. A small green lizard traversed the wall, eyeing me nervously.

A crack of thunder, like the splitting of a giant redwood, rent the air. Andrea let out an involuntarily scream as the room was plunged into blackness. In a flash of lightening I saw the silhouette of the little man who stood on the patio, bow slung over his shoulder…and someone else, hovering near the bushes. The little man saw him, too. In the next instant we heard the sound of footsteps pounding around the house.

"Hope the fellow escapes, poor sod," said Tony, rummaging around for candles. "I can't understand why anybody would chance a break-in when he knows the consequences. Just shows you how bad things are in this country."

I pictured the iron gate at the entrance to each group of houses, secured by a heavy metal chain and unlocked by a guard every time you went in or out. I wondered how this man had slipped through without being detected. And once in, how would he ever get out, with all that barbed wire?

All night long I tossed and turned, wondering what had happened to the intruder and dreaming that my beautiful old home was being destroyed by raging wind and pounding rain. Just before I woke up I was standing in the turnaround by the flagpole, sopping wet and weeping, as the cathedral roof cracked apart, collapsed, and fell in a heap onto the side patio. Only one rugged pine remained standing to witness my despair.

At 8 A.M. Jim delivered me to the new airport. I sat in the modern waiting room wearing the hand-painted, sleeveless shift and heavy hoop earrings I'd bought the day before at a sheltered workshop. I was finally cool. In fact, with the air-conditioning on I was freezing!

The thought of leaving had sparked the return of my mental and physical energy. I was grateful to my hosts for giving me my first taste of life as a "colonial" in the new Africa. But I couldn't have stood that kind of life for long—the oppressive heat, the constant delays and dirt, the black market economy, the hopeless poverty, and the sense of being a prisoner in a small, circumscribed world. Visiting Dar had been good for me. It had made me appreciate home.

I was shocked when I entered the plane's cabin. "Sit wherever you wish," said the steward. "There are plenty of seats."

I looked at the half-empty plane. For two days I'd been whipped around by officious clerks with tales of full occupancy and waiting lists. Why? I was furious!

"Going to Lusaka?" asked the portly, bespectacled man who sat down beside me.

"I wanted to," I answered. "A friend invited me but I haven't heard from him lately, and I've been told it's dangerous for foreigners, especially if you're white. So I decided not to go."

"You're right," he said. "It's been difficult this past year due to the South African bombings. But you wouldn't have a problem now as long as you didn't go to public buildings after dark, didn't take pictures in restricted areas, and cooperated with all the roadblocks." He smiled, thinking he was being helpful. I prayed that Zimbabwe would be better, but was prepared for anything.

"I'm in the poultry business," the man continued. "I buy and sell machinery around the world. Perhaps I know your friend."

"He's an ethnomusicologist at the university—Mwesa Mapoma."

"By Jove," he said, slapping his thigh and throwing his head back in disbelief. "He's my next door neighbor. Yes, he's been very busy, lately, starting a pig farm. That is, when he's not flying around to international meetings."

"Please tell him I'll try to call him from Victoria Falls," I said, overjoyed to know that Mwesa was all right.

I felt as if I were back home when I stepped off the plane in Harare. A banner welcoming the International Convention of Meteorologists of Africa stretched across the entrance and a map of the world advertising Barclay's Bank covered one side of the waiting room. Friendly officials greeted me at customs and the tourist office leaned over backwards to please. They had a working computer and an efficient clerk, and booked me into a reasonably priced hotel—fifteen dollars a night—in minutes. They also booked a trip to Victoria Falls for the next day.

As I was rushing to board the airport bus I heard a shout. I turned and saw an official of the bank where I had just changed money. He was running toward me, frantically waving my leather packet containing $1,000 in travelers checks.

"Madam, you forgot these," he said breathlessly. "I believe this is your money. We're not allowed to take such large tips."

A banker with a sense of humor! I was right. Zimbabwe was going to be better, much better.

18

GOING NATIVE

I could hear the roar of the falls over the sound of the plane's engine. I looked down and there it was—a foaming, mile-wide gash in the earth, with tons of water pouring from the Zambesi River into a narrow gorge and escaping around a jumble of jagged rocks on its way to the eight zigzagging gorges beyond.

Victoria Falls looked exactly like its African name—*Mosi oo Tusuya*, the smoke that thunders. It was this fabled geological mystery, hidden deep in the jungle and never before seen by a white man, that Dr. David Livingston was searching for in November 1855 when he made his way down the Zambesi River, stopping inches short of the precipice at the northern end of a small island, later named after him. When I saw this tiny spit of land poking out from the middle of the falls I shuddered to think of the great explorer's fate had he missed the mark and been carried by a mountain of swirling water into the gorge three hundred feet below.

I waded a few yards from the top of Devil's Cataract, where the river was shallow and clear. A swarm of minnows darted around my feet. It could have been any one of the gentle streams I'd played in as a child at the foothills of the White Mountains. Except for the incessant roar, there was no indication that this peaceful river would suddenly speed up and plummet with such violence over the rocky embankment, flattening the long grasses in its path.

"Everyone to the lower level!" shouted the guide. We scrambled down until we were nearly under the spray. How could trees still grow out of the rocky face and withstand this rampaging water?

"We're going to look at each section of the falls and see how it influences the flow of water," she continued, her voice almost lost in the deafening thunder. "For example, notice how the Devil's Cataract shoots directly into the main falls from an oblique angle, creating dramatic double and triple rainbows as the individual sheets of spray collide...."

I moved away from the group and climbed to the opposite bank. I wanted to be alone as I walked the thousand feet to the end of the falls, using only my map as a guide. I chose a path dangerously close to the edge. It was scary, and the scariness added to my excitement. There were no guardrails and the pull of the yawning chasm was strong, like the unreasonable urge to jump from the top of the Empire State Building. Wet with spray, I stopped, intermittently, to sit on a rock along the grassy rim and peer into the deep gorge. The foam was so thick I could hardly see the bottom. I didn't dare watch any one place for too long.

Sitting on the edge of Victoria Falls, Zimbabwe.

Across the gorge Devil's Island jutted out, followed by the main falls, then a large protruding rock called the Armchair. The steady flow of the falls was interrupted again and again by a fountain of spray that burst from around Livingstone Island, perched precariously on the edge, and by individual falls, like Horseshoe and Rainbow, each with its own special configuration.

The path led into a tropical rain forest, formed entirely by the continuous spray. Clothed in waterproof gear, I strolled through this Rousseauian fairyland of squatty palms and tangled vegetation, breathing in the sweetness of the damp earth and listening to the chatter of monkeys. The sun shone through the downpour, creating a mist of miniature rainbows that popped up from every direction like flashing neon bouncing off the rain-soaked streets of a big city.

Minutes after I emerged from the forest, drenched, I was dry in the noonday heat and continued on to Danger Point and the Eastern Cataracts opposite Knife Edge. At the farthest end of the falls I looked down into the terrifying Boiling Pot, where the river swirls around a giant pinnacle of rock and empties into the waiting gorges, which wind for fifty miles before coming to rest in Lake Kariba. I could see only three of these eight massive clefts, composed of hard basalt that reached several feet into the ground. And to think that each one had been—over the past two million years—falls even bigger than the present Victoria!

No natural wonder had ever affected me like this. It awakened every part of my being. Emotions like reverence and joy crowded my consciousness. I yearned to see it over and over in all its moods.

"Lunchtime, folks. Everyone gather at Livingstone's statue." The demanding voice of the guide jolted me into a different reality. How I hated tours and their unrelenting schedules.

Lunch at the swanky Makosa Sun Hotel seemed a vulgar intrusion, but turned out to be a festive occasion shared with Kevin and Carmen Mountjoy, a young South African couple I'd met on the early morning flight from Harare. Delicate red and white streamers adorned an anemic potted pine near our table—my first Christmas tree, Zimbabwe-style. To add to the festivities a xylophone combo struck up a tune from the raised bandstand. It was a pathetic attempt to harmonize traditional Christmas songs. The players seemed almost comatose as they struggled with the unfamiliar rhythms. Listening to it was painful.

Impulsively, I jumped up and ran over to the leader. "Please, play *your* music," I pleaded. "African music. I want to record it." I thrust my tape recorder in front of him. He smiled, shrugged, mumbled a few words to the musicians, and moved his body to a new beat. The band came alive. Softly hammered woods blended with the percussive brightness of metal bars. Close harmonies moved in and around the polyrhythms. The sound was infectious. Who could sit still?

"Come on," I said to the Mountjoys. "Let's dance." Hesitantly, Kevin reached for Carmen's hand. More people joined in, some with partners and others alone. We whirled and swayed and clapped our hands. And all the while we were dancing I could hear the roar of the falls—a steady, mesmerizing accompaniment to the pulsating music.

The sound lured me—like the singing of the Lorelei—down the half-mile path for one last look at the falls. Racing, sweating, I reached the Devil's Cataract just as the sun burst from under the clouds, casting a million dazzling jewels onto the thunderous spray. Above the foam a brilliant arc appeared, duplicated by smaller ones that became more and more muted until they disappeared into the pale blue atmosphere.

My mind was still full of the sounds and faces of Victoria when I said goodbye to the Mountjoys and boarded the bus for downtown Harare. I chuckled as I recalled the expressions on the faces of the band when all the tourists started gyrating around the floor at lunchtime. I thought back to fifteen years ago when I was selling musical instruments at a teacher's convention in Boise, Idaho. One evening a fellow exhibitor and I decided to liven up a boring party by dancing barefoot in the sunken bathtub of the Royal Suite at the Rodeway Inn—a most unlikely place to find bathtubs the size of swimming pools, supported by canopied ionic columns. Guests, half-asleep, sitting around on chaises, suddenly jumped into the water—some even forgetting to roll up their pant legs—and began to move with the music. It livened up the party all right! Fortunately, my friend and I were long gone before the police arrived.

Tentacles of orange and crimson reached into a cloudless sky and had vanished under a blanket of purple by the time we reached the downtown terminal. I walked to my hotel. The air was fresh, the streets were clean, and the people orderly. The only disorderly place in town seemed to be my hotel, the New International. It was hopping!

I started up the steps to the entrance as two men were coming down. They blocked me. I moved over to let them pass and they moved, also, blocking me again. This went on two more times. I laughed as you would when two people try to get out of each other's way and only manage to get more tangled up. I was clutching my camera bag across my chest as I always did, and one of the men knocked into it. At that moment I heard a shrill yell: "Stop them, they're *tsotsis!*"

The two men pushed ahead, almost toppling me, as a short, elderly lady started down the steps after them. "You dirty thieves, you *tsotsis!*" she yelled, shaking her fist. "Don't ever come back here or I'll call the police."

They disappeared around the corner of the building. She turned to me, still red in the face and puffing. "Young woman (that always comes as a pleasant surprise), didn't you see what they were doing?" I shook my head. "That's an old trick with *tsotsis*. You're lucky I saw them."

"I'm very grateful to you," I said, "but nobody could get this bag away from me without taking my arms, too."

"Do you want to take that chance?" she asked.

Shaken, I walked into the lobby. The bar and English dart room were loaded with well-dressed professional men jammed so tightly together that sitting was out of the question. The desk clerk told me the partying had started at three. I was sure the low cost of a bucket of beer had a lot to do with the increased decibel level as the evening wore on. Cautiously, I pushed my way through the bodies and into the elevator cage and watched the heavy ropes pull me to the third floor.

It was ten o'clock when I ventured back downstairs. I surveyed myself in the hall mirror. Not bad, considering that I'd been fighting diarrhea all day—probably the result of the one glass of water I drank at Jim's office before leaving Tanzania. God, I'd been so thirsty in Dar! Here I just decided to drink out of the faucet and take my chances. What more could I get? My back was killing me from two nights on a soft mattress, but at least my belly felt better. I stepped out of the elevator to face the crushing crowd flowing from the dart room.

As I entered the dining room a tall, fortyish man with a Fuller brush moustache and olive skin stood up and strode toward me. He was handsome, indeed, with mounds of wavy black hair and a thin straight nose guarding high cheekbones and almond eyes.

He bowed grandly and reached for my hand. "Hello, my name is Vasco de Sienna. I've been watching you for two evenings and would like to make your acquaintance." Speaking slowly, in a distinctly European accent, he continued. "My car is parked outside. May I take you to dinner?"

"How nice," I said, wondering why I hadn't noticed this elegant man before. "But I'd prefer to eat right here."

There was a flicker of a smile. He took my arm and ushered me to his table. "The car can wait. I'll show you Harare after dinner."

◆   ◆   ◆

"You've just missed the last luxury express to the mountains," said the agent in charge at the Zimbabwe Tourist Bureau. I didn't care. I was determined to visit the famous Greater Zimbabwe Ruins over the weekend and didn't want a fancy bus, anyway. Ever since my wild ride in Egypt on that broken-down crate barreling through the Sinai, I knew that real adventure happens away from tourists and tour buses.

"But that's no problem," he continued. "There are plenty of local buses. Just get to the Mbare station by 7 A.M. It's first come, first serve. Takes a bit longer, but don't worry, you'll get a seat. They add plenty of extra buses for the holidays." He slid several brochures and a detailed street map across the counter.

I smiled. *No problem. Don't worry.* All that was missing was *trust me.*

He never told me that there was no ticket office at the station, that there were no assigned slots for the buses, that the buses had no destination marked on them until the last minute, and that only if you were extremely lucky could you find a spot to occupy on the small raised asphalt platforms. Otherwise, you sat or stood in the street for hours, more in danger of being trampled by people and small animals than by motorized vehicles. I didn't know all this yet, so I didn't worry.

It was now only one week before Christmas. How strange to see jacaranda and eucalyptus trees in bloom. I wandered around the center of Harare, window-shopping in the pedestrian malls and searching for a good pen. When I found one I couldn't believe the price. Eight U.S. dollars for a rolling ballpoint?

"We have to import them from the United States," the shopkeeper said apologetically. I reminded myself never to leave home in the future without at least two dozen.

Compared to Dar es Salaam, Harare was a flourishing modern city. The streets were wide. The center strips were lined with tall skinny palms. And traffic congestion was almost nonexistent.

At a large Woolworth store I bought watermelon chunks on a Christmas special. At Macey's, the biggest chain of supermarkets in Zimbabwe, I bought bread, cheese, fruit juice, and half a barbecued chicken. What a feast I had, sitting on a bench in the park underneath the yellow-blossomed gum trees. People nodded a greeting as they strolled along the path that led to a center fountain and formal English garden. On the way back to my hotel I walked by ornate buildings and private clubs, and peered into sedate courtyards shielded from the public by elaborate wrought iron gates. I felt as if a bit of London had been transported to Africa.

"I wouldn't go anywhere by local bus if you paid me, and especially not all the way to Masvingo!" warned Vasco, my Portuguese friend. He seemed to have unlimited resources, so I had accepted another dinner invitation. This time we drove through a classy residential area to get to a small smoky bistro specializing in spicy chicken and beer. Vasco was a strange man, very intense and nervous. I was intrigued to find out why he had gone to Angola and Mozambique "to keep the peace," as he euphemistically put it. Both countries, I pointed out to him, were now in shambles.

"If you get a seat, it will be a miracle. And if the bus goes ten miles without a breakdown, that will be another miracle," he said, his voice rising. "You'll wait for hours, and then you'll suffer through roadblocks, which can be dangerous, especially to a foreigner." He failed to mention the heat and the dust.

Since I wouldn't change my mind, Vasco insisted on driving me to the station the next morning. At 5:30 A.M. he arrived at my door, banging loudly and singing what I supposed were Portuguese popular songs. He'd been in the bar most of the night. Strands of black hair escaped from under a furry ten-gallon hat ("Just like Texas," he said), which gave him the look of a Mexican rancher.

"You're crazy," I said. "And who gave you my room number?" I was exhausted, having been awakened in the middle of the night by a fight outside my window. For a moment I had imagined myself back in New Orleans, with the knives and the epithets flying.

"The desk clerk," he answered. "We are friends."

As I stood half-asleep in the doorway Vasco thrust a bottle of home brew into my hand, saying it would be better than coffee for waking me up. Before I could stop him he proudly recited the entire recipe and assured me that it was the best, since he had sampled it for breakfast at 4 A.M.

I settled for instant coffee at the bar.

Just as the sun was rising we headed for the Mbare bus station. Vasco drove, and sang, and reminisced about his life as the third son of a farmer back in Portugal. Then he told me, very casually, that he had lost $10,000 a few days ago.

"How awful," I said. "Was it stolen?"

"Oh, it's nothing," he said. "Money means nothing to me. But I could save *you* money if you'd stay with me when you return Sunday night. Think about it…twenty-four Zimbabwe dollars."

I was thinking about it, and wondering how I could sneak back into the hotel Sunday night and change my room without being detected. This man was getting stranger by the minute.

"Then maybe I can drive you to Masvingo. I have a new Nissan."

The minute we reached Mbare I opened the car door and sprang out. "Please, Meg, you're being foolish. You'll be sorry." He was still pleading as I fled—without a backward glance—right into the eye of a human hurricane.

Imagine scenes from the movie *Grapes of Wrath*, or the refugees fleeing Eastern Europe after World War II, or the county fair in Rutland, Vermont. Put them all together with a backdrop of black faces and rickety buses and you have the picture. I inched my way through the mob, half stumbling over furniture, chickens, and sacks of oranges and potatoes. Large bundles of clothing tied with coarse bits of string rested beside rolled up rugs. Goats and children appeared to wander free. Enormous cardboard suitcases stood on the pavement haphazardly, or lay flat, providing a bed for a sleeping child. Everyone was going home for the holidays. I could feel the excitement.

In the midst of this confusion a bus pulled in, the driver posted a hand-printed sign on the dashboard, and people ran from every direction. A throng of pushing, shoving bodies crowded toward the door while others shouted the destination and formed a tight line around the bus, with no chance of ever penetrating the initial blockade. I found myself in several of these bone-crushing lines, part of a human chain held together by the sheer momentum of so many surging bodies. More than once my chin pressed into the cheek of a sleeping baby hanging in a cloth pouch on its mother's back.

The women said very little. I received only polite shrugs in response to my complaints. It was the men who were the aggressors, storming the door and yelling their names at the man inside the bus, who was laboriously writing out individual tickets. With raised arms they held out money and tried to thrust it through the door. Once, tempers flared, and the police were summoned. They tried to pull the men away by grabbing an arm or a leg, but friends inside the bus held on, turning the scene into a mock tug-of-war. The crowd outside was laughing and cheering them on. It flashed through my mind that if a news photographer had snapped a picture, it would look like police brutality—Black against Black—that is, unless you looked closely and saw the smiles on the faces.

While this pulling and shoving was going on the driver tried to close the door and stop those attempting to enter the bus by threes. Sometimes he caught a would-be passenger's foot or hand, causing its owner to send up a yowl of protest. It didn't seem to occur to anyone that only one person could fit through the door at a time.

I watched the fracas in disbelief. Why not sell tickets ahead of time rather than have the ticket writer inside the bus? And why not line up in an organized fashion? Then the bus would be full in a short time and could depart quickly. Too logical? Yes, for I soon realized that this was a game of chance. High drama. Some men were able to force their way in and hand tickets out the window to their relatives. The bargaining position inside the bus was powerful.

In the meantime, others climbed onto the roof and loaded their belongings, piling them high until they were in danger of toppling over the shallow railing, only to have them thrown down if their family couldn't get seats. This caused further delays. But through it all everyone was good-natured. They were just having fun.

The sun beat down. My clothes were soaked with perspiration. I began to feel dizzy. I hadn't brought a lunch and there was nothing to buy but unwashed produce. Not even a bottle of seltzer. And nowhere to sit but the steaming pavement. I was discouraged and felt very conspicuous in my drab outfit and limp safari hat—like a brown wren that had wandered into a convention of flamboyant peacocks. Uncomfortable, out-of-place, dull. I was the only white person in the crowd, but had long ago forgotten that.

Sister Francine, a young nun who had spent two years in Denver, Colorado, and her nephew, John, who hoped some day to study medicine in the United States (Perhaps at Harvard, he told me), became my buddies during three long hours of waiting. We visited a sprawling market near the station, where vegetables in large quantities were sold outdoors and meats and handcrafts hawked from booths in a colossal tin shelter. Or we amused ourselves under the broiling sun by watching the show as each bus came and went.

Rimming the station were billboards advertising soap and toothpaste—"2 Fluoride Colgate, for extra protection against tooth decay"—an incongruous reminder of another world poking its way into deepest Africa.

After being shoved out of two buses heading for the mountains I began to wonder if I really wanted to see ruins of an ancient civilization after all. I finally gave up, said goodbye to my new friends, and headed for the taxi stand across a parched field. Perhaps I could organize a car pool. How American!

A cab driver in the parking lot suggested that I hitch, and pointed me toward the highway. (I later found out that hitching is very common in Zimbabwe, with special locations designated for people to wait. However, you're expected to pay the driver for stopping.) As I approached the highway I spotted two motorcycle policemen pulling into a driveway. I told them I wanted to hitch and asked where the best place would be to stand.

"You can't hitch today," they said. "It's a holiday weekend and nobody will pick you up. You *must* go by bus. Come, we'll take you to the station and get you some help."

"No, no," I protested. "I can't go back there. No more 'first come, first serve' buses for me!"

They kept walking. I followed like an obedient puppy.

"There's no other way to get to Masvingo," they said. "Don't worry. We'll show you how."

Not those words again! How could I tell them that they were delivering me to where I had just been and explaining to me what I already knew. Feeling ridiculous, I greeted Sister Francine and John, thanked the policemen, and vowed to be patient.

By noon I was numb and sunburned. I had forgotten about food. I felt like a spectator, not a participant. It was probably this attitude that made the ordeal bearable.

At one o'clock my chance finally came. John raced around the bus and grabbed my arm.

"Hurry," he said. "Hand ten dollars through the window to Joe. He'll get tickets for you and Sister." Joe was a friend of the driver. John promised to help him load his animals and baggage onto the roof in exchange for this favor. I wondered, fleetingly, if I'd ever see the money again, but soon was handed two tickets with the promise of receiving change after the bus was on its way.

But how to get through the madding crowd? Like a worm, I inched my way around to Sister Francine, who immediately gave her ticket to a wizened old lady who seemed totally unable to cope. Two men lifted her up the steps. I didn't fare so well. Sandwiched between two mothers with babies, I was flattened against the side of the bus. I began to panic. Just then a policeman saw me waving my ticket and yelling. I'd lost all inhibition and joined the pushing, screaming mob. He smiled and pulled me inside—by my arm.

Weak, hands shaking, I looked around the almost-empty bus. I had survived the stampede. The sheer joy of this accomplishment was heady. A young mother greeted me. We smiled at each other like co-conspirators. We had made it. I took a front seat wide enough for two adults. It ultimately was occupied by three adults and one large baby boy.

So I sat and watched the circus from the inside, marveling at the patience of the ticket writer, who scribbled frantically on small squares of paper, handing them to the driver, who handed them to a passenger, who handed them out the window until the bus was filled to overflowing.

All during this boarding process the motor ran, shaking the old bus and filling my eyes and nostrils with exhaust fumes. As I settled into my seat I wondered how on earth we'd ever make the 300 miles to Masvingo. *Don't worry*, I thought. It's *no problem*....

19

ROADBLOCKS AND PEACOCKS

There was a holiday atmosphere on board as the bus clattered out of Harare and headed south to Masvingo through the acacia-covered hills and valleys. Passengers were stuffed into every seat and overflowing onto the steps of the front and back entrances. Soon the countryside turned wild and scrubby, with scarcely a house in sight. Everyone settled down, exhausted from the morning's excitement and hypnotized by the rhythmic bump-bump of the tires on the rough pavement and the hot, sluggish air pouring in through the windows. For a time, hardly anyone spoke. The shouting was over.

The baby next to me lay on his mother's lap and laughed and gurgled, content to amuse himself with whatever caught his eye—a shiny handle, a necklace, the catch on my camera bag. His mother attended him lovingly, reaching into the pocket of her voluminous skirt, whenever necessary, for a simple trinket or a cracker. She was very thin and pale brown, with hair pulled straight back into a pony tail that bushed out after it was free of the elastic.

I was jammed so tightly into the seat that I couldn't move. Every now and then the teenage girls sitting behind me would tap on my shoulder and offer me a cookie, or show me a game they were playing with string tied around their fingers, urging me to try it. We laughed, because I could not even raise my arms or turn around. "O.K., we'll show you at the rest stop," they said, and went back to playing with the younger children, who were crowded between their legs or on their laps.

I studied the faces. They were all so different. A handsome young father, tall, thin, with aquiline nose and very light skin, sat on the bench next to his wife, a short, very dark woman with heavy negroid features. They laughed and kissed and played with their baby. Another man looked like an Egyptian with blue-black skin, sculptured cheeks, and a long thin neck. Next to him sat a young woman with identical features and almost-white skin.

The dress was as varied as the faces. Brilliantly colored material, expertly wrapped around the body of some women, made a sarong or a full costume. Others were attired in simple western skirts and blouses with a splash of color in a kerchief or turban. The men, in contrast, wore light-colored summer suits and sports jackets, or drab work pants, open-necked shirts, and jaunty caps.

But it was the nursing mothers who fascinated me the most. They tended their babies with such joy and patience.

One chubby three-year-old sat straddling her mother, stroking her cheeks and neck. Once in awhile she'd peer at me out of the corner of her eye, then plunge her head into her mother's chest in a game of hide-and-seek. When I finally took notice and winked, she howled with delight, promptly reached into her mother's blouse, and pulled out a mammoth breast. She approached it, eyes rolled to the side to see if I was watching. All I could think of was that full set of teeth. After she had nursed she sat back and surveyed the nipple, which stood out about an inch. Then she started in again, holding the breast as if she were playing a bagpipe, squeezing with her hands as she sucked. The mother seemed oblivious.

I was offered fruit and homemade breads, which I cut with my Swiss army knife—an invaluable tool that was passed up and down the aisle, used and admired—my contribution to the feast. As we were cleaning up I fished several *Wash 'n Dries* out of my pocket and handed them around, adding to my growing popularity among the mothers. A month ago, when I hurriedly threw a handful into my backpack before leaving New Jersey, I could never have predicted the happiness this simple gift would bring.

Brakes screeched. The bus pulled to a halt. Oh, no, not a roadblock! My heart started thumping. The men standing by the front door ran to the back and the ones on the back steps squatted down as if to make themselves invisible. Then, utter silence.

A soldier in a wrinkled khaki uniform and visored hat appeared at the driver's window. The driver handed him a tin that he opened. He took a pinch and sniffed, then handed the tin back to the driver who sniffed also. Two other soldiers joined the party, passing the tin back and forth.

"What are they doing?" I asked the woman next to me.

"That's snuff," she said. "They're friends. Nothing to worry about. They all do it."

But suppose it was more than snuff. How did she know? "Why are they stopping us?" I asked.

"Looking for guerrillas, for soldiers who live in the woods. Sometimes they're dangerous. But don't worry. It's Christmas."

The first soldier pushed open the front door of the bus with his rifle and strode up the center aisle...very slowly. He looked down at the crouching men. He looked at each of us. He prodded the bundles in the luggage compartment. Nobody spoke.

"What you are doing is illegal. Do you hear me?" he shouted. "You are all breaking the law. There are too many people on this bus. It is not safe. The driver will be fined and you will go to jail...*if you do this again.*"

Still nobody spoke. "Do you hear me?" he shouted even louder.

The men on the steps stood up, heads hanging, like children caught sneaking out the window on mischief night. I could see that they were trying hard not to smile. Were they crazy? This man was pointing a gun at them. But I seemed to be the only one scared.

"O.K. *I have warned you.* This bus will break down and it is *your* problem." He clicked his heels, exited, and waved us on.

The minute the soldiers were out of sight laughter erupted. "This bus will break down and it is *your* problem. Do you hear me? You will go to jail—you and you and you." The men mocked the officer and pointed to their friends in turn. Just another game.

The khaki uniform with its frayed red trim became a familiar sight by the fourth roadblock. The drama was repeated and the hilarity increased after each encounter. Thank God for a rest stop so the men could walk off some of their excess energy.

The heat—far more intense once we had stopped moving—enveloped me as I stepped off the bus onto the unpaved parking lot. My bladder was bursting and I was hungry and thirsty. I headed for the outhouse behind the Nemabweyi Variety Store. The smell hit me as I rounded the corner. The toilets were large holes in cement, set so far back that nobody could possibly sit on them except the Jolly Green Giant. No wonder they stank! There was no way I would go in there. And there were no bushes or trees in sight, except a bank of acacias under which sat a small colony of merchants. Painful as it was, self control was the only answer.

I walked toward the trees and past the pots of beans, roots, and vegetables cooking over open fires, tended by children who sat cross-legged on the ground. Roast corn—ah, that looked good. I peeled the black, thick husk and took a bite of the soft yellow kernels. Surprise! It tasted like potatoes. Everything I tried tasted like potatoes. But I didn't care. I was hungry.

"Come, Missus, we'll show you our tricks," shouted one of the teenagers who had been sitting behind me on the bus.

"I'm not good at this," I said, as they placed a loop of string around my hands. I tried to work it with my fingers.

Giggles. At least I was providing entertainment as I struggled to make sense of the spider web encasing my hands. It looked so simple when they did it, singing a little rhythmic chant as their fingers manipulated the strands.

"I'm hopeless," I said. "How do you do it? You're great."

More giggles. They reminded me of Nderi and her friends, nudging each other, joking, whispering. One girl grabbed me around the waist and we walked back across the dusty parking lot together. I felt their warmth deep inside, and an unconditional acceptance that needed no words.

The bus was growling and choking as we boarded. How I wished I had a surgical mask!

I watched the mothers skillfully remove their babies from their backs and settle into the narrow seats. Earlier I had marveled at how they made their own baby pack—a flexible pouch—from a large towel or cotton blanket. They would lean over, trunk horizontal to the ground, lay the baby on their back, place the material on top of the baby, and tie the ends tightly at their waist and chest. The baby would automatically wrap its legs around the mother and sleep through the whole process. When she stood up, the baby slid down to the small of her back just above the hips, and hung there. I was intrigued, as I traveled through Africa, to see that each country had its own special "baby backpack" design.

The bus was chugging away when the mother who sat next to me jumped on. At the last minute she had decided to buy one of those large ears of corn for her baby, along with *Fanta,* the favorite drink. *Fanta* for a nursing baby?

She grinned. "See…he likes this orange juice." The baby gulped from the can, spilling it down his chest and coloring his clothes and arms bright orange. Without a word his mother gently wiped it up with her skirt.

Shortly before we arrived in Masvingo the landscape changed. Flat terrain gave way to jagged hills out of which emerged smooth rock formations like gigantic primitive sculptures. It was while I was enjoying the scenery that we ground to a halt amid hoots and hollers. I was certain it was a flat tire this time.

There in a deep ditch lay an army truck. It had taken a flimsy utility pole with it when it crashed, and wires were hanging dangerously low over the road. With mounting excitement the men piled out of the bus and crowded around the vehicle, mixing with the soldiers. Together they heaved and pushed, while the women hung out of the bus, offering suggestions and holding back the children.

I thought the driver would never get the men back on board. He carefully drove in and out of the opposite ditch to avoid the wires, and honked for a full five minutes before slowly starting down the road, the men running to catch up, shouting and waving their arms. The carnival mood prevailed all the way to Masvingo.

I leapt off the bus. "Come with me," said one of the teenage girls. "I'll show you where to get a taxi to the ruins. And don't take the first price. These drivers will try to cheat you."

We hugged. Goodbye, goodbye.

The second price wasn't any better than the first, but I didn't care. I wanted a bathroom, a cold drink, and a meal. Twenty minutes later I walked into the plush lobby of the Greater Zimbabwe Ruins Hotel. The manager bowed. How had I gotten here? Why was I so dusty?

"I came by local bus from Harare. Five-and-a-half hours, four roadblocks, but no flat tires," I said, proudly.

"But a luxury bus arrived this morning. The people are touring Lake Kyle at this very moment. You could have had air conditioning, tea, cookies….You must have had a terrible time. How awful."

"No," I said, smiling, "I had a wonderful time. I wouldn't have missed it for all the tea and cookies in Zimbabwe!"

In five minutes I was on my way across the velvet lawn to a thatched guesthouse, accompanied by two aristocratic peacocks that shook their electric-blue heads nervously as if to say that this was the saddest human specimen they'd seen in a long time. Strutting ahead, they'd stop intermittently to spread their fan of feathers, as if further sizing me up with flat, iridescent, turquoise eyes.

I stood in the cool breeze blowing out of the valley and the physical discomfort of the past eight hours evaporated. But I had no time to linger if I wanted to explore the trails around the hotel before dark. Tangled brush grabbed at my legs as I scrambled onto great slabs of black rock overlooking a ravine, where fat monkey cacti peeked out from among flowering trees and wild hibiscus. Ahead of me, deep in the valley, stretched a slender gray-green ribbon of lake dotted with small dark islands. It looked like my own Lake Winnipesaukee plunked in the middle of a tropical New Hampshire.

Delighting in the sweet air and the excited trilling of birds and insects, I made my way down the narrow path toward a native village. Standing at the entrance next to a fairy tale crooked stile were two stunning men—one tall and blonde, the other wiry and dark with an overgrown Van Dyck beard.

"Soren Anderson here," the dark one said, greeting me with a brilliant smile. "And my brother Alf. He's visiting me for the holidays. Thinks he can persuade me to come home." Another wonderful smile.

I felt an instant attraction to this man. "And where is home?" I asked.

"Norway. We're on holiday. It's hard for us Vikings to believe it's almost Christmas—with all this tropical vegetation—but we celebrate the season anyway."

We stood together, silently watching the sunset, then slowly walked back to the hotel and became acquainted over a gin and tonic. In an instant I was transported back to the frenetic life I'd left behind. How similar the three of us were—the way we talked, the way we analyzed our problems, the way we laughed at ourselves without an ounce of pretense. By the time dinner was served—under a string of lanterns on the stone patio, watched over by the same two peacocks—we were old friends.

"It's been ages since I've talked with anyone this frankly," Soren said. "I'm really out of touch with western culture most of the time, and that's a good way to avoid problems. Take on other peoples and yours don't seem so bad. Everyone at home thinks I'm a self-sacrificing hero for leaving a thriving practice to come here. But I'm no hero. I love it. I've never been happier."

Alf sat quietly, watching his brother with obvious admiration. With long thin fingers he slowly and repetitively smoothed down his unruly blond hair.

I found myself entranced with Soren and his tales of starting a school for the blind in Botswana, and of his exploration into the wild territory populated by the little bushmen. He was appalled at the invasion of their privacy by curious Westerners in the wake of the movie, The Gods Must Be Crazy.

"It's rape," he said angrily. "Why can't these people be left alone? Last month when I was camping nearby, the Germans flew in an entire television crew—interpreters and all—stayed for two days, filmed a documentary, and departed. They disrupted everyone's life for forty-eight hours and left behind a lot of cheap souvenirs and promises. Promises of what? A chance to ride on the "iron bird" to see a new, exciting life in the city, where everyone's always in a hurry? How long will it be before they destroy this happy, self-sufficient, peaceful culture?" Soren sighed.

"I'm dying to go to Botswana...especially that part," I said, trying to lighten things up a bit. "I hear it's quite different from other African countries. Never was a colony...."

"It's special, all right. There are no roads, so if you don't have a helicopter you'll need a helluva good four-wheel drive, preferably one that's rhino-proof.

You'll sleep under an unpredictable sky or in a tent with possibly a snake or two, and you'll never know whether a wildebeeste or an elephant will pay you a visit in the middle of the night."

"I guess that takes care of my trip into the bush," I said. "It sounds as if you want to keep it all to yourself."

Soren fell silent, observing me. His penetrating brown eyes had a trace of humor at the edges. I couldn't figure out whether he found me intelligent, or attractive, or just amusing.

"I've been looking at you all evening, Meg," he said, as if to read my mind. "And do you know what I've been thinking?"

"I'm afraid to guess," I replied warily. I could feel my cheeks begin to burn and my heart race. He looked at me impishly. "You are so much like Jessica, the redhead in that TV show, Soap. The way you laugh, and interrupt, and...."

"Oh, no," I said. "Please don't say that. She's so crazy and bubble-headed." Once again I saw myself in the role of clown—one I had played to the hilt as a child. And I didn't like it.

"She's great," said Alf. "And you're wrong, Meg. She's not dumb at all...but I think you look more like Shirley MacLaine."

"How do you two know about these people?" I asked, ignoring his comment.

"Television and movies, of course," replied Soren. "Don't you know that Norway is an entertainment colony of the United States? That's why we're all beginning to talk and act alike. We now have a common language...and common neuroses as well. But I can't blame it all on America. Civilization is partly responsible. Look at the three of us. I'm a family therapist who's come to Africa to run a school for the handicapped. A do-gooder, some say. And Alf is a lawyer who works as a public defender. You run a philanthropic organization, and we're all three divorced and looking for the perfect career—our 'contribution' to mankind—and, at the same time, the perfect relationship. What's more, we believe it's possible. We believe everything is possible."

That's because we're Protestant," I said. "Not because of television. And it's also because we have a little extra money, at least compared to most of black Africa. And that gives us the luxury of time and choice. We can face our problems and try to solve them. Or choose to wallow in them."

"Well, it's not quite that black or white, except, of course, in Africa," said Alf, laughing.

Soren ignored the pun and leaned forward, looking at me with an almost frightening seriousness. "O.K.," he said, "let's see how good you are at facing your problems. Alf says he came to Africa to see me. But I think he's really running away from a failed relationship. Tell me, Meg, what are *you* running away from?"

Was this a rebuke, or curiosity? Suddenly I felt the need to defend myself. "Who says I'm running away?" I countered, my voice rising. "I'm not. I love to travel. I'm exploring new places. Testing my strengths. And I'm becoming comfortable with myself as a single woman. It's as simple as that. Don't be so negative."

Silence. Soren's face was expressionless. Alf shifted slightly in his seat.

"Since you mentioned it, who's the negative person in your life?" he asked.

"Jesus. Is this becoming a therapy session? Sorry, but I forgot to bring my money with me."

"Why don't you just answer my question and not make jokes?"

There was a long, uncomfortable pause. "My ex-husband is the negative person." Soren sat with his hands folded, looking steadily at me. "I think I'm going to cry," I said, trying to steady my voice. I was surprised at the powerful emotional response his remark had triggered. "The pain is still so close to the surface. You'd think by now I'd have forgotten all the put-downs—put-downs I didn't even recognize. But that's the worst part. For a long time I didn't realize what was happening to me, and now I'm dreadfully ashamed, and damned angry that I allowed it. Funny, but when you asked me that question all I heard was Glen's voice saying to me, thirty-five years ago, after he'd read my Fulbright application: 'Why do you *really* want this scholarship? And don't give me any more sociological bullshit reasons like world peace. You say you want to study economics, but you really just want to go to London.'"

"Soren, you did the same thing to me, and to Alf. You assumed you knew our motivation better than we did, and told us so."

"I apologize, Meg. I was out of line." He reached over and took my hands in his, gently squeezing them as he drew closer. I felt his strength, sensed his concern. Wow! This was the first time in a month that I'd felt like a woman, a desirable woman, and I allowed myself to enjoy it. The feeling between us was so strong that I thought I'd faint. Pull yourself together, I told myself. And don't drink any more wine.

"I'm used to my big brother," said Alf, throwing his hands up and shrugging like a defeated merchant at a flea market. "And most of the time he's right. But he's not a diplomat."

I tried to withdraw my hands, embarrassed, hoping my feelings weren't too transparent. Soren released his hold, and for a moment his fingers lightly touched my palms. Pain, understanding, and longing welled up in an instant, a mute message, eye to eye.

"Well, he was right again," I said, turning to Alf and freeing myself from Soren's gaze. He looked at me questioningly. "I admit that escape did figure in my plans. Running away from my reliance on men, from rejection or the possibility of it, and from my everyday routine and conflicting career choices. Have I left anything out? But the irony is that no matter how hard I run, there's one person I can't escape. Me. I keep meeting myself around every corner, like right now. I knew I would and I'm glad. So now I'll have to deal with myself all alone. No distractions, no excuses."

I turned to Soren, who was looking with amusement at the two of us. "And what are *you* running away from?" I asked, "as long as we're minding each other's business."

"That's easy," he said. "The complications of civilization, the never-ending minutiae, the morass of 'shoulds' and 'oughts.' I love the simplicity and straightforwardness of Africa. I find peace under its vast silent sky, and I love the certainty of the tribal values and the strong, all-embracing family. I pray that the West doesn't ruin this. We're great at exporting the worst features of our society—divorce and excessive materialism for starters."

How I liked this man—genuine, altruistic, and complicated. I was aware that he also liked me, but I wondered if he ever let anyone get very close to him.

It was after midnight when Soren stood up. "Do you realize that we're all alone? Guess everyone else is asleep, preparing for an onslaught of the ruins tomorrow morning."

The moon had worked its way across the sky and was hanging over the pool, inviting us to follow its rays to where they disappeared into the deep water. On one side was an elaborate garden and on the other were cottages, all of them dark. The two peacocks stood in the shadows, now and then letting out a hideous, piercing screech that caused a tiny, involuntary shiver to run through me.

Soren reached the pool first. Without a word he started to undress. Silently he slipped in. Alf followed. No time for modesty, I thought, and abandoned my clothes, letting myself quickly into the cool water. I couldn't imagine doing this with strangers back home, but at the moment it was as natural and innocent as taking a stroll in the garden.

20

ON THE ROAD, AGAIN

A sudden wind rustled the delicate shutters of my cottage. Half awake, I lay on my bed, luxuriating in the afterglow of last evening. The first rays of sun peeked through a small gap in the thatched roof and lit up the sitting room, its two slender chairs casting solitary shadows on the heavy woven floor mats. I hung onto the moment, wanting to postpone the day a little longer.

I felt utterly alone and utterly tranquil. In the past this would have seemed a contradiction, but at this moment I was content in my isolation, not wishing to change a thing, eager to welcome each day as it came along.

The two inquisitive peacocks greeted me as I hurried across the lawn to the large breakfast room. In one sweeping glance I took in the lavish buffet, my eyes moving from the small seeded buns and croissants past an assortment of cheeses and meats encircled by a variety of breads—tan, dark brown, egg-yellow. A colorful mound of tropical fruit piled high, and looking like Carmen Miranda's hat, rested in the middle of the table. Carved wooden legs, powerful and polished, thrust themselves from under elegant starched linen.

I heaped my plate with thick-crusted bread, an exquisite mushroom and cheese omelet, and exotic fruits, and headed for the corner table where Soren and Alf were devouring a round of dark bread and cold cuts. They looked up unenthusiastically.

"If I have to listen to the same three American Christmas tapes one more time I think I may be sick," said Soren.

What a greeting. Not even a "good morning."

"Sorry fellows," I said, "But I can't take responsibility for Bing Crosby's rendition of 'White Christmas.'"

They motioned for me to join them, but the magic was gone. The conversation was as desultory as it had been exciting the night before. Were these the same crazy, talkative Norwegians I had gone swimming with? Perhaps they regretted their openness, or were ashamed of having revealed so much of themselves. I chuckled, inwardly, as I remembered Soren's bare bum in the moonlight. That wasn't really the kind of revelation I meant, but it was an amusing image. I wish I'd asked them about their sudden change in attitude and personality, but it was such a shock that I was caught completely off guard. I kept expecting the good feelings to return. But they never did.

After Alf and Soren left I tried to block out the disappointment of the meal and remember only the warmth and spontaneity of the previous evening. But feelings of loneliness kept cropping up. This was not the same aloneness, the glorious freedom, I had felt early in the morning. This was unexpected rejection that mystified and hurt. I wondered what I'd done wrong. But wasn't that just like me? I always laid the blame at my feet, never considering that it might be *their* problem.

The ghostly ruins of the once-thriving 16th century capitol fit right into my mood. The day was hot and the morning mist was still rising above the bougainvillea and jacaranda as I made my way through the unspoiled wilderness, up and down the well-worn paths built into the gentle hills. I stopped to rest under one of the gnarled old trees—its lacy branches spread wide, a promise to hold back the worst of the heat—before climbing up a spiral stone stairway which narrowed artistically as it reached the hill complex. Man-made walls of rough stone, each piece cleverly wedged together, blended with huge slabs and boulders that protruded from the red soil and overlooked the valley. Together they made a formidable fortress, fashioned by the *Shonas*, the indigenous Africans, who were 20,000 strong before their culture mysteriously vanished.

I stooped low to go through the ten-foot-thick entranceway to the tower enclosure. Once inside I felt dwarfed standing next to a segment of crumbling wall, sixteen feet deep and thirty-six feet high, that had once stretched for 825 feet around the entire city. It was here that the skilled artisans of this lost civilization had fashioned the brightly colored, stylized Zimbabwe birds that graced the towers of the lower valley and have become a symbol of pride throughout the country.

For the next three hours I poked around the great enclosure, photographing the high conical council towers and the curved stone entrances of the grand dwellings, now in ruins, that spread out on either side. As I left I wondered about these once-powerful people, whose influence had reached into Botswana, Mozambique, and South Africa. What had caused their downfall? Was it overpopulation and starvation? Disease, hostile tribes? This was the largest single ancient structure in sub-Sahara Africa and the most advanced civilization, yet it had disappeared without a trace.

The great wall at the Zimbabwe ruins.

At 3:30 P.M., without confusion or delay, I boarded the luxury bus for Harare. It sped smoothly over the roads that only yesterday seemed full of potholes. What a contrast between this calm, comfortable ride and that chaotic, clattering journey! Not even one roadblock to break the monotony. There were just as many black people surrounding me as on the local bus, but they dressed and acted differently. And the children displayed the whining and restlessness of a lot of overindulged western children. Nobody tended anybody else. The parents seemed preoccupied with keeping the children quiet so they could read and relax. I missed the laughter and the horseplay that had rocked the rickety old bus. Of course, I *did* get my biscuits and tea, served by a courteous, hovering hostess.

I sat back, drinking in the view and appreciating the air conditioning. My thoughts returned to last night. Soren's remarks still irritated me, but he hadn't been totally wrong. In part, I *was* running away from rejection, or the fear of it. Just like Alf, I'd had a failed marriage. Failure, for whatever reason, spells rejection to me, and rejection spells failure—a hapless circle. And there is Glen, who always seems to be looking over my shoulder. Could I ever really commit myself to another man or was my past disillusion too deep? I didn't want to make the same mistakes again. I was terrified of being swallowed up, my creativity and independence wiped out.

"It's beautiful here, isn't it?" I turned to face the young woman who shared my seat. Her black features had the fine, chiseled quality of a Nubian, and her deep-set eyes danced as she spoke. "I've saved for three years for this trip and if my husband and son weren't in Mozambique, I'd never go back. I'd stay in this peaceful country forever."

Elizabeth was married to a Portuguese and worked at the British Embassy in Maputo. This allowed her to travel and have more freedom than most of her compatriots.

I was immediately drawn to this stately young woman, and told her about my experience on the bus the day before.

"Oh, so you must be a foreigner," she said. "Otherwise you would never have attempted to board a local bus at holiday time."

"How else can I get to see the real Africa?" I asked.

"Why would you want to see the real Africa? It is not a pretty sight in these times, especially in my country."

Elizabeth told me of her harrowing life since "liberation." War on a daily basis, shelling, deprivation, and fear. It was not that much different from the tales other Africans had told me, especially from Nigeria, Uganda, and Zaire—hardship suffered at the hands of corrupt, tyrannical governments. But it touched me more personally this day. Elizabeth was the exact age of my eldest daughter, Cary, but she had had her education cut short, her dreams of freedom squashed, her hopes for the future destroyed.

"At first we were ecstatic when the Portuguese left," she said. "We wanted to be free. Instead, we are 100% worse off. We had no idea what was going to happen. Now our beautiful country is completely run-down, its thriving industries destroyed or nationalized. And most of the qualified workers and teachers have fled. Along with my friends. The missionary hospitals have been dismantled and the doctors fired, and now that the government wants them back, they're gone...or they're dead. I used to work for one of those doctors. He was such a good, kind man."

She sighed and looked out the window for a long time before continuing. I sat in silence, feeling depressed and uneasy.

"Taxes are high, salaries are low. And if you think the roads in Zimbabwe and Tanzania are bad, you should go to Mozambique. But the worst thing for me is that I'm not free to say what I think, or worship my God as I choose. Can you, an American, imagine that?"

I had no answer. But she was right. I couldn't imagine that.

"You know, it's ironic. Everybody blames the South Africans, but many of our people are trying to get over the border—despite the danger of wild animals—just to find a job. Apartheid is not our problem. Communism is. It may be good for the Russians, but it isn't good for Africans. I wonder if it's good for anybody." Elizabeth was soft-spoken, even in her anger.

I squirmed in my clean, commodious seat, wishing I could bring some measure of encouragement to this distraught young woman. I took out the bread I'd saved from breakfast. Its thick crust and pale center were still fresh.

"Suppose we break a little bread together," I said. "I've found that when life is bleak, the fellowship of friends can be very healing."

She smiled and took half of the bread. Together, each in our own way, we shared the familiar ritual.

As we neared Harare I thought of Vasco. How could I sneak into the hotel without bumping into him? I couldn't cope with any more of his crazy stories, not after talking with Elizabeth. And that African moonshine he was swilling. Just the smell of it must have had my saintly Salvation Army grandmother spinning in her grave.

At the hotel I was met by a wall of black males, arms outstretched, clamoring for the Friday night special—beer at half price. The desk clerk greeted me warmly and handed me my pack and a room key. He promised not to give my room number to *anybody*. I lost myself in the overflow from the bar and worked my way to the elevator. The thud of the darts hitting their mark provided a soft rhythm behind the metallic scream of the music.

Just what I needed! Another soft, swayback bed. I had hoped that this room would be better. I lay down, pretending it was a hammock. If I just curled up like an embryo I could make it through the night. What did I expect, anyway, for fifteen dollars a day?

The steady beat of the music, accompanied by the click of heels on the cobbled streets below, filtered through my open window. How unlike Soren's description of the little people of Botswana were these modern Zimbabweans. Why had this suddenly entered my mind? Because the serenity of the *veld*, of Soren's idealized Africa, was definitely not apparent in Harare this evening. At least not in my section of town. Soon those proud bushmen, too, would be swallowed up by "civilization." No longer would they remain simple people living in a country inaccessible by road, shooting their game with a poison arrow as they needed it. Just enough to eat and no more.

"Sometimes it takes the poison a week to kill," Soren had said, so the little people follow their prey through the bush until it dies. They feel great reverence for these animals."

"How awful. Why don't they get a speedier poison?" I had asked.

"Yes, Meg, I'll tell them to dip their arrows in the fast stuff and cut out all the foolishness."

I laughed, realizing how absurd my impatience had sounded. If it needs to be fixed, it must be fixed. If it needs to be done, it must be done. And it *can* be done. Now. All things are possible.

The day had been exhausting. Yesterday morning seemed so long ago. I rolled over, not bothering to undress, and fell asleep, caressed by the warm evening breeze.

In my dreams the massive stone ramparts of the Zimbabwe ruins were protected by little people who held their bows high against savages and kings and the lure of the modern world. Smartly dressed Elizabeth kneeled outside the great wall, sobbing before the grave of her doctor. And all the time I was watching, trying to hold onto the moment. Suddenly, a dark swirl of clouds rolled toward me, pushing me back. I ran to get away but the clouds were gaining on me. I stumbled through tangled tropical forests until I reached the comfort of pine and hemlock. I was a little girl, again, sitting on my father's lap. "Daddy, I don't want to grow up," I sobbed. "I don't want to get old. I want everything to be happy, just like now."

The telephone split the silence. I jumped up. The faint glow of morning lit the room. Who could be calling so early? Dear God, please, not Vasco….

"Mrs. Peterson, Benjamin Ndlovu returning your call," said a deep voice on the other end of the line. "The day you called I had an office full of people, but I did try to reach you yesterday."

"Oh, I had so hoped to meet you. Frank speaks so highly of you. I was at the Greater Zimbabwe Ruins overnight, and, unfortunately, I have to leave for South Africa this afternoon."

My brother-in-law, Frank Magill, used to work in a clinic in Rochester, New York, with Dr. Ndlovu, who returned to his native land when it gained its independence. After talking about the critical shortage of doctors in Zimbabwe, he said, casually, "I called you, yesterday, to invite you to my home to meet some friends who have a South African band. You may have heard of them—the Ladysmith Black Mombaza. They're giving a concert here on Sunday."

"When will they be coming? I'll change my ticket. I'm a musician, you know. And I believe in what they're doing. I'd kill to meet them." I must have sounded like a star-struck teenager.

He chuckled. "That won't be necessary. They were here all day yesterday, but, unfortunately, are unavailable today. I'm so sorry. Maybe, when they go to your country...."

I wanted to cry. Now I'd have to catch the group in the U.S...with Paul Simon. A far cry from the intimacy of Dr. Ndlovu's living room.

This was right up there with lost opportunities I've had in my life. In college I refused an invitation for an all-night jam session with Gene Krupa and his band. (Someone said they smoked marajuana, heaven forbid!) Then there was the time I left my hotel in Los Angeles and returned in the late evening to find this message from a fellow musician: Call me. I think you'd enjoy spending the evening with Heifetz, Piatagorsky, and me. We're playing trios at Heifetz's house.

I found out the next day that the only other guest was Danny Kaye.

I washed my hair and ordered a coffee. Suddenly, I remembered my South African visa. Where had I hidden it? I panicked. I'd been told in New York that my passport would be lifted by other African countries if a South African visa was in it, or could be located in my belongings. So I had purchased a special loose-leaf visa. But if I wasn't allowed to carry a South Africa visa, how come I was sold a ticket to Johannesburg? How did they think I would get into the country? What kind of hypocrisy was this?

I started searching, slowly and methodically. And there it was, nestled in the instruction book for my Canon camera, alongside Dr. Manwe's letters and the addresses of ANC members.

With only three Zimbabwe dollars in my wallet I started for the airport. Perfect planning. I had just enough U.S. dollars left to pay the hated airport departure tax.

Two blocks from the bus station I bumped into Vasco. He put up his hand to stop me. He looked weary, but when he grinned his vitality seemed to return. We stood, silently, for a moment. I felt uncomfortable, perhaps a little guilty for having avoided him.

"You're leaving?" he asked. I nodded. "You are a wonderful and different woman," he said.

Different? I hoped that was a compliment. Without waiting for a reply, he tipped his ten-gallon hat. "Just like Texas," he said and walked on.

21

PARTIES AND APARTHEID

With a good deal of trepidation I entered customs in Johannesburg. I'd heard scary things about South Africa, so I was pleasantly surprised by the courteous, smiling officials. "Nothing to declare? No problem." I was waved through without incident—perhaps because I was white.

I walked through the wide, windowed corridors and peered into a variety of fashionable shops. This could have been St. Louis, Houston, or Atlanta. Only the conversation was different—intensely political with unfailing candor—and instigated by any number of casual acquaintances I met while waiting for my flight to Durban. Everybody wanted to talk about sanctions, which had just been levied on South Africa, and everybody wanted to propose a solution to apartheid, or say there was no solution…that it was already too late to avert a catastrophe. I listened. In fact, I listened for the next seven weeks. For me, an avid talker, that was difficult, and hardly enough time to scratch the surface of a culture far more diverse and complicated than any I had ever experienced. Juxtaposed to its modern, affluent side was a dark, ominous side—squalid black townships, desolate homelands, and housing projects created by the repressive Group Areas Act for the sole purpose of keeping people of different racial backgrounds segregated.

It was two days before Christmas. I awoke at 4 A.M. to the buzzing of mosquitos, and went rummaging through my pack for the smoke coils given me in the Amboseli by a couple from Tulsa. How strange it was to be in this charming, airy room, sleeping on a firm mattress and hearing nothing but the sounds of insects and the occasional screeching of a fruit bat. No traffic, no shouts from the street, no drunks thumping down the hallway.

The sweet smell of bougainvillea hung in the air outside my window. I lay thinking about my arrival the previous evening, and the ride over rolling terrain to Cowies Hill, fifteen miles from Durban in Natal province. It was here that my hosts, Sheila and Lionel Astill, resided in a comfortable English country home much like the old coach houses I'd seen in Sussex, England. I had met the Astills and their two daughters seven years before in Florence, Italy. It was a friendship undiminished by lengthy separations. Lionel, a prosperous businessman, and Sheila, a song writer, floral arranger, and chef extraordinaire, entertained me on the patio, where surrounding poinsettia bushes pushed their way between feathery eucalyptus. The lights from the Christmas tree had shown through the small glass panes of the den. Their fractured glow spread its message of hope over the warm reunion of old friends in this troubled country.

At seven I awoke again, this time to the redolent smell of bacon cooking on the grill. I stuck my head out the window. Monkeys, which I could hear but not see, chattered high in the trees, while Lionel floated luxuriously in the pool below.

He spotted me. "Get into your bathing costume, Meg, and get down here!" he shouted.

Swimming at Christmastime? How incongruous! Sitting around the pool, the sun streaming through a loose canopy of tangled flowers that hung from crosspieces over the patio, I enjoyed a respite for a few hours from the intensity of the past five weeks. My eyes wandered down the sloping backyard to a dense garden, where scarlet anthurium nodded their waxy blooms like praying nuns in a field of Prince Edward ferns. Birds of paradise poked out from under ficus and fig tree. On the lowest tier were stonewalls and trellises, built by Sheila to house her exotic plants. It was like everyone's secret garden, a fairyland of indigenous flowers and rare plants that can only be found in the southernmost part of Africa.

For the next week I was a spoiled guest. Nobody let me do a thing. "You're on holiday, Meg," said Sheila.

What a wonderful way to look at it. I'd always had trouble relaxing—it was somehow not worthy, a carryover from my grandmother's old-time Protestantism and my mother's caveats about keeping busy doing what is productive and creative…at all times. What a heavy burden that can be! I always envied people who could just lie back, "chill out," relax.

Being with English people in South Africa was like being in upper crust England, although a great deal less formal. There were large and lively outdoor parties, where the whiskey and beer flowed, and an enclave of men hovered around the "telly," watching a game of cricket, which looks a lot more strenuous than baseball, and which nobody could ever adequately explain to me. The women, well-coiffed and cheery, presided over elaborate feasts, where quantities of barbecued meat were served, accompanied by lavish salads, vegetables, and sweets.

But for all their fun and frolic I'd never met a group of people more concerned about what was happening in their country, nor more aware of the problems brought about by the insanity of apartheid. They lived it, breathed it, argued about it, and agonized over it. It was on the television constantly. Opposition papers took the president to task daily, and interviews on television openly ridiculed officials who referred to the ANC as an "illegal organization," rather than by name. Full-page ads admonished the government to free Mandela or face disaster. "The situation" was the center of heated discussion at every party. There was no escape, no place to hide. Change was on everyone's lips and as inevitable as the howl of a newborn baby.

As a foreigner I was constantly besieged by explanations of what was good and what was bad and what could be done to change the social and political inequities short of civil war. I felt tension, unrest, and turmoil spilling from the hearts and minds of everyone I talked to, black or white. Many of the young people I met—English and Afrikaner—were planning to leave in disgust at the government's stupidity, and many had returned—as Rian Malan so poignantly describes in his book, <u>My</u> <u>Traitor's</u> <u>Heart</u>—to tackle the problems of their homeland, not run away from them.

This was before Nelson Mandela was released from prison and President F.W. De Klerk called for free elections. To visit the townships and see the destitute black homelands was to know that this transition would not be easy. But all you had to do was open your eyes to see that the end of legal oppression was at hand.

Sheila and I spent hours by the pool, talking and enjoying the warmth of high summer. She felt discouraged about the overall picture in South Africa, but like her friends, she was doing what she could in a personal way to help the Blacks she knew and those who worked for her—like paying for the education of the children of her longtime maid, Thembi.

"You know," she said, "the rest of the world has very little idea of the problems we face or what is being done to remedy them."

She went on to tell me harrowing stories about the tribal rivalries and the brutal killing of Blacks by other young Blacks in her own Natal Province, now renamed Kwa Zulu.

"But there already have been some changes," she said. "Beaches desegrated, 'For Whites Only' signs removed, and schools, especially universities, opened to all who can pay. This doesn't erase all tension, but it's a long overdue beginning."

She sighed and looked out over the rich green valley beyond the flaming gum trees. "It'll be a long and terrible struggle to attain real freedom. And it'll take a great deal of courage and hard work to make it happen. And there will be a lot of pain in the bargain."

The fervent hope was that peace could be maintained while it was happening, and that bloodshed could be avoided.

The day before Christmas we hopped into Lionel's GTI and wound along mountain roads, past valleys and waterfalls, to a remote farm where Sheila bought armloads of flowers and exotic ferns for 22 Rand (about $11.00). That afternoon I watched in awe as she deftly put together exquisite arrangements and placed them throughout the house or gave them as gifts to friends.

It was a joy to see the way Sheila and Lionel interacted. Like the Wasims they had a solid marriage, a partnership of twenty-four years built on good humor, understanding, and love. How could I help but envy them? Sheila had told me that she didn't think disagreements needed to be divisive. She believed that trouble shared was trouble halved.

I wondered how these two would fare without each other. They were such a close unit…like my parents. One complementing the other. Yet each one retained his or her individuality, which belied the notion that in marriage two people had to become one. With them, one and one still made two. I had wrestled with this for thirty-three years, finding myself stifled by the rules of a traditional '50's marriage. It took me far too long to realize that I didn't need someone else to validate me, to complete who I was. In all fairness, this was *my* problem, not Glen's.

That evening, at a neighborhood Christmas Eve party, I had my first argument. Most of the English were not South African citizens. They seemed to be retaining their British citizenship to be on the safe side. I found this rather hypocritical, since they all made fun of the central government, calling the Afrikaners stubborn, and labeling apartheid suicidal.

"Why not make your voices heard by getting into the political arena?" I asked.

"We're only one million compared to three million Afrikaners. We'd have no influence," was the answer.

"So you won't even try? Perhaps you'd find a lot more agreement from the other side than you imagine," I countered, aware that I wasn't making myself very popular.

A recently arrived English businessman started railing against sanctions, shouting at me as if I were personally responsible. "Don't you Americans realize that your precious Blacks are losing jobs by the hundreds because of this? It's madness. I just bought an American business for half its value, and I can get rid of all the expensive educational programs if I choose, which does nothing but damage the people you want to help."

"Most Blacks I've spoken with are willing to suffer short term economic pain for the greater goal of freedom," I said. "And why are you so angry, anyway, when you just admitted that you're profiting big time from the situation?"

Sheila got me out of there as fast as possible.

"Now you know that not every Englishman is a gentleman," she said. "I'm glad you told him off. He's full of *codswallop!*"

I looked puzzled. "That's our word for b.s.," said Lionel.

Two days after Christmas, Dr. Prudence Winthrop came to pick me up and take me to McCord Zulu Hospital, located on a narrow, tree-lined street in Durban. My brother-in-law, Frank, had been the physician in charge of the pediatric program twenty-five years ago. It was a hospital with a mixed resident staff where non-Europeans—Blacks, Coloreds (people of mixed parentage), and Asiatic Indians—could be treated. It also trained non-Whites in nursing and midwifery. It was from Frank and my sister, Anne, that I heard my first stories about the horrors of apartheid and the hardships suffered by the non-Whites living in restricted areas, faced with inferior education and the tyrannical pass laws.

Dr. Winthrop, a close friend of Frank's, was plain, unadorned, and erect. Although her accent was British, she was proud of her South African heritage. She talked with great admiration about the work of Dr. McCord, the religious convictions which inspired the hospital's humble beginnings, and its powerful impact on the hearts of black South Africans. She introduced me to the black matron and a group of nursing sisters. We met in the lunchroom.

The women were warm and accepting, but wanted me to relay their continued anguish over problems in their country to Frank, whom they remembered and loved. I found their honesty courageous.

I toured the pediatric ward, which was very simple compared to our sophisticated hospitals, and full of children who suffered from pulmonary diseases (pneumonia and TB), malnutrition, and diarrhea. The atmosphere was relaxed and friendly, largely because of Grace Rametsa, the capable young woman in charge. Dr. Winthrop filled me in on her story. She had had to drop out of her training when she became pregnant. She lived in a township and would nurse her baby at midnight, and again at four A.M., then take a bus to Durban to work in the milk room of the pediatric ward. She set up the lab, or sterile kitchen, herself. It was necessary because so many black women—in an attempt to be like white women—had discontinued nursing and mixed widely-advertised formula with polluted water. This had led to a dangerous increase in infant death and diarrhea.

While working in the lab Grace completed her nursing degree. She now had three children.

"Why make so many travel so far to work each day?" she said. "Can you imagine leaving your family and small children at four in the morning in order to ride miles in an old bus to get to work by seven? And then turning around and adding another three hours to the end of the day. How can there be any stable family life?"

She looked at me imploringly. "Why go to so much trouble to keep people separate? And this government calls itself Christian?"

I spent the next hour with the matron. She asked some of the same questions as Grace Rametsa, but a touch of optimism crept around the edges of her story. "There's been a great deal of progress with our people," she said. "Not as many women are going to witch doctors, but there is still a great need for programs educating them in proper nutrition, prenatal care, and birth control."

She told me that there are large numbers of black women who want to use birth control, but are afraid of the men, who block them from entering the clinic. This was reminiscent of what Hamal Wasim had said to me in Egypt. The male feels he must father a child to prove his manhood. The more he feels unable to cope, and the poorer he is, the more children he wants. He thinks it's his insurance against old age. It gives him some semblance of power, some feeling of control. Women see it differently. They're becoming stronger and beginning to assert themselves.

The ice broken, we began to talk about the real nitty-gritty of South Africa. Perhaps she now felt she could trust me. Too soon Dr. Winthrop appeared and seemed to be in a great hurry to whisk me away. As I passed the matron she whispered under her breath, all pretense stripped away, "Things aren't good. Tell Dr. Frank"

We looked for a long moment into each other's eyes, then she turned and left the room. I felt bereft. Evidently, despite the freedom of expression here, a white doctor was still intimidating.

When Dr. Winthrop left me her words were chilling. "When it happens, when the Blacks finally rise up and strike back, it will be a blood bath. There will be no distinction between the good and the bad. Why do you think so many Whites are emigrating? But I have nowhere to go. This is my country. I love it and I'll stay."

Fortunately her gloomy prediction did not come true.

I felt heavy with the unsolvable problems I was hearing and even worse when I was told that I couldn't meet with the lawyer for whom I had letters from Dr. Manwe. It would be too dangerous, he told me over the phone.

That afternoon Sheila took me to the American Express for my mail. I opened my letters eagerly. My daughter, Cary, communicated in writing more freely than in conversation, and my trip was drawing us ever closer. She and I were about on a par when it came to self-exploration. She shared her struggle to peel off unnecessary layers in her life and let go of old patterns that didn't work for her any more. That was good for me to hear. The last part of her letter tickled me as well. Of all my children she seemed the most concerned about my exploits *and* my safety.

> Just received your letter, and your trip is now much more alive for me. You sound like you're doing well in one of the more difficult places in the world to travel. Bravo! I'll cease worrying about you, but just send lots of loving and warm energy to keep you going if you get lonely. One thing I really admire about you is how you can soak up so much and truly be somewhere with all your heart and soul.
>
> As for me, right now I have the urge to go to China and continue the study of shiatsu and acupressure. And ride my bike wherever I go. I get fed up with our society at times—the frantic pace, the traffic, the pollution, the greed. Now is one of those times. As much as I love my country and am irrevocably American, in many ways I don't relate. Maybe I lived in Europe too long....

The next day we headed for the Drakensberg Mountains. We drove along the road to Ixopo, the very road mentioned by Alan Paton on the first page of Cry The Beloved Country. He called it the most beautiful stretch of highway in South Africa. We traveled west toward Pietermaritzburg, through hills and valleys, orange groves and manicured farms. Cattle with white tickbirds perched saucily on their backs grazed languidly in meadows. Deep red soil, like that in the Great Rift Valley of Kenya, lined the streams and outcroppings. And always up ahead were the mountains, flat-topped and rugged, one of the scenic wonders of South Africa.

I arose early on the 29th of December, brushed the Astill's beagle and two Siamese cats off my bed, and took one last swim in the pool. I lay on my back watching the first rays of sun appear and wondering when I'd see my friends again. Saying goodbye would be difficult.

I blew Sheila a kiss as the bus pulled away from the city square, still festive with its holiday decorations. Leaning back in the comfortable seats I reflected on my days in Durban. Exciting and intense, but not light-hearted. I was spinning from the emotionally charged atmosphere. All those parties. All those heavy conversations. It was hard for an outsider to even attempt an evaluation. So I concentrated on the positive. The gala English Christmas with all the trimmings. Swimming in a pool surrounded by good friends. And the ever-present perfume of tropical flowers. This was more than most northeasterners could expect even in the best of times. But I had to admit that I was homesick for the snow, and for my family, and for a crackling fire. I even missed the freezing ride to attend the Christmas Eve candlelight service at the little stone church where Allen Tinker, my minister, joyously proclaimed, "It's now Christmas morning. Go in peace...."

22

I'M ONLY A HIKER….

"You'll never know just how much I love you," the music wailed. Moments later Sinatra's impassioned "Strangers in the Night" oozed out of the loudspeaker above my head. The luxury bus hugged the coastline high above the Indian Ocean, where easy waves lapped the layered rocks. I looked out of the other side of the bus toward burgundy hills and jagged mountains. "Don't Rain On My Parade," pleaded Streisand.

Save me, oh, someone please save me! The pretty blonde hostess smiled sweetly when I told her that I was a musician and couldn't stand to listen to fourteen hours of canned American music, including entire soundtracks of Broadway musicals. "I have to listen when music is playing," I said. "I can't talk or read or write. I'm going bananas. Do you know what that means?"

She continued serving coffee and tea. "I'm sorry about the music, Madam," she said as she placed a small 'tasteful' basket of sandwiches on my tray table. "But it says on the brochure, 'relaxing music during your journey,' so we have to play it."

I wasn't the only discontented person on the bus. Terry, a dancer from New Zealand, who was sitting next to me, suggested that we confront the driver at the next rest stop.

"I don't ask you to play Beethoven," I said to the bewildered driver, "so please don't subject me to *your* taste in music."

"She's right," chimed in Terry. "If you keep this up I'm going to insist on heavy metal."

We were given a one-hour respite. I lay back and enjoyed the changing landscape. Green valleys alternated with sloping hillocks where bald-headed ibis played. The rusted tracks of an old railroad, used in the days when timber was transported to Port Elizabeth from the Wild Coast, snaked along the coastline. Acres of neatly cultivated sugar cane and maize fields, interspersed with stands of tall evergreens and spindly deciduous trees, made a subtle mosaic in shades of green.

It was great to be able to talk—unaccompanied. Terry leaned toward me in a conspiratorial way. He was strikingly good looking, with impeccable manners and a dancer's muscular body. Intense eyes peered out from under deeply arched brows and a mop of unruly black hair, which he kept trying to smooth down. His good humor had slowly vanished, and in a surprising burst of candor, he said, "I'm having real problems in my marriage. You said you'd been married a long time, so I thought maybe...."

"I had a few answers?"

"Yes, something like that," he replied.

"Well, Terry, I've been divorced for three years, and I still haven't figured it all out...where it went wrong and how I could have changed things. Everybody's pain is different, but maybe I can shed some light on yours. Fire away."

He nodded gratefully. "For the last two years I've been pulling away from my wife. It's as if a chasm has opened up between us—and it keeps getting bigger. We can hardly talk anymore, and now sex...." His voice broke.

"What about sex?" I asked tenuously.

"You see, she's gorgeous," he said. "She has everything. It's my fault, but I can't help it."

"You can't help what?" I asked.

"I don't want to sleep with her anymore. I come home after a long absence, and you'd think I'd be dying to get her into bed. But I'm not."

"Do you find other women attractive?" I asked.

"No. It's not that."

"How about other men?"

"What a terrible thing to say!"

"It's only a question."

For the next few minutes neither of us spoke. Then Terry turned toward me. Trying to control himself he said, "You don't know my family."

"Families are difficult," I said, "but you have to give them a chance. It sounds, just maybe, as if you don't know *yourself*."

It started very quietly, then the tears began to flow, and the next thing I knew Terry had buried his head in my lap and was sobbing. Where was that music when we needed it? I sat there feeling compassion...and embarrassment. Nobody around me moved, but I could feel their eyes.

"Terry," I said quietly. "Please don't think me unfeeling, but I don't see this as the catastrophe you do. Perhaps that's because I've lived with it a long time. You see, my eldest son is gay." I wondered if he heard me. Slowly, he sat up.

"And your husband? How did he take it?" he asked.

"You don't 'take it,' you accept it as part of who the person is. Actually, my husband was wonderful. He said, 'I have a gay son. I can either accept him, or I can lose him. I choose to accept him.' That was all there was to it. I really loved him at that moment. We think our son is terrific. He's had many problems over the years, but being gay isn't one of them. In fact, he told me during a particularly tough time in his career, that being gay was the only thing he felt good about."

A picture of Chris flashed through my mind—tall and blond, outrageously funny, artistic, exacting, hot-tempered. "Terry. It's not the end of the world. It'll be difficult, but, first, you have to confront who you are...honestly, and without shame."

"I've never talked with anyone this openly," Terry confessed toward the end of the afternoon. "I wonder why. I hardly know you."

"That's easy," I said. "We'll probably never see each other again, so our secrets are safe. And you've done me a favor. For the first time in a week I've talked about something besides politics. It's refreshing."

"You're about to enter the homeland of Transkei," announced the driver. We were grateful for any interruption in the music, which had resumed its attack with increasing fervor. He talked in a patronizing way about this recent experiment in black self-government. It was obvious to all of us that these shabby towns were a far cry from the neat, prosperous cities of South Africa. But the countryside, itself, was exotic. Dense forests and imposing mountains—some serrated like the knife's edge on Mt. Katahdin in Maine, and others blanketed with grass like the rolling hills of Vermont. Black widow birds, ebony-tailed with orange feathers on their backs, mingled with clusters of crested cranes. And clumps of pink and violet wildflowers lined the road.

We passed through Xhosa territory, where many houses were covered with bright blue and white tiles. Our driver pointed out an especially imposing residence. Two stone lions sat on either side of the long front walk. "That's the home of the greatest witch doctor in South Africa," he said.

As we neared our destination the commentary resumed. "And now we're entering Umtata, meaning 'taker,' the capital of Transkei. The city was named for the Umtata River, where thousands of native Africans were slaughtered in a bloody battle, their bodies left to rot." I had read about this terrible time in South African history, and I wished he hadn't gone into such detail.

At 9 P.M. we pulled into Port Elizabeth, ending the luxury leg of my journey. Terry and I hugged for a long time before parting. Early the next morning we were escorted onto a modest Inter-City bus—*sans* toilet, but with the customary uninterrupted music. This time I didn't fight it. I lost myself in a surfeit of diverse landscapes. Dusty yellow pastures covered with grazing sheep reached to the foot of the Swellendam mountains, which hovered in the distance like great metallic elephants. Small villages and seaside resorts dotted the coast. Further inland we passed through orderly towns where I saw my first Cape Dutch houses, stark white and symmetrical, surrounded by multi-colored *protea,* the signature flower of South Africa.

We entered Cape Town through Sir Lowry's Pass. As we sped toward the bus station our driver proudly pointed out the famous Groote Schur Hospital where Dr. Christian Barnard had performed the first heart transplant. Everything looked bright and clean. And above the skyline, filling the horizon, loomed Table Mountain, flat-topped and formidable.

Forty-eight hours after leaving Durban I stepped off the bus to be greeted by Matilda Rush, an old friend and professor of music therapy at Cape Town University. There she stood, beaming contentedly—tall, robust, with a halo of saucy red hair.

"Happy New Year's Eve," she shouted.

We embraced. "Oh, Matilda," I wailed. "I'm about to take out a contract on Frank Sinatra and Barbra Streisand. Take me somewhere peaceful."

"I have just the place. But first, I have to buy champagne."

We headed for Camps Bay, a secluded crescent of shore with houses layered into the rocky hillside overlooking the ocean. I wasn't prepared for the beauty of this city nor the magic of the bay, which is reached by winding roads that lead past Lion's Head rock, high on a bluff, to the beaches, inlets, and coves below.

We walked up several flights of stone steps, passing through small courtyards and under vine-covered trellises to the very top, where Matilda's modern, two-tiered house was perched. Norfolk pines and flowering gum trees clung to the sides of the cliff. Inside, an expanse of front windows looked out onto rocks, beach, and crashing waves, with ocean as far as you could see.

New Year's Eve was in full swing. The barbecue, or *brei,* was sizzling on the grill, nestled in one corner of the overhanging front deck. A large birdbath stood in another corner. Several high-spirited tropical birds swooped down, fluttered in the water and flew off. It was their home, too.

James, dark-haired and elegant—one of Matilda's colleagues—greeted me. Michel, Matilda's cousin, gave me a hug. Magda, his sister, threw her arms around me. Matilda was part English and part Afrikaaner. These were the Afrikaaner relatives—a boisterous, fun-loving lot. Three teenage boys, sons of Michel and of Magda, wrestled on the sunporch. Josina, a ferocious-looking bulldog, and Janos, a bright-eyed Staffordshire bull terrier, covered me with wet kisses. And Herman, an old family friend, nodded politely from the dining room. I felt at home, instantly.

Matilda led me down the hall to a spacious bedroom with glass from floor to ceiling on the ocean side. "Here it is. Yours for as long as you want it," she said.

"Are you certain you have enough space for me—with all these guests?" I asked.

She threw back her head and hooted. "There's an old African expression: you can get a lot of tamed goats in a small enclosure. Does that answer your question?"

"Yes, but I can't imagine you know any tame ones."

I was eager to get back to the party. After two days of confinement my sanity was returning, and I was ready for anything. Matilda grabbed my arm and motioned toward Herman, who had moved to a corner of the dining room and was reading a paperback. He had a tape of Beethoven's seventh symphony playing softly.

"Large groups bore him," she said, "but you two will get along fine. Mountain climbing is his passion. He can climb the socks off all of us, including Michel." She introduced me.

Herman put his book down. "You climb?" he asked.

"Well, not much so far. I couldn't go up Mt. Kenya because of the rain and fog, and I missed Kilimanjaro because there was no transportation to Moshe, but I hope...."

He interrupted. "Never mind Kilimanjaro. That's not climbing. But Kenya—*there's* a mountain! I did it in 1960 when I was forty-five years old. Well, now you know my age. I was in shape then." He made a gesture of resignation with his hand.

He looked in shape now. Wiry and muscular, he could have been in his late 50's.

"You have to watch Kenya. It's tricky. But once you get acclimated and complete the training—you know, ropes, rappelling, survival skills—it's well worth it."

Kenya, a technical climb? How come my nephew, Chip, never told me that? He said I'd have no trouble. He must have taken a different trail or wanted to give me a good scare.

"I'm not a technical climber, Herman," I said. "Just a strong, steady hiker. I don't like the idea of hanging from a cliff on the end of a rope...."

He wasn't listening. He was telling me about his youth in Germany before the Nazis, and his escape to South Africa fifty years ago, and the wonderful climbing around Cape Town.

Just before midnight Herman left. "I'll take you up Table Mountain day after tomorrow," he said excitedly. "It's a great climb."

We celebrated New Year's Eve three times that evening—once for the U.S., once for England, and once for South Africa.

The next morning I awoke to the roar of the ocean. An insistent wind rattled the windows. I snuggled deeper into my down comforter. It was definitely a New Hampshire mountain day.

Michel bounded in like a big teddy bear. "Magda...Meg...hurry. We're headed for Hout Bay and Seal Island. The boys already have the boat. Put on your rain gear. It's windy out there."

The boat ride was harrowing! All this to observe a few offshore seals? I was sure the small craft would capsize as it pitched and coughed in the rough sea. I hung on to anyone and anything, trying to duck each mammoth wave that broke over the bow pouring water onto the deck. I was so scared that I forgot to be seasick.

It didn't take me long to realize that being with Michel meant danger, excitement, and lots of laughs. How attractive he was with his robust good looks and lack of inhibition. His sons, Anton and Hendrik, adopted me for the rest of the day, which was spent celebrating the New Year with an assortment of their father's friends—artists and writers—at Kommetje Bay, further south on the cape. It was only a little less strenuous than fighting the open sea.

The surf in the bay was bewitching—five banks of waves waiting, like stacked planes, to roll onto the beach. They'd hang, suspended, for one brief moment, then break at intervals and spray foam high into the air. I'd never seen an ocean this wild. Along the shore sand dunes and tall grasses mixed with tangled underbrush and ancient trees. Flocks of gulls and egrets swooped down from an adjoining bird sanctuary. We chased them toward an old lighthouse, across the sand and over a breakwater already half-submerged by the tide. In my enthusiasm to keep up with the teenage boys I smashed my little toe against a sharp rock. Now how could I climb Table Mountain the next day?

Shortly after I hobbled back from the beach the party moved next door to an exquisitely decorated modern beach house—cathedral ceiling, mirrors, marble floors, and chandeliers. When we entered, our host, Norman, was sitting in an antique bathtub on a raised platform. The door to the bathroom was ajar and the scene was transmitted in perfect detail by the mirrors. Sari, a flamboyantly dressed opera singer, was regaling him with excerpts from The Magic Flute. Gestures and all. Nobody spoke until she was finished. Was I in South Africa or San Francisco?

"Bravo and welcome," Norman said. "Carry on. There's food on the table and records in the library."

The music blared. We danced. Norman bathed.

Michel took the precarious mountain road back to Camps Bay, reaching the highest point, Chapman's Peak, in time for sunset. Stretched out below was the graceful curve of the cape. We stood silently on the edge of the bluff until the final burst of orange had faded and the sky was dark. Stars began to appear, as if to compete with the flickering lights springing up from houses all along the coast.

When I awoke the next morning my toe was purple and swollen, but could still fit into my hiking boots. I had carried them this far, and I would use them!

Herman arrived early with Michel and Magda. Matilda had decided to sit this one out. She was smart. We would be going up Woody Buttress, one of the cliffs leading to the lower plateau of the mountain. I could see the trail from Matilda's dining room. Twelve rugged peaks, appropriately named the Twelve Apostles, stretched from the main mountain down the peninsula. Later, I found out that more than a few lives had been lost attempting their ascent.

As we got out of the car Herman turned to me. "Do you want me to bring the ropes, Meg?" he asked.

"Hell, no," I answered, not realizing why he had asked. I thought he was asking whether I wanted to do a technical climb—not whether I wanted to do a technical climb with or without ropes. I soon discovered my mistake.

After a short walk to the base of the trail we started scrambling hand-over-foot up the steep "chimneys" that connect each ledge. I found myself high above the ground, searching for footholds in sheer rock, handholds in rough stone. I started clawing at the rock face, grabbing for bushes, roots, anything I could hang on to. Herman was racing ahead like a monkey, but Magda and Michel were clearly worried about me.

"Don't use your arms to pull yourself up. Use your leg muscles to push," said Michel, forcing himself to sound casual.

"Grab onto the rocks, not the bushes," instructed Magda. "We're right behind, Meg. Nothing can happen to you."

Nothing? I could miss a foothold and bounce off the cliffs on my way to eternity. Or I could faint, with the same result, but it might not hurt as much. This is what it must be like to walk on the ledge of a thirty-story building. I tried not to look down. It made me light-headed. At one point we had to negotiate a massive overhang by walking on a narrow path, our hands clutching the outside of the rock, inching along, with our backs arched over the crevass. And what was behind us? A sheer drop to the valley. Sweating, I completed the exercise only to be told by Herman that we'd gone the wrong way. Go back around again?

I panicked. I thought of my old friend, Sylvia, who had died the previous spring. She used to hike with me in the White Mountains of New Hampshire. Was she standing by in spirit, laughing and telling me to act my age? Well I can't die young, I whispered to her as the wind began to blow fiercely. My safari hat blew off, but was held by its chinstrap. It pulled at my neck. I didn't care. My legs and arms were bruised and bleeding from rocks and thorny plants. I didn't care. I couldn't even feel my toe. Every ounce of concentration and energy was focused on survival. I knew that one mistake could be my last. I had never before known such terror.

My companions thought this was a relatively simple climb. Magda, heavy, muscular, kept bopping along, never looking down, while Michel relished the danger as a challenge. There were places where the trail simply disappeared up a rock face. Maybe if I hadn't tried to figure out how to tackle each new obstacle, but just plowed ahead like the others, I would have done better. I couldn't go back, so I listened to Michel's sympathetic instructions, which admonished me *not* to use my knees while scrambling for safety and to keep my legs stretched in such a way that I was "balanced." I was to do all this while I was hanging, spread-eagle, across a rock above a ravine, paralyzed with fright.

Michel reached for my hand just as my legs gave way. It was like the hand of God. He put his other hand under my arm and pulled me up over the ledge. I sat there, fighting the tears. There's no way I'm going to survive this, I thought. But I promised God one hundred years of dedicated service for any help He or She could give.

"Meg, you have guts," Michel said. "It's easy to do something if you're used to it and not scared. But it takes guts to keep on when you're terrified. Don't worry. We'll get you out of this."

Dear, dear Michel. I hope you're right.

Herman sidled over to me. "I'm sorry about this, Meg, but you said you didn't want me to bring the ropes."

Just then a young Frenchman appeared with his wife, son, and mother. They were roped together as any sensible person would be.

"Can you give us a hand?" yelled Herman. "We have a woman here who needs help."

"*Certainment*," he shouted back and threw down a coil of rope. I immediately started humming *La Marseillaise*.

Michel put the rope around my waist. My hands were still shaking, but I did well on the most difficult part, thanks to the blessed security of that rope. I used it on one more ledge, then had enough confidence to go it alone. Herman was very complimentary about my progress, which pleased me. He kept saying there were no more difficult sections. He lied. But my fear had subsided. At least I wouldn't be killed—only maimed—if I fell.

With the wind ripping at our clothes we reached the wide plateau and saw a hut in the distance. I was ecstatic and started to jump and leap through the tall grass. We were all giddy with excitement. Even Herman.

"You see, Meg. I said you were fit, didn't I?"

I smiled. "Fit to be tied, that's what." Suddenly I felt very close to these warm, strong, fearless people.

After lunch I lay in a field of flowers, arms outstretched, and looked at the sky and the surrounding mountains. The symbol of my adventure would be the delicate *agapanthus*, which was everywhere, in purple, blue, and white. Its tiny bell-like blooms amass into a large ball, which dips in the wind as the long thin stem bows to its weight, bounces back, but never breaks. I felt like the long stem. Bowed, revitalized, unbroken.

We climbed down Kasteel Spoort, a steep, non-life-threatening trail. In the distance was Robben Island where Nelson Mandela was being held prisoner. We paused in silence. Behind us stood a simple memorial to Jan Smuts. To the right of us was the dramatic silhouette of Lion's Head.

The climb was almost over. Like childbirth, like rafting down the Colorado, like being caught in the Himalayas in a blizzard, the struggle had been worth it. The pain and fear would soon be forgotten, but the exhilaration and joy would last forever.

I turned for one last look at the mountain. Billowing clouds were rolling over the top, forming the famous "table cloth." How benign it looked.

I hurried ahead. There was a lot to do. After all, I'd just promised God one hundred years of service. Better get started.

23

MRS. BOTTOMLY'S GAMBLE

Matilda was furious at Herman when she heard about our climb. "He has to be out of his mind," she said. "The idea...."

"It's all right," I interrupted. "Just a little misunderstanding. And even when I realized what was happening, I said to myself that everything would be fine. You know I'm a great one for denial. Otherwise, how could I have lived with an alcoholic for so many years?" I laughed and grabbed Matilda by the arms, twirling her around the living room and chanting, "Call me Mary Sun-shine. Lit-tle Mary Sun-shine. Don't complain. Try to please. Just like Mary Sun-shine."

Matilda pulled away. "O.K., O.K., take it easy. I get it," she said breathlessly.

"And don't forget....I hate to be a quitter," I added, looking out the window at the Twelve Apostles, and remembering the rush of excitement when we reached the top of Table Mountain. "So take it easy on Herman. He's a helluva guy."

Early the next morning I walked the dogs. Josina plodded heavily, nose to the ground, groaning and wheezing with each step, while Janos leaped and frolicked, his powerful shoulders straining at the leash like his famous look-alike in the film, Jock of the Bushvelt The beaches were deserted, except for an occasional jogger, but you could see the remnants of sand castles, reminders that children had picnicked with their families the day before. On Matilda's stretch of beach were large saw-toothed rocks reaching into the ice-blue surf. The rocks defined the beach, separating it from the road above and giving it a mysterious, secluded ambiance. Segregation had been abolished on the beaches in Cape Town.

When I returned, the mourning doves were fluttering in and out of the birdbath flicking droplets of water on the stone patio. Matilda greeted me.

"Mrs. Lillian Bottomly from the local Association of University Women just called. Seems they're planning to roll out the red carpet for you tomorrow. And I'll wager there'll be a bit of brainwashing in the bargain. I don't envy you. Those ladies are a bit too proper for me, but you'll get a taste of English affluence and a healthy dose of the status quo."

I was glad she'd called. AAUW certainly had a superb international network. This was the third country to respond to my letter of introduction. First Kenya, then Tanzania.

After breakfast we drove to Cape Town to get my mail and do some shopping. We strolled through the gardens, the quiet pedestrian malls, the parks. Streets were spotless and uncrowded. Flowers were everywhere. A few Christmas decorations still lingered, but to me it was summer, and I was infected by a vacation, not holiday, spirit.

After buying a *kanga*, an African sarong to wrap around my body after swimming, we settled down in a small outdoor café at Green Market Square, sipping tea and watching a group of Zulus playing homemade wooden xylophones and drums. Their spirited dancing added to the festive atmosphere.

I opened Martha's letter and hooted. "I knew it, Matilda, I knew it. She's pregnant. My God, I'm going to be a grandmother!"

My mother had fourteen grandchildren by the time she was my age—from three daughters. I had five children and only one was married. I never realized how much I'd wanted this, always joking that I was too young to be a grandmother. Now it sounded great to me. How I hoped I could be there at the birth.

"Matilda," I said after the first flush of excitement had subsided, "for all my joy, there's still something lurking in the background that makes me sad. And don't tell me I'm asking for trouble. On the contrary, I'm trying to face my feelings and deal with them, not deny them."

Matilda looked at me and shrugged. "Hey, I envy you," she said. "I couldn't last long enough with *any* man to even get a family started. Marriage suffocated me."

"It's expectations. That's the problem," I said. "This brings back all my old demons about divorce and failure and what might have been. On the one hand I cherish my freedom. On the other I've idealized the *idea* of home and hearth—the happy couple delighting in their children and grandchildren and watching the new generation grow—and it's tough to let go of that dream. There won't be a grandfather at my side, and I'll have to explain why, and…."

"Haven't you learned by now that expectations are deadly?" interjected Matilda. "And what makes you think you're so different? You have a lot of company among the disillusioned 'til death do us part' contingent. Fortunately, I was able to overcome that one long ago. But I'm not putting you down. Sure you feel some sadness. It's natural. Just remember, you think it's a lot worse than your grandchildren will. Guaranteed."

Good old philosophical Matilda.

"Let's go," I said. "If we hurry, we can get to the post office before it closes. I want to send a cable to Martha and Russell." I quickly composed a little ditty that went like this:

Hooray for the wonderful life that's inside;
Hooray for our Russ and his beautiful bride;
Hooray for the love of this boy or this girl;
Hooray from the grandma who's circling the worl.'

The next morning Matilda dropped me off in town and I hopped a train for Deep River, where Mrs. Bottomly was to pick me up. The shiny clean station and the punctual trains made me think of Germany. But for the first time I was faced with evidence of apartheid. Large signs proclaiming NET BLANKES: WHITES ONLY hung on the rest rooms. Sadly, it made me think of Richmond, Virginia, in the 1950's.

The only graffiti I saw was scrawled on the side of an old industrial building along the way:

FREE MANDELA.

Mrs. Lillian Bottomly, sixtyish, was a South African of English stock—reserved, genteel, and very self-conscious about what the world thinks of South Africa. Her attire was tailored and neat, and her explanation of the reasons for the existence of apartheid and the present struggle in South Africa had a decidedly paternalistic flavor. She spent a good deal of time trying to persuade me that the good works of her friends did much to improve those "less fortunate."

I was treated royally, although it was a bit embarrassing to be introduced as a V.I.P. from Syracuse University, and futile to try to correct the impression. Sitting in Mrs. Bottomly's elegant living room I was immediately aware of the hostility between those representing the old guard and those advocating drastic change. Several young women, university students and teachers, were noticeably ill at ease with the older group. This highly charged atmosphere permeated the day.

After tea we left for the famous Kirstenbosch botanical gardens, where Lillian expertly squired me through the labyrinth of beds, explaining each unusual plant, herb, and blossom.

"Here's something you may not have seen," she said, taking my arm and leading me into an area of thick vegetation. "This is a path for blind people. The foliage is pleasing to feel and the plants are selected for their fragrance. Close your eyes and move your arms from side to side as you walk. I'll guide you."

It was amazing! I ran my hands over soft ferns, tall spiky reeds used in thatching, and stalks with furry heads like giant pom-poms. The smells of the damp earth mixed with the honey-sweet perfume of the flowers filled my senses.

From the gardens I could see the other side of Table Mountain, castellated over the years by the weathering of the soft sandstone. I photographed Skeleton Gorge, through which I would climb the next day. Herman had picked a "sensible" trail up to Castle Rock, in search of a rare variety of early *protea*. He was determined to show me another face of the mountain. We would be joined by several university professors, some of whom belonged to the Black Sash, the women's anti-apartheid movement, whose members wore an identifying black sash across their chest.

At lunch Lillian kept emphasizing the monumental problems with the young Blacks: street gangs; loss of a sense of family and neighborhood; lack of respect for their elders; and mounting violence. As she talked, Judy Weinstein, a college student from Rhodes in Grahamstown, looked more and more pained.

"Of course families are being split up," she said. "How can a woman work all day miles from where she lives and still have time to care for her children adequately? And don't forget that the men are moving to the cities for whatever jobs they can find, leaving the women to run things the best they can, with what little time is left."

Lillian made no comment, but the color rose in her cheeks. Quickly she ushered us into the lobby. A small van was waiting out front. She had arranged with the government for an extensive tour of Mitchells Plain, a "Colored" community, and Khayalitcha Township, an area far from town where thousands of Blacks had been relocated. Ten of us piled into the van and headed down the narrow coastal road. I was nervous, having heard of the violence toward Whites that occurred with regularity when they entered the townships.

On the way I asked Lillian about District Six, a section of Cape Town where Coloreds, Malays, and Indians had lived. According to Matilda it had been a quaint, bohemian area full of artists and hippies of various backgrounds and religions. It had also been a meeting place for the *avante garde*—a kind of rundown Greenwich Village on the periphery of white, comfortable Cape Town. Perhaps that was its downfall. The government said it constituted substandard housing, and ten years ago had it bulldozed and the people moved to a new area, Mitchells

Plain, where modern homes were built on reclaimed land. Matilda and I had driven by. All that remained of the district were a couple of steeples and the onion-shaped dome of one mosque. The rest was rubble. Matilda said that even the white people were so enraged over the government's action that nobody has bought or built on the land in ten years. It was open defiance, decent people's way of protesting the insane policy of wantonly destroying other people's homes, all in the name of the Group Areas Act.

"That was a long time ago, Meg," Lillian said, fairly sputtering. "I don't know who you've been talking to, but you must get your facts right. It was a slum."

We rode for a time in silence. Then Judy turned to me and said, in a hushed voice: "You can't imagine the conflict in the minds and hearts of young people today. I just returned from the Middle East with all its problems, and I could feel the tension in South Africa the minute I stepped off the plane in Johannesburg. This is my home. I love it, but I'm constantly drained. And what's really insidious is that many of us—if we'll be honest—love our life of privilege. We're afraid that our beloved country may be turned into a Mozambique or an Angola. It's this unknown we fear."

The van glided into the parking lot at Mitchells Plain, a carefully planned development with new facilities and outstanding P.R. We were ushered into the main activity building, where a well-spoken "colored" lady, Mrs. Andrews, addressed us. She had been one of the first occupants of the area and was the mother of eight, with fourteen grandchildren. She exuded dynamism and energy. And her pitch was well honed. Maps and graphs lined the walls. We were told that there was a waiting list of 55,000 people who wanted to buy or rent in Mitchells Plain.

We toured the community, starting with the civic center, where all kinds of educational and self-help projects were displayed. The area had been carved out of a thirty thousand acre sand dune wilderness southeast of Cape Town, with frontage on False Bay. What a lot of effort and money had gone into keeping people separate.

Mrs. Andrews joined us as we drove to Khayalitcha. She had a permanent smile pasted on her face, and even the obvious discrepancy between her lovely new home and the less fortunate black community didn't seem to faze her.

As I was staring out the window I overheard one vocal lady behind me. "The only solution to the overpopulation here is to require every black male over twenty-five to have a vasectomy."

I couldn't keep quiet. I wheeled around. "What an abominable thing to say!"

"Well," she countered, as if it was somehow related. "In China they only allow two children to every family."

"No," I said, "only one, and they force women to have abortions if they disobey. But that's a communist dictatorship, and the rule holds true for everyone. How does that relate to what you're advocating?"

No answer.

Mrs. Bottomly became agitated whenever she smelled controversy. "We've done a great deal to encourage education among the Blacks in the last ten years," she said haughtily. "And all they do is boycott our efforts. That's why they're so behind. I think the problem is hopeless."

A young teacher was sitting next to me. "I've almost given up on these women," she said under her breath. "They may be university graduates, but most of them have never taught and they believe only what they want to believe."

She turned to Lillian. "I've worked in black schools for five years, and I can tell you that they're *grossly* inferior. It's no wonder these people are angry. I think they realize, now, that it was a mistake to boycott. But you wouldn't have wanted *your* children to go to those schools."

Mrs. Bottomly fidgeted nervously with a handkerchief. Her lips formed a thin, straight line.

By the time we arrived at Khayalitcha, I was not only nervous about the smoldering anger I could sense as we passed the groups of young people gathered around the student health and welfare office, but I felt embarrassed to be riding in a fancy government vehicle through the dusty, unpaved streets, like a tourist gawking at someone else's misery. The township was a mere six months old and the rows of flimsy dwellings were little more than makeshift shantys.

Mrs. Andrews announced that we wouldn't stay...just drive through. "We don't want to take any chances," she said cheerily.

"Oh, look," cried Lillian, pointing to a miserable hut, where an old black man was tending a small fruit stand and overseeing two rows of drooping beans. "That just shows you the ingenuity of some people. He has his own little garden and house and has started a business. How wonderful."

I thought I might vomit. Not even a chicken would want to live in that tin shack in the broiling sun. No floor. A tar paper roof. And no hope. I tried to scoot down in my seat so nobody would see me as we drove past groups of men and women milling around with nothing to do.

Evelyn Woolsey, a retired teacher from an exclusive girl's school in Paarl, leaned over. "The government *is* trying, but they haven't a clue. Each person gets a small plot of land and can buy materials and get help in the construction of the house. But they have to live surrounded by these ugly wire fences. It's the basic premise of inequality that's so damaging."

After the tour, Judy took me aside. "I think you've had enough of our problems for one day. What do you say we run over to the Groot Constantia museum and vineyards for an hour? If we're lucky, we can grab the last wine tasting of the day."

This sounded great to me. I was spinning from the emotionally charged events of the last few hours. I felt like a sponge, full to overflowing.

I was also conflicted about what to say to Lillian and her friends. She had been most gracious, and had planned an interesting day for me. For this I was grateful. But she knew how upset I had been during our visit to the township, and that I was not taken in by her protestations of good works, her patronizing attitude toward the Blacks. Her gamble had failed. I would not be going home to write glowing reports on the progress of race relations in South Africa.

I took her hand. "The gardens were lovely. I really appreciated your knowledge of botany," I said. "I wish you peace, and an end to strife in this beautiful land."

She nodded. Her farewell smile was tight.

24

MIXED MESSAGES

"We're taking a holiday…just you, Jenny, and me," Matilda announced at breakfast. "It's that time of year. And, besides, I have to check on my cottage."

Jenny Moffit, an old friend of Matilda's, had arrived the day before from Johannesburg. She'd been a godsend to me, listening with great sensitivity as I regaled her, long into the night, about Mrs. Bottomly's disastrous "tour." She was as concerned as everyone else about the outcome of South Africa's insane governmental policies, and wondered whether she ought to pack up her three teenage sons and return to Australia.

Jenny had divorced much younger than I, and was having the usual difficulties of a single working mother. The only difference between her and other friends of mine in similar circumstances was that child care was inexpensive and easy to come by in South Africa.

We left Cape Town by way of District Six and over a highway where, only a year before, young Blacks had lain in ambush and stoned passing cars. These same "toughs" would enter black homes in the township and drag out the children, forcing them to join in the vandalism. Parents felt helpless, knowing that non-cooperation meant certain retribution. In some instances the youths, protesting substandard housing, would try to bar tenants from paying their rent. If the tenants disobeyed, their houses would be burned down. The anger and frustration that led to these extreme tactics was obvious and understandable, though not condoned by the majority of the black community. On the contrary, it filled them with terror. But to these young men it seemed their only way of fighting back. Necklacing, encircling a person's body with a tire, then setting fire to it, was also common at that time—a gruesome way to punish anyone suspected of collaborating with the white police.

It was a relief to leave the urban area and its problems behind and focus on the peaceful countryside. We could see the Stellenbosch mountains in the distance, and three more ranges close by, whose irregular contours were now familiar to me. The road continued south through Fals Bay and Sir Lowry's Pass, then hugged steep, rocky cliffs all the way to Hermanus, a sleepy resort snuggled among Norwegian pine, eucalyptus, and palm.

"Now you'll see a real farm gate," shouted Matilda, as we came to the end of a winding dirt road. She leapt from the car and ducked under a canopy of flowering bushes. The gate squeaked and groaned when she pulled on the heavy wooden crossbars that sealed the entrance to a barbed wire enclosure where sheep and ducks roamed free. I had never seen her so animated. She opened her arms wide and said with great drama, "Behold, fair maidens, my own private paradise."

On one side of the fence was a green pasture where neighbors kept their horse. On the other was a farmyard tended by an eccentric lady named Maven, who lived in a small shack and paid very little rent.

"She's terrible about making her payments, but I don't have the heart to evict her," explained Matilda. "She's such an individual. A communist who can't keep a job because she's always at war with the boss. And a capitalist farmer who champions the downtrodden. Don't you love it?"

A river ran deep into the tangled woods behind Matilda's modest little house. And far to the left, smack in the middle of a luscious flower garden, sat an old Cape Dutch manor house. Near the entrance to the property, in a one-room stucco dwelling, lived a colored family—Elizabeth, her husband, Carl, two children, and assorted cousins, nieces, and nephews. (It's hard for me to get used to the nomenclature "colored," because its meaning in the United States is so pejorative.)

Family members drift in and out," said Matilda, "They live cheek by jowl. And I say nothing." She shrugged. "They have nowhere else to go."

By the time we started unloading the car the sun was heading for the horizon. "Better hurry," she coaxed. "I have no electricity."

Matilda's house had been one large room and a chicken coop. She'd added a front porch, stuccoed the entire structure, painted it white, put in old windows—rectangular and crescent-shaped, which she'd collected from dismantled Cape Dutch homes—and installed an old-fashioned bathtub and toilet, transforming the chicken coop into a cozy dressing room and bath. A gas stove and a gas hot water heater completed the remodeling.

After supper we walked on the beach just beyond the woods. The rock formations had a fluid quality, shifting in the moonlight, beckoning us to follow. The steady crunch of the sand underfoot provided a counterpoint to the crashing waves, alive with myriad glowing creatures. A soft breeze bent the palms and soothed our bodies. Not another person was in sight. We had only the moon to guide us.

Jenny and I spent the evening lolling on mattresses on the floor while Matilda read by flashlight. Candles flickered on the nightstand. A scrawny black cat stood on hind legs and batted the fringe of the bureau scarf, casting jumpy shadows on the wall.

"Can you imagine a husband who would insist that you get a tummy tuck six months after giving birth?" Jenny said. I shook my head. "Well, that's my husband. I had a few stretch marks and my stomach was a little saggy. So what! I'd just had twins. He couldn't even wait six months to let me get back in shape, even though I was exercising like mad. He criticized me, constantly, until I felt ugly and misshapen. And the worst part is, I knuckled under. So instead of an ugly belly I have a great big ugly scar to show for my folly."

I thought of the terrible pressure a man puts on a woman. And then I stopped to realize that most women, if they're honest, put that same pressure on themselves. Otherwise, why all the plastic surgery, all the cosmetics, all the compulsive dieting, all the hysteria when each new decade rolls around? Is beauty—spelled y o u t h—all that makes us worthy?

And who is the real culprit? Men, society, economics, human nature? All of them? I guess it boils down to how much each one of us will allow popular mores and the media to influence who we are. Or who we think we *should* be. Meanwhile, very little of our attention is spent on accepting who we *really* are, and feeling good about it.

"My husband was quite the opposite," I said, reaching over and pulling the cat away from her perpetual playing. "Glen said, when he first met me, that I'd look beautiful pregnant, and he never once criticized my body. But then he started to use my looks *against* me...called me vain because I cared about my appearance. I now see it as control, but what did I know thirty years ago? He said I was the first pretty face he'd come upon with a brain attached. And I was supposed to be flattered? He then proceeded to belittle and bully that brain until there was very little self esteem that didn't revolve around the pretty face. It was a slow, almost imperceptible process, and, what makes me furious at myself is that I put up with it."

"Since my husband didn't seem to give a damn about my body *or* my brain, I started looking for someone who cared for the whole me. I was your age, Jenny, and should have had the sense to leave then. But remember, there were five children. And the prospect of being alone and 40-something....Maybe that's why I was so concerned about the first gray hairs. I said I didn't care, but I started dying my hair. Said it was just for fun. To be crazy. So why don't I stop it now?"

"And why don't I?" said Jenny.

We hugged goodnight and lay back on our mattresses. Matilda was snoring softly. The candles had sputtered out, leaving conical heaps of folded wax from which sweet-smelling wisps of smoke curled upward. I felt tired and perplexed, as I always do when I examine my inconsistencies. There was that inner voice, again: So you're not perfect. Just keep moving ahead, that's all you can do. And confront those tiresome old vanities.

Five A.M. Cock-a-doodle-do! I had *never* heard such a loud rooster. Then came an answer from another rooster…and another. By eight A.M. I wanted to strangle all three. They were hoarse, and I was exhausted.

A large man appeared at the door. "Dr. Engelbrecht, M'am," he said to Matilda, who quickly threw on a robe and stepped into the barnyard. "My two assistants are here. It'll take your help, too, if we're to get these sheep vaccinated."

As Jenny and I started for the beach, Matilda, three men, and Maven were engaged in the unceremonious corralling of a dozen recalcitrant sheep. A large turkey, standing faithfully by his mate while she sat on several large eggs, blinked vacantly, but never moved. The three roosters were perched haughtily on Maven's roof, nursing severe cases of laryngitis.

"If you wake me tomorrow, you're dead meat, you miserable creatures," I yelled, shaking my fist ominously.

"I'm sure they're scared witless," said Jenny laughing. "Now they'll really turn up the volume." She was right. They harassed me unmercifully the entire week. But, I observed with pleasure, each morning they were getting hoarser and hoarser.

"Today we make the journey to Barrydale with Hendrik," Matilda said when we returned from swimming. "School starts tomorrow, so this is his last free day."

Hendrik was a fifteen-year-old boy related to the family living in the stucco house near the front gate. Matilda had watched his development since he was a small boy. One of the reasons for this trip was to take him to visit his mother, who worked on a large farm near Barrydale. Hendrik was under the supervision of the government welfare service that had taken him away from his parents because he was starving and the father was abusive. Matilda spoke highly of the service and the way they kept tabs on the children. She was overjoyed to find out that Hendrik had been given a new foster home and would now have a chance for a decent life and a good education.

"You can't imagine how excited he is to see his family," Matilda said. "It's been over a year. Now you see why I couldn't let him down."

Hendrik appeared at 10 A.M. with Elizabeth and her four-year-old daughter, Carol. He was slight for his age and had the yellow-brown skin and high cheekbones of his Hottentot ancestors. Both children were quiet and well behaved. Not once did they ask for food or beg to stop.

Elizabeth, at thirty-three, was already stooped and careworn. "Carl gets drunk and beats her," Matilda had told us. "I warned him not to do it again or I'd have him thrown out. And I will. You see why I'm glad to get Hendrik out of there? He's seen enough abuse from his own father."

We drove alongside a turbulent mountain stream until we reached a wide plateau. Enormous Afrikaaner farms stretched out on both sides of the road and blue-gray mountains watched over us from a distance. We passed through the old Cape Dutch town of Swellendam and reached the Breede River, where newly blossoming thorn trees—like the ones I'd fallen in love with in Kenya—were heavy with fiery red and yellow flowers. This dazzling display of color followed us all the way to Tradouws Pass, 1,000 feet above sea level.

"Look around," said Matilda. "This is just like the *bushveld* of the Transvaal."

After the pass we were again in farmland. I was about to point out the largest farmhouse of all, an unusual old structure with decorative doors and windows unlike any I'd seen before, when Matilda turned into the long, circuitous entrance.

Hendrick was leaning forward, his hands clutching the seat, his face beaming. We passed the main farm complex and stopped at a group of one-story stucco houses, where the workers and their families lived. Hard-packed earth and matted tufts of grass surrounded the dwellings.

A tiny brown-skinned woman came forward. Hendrik rushed to her. I'd never seen such joy! Tears were running down Matilda's cheeks as she watched the tender reunion. I noticed that there was a lot of kissing on the mouth, and horseplay with siblings and friends, but very little hugging. I photographed several family groups at their request, and took close-ups of a variety of faces, some with the rounded foreheads, squinty eyes, full lips, and delicate bone structure so reminiscent of the proud bushman Laurens van der Post wrote about in The Lost World of the Kalahari. Thinking of these scattered descendants of the vanquished little people made me sad. Their systematic slaughter was one of the most brutal cases of genocide in recorded history.

Matilda chatted with the mistress of the farm about affairs of the family, then the three of us left for lunch. Elizabeth and Carol would remain with their relatives, but we would return for Hendrik at four o'clock.

We'd barely finished an elaborate Afrikaaner luncheon of meat and onion stew with custard tart when it was time to return for Hendrik. As we drove up the road his entire family, led by him, came running to greet us. They swarmed around the car, laughing and pointing. Hendrik beamed, obviously enjoying his position at center stage. His mother was carrying a large box of peaches on her head and stopped in front of Matilda, who had gotten out of the car to greet her.

"Here, Madam Professor, for you…from Hendrik and me." There was a hush as Matilda took the two small hands, and held them tightly in hers.

Back in the car once again, Hendrik pressed his face to the window, watching and smiling. The family waved and shouted until we were out of sight.

It was almost 7 P.M. when Matilda discovered that Hendrik hadn't eaten all day. He had arrived after the family's lunch and been given a peach. Jenny and I were aghast! I couldn't imagine any of my children sitting quietly without complaining. And I wouldn't have wanted them to. Matilda stopped and bought him a hamburger and some milk. She also tucked in a special treat for the first day of school. He was thrilled.

We dropped Hendrick in front of his new home. How handsome he looked. Close-cropped hair, wide cheekbones, captivating smile. The house was modest, surrounded by flowers and trees. He'd never been there before, but I saw no trace of fear. I picture him in my mind, still waving.

"Tomorrow they'll issue him a school uniform," said Matilda happily. "He'll get food and a decent place to live, and, most important, an education. Yes, he's one of the lucky ones."

I looked at Matilda as she drove down the road, red hair blowing, the hint of a smile on her round face. Practical, honest, strong, warm…and funny. Quite a list of virtues. She seemed to take care of everybody, without fuss or fanfare. She even let a colored woman and her daughter live downstairs in her spare room. A dangerous thing that was forbidden in her part of Cape Town.

"She works for me. Why should she commute five hours a day?"

"What if you get caught?" I had asked timidly.

"Somebody has to take a risk, or we'll never have change." That was all she had to say.

For the next week we played—explored caves, went for long walks on the beach, and battled with the surf. The chemistry among the three of us led to hilarious escapades. We tried to keep the conversation light, but it was impossible. This was South Africa.

◆   ◆   ◆

Two days before I left, Matilda dropped me in town to buy more notebooks and pens. By 6:20 my feet felt like hot coals. I ran all the way to the Bakoven Stop, arriving just in time to see the 6:30 bus for Camps Bay disappear up the wide, sloping boulevard.

The street was abandoned, except for three men horsing around in front of a liquor store. The proprietor, a slight, gray-haired black man, seeing me standing alone, offered to look up the bus schedule. "If you need any help, just come in the store and get me," he said reassuringly.

Just then a young fellow, who had been sitting in his Porche, sauntered across the street and stood next to me. "I'll stay with you until the bus comes," he whispered conspiratorially, "so you'll be safe."

"Thank you, but I'm perfectly safe," I said. He rolled his eyes.

"You must be an American. You're all so naive."

I soon discovered that he was a German farmer from Windhoek in Southwest Africa and had come to Cape Town to get his Porche repaired. We talked for half-an-hour and I listened as he told about the little bushmen and their "ways." When the conversation got around to life in South Africa, he lamented the presence of non-whites as polluting the racial purity of the region.

"You might say that it's we who spoiled *their* racial purity," I said. "And what do you suggest…that we ship them all over the border into Mozambique?"

"No, no," he answered. "We need the Blacks. Otherwise, who would clean the streets. That's all those dumb bastards are good for."

"You're full of *codswallop*," I said, surprised at my sudden boldness, and hoping the men, still standing in front of the store, hadn't heard him.

A look of utter contempt distorted his face. Without a word he turned on his heel and left.

The next evening Matilda threw a farewell party for me. Twenty friends wandered in and out. I could hardly bear the thought of leaving. I'd fallen in love with Camps Bay. It had everything I'd always wanted. The ocean on one side and the mountains on the other. I could see why my sister, Anne, loved South Africa so much. I really fed on its natural beauty.

Sleep that night was almost impossible. The rhythmic thunder of the waves, usually soothing to me, now made me sad. Had I upset Matilda with my pointed questions? Was I foolish to ignore the advice of her friends? They had begged me not to get in touch with ANC officials in Johannesburg and risk antagonizing the government. I was beginning to question my own judgment. And already I missed Matilda. Loneliness was creeping in. Stop it, I told myself. Your adventures are just beginning.

Cape Town was lovely in the morning, and the drive to the train station was especially poignant. At my request we stopped on the way so I could take a picture of Bishop Tutu's church. After clicking the shutter I turned to Matilda. "I wonder what will happen to this man and this tortured country before it's over."

Matilda sighed. "Meg, the situation is enormously complicated. There are no simple solutions."

Just as the train was pulling out Matilda rushed down the platform and thrust a newspaper through the window of my compartment. "Surprise," she shouted. "A little gift from home to speed you on your way. Bet you haven't read one in months." I looked down at The New York Times.

"Matilda," I shouted back. "You are a *most* extraordinary friend."

25

OUT OF AFRICA

How lucky I was—a luxurious two-person compartment all to myself. Through the wide expanse of window I watched the scenery change from thick vegetation to sagebrush and stubble. I could hardly contain my excitement. This was the legendary Trans Karoo Express, which would take me through the heart of South Africa in twenty-four hours, covering a thousand miles of sun and stone before reaching the plateau on which Johannesburg rests. We chugged along at forty miles an hour. But I didn't mind. It made me feel a part of the shifting landscape.

The afternoon heat was unbearable, and opening the window only made it worse—like entering a blast furnace. So everyone piled into the dining room, where the food was excellent and the air-conditioning heavenly. Teatime blended into suppertime. Nobody wanted to move.

"It's hard to believe that two hundred years ago this desolate looking land was the hunting ground of the bushmen and the summer pasture of herds of game—elephants, lions, wildebeest, the whole lot," said Elvira Hale, a silver-haired octogenarian with whom I was having tea.

"And look what's happened since those poor buggers were wiped out," added Reginald, her husband of fifty-five years. "It wasn't but ninety years ago that the British army rolled over the land and seized the gold fields of the Transvaal." He looked out the window and shook his head sadly. "Never forget, this was a hotly contested area during the Boer War. If you look carefully you can still see the remains of old army forts." He indicated several distant piles of rubble.

The Hales had invited me to join them for tea and scones. They'd made this trip many times, traveling from England to visit their daughter in Cape Town. Their understanding of the land and its people was prodigious, and I was a willing receptor for their knowledge and insight. Reginald, a retired civil servant living outside London, had spent every holiday abroad, trekking with his wife in the great mountain ranges of the world—in Russia, Norway, France, Austria, and

India. They were both thin and agile, belying their eighty years. But recently Elvira had broken her hip, causing a momentary halt to their adventures.

A whistle shrieked and the train lurched to a stop. Dust swirled. I could feel the heat radiating off the parched platform. It seemed like the middle of nowhere. As we started to leave, two small black children appeared and ran alongside the train. They held their hands in a praying position, moving them up and down rhythmically. I knew they were asking for money.

Elvira pressed Reginald's arm. "Hurry, give them something."

He pulled open the window as we were gathering speed and threw out a handful of bills. I watched, sadly, as the children scrambled for the money, like a swarm of minnows diving for bait.

After dinner we lingered over coffee. Whenever Elvira told about their travels together Reginald gazed at her adoringly. Age was never mentioned. Instead of looking back they focused on their next project—a trip to the Italian Alps or to Thailand—anywhere to get away from the damp English winters. I was filled with admiration for these two vital people.

Suddenly Elvira touched my hand. "Look out there," she said, motioning toward the window. "You've never seen a sunset until you've seen one in the Karoo. It's worth the whole trip. Doesn't it seem as if the sky and the color go on forever?"

We watched. The mountains, multi-layered, pyramidal, had turned light purple with patches of deep blue. They stood finely etched against a blazing sky. Soft full clouds hung above the spires, reflecting the changing hues. In front of the mountains stretched an ocean of sand with scattered rows of sage grass growing on the diagonal—wispy feathers cross-hatching the gently rippled surface of the earth—casting outsized shadows. Spindly telephone poles, looking small as matchsticks against the mountains, marched before them in a continuous line, like undernourished foot soldiers. Soon the afterglow faded into inky stillness, lit only by a half moon. All was silent, except for the clickety-clack of iron wheels.

Hours later I lay on my bed watching a sky overflowing with stars. The night air was cool. What a treat to sleep under blankets after having sweltered during most of the day.

Sunrise began at 5:30, the faintly tinted sky deepening into fiery tentacles before the sun broke out in blinding intensity, obliterating all color. We'd crossed the Hex Mountains and the scenery was once again luxuriant. Fields of corn and a mass of yellow flowers covered the land like a blanket of gold. Clumps of sunflowers waved their heavy heads, bending low in the wake of the passing train. In the distance were ugly slag heaps, the detritus of worn out mines.

Mine dancers, Johannesburg, South Africa.

The Hales had recommended the modest Victoria Hotel near the Johannesburg central station. I booked a large, high-ceilinged room with a view and a bath for $18. Upon my arrival I phoned Alan Paton's son, Jonathan. As a young woman living in Virginia in the 1950's, my eyes had been opened to the struggle in South Africa by Alan Paton's searing books. Dr. Manwe had assured me that his son, also involved in the anti-apartheid movement, would welcome my call. No answer. I tried, again. Busy. For the next two days the line was busy whenever I tried. This was a huge disappointment, but said to me that Jonathan Paton wanted to be left alone. The steam had gone out of my resolve to meet with ANC members. I had no other contacts in Johannesburg.

The desk clerk warned me not to walk around my hotel area alone, day or night, so I took a cab to the posh Carleton Center, where there were several streets of shops and restaurants on three levels, forming a series of modern malls. There I met Jenny.

Jo-burg, as it's called by many, is known as the city of gold. It has the energy of a New York or a Chicago. People come from all over the continent to gather in its coffee houses and cafés to talk about politics and the future, to invest, to gamble, to hide. Here I saw the faces of Mozambique, Angola, Nigeria, Malawi, and Zimbabwe. Excitement and change were in the air. For the next two days Jenny proved this to me. We visited the mines, enthralled by the mine dancers, their pantomimes and their biting, satirical skits. We enjoyed *avant-garde* theatre of the Sam Shephard and Athol Fugard variety at the Market Theatre, where four simultaneous productions were being presented. We roamed through Gold Reef City, a Disneyland-type tourist attraction on the outskirts. And we talked with several newspaper reporters who explored everything from AIDS to insurrection.

"If I really wanted to get the scoop I wouldn't read the newspaper," said Jon Lipscomb, the science editor for a leading Jo-burg paper. "I'd either turn on my short wave radio and get the news from abroad or call up one of my black friends in the township. That's how you find out what's happening and what's going to happen."

Jenny drove me to the airport on Sunday evening and the next morning I was in Cairo. Customs seemed more zealous than ever in rifling through my toiletries. And passport control wanted to bar my entry unless I cashed $150.00. But I'd learned my lesson. I purchased forty pounds and walked out. Try to stop me! The old "walk with authority" stance had finally worked.

Once again I was completely on my own and loved it. I even enjoyed bargaining with the cab driver. This time the ride to Dokki was only eight pounds and took half as long.

I'd forgotten how dirty and chaotic Cairo was. Children playing in pools of muddy water, donkeys defecating on the streets, garbage piled in the gutter, cars and trucks spewing forth clouds of exhaust. How different from the pristine streets of Cape Town.

"She's here, Hamal," shouted Judy, giving me an enormous hug. "She survived the wild animals and the Afrikaaners."

"Yeah," I said. "Only to be traumatized by the terrifying traffic of Cairo."

Tired as I was, I decided to get my ticket reconfirmed at the TWA office in the Hilton. The sky suddenly turned black as I was working my way down the side streets. What was this, a tornado? I tried, desperately, to get across a busy intersection before a blinding sand and rainstorm struck. But it was too late. The sky had opened up. Anything not tied down was blowing around. In the midst of all this, as I was leaning into the wind and attempting to reach the Hilton, a man came alongside me and asked, "Change dollars?" Good grief, at a time like this?

I was wearing my precious safari hat, red sweater, and faded jeans. All were dripping wet. Rain and sand were pelting the windows of the TWA office as I opened the door and fell inside.

"Oh, another Aussie come to see our fabulous pyramids?" said one of the clerks.

"I'm flattered," I said, "but, actually, I'm a Kenyan. Can't you tell by the hat?"

"Yes," said another clerk. "Straight out of Nairobi, New York. Right?" Laughter.

It was a congenial lot and I needed a little humor at that moment. By the time I'd concluded my business the rain had stopped, leaving large filthy pools of water clogging the streets. Traffic was at a standstill. When the lights changed and gridlock eased, each vehicle would push ahead as fast as it could, honking wildly. The only way to get through the mess was to walk in front of the slowest car and look directly at the driver, defying him to run you down. It was scary as hell!

A young man noticed my dilemma and offered to help me cross. I was glad to see him, even though it occurred to me that his sister probably owned a perfume factory that was going out of business. Nevertheless, at this point he was my savior. We started across. Halfway to the opposite curb we came upon a veritable river and reversed ourselves, but couldn't get back in time. So we turned left and, with the man pulling me by the hand, started running down the middle of the street. It was slippery and there was a phalanx of cars chasing us. Like the bulls of Pamploma. I didn't know where we were going, but we were leading the pack! It must have looked funny—a wall of cars chasing two frightened pedestrians. Keystone Cop material.

Just as I thought we'd be overrun, the man lifted me over a deep puddle and spun around to avoid an oncoming car, slipping as he did and plunging into a police booth. I went flying, landing spread eagle, after having slid on my stomach over a mountain of construction debris left lying in the street. I lowered my head, expecting a car to roll over me at any moment. My hands and knees were bleeding, my jeans were torn, and there was a gnawing pain in my right hip, reaching to my stomach. Please, God, no broken bones. Please.

I must have looked like the survivor of a bar room brawl. Mortally embarrassed, I picked up my drenched camera bag, smiled apologetically at my savior, who was attempting to recover his dignity, and inched my way back to the Wasims. I had assured the startled policeman, who came rushing out of his booth, that I would be O.K. I was only three blocks from my destination, and there were no more streets to cross.

"What the hell…." said Hamal when he opened the door. "What the hell happened to you?"

"Well, I was directing traffic down by the Hilton in the middle of a sand storm. And I had a little argument with this car." It wasn't funny, and neither of us laughed. "I'm glad you're a doctor," I said, suddenly feeling teary. "I have a few cuts that need attending."

There was a wicked abrasion on my abdomen. I wanted to scream when Hamal cleaned and dressed it, adding sterile gauze and quantities of adhesive. My hip was badly bruised, but this would pass in no time I told myself.

"I think you'd better stick around for a few days," said Hamal. "Doctor's orders. That's a nasty scrape. You're lucky it didn't puncture the skin. Even so, you *do* have to keep it clean."

"There's only one plane out this week, and that's day after tomorrow," I said. "I'm all set to go, and I *must*. Just give me some antiseptic and bandages and I'll be fine."

"Sure, in India, the sanitary capitol of the world," he said cynically. "I don't advise it."

"I know, but that's how it has to be. I'm way behind schedule." There was no dissuading me.

I slept well for the next two nights and used up all my mosquito coils, despite the relatively cool weather. Although a little stiff, I was overjoyed to be ambulatory, and spent a lot of time roaming through the streets and bazaars of old Cairo. One afternoon I arrived home to find the doors locked. I sat down on the curb to wait, tucked my voluminous black skirt between my legs, and watched four boys playing a rousing game of soccer in the street, skillfully avoiding parked cars, pools of water, and a variety of moving vehicles that came and went.

As I was sitting there a man came from across the street and asked me, in broken English, if I wanted a chair. I declined, but he brought me one, anyway. Then he tried to get me to come to his house. He said he was Hamal's friend and it was "unsuitable" for me to sit on the curb like that. How considerate. I thanked him and stood up to follow just as the Wasims returned.

"I just had a lesson in Egyptian manners," I whispered to Judy, telling her what had happened. "I hope I didn't disgrace you in front of the neighbors."

"Meg, I've been raising eyebrows for twenty years. You have to be dead not to!"

Flight 800 to Bombay was a Lockheed 1011 with only nine passengers. Before being allowed to board I was asked by three different agents to "Let me check your *bawdy*." I had to bite my tongue to remain respectful. But I'd learned never to laugh at security guards, especially the ones with the carbines. They took my bags apart. What would they have done had they discovered my bandages? Rip them off to see if I was concealing a knife?

I looked out the plane window at the shifting desert, pale magenta all the way to the tip of the Red Sea. The sun had begun to set and down below it seemed as if a thousand tiny volcanoes had sprung out of the rippling sand to capture the last rays of light and hold them till morning.

I stretched out across the wide seats and plotted my return to Africa, and all the places that had escaped me—the Serengeti, Mt. Kilimanjaro, Mt. Kenya, Malawi, Botswana, the Gold Coast. And I thought of Karnach, Lamu, Mt. Moses, the Masai Mara, Victoria Falls, and South Africa, places that were already a part of me. I had seen a lot and I had learned a lot. That there are no quick fixes, no easy answers. That preconceptions are often misconceptions. That we're all just people—those struggling to understand and those struggling to survive. And we can't ignore or escape the struggle, no matter where we live.

I fell into a deep sleep. At 1:30 A.M. the thud of the landing gear awakened me. Spread out in every direction, like an earthbound Milky Way, were the lights of Bombay.

26

BOMBAY BLITZ

A cardinal rule when traveling in India: Make your hotel reservations at a reputable tourist office in the airport. Don't try to economize by accepting unseen lodgings, especially in the middle of the night. And refuse all "free" rides, because they aren't really free. There's *always* a catch.

I was exhausted when I finally cleared customs and secured a reservation for the moderately priced Hotel Apollo in Bombay. As I was waiting outside for a cab, a young man approached me.

"Madam," he said, bowing deeply. "Let me introduce myself. I am Niranjan, and I offer you a free limousine ride to the Hotel Metro International where a new, modern room awaits you for only $15.00. And it is twenty minutes from Bombay. The savings in cab fare alone will be $10.00." He handed me a fancy, engraved card.

How could I resist?

When a 1930's "limo" rolled to a stop in front of me I should have declined and gone back to my original plan. But I was too tired. Fifteen minutes later we pulled up in front of the hotel, a remnant of urban renewal perched in the middle of a wasteland—an industrial area that might someday be rebuilt.

There was no window in my "modern" room, no hot water, and a useless, clanking air conditioner suspended from the ceiling. It was 4 A.M. before I could sleep. Two hours later the sound of jackhammers awakened me. My appraisal of the location had been on target.

"Please, Madam, you *must* stay for breakfast," said the desk clerk when I asked for my bill. "We have real filter coffee, which is served on the elegant roof garden." He rolled his r's and bowed in such an enticing manner that I headed for the roof.

Indoor-outdoor carpeting and a phony pagoda were not my idea of elegance, but the panorama gave me a poignant introduction to India. I leaned on the stone railing and looked across the barren field. Several men were digging in an unfinished roadbed. A dozen young women, barefoot and dressed in delicate *saris*, were lined up, each holding a shallow pan. They filled the pan with pieces of broken rock and pavement, placed it on their head and carried it up and over a mound of debris, emptying it on the other side. They marched with slow dignity, like a row of monks on a sacred pilgrimage, repeating the task over and over, never breaking the rhythm of their movements or the shape of their elliptical path. The new pile being made was only eight yards from where they'd begun. I wondered if the next day they would move that pile a little farther, going through the same repetitive motions. To me, a western woman, this defined drudgery. But I soon learned that this was called labor intensive—the hallmark of the Indian economy. It seemed more like a euphemism for inefficiency. No, I was told. It's better to give people work than displace them with a more efficient machine. At least they can earn enough to buy food. I kept quiet. I was here to observe, not judge.

My breakfast finally arrived. Weak instant coffee, canned orange juice, and an ossified omelet on limp white bread.

The drive to Bombay took one hour, not the twenty minutes promised by Niranjan. But that was fine because it gave me a chance to see the countryside in daylight. I noticed dozens of three-wheeled, open-air cabs, which looked like motorized rickshaws or modified beach surreys. They had a curved black leather top that arched over the passengers, who sat behind the driver. The fancy ones had rumble seats. These were strictly local cabs, not allowed in Bombay.

The wide road leading to the city was lined with shacks made of tin and tarpaper. Some were scant lean-tos with cloth or cardboard thrown over wooden poles—a makeshift cover under which whole families squatted in the dirt. Children played perilously close to the highway, where cars careened through traffic, belching black exhaust. Sanitary facilities were non-existent. It was worse than anything I'd seen in the squalid townships of South Africa.

Behind these temporary shelters, incongruous billboards loomed. The most popular pictured a huge TV screen proclaiming:

TALL, DARK, HANDSOME AND NO.1: BUSH T.V.

We drove in and out of side streets looking for the Hotel Apollo. Each time we stopped at a light the driver turned off the motor to save gas. This signaled the beggars to move into action. They'd even stick their hands into the open windows. One woman, a baby clinging to her neck, grabbed my arm. I begged the driver to send her away. He ignored me. She opened the door as if to get in. I moved to the other side of the cab. She ran around to meet me. I was starting to panic when the light changed and the driver sped away, almost hitting her. This filled me with pity...and guilt. Get hold of yourself, Meg. You can't help everyone. But I was deeply disturbed by my irritation.

It was suffocatingly hot by the time we found the Apollo, stuffed between a restaurant and an alley in a nondescript, rundown neighborhood. The driver stuck out his hand. "Five dollar, please." Those had been his only words for the last hour.

I gave him the equivalent in rupees, and he glowered.

"Sorry, no more dollars," I said, and hurried into the hotel. I hadn't known how cheap cab fares were in Bombay. You could go almost anywhere for sixty cents. Again, I thought of Niranjan, who had touted the splendid savings I would enjoy by using his free "limousine." He had certainly taken *me* for a ride!

My basement room was dreary. It had no ventilation and when you turned on one faint light bulb the other went out—like cheap Paris hotels in the 1950's. But at least it was away from the noise and the crowds. I lay down on the narrow cot and tried to sleep, but the scrape on my stomach had begun to throb. I'd forgotten to change the bandage and had very few sterile pads left. I dragged myself off the bed. Better get to a pharmacy right away.

I walked through town. No pharmacy. There was a plethora of fruit stands and small stalls nestled under archways or next to the curb. Some were covered with tin roofs and some with volumes of material that billowed in the breeze. Eager merchants sold *chapatties* (a pancake-like unleavened bread baked on a griddle), sugar cane juice, fried potatoes, curry, an assortment of leaves for "turning on," and exotic, spicy foods. What a wonderful combination of smells!

But still no pharmacy.

I reached the river, and before me stood the luminous Taj Mahal Hotel, a white square building with an ornate facade imitative of its namesake. I walked in on the pretense of looking up my old friend, Richie Berek, who stayed at the hotel when traveling in India. No Richie, of course, but I was in. Swanky Third World hotels are very fussy about letting the "rabble" enter. I guess my all-black outfit gave me a certain air of authority. I had "passed" for the moment.

My next stop was the Ladies' Room. To my surprise, spread out in front of me on the marble counter was a basket full of sterile bandages, adhesive, and packets of antiseptic. I wanted to shout for joy. Thank you, God. Thank you, Richie.

For the next three days I returned to the hotel each afternoon, dressed my wound, stocked up on toilet paper and pharmaceuticals, and lounged by the pool, which was surrounded by marble columns, giving it the look of a Roman bath. I watched wealthy tourists sunbathing as they sipped their drinks in the blazing sun at the edge of the pool. And I wrote in my journal, read, or snoozed in one of the high-backed wicker chairs secreted in well-lit alcoves on the portico. Each day the doorman greeted me and mumbled a suitable pleasantry. He must have figured I belonged to the casual rich, dressed as I was in the same drab outfit.

I was readily accepted by several patrons, one of whom asked me to join him for tea. He seemed much more interested in telling me how wonderful he was than in hearing about my travels, so I sat quietly and enjoyed the tea and cakes.

"You *will* come for a swim," he said, finally, "and, by the way, tell me your room number."

This made me a little nervous. He was a *Sikh*—I could tell by the turban and beard—and I did not like his dictatorial, demanding attitude. In the past three days I'd been rudely jostled by many such men, large and small, who saw no reason why women should enter a bus or a building first. Neither did I, but it was disconcerting to be forcefully pushed aside by the mighty man in a mini-struggle for power at every entrance. They wanted women on their terms and in their place. Manners were not part of the deal.

I grabbed the remaining cakes and excused myself, saying that I had to leave for Pune the next afternoon and needed to buy my railroad ticket. I didn't know this would take the rest of the day. But I had no intention of spending it with him.

Carmela, my travel agent, has done me many favors, one of which was to insist that I buy a green Indrail pass for two weeks of travel in India. Even if I bought only a few tickets it would speed up the reservation process and give me a tourist's advantage. I stood in the crowded waiting room of the cavernous Bombay railroad station and watched the long lines, the harried clerks, and the frantic tourists. One in particular caught my eye. He had come to the head of a line, talked to the agent—with no apparent success—thrown up his hands in disgust, and was rushing toward the door. Maybe he could tell me what not to do.

I grabbed him on the way out. "Excuse me…what's the problem?" I asked.

"I've been here off and on for the past two days and I still don't have my ticket to Kashmir. It's one run-around after the other," he said. "A bloody nightmare, that's wot."

His name was Andy Reynolds—young, blond, very British, and obviously non-aggressive. He had been an accountant in Cornwall, but became fed up with his work and decided to tour Asia.

"About now I'd give anything for the British railway system," he lamented.

I persuaded him to try again.

Buying a train ticket in India is like taking the census. You have to fill out a long form for every trip, including the dates coming and going, your age, your passport or local identification number, and your home address, Bombay address, and nearest relative in case of accident. I put down Chris's Jersey City phone number, wondering if they'd call him in the event of a train wreck.

But it doesn't stop there. Once you've filled out the initial form you have to stand in line to show it to another official. My Indrail pass put me in the short line, but I still had three more lines to negotiate before reaching the man who was to take me to the supervisor.

My experience with the airlines in Egypt and Tanzania had prepared me well for this.

"Just a minute," I said, sternly, as I reached the head of the third line. "I will *not* stand in another line. Take me to your supervisor or write the ticket yourself." Our eyes met. I wasn't going to budge and he knew it. "And by the way," I added, "this man has something to say to you." I motioned to Andy, who turned scarlet. "Go ahead, Andy. Don't you have a question?"

Half-an-hour later we walked out, jubilant, with two tickets. "How can a simple purchase like this make you feel as if you've just climbed Mt. Everest?" I asked.

"I'm sure Everest is easier," he answered wryly.

We walked around, enjoying the hubbub of early evening. Andy stopped at a fruit stand and bought some bananas. I'd never liked bananas, but perhaps I could make an exception. They were cheap, filling, and safe. Most of the foods sold on the street looked dubious, and I was getting tired of tandoori chicken and *chapatties*, the only restaurant food mild enough for my palate.

"I'll give it a try," I said. "I like to live on the edge." The bananas were smaller and sweeter than ours. And rather good. After that I ate them regularly while in India.

The city was energetic, kaleidoscopic. Large billboards screamed from the sides of buildings and decaying fences. Triangular flags, strung high above the streets, fluttered in honor of one celebration or another. Grizzled old men in dirty turbans and voluminous *dhotis*—those draped loincloths that are the male equivalent of *saris*—lay on pallets beside the road, tending their cubicles of dusty merchandise. Artists sat in front of their easels, hardly noticing the hurrying people who jammed the sidewalks. Skinny men pulled wagons loaded down with blocks of ice and mounds of wheat.

We covered several city blocks, walking on ancient pavement made of smooth stones, shiny and worn, and maneuvering through a maze of hucksters and beggars. Emaciated men and women sat or lay at intervals on the pavement. It was difficult not to stumble over them, and impossible to ignore them. My anger and frustration at their situation mounted, but all I managed to say was, "What'll I do with my banana peel, Andy? There's not a trash can in sight."

"Find the biggest pile of garbage and throw it on," he answered. "It's biodegradable, isn't it? And stop fretting. The first time's always the hardest."

Just before we arrived at the Apollo we spotted a young woman sitting on the dirty pavement. Two pretty little girls were playing in the gutter next to her. Their toys were bottle caps and extraneous debris. A man held the woman by her long tangled hair and was trying to get her to sit up straight. He jerked her roughly.

Andy turned to me. "She's on drugs, you know. She doesn't even notice the children, and they don't seem to notice her."

I recalled my visit to Haight-Ashbury during the late 60's, and my horror at seeing the neglected, soiled tots of Flower Children playing in the street next to their stupefied mothers.

I said goodbye to Andy and walked on past the Apollo. The moon was up by the time I reached the sea. The wide walkway adjoining the retaining wall was almost empty, except for one thin little boy, who stood naked and alone. He looked all around, but nobody paid any attention. I wanted to take his hand, but as soon as I went toward him he turned and ran into the shadows.

The next afternoon, on my way to the station to catch the 5:10 Deccan Express, I caught sight of a dark-skinned little girl in rags, perhaps eight years old. She was standing at a bus stop with a miniature wirehaired terrier, hitting his legs with a stick to make him perform. First, she shook his paw, then she hit his legs and he mounted a large can. Then a smaller can on top of that one. And so on, until, after several switchings, he hopped up, whimpering, and stood on his hind legs on the tiniest can at the top, while the little girl stood next to him and delivered a piercing chant. The crowd clapped and threw coins. She smiled and bowed. I was intrigued by her ingenuity, appalled by her cruelty.

My destination was Pune, a bustling city three hours from Bombay in the famed Rajasthan district. I was going to visit the family of Madhura Chako, an Indian friend from my exercise class.

To my surprise, the train, a first class commuter express, had the unmistakable smell of urine. I felt as if I were sitting in a New York City phone booth, although the seats, a kind of old-fashioned rattan mesh, were far more comfortable. I couldn't wait to get going so there would be a breeze. Happily, I counted twenty-six ceiling fans, which helped a great deal in clearing the air.

A handwritten list of all the passengers was posted in each car. Since reservations are needed for every journey, this must keep many people very busy. Labor intensive. Indeed.

The train left the yard and made its way through the suburban areas past scores of people sleeping under bridges and on the grass. Neat little gardens and small shacks with roofs of straw dotted the landscape. Soon, larger cement houses, surrounded by tall trees, appeared. Thick walls and gates with elaborate see-through designs protected each house. In the distance, high mountains were faint outlines in the afternoon haze.

The countryside became brown and terraced with an occasional stream running through it. Children played with Brahman bulls sporting fearsome horns. How dark these children looked as they scampered through the fields. Already I had seen many different faces in India, and skin color ranging from light, to brown, to gray, to ebony. But no matter how the people varied in height and age, they were almost all thin. I longed to photograph them. But when I tried, even with my telephoto lens, I was invariably noticed, and there was visible displeasure.

As we moved westward the terrain turned wild, with tangled brush, clay-red soil, and rugged mountains. Poinsettia bushes—abundant splashes of crimson—dominated the undergrowth. The train continued to climb until we were on a high wooden trestle with a deep gulch on either side. At sunset I watched the trestle snaking ahead, its cross-hatching charcoal against the apricot sky. Then the moon came up, and for one brief moment I was back in Austria with Glen, listening to the click of the wheels as we lay in our compartment looking at the moon above the Alps. The memory was unsettling. I was glad when the train slowed and the sign for Pune came into view.

This was my first experience in a semi-rural Indian railroad station and I was excited. The station wasn't as picturesque as some I saw later on, where cows and sleeping bodies covered the platform at 5 A.M. and boiling tea was served from huge metal caldrons. But there was plenty of atmosphere in the mammoth turn-of-the-century structure, including two long-haired pigs who refused to leave the tracks, thus holding up the departing train for an indefinite period of time.

Elderly men were sitting cross-legged on the floor by the entrance, peering at me strangely, their bony legs protruding from the multiple folds of their short, draped garments.

I was wearing white slacks and a new V-neck T-shirt purchased in South Africa. Sick of looking drab in my black traveling outfit, I had picked a shirt of shocking fuchsia. The color, I found out later, was also worn by the *Rajneesh*, a cult reputed to endorse free sex and unorthodox communal living. It had been formed in Pune and had now moved to the west coast of the United States. Most people in town were very upset about the group. Perhaps the color of my shirt was the reason for the old men's stares.

The stationmaster was still trying to prod the pigs off the tracks when a diminutive man walked up to me. He was dressed in a shiny black suit and wore a tall, old-fashioned top hat.

"Hello, Madam. I am a bachelor, and I have just returned from Nigeria," he announced, tipping his hat and bowing gallantly. "Let us go somewhere to talk."

His grin was a bit too broad and his eyes focused, disconcertingly, over my shoulder. A narrow moustache, combined with the black outfit, gave him a distinctly sinister look. Ordinarily I'd have ignored such a bold pronouncement, but I was eager to talk with anyone who might have firsthand information on Nigeria. The French family I'd met on safari in Kenya had told me about some outbreaks of cannibalism while they were there and I wanted to check it out.

"Great," I bubbled, "I've just come from Africa, myself, and I have some questions I'd like to ask you."

"Then we must go where we can talk alone," he said with exaggerated formality. He led me to a bench in a secluded section of the platform.

I started by asking if cannibalism was still practiced in parts of Nigeria, but he evaded my question. He was more interested in asking his own. "Have you had any happiness since you arrived in India?" he said.

"Well, for a Westerner it's somewhat depressing—the poverty, the beggars, and the sickness everywhere—but I've visited some beautiful temples, and talked with many interesting...."

He interrupted me. "No, Madam. I am talking about pleasure—the kind you can experience only in India."

I began to feel uneasy.

"Would you like to know what *real* pleasure is?" he continued, not waiting for a reply. "I can introduce you to things you would never read about in travel books. I can lift you to heights of sublime physical and spiritual perfection. Oh, lovely madam, come with me and I will show you."

The little man sat hunched over, holding his hands in a prayer-like position, nervously locking and unlocking his fingers, and speaking with a rapidity I found difficult to follow.

"You're very poetic," I said, "and I appreciate your hospitality, but my friends are coming to pick me up any minute." I kept returning to the subject of Nigeria, but received no answers. I finally stood up to leave, convinced that this man had never set foot in Africa.

As we were returning to the waiting room he stepped up his descriptions of pleasure Indian-style, becoming more graphic until, finally, the real nature of his interest dawned on me. How could I have been so naive? Once, again, I'd been taken for a ride. Not wanting to cause an international incident, I told him to get lost in as few words as possible. Then, feeling like a fool, I stood under the arch at the entrance, enduring the nods of the old men, and wishing my friends would hurry up and arrive.

Suddenly, like a scared mouse darting out from under a chair, the eager bachelor appeared once more in front of me. The top of his head was level with my chest. He had removed his hat, revealing long strands of black hair bisecting his scalp. The grin was still pasted on his angular face. In a voice much louder than a whisper he blurted out, "Madam, your tits are so sweet. Do you know that I like them?"

"You miserable creep!" I screamed. "Get out of my sight!"

Several old men jolted awake while the others just turned their heads wearily. I grabbed my backpack and rushed to the curb just as my friends drove up in their new Ambassador.

"Meg, are you all right?" asked my host as he lifted my pack into the trunk of his car. "You look so flushed. Sorry you had to wait so long. It's awfully warm in India this time of year."

The nasty little man scampered back into the station. Yes, I thought. Very warm.

27

PUNE

"I think it must have been the color of your blouse," said my host, Sham Kirloskar, after I related my unpleasant encounter with the little man. "He probably thought you were one of…you know, the *Rajneesh*. I'm truly sorry you were treated in that manner."

Sham was broad-shouldered, over six feet tall, and light-skinned. He spoke in a gentle soothing manner. His wife, Sheila, had a delicate build, which was draped exquisitely in a silk *sari*. She looked at me through wide expressive eyes. Her black hair had been smoothed back and knotted at the nape of her neck. No wonder Madhura was so pretty.

Suddhir, their twenty-five-year-old son, was as imposing in stature as his father. Dark hair. Luxuriant moustache. Easy charm.

"The family is going to a classical concert," Sham announced. "Several cousins are waiting for us at the hall." He turned to me. "I understand you are a musician." I nodded, eager to hear classical music after all these weeks.

We piled into the small white sedan and headed for Pune University. I'd never ridden in an Indian car before. It looked like vintage 1930's with its rounded hood and bulbous trunk. But it was the classiest car on the road. Not at all like the flimsy-looking Fiats and Japanese Mutaris.

I had visions of the familiar melodies of Beethoven and Mozart as we made our way through the gates of the sprawling university. Instead, we walked into the middle of an Indian opera, with all the characters sitting on the floor of the stage, playing instruments I hardly knew, and singing in ways that were definitely not *bel canto*. The voices had a howling, nasal quality. I stood, transfixed. Sheila placed her hand on my arm. "This must sound strange to you," she said. "I'll explain it later."

She was right. This was an art form that required a lot of getting used to—for a Westerner. I reached into my bag and activated the tape recorder. I didn't want to miss a note.

It was 10 P.M. when we left. Traffic still clogged the streets. Does India never sleep? Of the one million inhabitants of Pune, it seemed that half of them were out on the town. At every stoplight a phalanx of bicycles and bicycle rickshaws competed for space with smoke-spewing taxis and trucks. Lining the road leading out of town were the now familiar shelters made of rough cloth draped over skinny poles. Families squatted in the dirt before open fires, which flickered intermittently, puncturing the darkness. Soon houses began to appear, many of them decorated with a single string of colored lights. I watched the changing panorama from inside the comfortable car. Surrounded by friendly, prosperous people.

The Kirloskar home was large, with a spacious front veranda and an elaborate garden of flowering bushes and palms. I shared a large bedroom with Kashmi Karode, Sheila's sixteen-year-old niece, a student of religion at Pune University. A small shrine stood on a table in one corner of the room. As soon as I expressed interest in this symbol of her religion she took it upon herself to interpret Hinduism to me. Snuggled under our individual canopies of mosquito netting, we talked in hushed tones late into the night, sharing stories like teenagers at a slumber party. Despite her sober religious ponderings Kashmi exuded the enthusiasm of any young student as she described college life in India. It sounded much like college life anywhere in the world.

When I awoke Kashmi was sitting on her bed, reading a book of Indian poetry. She was eager to return to our conversation of the previous evening. Convinced of my genuine interest, she read aloud—with the intensity of youth—the translation of an ancient poem.

> The singer only sang the Joy of Life,
> For all too well, alas! the singer knew
> How hard the daily toil, how keen the strife,
> How salt the falling tear; the joys how few.

> Oh, roseate lips he would have loved to kiss,
> Oh, eager lovers that he never knew!
> What should you know of him, or words of his?—
> But all the songs he sang were sung for you!

"Oh, Kashmi, what a wonderful way to greet the morning!"

We talked of love as we took down the four poles holding up the netting and put them away, along with the blanket and top sheet, which were artfully folded together in a smooth triangle. When evening arrived they would be placed at the bottom of the bed, ready to be pulled up if needed. In no time the bedroom had been transformed into a sitting room, ready for the day.

Breakfast was cream of wheat, coconut, fresh peas with spices, and *dosa,* a southern Indian dish made with potatoes. Grandmother had carefully sorted the cereal grain and cooked it into a thick pudding. There was also regular toast with homemade butter, not at all like the Indian *ghee* served at the previous night's dinner.

Right after breakfast two little boys appeared at the back door. "Ah, here are my helpers," said Sheila. "I give them work chopping and cutting. Their families need the money and I can use help with the chores. It's only for a few hours each day." She patted each one on the head lovingly.

The boys greeted me, pressing their hands together in a praying position and bowing ever so slightly. I saw variations of this "hello" all over India and Nepal. They regarded me curiously, smiling and moving their heads rhythmically from side to side as if their necks were on an invisible spring. Later on I noticed Sheila making this same gentle movement as she talked with me. It was a gesture of friendliness and of agreement, not nervousness as I had first thought.

I hovered around the kitchen, fascinated by the preparations. Meal planning looked like a formidable task with complicated menus. This brought back the biggest nightmare of my years of childrearing—deciding what to cook and how to make each meal interesting as well as nutritious.

"Sheila, you're amazing," I said as I watched her supervise the cutting up of herbs from the garden. "How do you decide what to have each day?"

She smiled at me. "Each morning I wake up and ask myself what kind of day it will be. Before I start cooking, the taste I want has to come to my mind—the spices, the particular flavors. Once I decide on a theme I plan everything around it."

Dinner was at ten. Thank heaven for afternoon tea! This was even more continental than the Continent. After Sheila had made all the preparations, a thin, dark man arrived to complete the cooking, make the bread, and serve the meal. He had been trained by Sheila. During the day he worked as a rickshaw driver.

"He needs the money," she said, "because he has three daughters and an infant son. He wouldn't stop having children until he got that boy. That's essential for most Indian men."

There were two homemade breads—one thick and one thin—cooked on a dry iron skillet, various vegetarian dishes with mild spices, rice, cowpeas in saffron, and fresh greens from Sheila's garden. All of this was served with heaping quantities of yogurt, which resided in bowls around the table. Dessert was a sweet, very hard round ball filled with exotic nuts.

Sham looked at me as we sat down. "If you wish a fork you may have one," he said.

"Well," I said, hesitatingly, "how will *you* eat?"

"With my fingers, of course." He grinned mischievously.

"Then so will I."

Now I knew why there was a small sink in the alcove outside the dining room. Forks, spoons, and knives were used for serving, not eating. I marveled at the skillful use of fingers to negotiate even the most difficult of combinations—rice and yoghurt. And I was glad for the large napkin ready to cover up my mistakes.

It had finally turned cool—a blessed relief from the scorching day—and we all moved to the parlor for an evening of talking and music. Grandfather played the organ, a beloved hand-carved instrument that he pumped by foot, and Sheila sang. It made me think of the Sunday nights of my childhood spent glued to the radio, or playing piano trios with my sisters, or listening to my father ham it up on the piano. That was our special time together. Sometimes Mother read O. Henry stories, or recited poetry, or acted out a monologue. In the summer months, when Grandpa and Grandma lived with us at our cottage in New Hampshire, there would be hymn singing at dusk as we sat on the high, wrap-around porch underneath the pines. "Now The Day Is Over." "Day Is Dying In The West." How many times I had watched, solemnly, as the mystery of the dying day repeated itself and the sun disappeared behind the islands, sinking deep into the lake. Or so it seemed to a six-year-old.

Being the honored guest all evening had been exhausting, and in my eagerness to get to bed, I made the mistake of walking too near the bedroom shrine with my shoes on. Kashmi admonished me gently and began another lesson in Hindu customs.

Sheila came to say goodnight. Barefooted, she walked to the shrine and lit two small candles. Next to them were two framed photographs and brass images of several Hindu gods.

"These are pictures of my parents," she said. "The shrine is out of respect for their memory. I loved them very much." She knelt silently and bowed her head. "When I light the candles, they are with me, again." She rose, touched her cheek to mine, and was gone.

The wound on my stomach had flared up and looked worse than ever. Kashmi walked into the bathroom as I was cleaning it.

"Oh, what happened, Meg? That's awful. We must get you some sterile bandages," she said.

"That's not easy, I've discovered." I didn't want to elaborate. I'm sure my daily trips to the Taj Mahal Hotel in Bombay would have shocked her.

"I will speak to my aunt. She will find something."

"Please, Kashmi. Not now. It's late. It'll be fine."

The next morning there was no time to deal with my infection. We were all concentrating on getting dressed for the wedding of a close family friend. Since the women were wearing *saris*, I insisted on trying to make the broad swath of silk adhere to my body. But it was impossible. You not only had to be skilled in draping the slippery material, but you had to know how to carry your body so the garment wouldn't unfold. Even Sheila gave up on me. All I had to do was take a couple of steps and everything came apart. I didn't want to unwrap, suddenly, in the middle of dinner.

"Your black outfit is fine," she assured me. "Don't you mind at all. *Saris* take a lot of practice." I appreciated her generous words and returned, full of regret, to my drab trappings.

The Kirloskar family spoke three languages fluently. English, Hindi, and Marathi. I was impressed as I listened to them move effortlessly from one to the other, greeting old friends and guests at the large hall where the wedding took place. The walls were washed with bright colors and hung with reproductions of Hindu gods in their human form. The art was bland, faded. Primitive without being exciting. And whose photograph was that staring out at me from a place of prominence? *Hari Krishna*—the man whose movement had begun in Pune.

The bride and groom met us at the door. They seemed much older than their twenty-one years. Cool, sophisticated, poised. What a contrast to my wedding day, characterized by unbridled excitement, confusion, tears, kisses. But perhaps these modern young people had a more realistic view of marriage than I did.

The ceremony was a shortened version of the usual three-hour Hindu wedding—more like a civil affair with a nod to the gods. I was disappointed. I'd been looking forward to music, dancing, and nonstop festivities. Instead, flowered garlands were placed over the heads of the bride and groom as they went through some simple rituals. The mournful singing of a man and a woman, accompanied by a sitar, continued throughout the half-hour ceremony. Then, after a bit of marching around and a few words in Hindi, it was over.

Kashmi, who had been my interpreter, escorted me to the lavish buffet. It was a relief to use a fork. I could eat so much more. The names of the foods all blended together, but Sheila did her best to acquaint me with them. "The philosophy is that you combine foods," she said. "For example, you put dry breads with sauces. The tandoori chicken is dry, so you combine it with rice and yogurt or curried vegetables. And here is southern Indian cuisine. It uses more rice because they grow it. And this is northern. It uses more wheat." She moved deftly down the line, explaining each food in turn.

I sampled every pea and bean dish in sight, scooping small portions into separate pewter bowls. *Chapatties* of all sizes were stuffed with exotic-tasting cheeses and vegetables. And for dessert they contained *pulse* and raw sugar.

That night I went to bed joyous and content. But the dreams that sprang from my subconscious told another story. Glen was visiting my family in New Hampshire. He was young. The cottage, once cozy and inviting, was now falling apart. The fireplace had crumbled. The dock was under water. My father was near death, and there was nobody to care for him. Nobody even noticed him. It made me so sad. Glen wandered in and out of the background. I watched as he grew older, then finally disappeared, leaving me all alone with my dying father.

I awoke in a panic, fighting to make the transition from the New Hampshire woods to a steamy room in Pune, India. Kashmi greeted me cheerily and asked how my infection was. I closed my eyes in an attempt to sort out my feelings. The dream was the death of the old. And the sadness of parting. Let go, it was saying to me. Move ahead. Tend to the present and forget what's past, what's dead. A great heaviness lifted. Energy and optimism returned.

"I'm ready to take on the world," I said to Kashmi. "But first I'm going to brush my teeth." She clasped her hands gleefully.

This had been my most luxurious experience in India and how lucky I felt. Until now, I had had a tourist's view of the country—a view that held only questions, no answers. Here was a chance to see another side of the society, to appreciate the magnitude of the problems being faced, and to taste the life of the privileged—a life that was not without conscience.

Sham Kirloskar managed a large factory employing 3,500 workers. It had been started by his grandfather as a small smelting business and now was making diesel engines in plants all over India. This was a man who worked along with his men. He was acutely aware of the problems of a young democracy and the shocking inequities all around him.

"We have to be labor intensive, Meg," he said, when I talked about the inefficient bureaucracy I'd encountered. "We have too many people and too few jobs. Some day this may not be so, but we are dealing with the moment, and that is how it is."

That afternoon Sudhir was elected to drive me to the station to buy my return ticket to Bombay. I didn't realize that "drive" meant a ride on the back of his motorcycle. It was a replica of the one-lunger Glen and I had bought on our honeymoon for fifty dollars in front of the Paris American Express...from a Yale student, who is probably still laughing. It was so gutless that I had to walk up every hill in northern France. These flimsy machines scare me now as they did back in the 50's when I had youth on my side.

"Why can't I buy my ticket when I get to the train?" I asked, not wanting to brave the highway without a car roof over my head.

"No, no," he replied. "Everything in India is done ahead of time. If you wait until the last minute, you'll have to pay *baksheesh*...that's a nice word for bribery."

To break up the trip to town, Sudhir took me on a tour of the main campus of Pune University, which housed the residence of the former British governor of the state of Maharachtra. The ancient buildings were a perfect marriage of Indian and gothic architecture, and looked to me like an Indian Princeton. We wandered through the formal gardens and lounged on the velvet lawn.

Sudhir told me about his year in Israel, where he'd studied the latest irrigation systems. His plan was to introduce modern ways into his own country. Like his father, he was a man with a conscience. And his idealism was firmly planted in the possible.

When our idyllic interlude was over I had to face the reality of Sunday afternoon traffic. How could there be so much congestion on the once-proverbial day of rest? Worst of all, I found myself in close proximity to elephant tails. Close enough to touch.

This did not faze Sudhir, who kept up a steady stream of chatter. I tried to concentrate on what he was saying, but I didn't care if *banyan* trees abounded in Pune or if their long tendrils had been cut so they couldn't reach the ground and uproot the pavement. I was only interested in one thing—survival.

"Oh, my God. Watch out!" I shouted as we narrowly missed a newly deposited mountain of elephant dung. I clung to Sudhir and closed my eyes, attempting to steer the bike with my body. The noise of vehicles honking and braking and gunning their motors as they wove in and out, inches from my legs, was deafening.

"Meg, if you don't stop squeezing my chest and moving from side to side, we'll surely have an accident. I can't breathe!"

"And I'm choking from exhaust fumes! Sudhir, am I going to die or just be horribly maimed?" I was consumed by fear, like a kid on a bucking bronco headed for the last roundup. But I forced myself to relax my grip and lean into his strong body. "If I do survive, please don't make me ride back home like this."

"You can walk behind, like an Untouchable, if you wish. That will give you a real Indian experience before you die." He swerved and stopped abruptly in front of the railroad station. After securing the cycle, Sudhir bowed and offered his hand, as if helping me off a great white steed. I knew by his eyes that he found me amusing, but good manners kept him from laughing out loud.

"Don't worry, Meg. After you've finished getting your ticket, you'll be too tired to notice the traffic."

Even in this homely setting he displayed the grace and manners of a man far beyond his years. "You're an officer and a gentleman," I said, returning an exaggerated bow. "Remind me to send all my suicidal friends to you." Now he laughed.

Purchasing a ticket in Pune was no different from Bombay, except that I had Sudhir to run interference. He and I sat outside the station on a large packing box while he fired questions at me and filled in the endless questionnaire. Age, home address, next of kin, destinations, profession. Although older is better in India, I hated to tell Sudhir my age. So I cheated...one year, as always. I'll probably still cheat when I'm ninety.

The next morning I stood by the train, steam billowing from between the iron wheels. Mist and soot mingled with the smell of burning coal. I wanted to hug everybody goodbye, but knew that open displays of affection were frowned upon in this society. Sheila had told me that I was allowed a certain enthusiasm, however, because I was a foreigner, and Americans were known for their boisterousness. A nice way of putting it. So we shook hands all around, until I came to Kashmi. Sorry, folks, this enchanting little lady is getting a hug. It was long. And tearful.

28

THE TRAIN TO UDAIPUR

I've never been good at farewells, at saying goodbye to people or places or segments of my life. I try to hold on to a season, to a sunny afternoon, to a child's special look, to a loved one's words. But they hover fleetingly, as if mocking my presumption, and are soon gone.

I sat for awhile thinking about my new friends, picturing their faces as they stood on the platform, and tucking the memories away before moving on. I settled into the rhythm of the train, but the pain in my side returned, increasing with each jolt, until it became a continuous, insistent throbbing. I must get to a doctor.

"Are you an American?" The voice came from a lady sitting on my right. "I have a son at Harvard." Why was I pegged as an American wherever I went? I hadn't even opened my mouth.

She introduced herself as Dr. Anand, the medical officer for the Bank of India. She'd lived in many countries with her two sons and her husband, a military man. My interest was piqued when she spoke of Nigeria. Perhaps I'd finally get my questions answered. I couldn't shake off the disturbing stories told me by the French couple in Kenya.

"Your French friends were right," she said. "There *are* places in Nigeria—dark alleys, warehouses near the waterfront—where human meat is sold, but this practice is not widespread. Of course Westerners are horrified by this, but I had one lady from the British embassy offer to give me a shrunken head from her coveted collection. Over a cup of tea, if you please. I'm sure she wouldn't see the connection." She shrugged ruefully.

I was glad when the conversation turned to new ways of approaching health care. Dr. Anand was a strong advocate of holistic medicine and meditation. "My whole life was changed by the course I took with my nephew, Deepak Chopra, an endocrinologist who lives in Massachusetts. He teaches about *Ayurveda*, the science of life being. Western medicine can be used to cure a disease once it is

217

entrenched in the body, but certain medicines can also destroy the natural immune system and cause toxic effects. We should use nature's basic intelligence to heal, to balance our system. After all, what is disease but dis-ease, a lack of balance."

I couldn't wait to relate her words to my daughter, Martha, who is a strong advocate of herbal and homeopathic remedies. It wasn't until I returned home that I discovered the writings of Deepak Chopra.

"Good luck on your journey," said the gentle, eloquent doctor as we left the train. She clasped my hand warmly and turned to signal a red-turbaned porter. I hoisted my heavy pack and watched her disappear into the crowd, followed by a tall figure draped in white, carrying her light woven basket on his head. Despite her democratic ideas, she was still a member of the elite.

I was getting used to the confusion of Bombay, but not the pollution. It helped if I practiced shallow breathing while waiting in line for a taxi to carry me to Bombay Central Station. Once there I stored my pack in Left Luggage, made a quick stop at American Express to pick up my mail, and an even quicker one at the Taj Mahal Hotel for a replenishment of sterile bandages.

One of the few restaurants in Bombay where the food didn't bring tears to my eyes was at my old Hotel Apollo. I had just been seated when a lanky, red-haired man walked over to my table.

"Graham Starr from Australia here." He thrust a hand in my direction. "American?"

I groaned. "How did you guess?"

"The way you walked in…kind of like you owned the joint. And the camera bag. All Americans have camera bags. Large ones." I laughed and motioned for him to sit down.

"This place has the only food in Bombay that doesn't burn my gullet. I'm not a hot spice person. But there are times when I'd like to try something besides tandoori chicken."

He offered to buy me a beer. "It'll put out the fire if you change your mind and decide to live dangerously. And if you come to this country on your own that's a given."

Graham had the brashness and charm of a Crocodile Dundee. And, best of all, I felt he just wanted to chat, not make me "happy."

I started to tell him about my sojourns to the ladies' lounge of the Taj Mahal Hotel.

"Oh, the good old Taj. Great lobby. I slept there when I arrived in Bombay three nights ago…at 2 A.M."

"How did you dare?" I asked, incredulous.

"Desperation. Told the cab driver to drop me off at a hotel in town. If you speak English they think you're rich. I didn't realize where I was before the cab had disappeared, so I just strolled in and curled up in one of the wicker chairs by the pool. A helluva sight better than the retiring rooms at the train station."

And to think how nervous I'd been when I first crossed that marble threshold and surveyed the sumptuous layout.

"What's a retiring room?" I asked.

"A place to flop if you have an early departure or a late arrival. Better than the street, aye?"

Together, we headed for the bazaar so I could buy a new screw top water bottle. My old one with the pop-up top was leaking.

"What you have to do in India," Graham said, "is find a YMCA. There's one in every good-sized town. I have a great room—bath, balcony, and breakfast—for nine dollars. Can your Apollo beat that?" I shook my head.

We left the bazaar with just enough time to race to the "Y" and pick up Graham's pack. We were leaving on the same eight o'clock train, but he was traveling in second or third class, wherever he could find a seat. "I'm here to see the real India, mate," he said, needling me. "Besides, have you seen first class? In my experience it's not much better."

I waited for Graham on the balcony outside his second story room. Flowering trees hung over the railings and tiny purple blossoms brushed my sleeve. For a few blessed moments I was insulated from the dirt and the noise of the city.

"You're right," I said. "This place is great. But let's get to the station. I have to retrieve my pack, and I have no idea how to purchase bedding or locate my sleeping car, or how long…."

"Hey, take it easy," he said. "Are all Americans this frantic? What makes you think the train will leave on time? It hasn't happened to me, yet."

"And if it does…and we're not there? Will you get me a room at the Taj?"

"No, but I'll protect you from the rabble in the retiring room…if you'll have me." Delivered with a rakish wink.

Once at the station we fetched my pack and hurried down the length of the platform past dismal second class cars bursting with people. Babies crying, bent old women draped in dark cotton, skinny men staring straight ahead. Hollow eyes. Children hanging out the windows, whole families crowded into each triple decker bunk.

"Don't forget about the 'Y'," admonished Graham as he hoisted himself into one of the cars. "You'll thank me, I promise." And he was off. I was sure that I was going to like Australia.

Half-an-hour later I had purchased a bedding ticket for forty cents, picked up two sheets, a pillow and a blanket, and was wading through a lengthy hand-written list to find my name on one of the two first class sleepers. Wandering through the narrow corridor looking for my compartment, I was appalled at the stink. What a disappointment! And after all the glorious literature I'd devoured about the great Indian railway, showcase of the former British Empire. This was *not* one of the luxury trains pictured in National Geographic specials. It was one of the new diesels. The huge, romanticized steam engines, now almost all retired or broken into scrap metal, were only used on the short runs into the smaller towns, or for long winding climbs into the Himalayas.

Had I been a contortionist I would have fared better. I made my bed on the top bunk and settled at the window end, stooped and cross-legged, watching the only other occupants of my compartment—an Indian woman and her small son—prepare for bed. She fed him juice and biscuits, washed his face, combed his hair, and put on his nightclothes. All the time cooing and kissing. Then she took two paisley spreads and a pillow from a large woven bag, wrapped the child in one and herself in the other. Like two cocoons, they snuggled together. Motionless in moments.

It would be an hour before we departed. Graham had been right.

A timid light from the platform filtered through the top half of the dirt-smeared window. I took out my flashlight and eagerly opened my mail.

Dear Mom,

The reason I've missed your last few mailing addresses and not written is basically because I'm in the process of falling in love and haven't been exactly the same person I was when you started your trip. In addition, my shiatsu massage practice quadrupled in February and I've made major leaps in my understanding and skill. Right now I'm totally exhausted and practically sick, rather disoriented, feeling confused and inadequate, having already gone through the emotions of elation and fear. So that's why I haven't written....

Cary's letter went on with two pages describing her boyfriend and the irrationality of falling in love. I felt a warm glow as I pictured my statuesque daughter in her out-of-control romantic haze. And I was glad she was concentrating on herself, no longer so involved with my trip. Everyone says that parents live through their children, but sometimes it's the reverse. Cary, back in her own country after seven years abroad, was settling down—as settled as any Peterson can be.

The next letter was from Chris. He started out by admonishing me to stop worrying that everyone was worrying about me. In fact, he was the only one who knew I was away, he said, because he had to field phone calls from my friends, send out my mail orders, and write to my strange customers. Then he described several vacation trips to the Mayan ruins, the rain forest, and the beaches of Tahiti before hitting me with this paragraph:

> ....Just as I'm feeling wonderful (having given up all my vices, including eight cups of coffee a day), it seems that the world is dying around me. The whole AIDS thing is really becoming awful. It's so sad to report, but Jay Purvis is in the hospital now and it's widely accepted that he's got it. I try to keep my optimism and not think negatively about it, but every so often reality sets in and I realize that he's most likely going to die. It's something I have no experience in. This is going to be hard for me, for all of us.
>
> That's about it. Joe sends his love. He visits every month, and I like it that way. I have the feeling I'm similar to you, Mom. Neither of us seems to want someone in our face all the time, even if we love him.

I thought about Jay, Chris's partner at NobleWorks, the card company they had started together. He was so young, so creative, so imaginative. By the time I returned home, he and several other friends would be gone.

More unhappy news from my baby sister, Cary. Baby at 55? She had been married for thirty-two years to a minister who burst her bubble of "happily ever after" when she discovered he'd been having a ten-year affair with one of his parishioners. Poor naive Cary. She was busy teaching music and raising her four daughters, never noticing, or perhaps not wanting to notice, the behind-the-scenes betrayal. There had been ups and down, as with every marriage, but she believed that if you just worked at your relationship and loved each other enough everything would be all right. We were so much alike, except that she left abruptly when she realized the extent of her husband's infidelity. That was eight months ago.

How my heart ached for her. When I called her from South Africa she had burst into tears. Like me, she was faced with a new freedom coupled with moments of anger and excruciating loneliness. I related to her anguish and to her dreams, though I despaired of ever finding the real companionship and intimacy she spoke about so honestly and longed for so earnestly. I thought about how I'd pushed her around when we were kids. She always said it wasn't easy being the youngest. Now it was my turn to listen and comfort.

By now the train had left the station and I didn't feel like reading any more letters. Misery seemed everywhere. I snuggled into my blanket and longed for sleep.

The small boy stirred and his mother flicked on the light. I peeked at my watch. Four A.M. I covered my head and burrowed under the sheets. A baby cried. Tea was poured. The boy squealed and ran to the door. A chorus of ablutions rose above the clatter and resounded through the walls. Sleep was impossible. It seemed that all of first class was awake and preparing for the day. Every human orifice was being loudly cleansed of mucous and gas. This was not your ordinary nose blowing, coughing, or throat clearing. It started in the sinuses, moved to the chest, and ended somewhere below the belt. After traveling back up through the entire digestive tract, it erupted in such honking and spitting as to terrify a small animal or child. The battle cry of rutting elephants. The spasms of dying consumptives. I wondered how so much excess effluvia could be stored overnight in the human body. This process went on with abandon for a full hour.

I never heard or saw an Indian woman engage in such a dramatic release of internal humors at the break of day. This appeared to be a well-orchestrated, well-rehearsed male tradition.

At 5:00 A.M. we arrived at Ahmadabad. Pitch black. I walked through the station and saw, up close for the first time, the sacred white Brahman bull strolling through the crowds, his regal hump lending credence to his nobility. Hawkers of food swarmed around me. People—wrapped in rags or blankets—were sleeping on one entire section of the dirty cement floor. (Were these the retiring rooms Graham spoke of?) It shocked me at first, but was soon to become so commonplace that I hardly took notice. Milk tea was being ladled from an enormous bubbling cauldron. I shuddered, and said a little prayer to the god of healthy immune systems, as I put my lips to the hastily rinsed tin cup, and dropped a few coins into a bony outstretched hand. By 6:40 I had climbed a long flight of stairs and reached platform ten, where the train for Udaipur was waiting, steam pouring from its underbelly. An old-fashioned train at last! On the posted list my name had been shortened to Mrs. Margarson, but I found my compartment without difficulty, and endured the interminable questioning of several conductors as to my true identity. I was too tired to be upset.

It had gotten very cold and there was no heat. And no blankets to rent. I quickly unpacked my wool socks, heavy sweater, and raincoat. Surely there would be a modicum of comfort in layers. I draped the coat over my shoulders, stuffed a couple of T-shirts under my head, and proceeded to freeze. My understanding of biofeedback was minimal. Neither it nor my belief in the power of mind over matter could convince my body that we were on a tropical island. Resigned, I spent a miserable two hours until the sun turned the car into an oven. From then on I baked.

My compartment companions were French. Jason, a photographer, and Mary Paul, a social worker. Both lived in Mulhouse near the Swiss border. Their English was minimal, but not as minimal as my French, so we hit on German as our means of communication.

The train had an authentic steam engine with a haunting old-fashioned whistle, shrill at times, long and dark at others, as if signaling its moods to those who gathered at every junction to watch it pass. The wheels began to turn slowly as steam was released—chook, chook, whoosh, chook—accelerating to an insistent booka, checka, booka checka, until they reached their stride and danced rhythmically over the rails. The brakes squealed and seething vapor clouds were released every time we approached a station, triggering early movie memories of *Murder on the Orient Express*, *Bhowani Junction*, and *Anna Karenina*. I didn't like the black soot that belched out of the smoke stack, but it made a striking picture as it mixed with steam exploding from the sides, encircling the passengers and giant wheels of the great iron beast.

You could see with what pride the engineers performed their duties. They were men of muscle with nerves of steel. Faces glistening with sweat, jaws set, eyes flashing.

Each train had its own exotic name etched on a brass plate, and each car was separated from its neighbor by a steel door—locked. Twice, Mary Paul stayed too long on the platform and had to grab the nearest car when the train pulled away. It wasn't until the next stop that we were able to retrieve her.

I'm sure that the reputation of Indian toilets is world-renowned. But you have to experience them to fully understand the impact on a Westerner. They are, simply, a hole in the floor. You take a deep breath, step inside a small cubicle, squat, and hope your feet don't get wet. When the train is moving you have the added fear that you might slip and put one foot down the hole. I was glad for my strong leg muscles, and equally glad that I hadn't worn what my daughter Martha insisted would be most convenient—one-piece jumpsuits. Can you picture yourself entering the toilet, undressing completely, and holding on to a strap with one hand while attempting to keep your clothes elevated with the other?

During the hours when the motion of the cars made it impossible to read or write, I'd relax by running melodies through my mind—the hypnotic ragtime of Scott Joplin, the frenetic finale of "Can-Can"—and incorporating the rhythmic click of the wheels into the music. I sat for a long time in this somnambulistic state, looking out the barred windows and watching the changing landscape through ripples of rising heat. Soft green fields, rivers, small villages, cotton plantations, and gray mountains resembling the hairy pates of elephants flew by with mesmerizing speed, further blurring my senses.

Abruptly, the train jerked to a stop in the middle of nowhere. "No cause for alarm, folks," the conductor announced. "A pig must have wandered onto the tracks…or perhaps a cow or a goat." People appeared on the platform. Little girls carrying bundles of sugar cane. A mother and child selling huge red carrots, beans, and apples, the child balancing the basket of vegetables on her head while the mother weighed out the produce on a hand-held scale.

We disembarked. I looked for pigs. There were none. Nor cows. Nor goats. Young boys approached us, selling the largest turnips I'd ever seen. How I yearned for some fresh vegetables. I hesitated and that brought on more eager children, hands outstretched, like spokes converging on a common wheel. The three of us had become a major curiosity. We were the only Westerners around. And so tall. Several children stared and pointed at our cameras, offering to pose for money. The scene was intense, noisy, festive. It was no coincidence that the train had halted in this desolate place. I was sure its passing was a predictable community event.

After the last stop we shut the windows and kept our heavy door closed to avoid the swirling soot. Even so, our clothes were soon covered with black ash, our arms and hands smudged and grimy, our bodies hot and sticky. As we neared Udaipur the train climbed higher into the arid mountains. At first it reminded me of the old Yugoslavia, the rock-terraced Adriatic coast where Glen and I had camped in 1951. But as the sun moved lower in the afternoon sky it reflected off a different kind of terrace—a tangled hedge of three-foot cacti intricately woven by nature into fences of silky green. At a distance, they looked like tufted Mohawk hairdos bisecting and encircling the dome-shaped hills.

Dusk was settling over the station when the train pulled to a stop. Indian music blared from a loudspeaker as a cadre of rickshaw drivers descended on us. Jason was a superb bargainer. He hired a rickshaw to take us to the Haveli, a small hotel on the outskirts of Udaipur. "Luxury with homely comfort" proclaimed the sign at the desk. An excellent choice. I opted for a "super deluxe" room with a marble bathtub (100 rupees, about $9.00), and immediately proceeded to soak off the layers of railroad ash. Within the hour we were rested and ready for an evening of exploration.

Mary Paul hung on to Jason's right arm and I hung on to his left as we careened around the traffic circles on our way to town. I kept shouting "Slow down, *puleeze*," but the driver only laughed and said, "No problem." This phrase was becoming a universal curse.

Motorized rickshaws, bicycles, and Vespas threatened to collide with one another as they squeezed through streets of mud and stone. Shops, looking like attached wooden boxes open to the public on one side, were interspersed with restaurants and small cafés, most of them decorated with strings of colored lights.

After a sumptuous dinner we started to search for sterile bandages. I had told my friends that if I didn't get my infection cleared up my adventures in India would be ruined.

"Did you ever see so many pharmacies or so many shelves of medicine?" said Jason. Pharmaceuticals were stacked from floor to ceiling, reaching into the far recesses. Clerks raced back and forth and shouted to stock boys who filled orders. How can it be that such an extensive warehouse has no sterile bandages?

"Let's fan out," suggested Mary Paul. "And meet back here in half-an-hour. That way we can cover more of the town in less time."

I was suddenly aware of my aloneness, my vulnerability. The insistent pain in my side fed a growing panic. I struggled to keep my mind on the task at hand.

An hour later we sat sipping wine at a sidewalk café and luxuriating in the cool evening air. I felt at peace. An unusual feeling for me. We had found no sterile bandages, but I'd settled for several rolls of thin gauze and adhesive tape, determined to make my own. And say no more.

"Look!" shouted Mary Paul on the way back to our hotel. "Did you ever see such an elaborate wedding procession?" We stopped the rickshaw and watched, mesmerized, as the groom came prancing by on an elegant white stallion, followed by a smiling, veiled bride, multi-colored streamers, and a Dixieland band. Behind the band came a crowd of ladies in flashy *saris*, singing and dancing. Bringing up the rear was an immense bejeweled elephant—a live replica of the tourist shop miniatures. This was the first of many wedding celebrations I was to see in India, but the only one with western music. I smiled at the incongruity. A far cry from New Orleans.

Just as I was drifting off to sleep there was a knock on my door. I staggered out of bed.

"Pardon me, Madam," said the concierge, a slight, pleasant man. His plastered-down black hair shone in the hall light. "If you put your soiled clothes outside your door, they will be washed and ironed by morning."

"Oh," I said, "And what will it cost?"

"I think it is not expensive for you," he replied. "Two rupees for a pair of slacks, and one rupee for a blouse, and...."

"Fine. That will be fine." I said, feeling cheap for asking.

I lay awake for a long time, listening to the faint sound of chanting interrupted occasionally by the ding-ding of the concierge's bell. It was soothing after such a frenetic evening. But sleep was fitful, full of dreams about scurrying children asking for money. Why couldn't they leave me alone? And shouting rickshaw drivers streaking through the night like insane chariot racers. "Stop! Let me out," I cried. Then I fell. A sharp object punctured my side. The throbbing pain returned.

29

ARE ALL THESE MEN DOCTORS?

The three of us had breakfast on the upstairs terrace, which was encircled by a simple geometric marble railing. Looking through the peaks and valleys of cut marble I could see Udaipur spread out below, stretching into the distance to disappear behind furry mountains.

It was love at first sight! There were lakes everywhere. No wonder it was called the Venice of the East. But Venice boasted of canals, and I was a lake person. That's what made this town so special. There were big lakes rimmed with mansions and sprinkled with islands, and little lakes—delicate transparent jewels reflecting the crystal bowl of the morning sun.

As I squinted against the brightness my mind carried me back to August 1974. I was camping with my children in Maine's Baxter State Park. We had just reached the top of Mt. Katadhin and were headed over the perilous knife's edge. A fierce wind was blowing and for one glorious moment the clouds parted to reveal miles of lakes on either side. Big ones, little ones. Some with cottages. Others a part of the marshy wilderness. Then a young climber holding a transistor radio rushed up to us. "President Nixon just resigned," he shouted. The news spread. Cheers could be heard up and down the trail. There was no escape. Nature and chicanery juxtaposed. Unspoiled beauty and the warts of everyday life. So I thought as I struggled up the rocky path from Katadhin to Pomola, the northernmost tip of the Appalachian Trail. And so I thought as I viewed ancient Udaipur with its lakes and palaces, its poverty and riches.

After promising to meet Jason and Mary Paul for dinner I grabbed a rickshaw and hurried to town. My first stop was the railroad station, where I found, to my delight, that a telegram had been received confirming my Thursday night sleeper reservation.

"Madam, come at five on the afternoon of your departure to get your bedding," said the station manager, rolling his r's with great authority. "Then there will be no problem." Remembering the frigid ride from Ahmadabad, that's exactly what I wanted...no problem.

My next stop was the Rajasthan Tourist office. Rajasthan is the state in which both Udaipur and Jaipur are located. There are still about six *maharanas*, or *maharajahs*, living in the area, but these former rulers are now merely figureheads with no political clout. They seem to be revered, however, and live in the splendid pads of the super rich.

I walked through a deserted courtyard to the tourist bungalow. The blood-red stains of beetle nut juice marred the beauty of the tranquil garden tucked away from the busy street and surrounded by white columns. I didn't dare sit on the beckoning stone ledges, so covered were they with the slimy residue. What was needed were a few old-fashioned spittoons of wild west vintage.

In less than an hour I had outlined three days of intense sightseeing and was perched in the front seat of a worn, brightly-colored bus ready for the next city tour. The smiling guide read from a sheaf of notes. "Udaipur stands 1,895 feet above sea level and was founded in 1559 by Maharana Udai Singh, whose last descendants lived in this sumptuous palace [we were about to visit] until 1947. Along with the attached museum, the gleaming structure is a model of ancient Indian architecture with its four levels of columned courtyards, white filigreed balconies and windows, picturesque cupolas atop octagonal towers, ornate arches, and sculptured gardens." Whew! That about says it all.

A surfeit of temples, monuments, museums, and palaces ensued. Between each stop we bounced over stone roads, worn with age. The bus inched its way through the narrow streets, sometimes having to back up and maneuver gallantly to avoid scraping a wall. Each such effort was met with loud huzzahs and claps from the patrons.

I trudged up dozens of stone steps to the golden spires of Jagdish temple, past the devout, who sat cross-legged on the floor, eyes closed, heads bowed. I marveled at the glass and mosaic work of the Lake Palace, the delicate wall paintings, the fountains. And I stood on a castle balcony where women hundreds of years ago looked down into a courtyard at their *maharanas* from behind marble latticework. Not to be seen. Not to be heard. I began to think of India as the birthplace of male chauvinism.

But it was the next day spent in the country that moved me the most. As the rickety bus labored over the rutted roads I noticed once more the tremendous expanse of unused land, the wild valleys, and the deserted mountains that cover much of India. Since the bus sat low to the road I felt a certain closeness to the passing landscape, its scrubby vegetation and twisted trees.

Thirty miles out of town we reached Haldighati, the site of an historic battle between the Moghul Emperor Akbar and the very popular Maharana Pratap of the Rasputs. Legend has it that nobody really wanted to fight, since the Rasputs were outnumbered two to one. But as peasants they felt obligated to defend their land. When both generals were killed, the conflict was declared over. During the battle Pratap's horse, Chetak, had its leg cut off by an elephant, but still forded a stream and rescued his master. An impressive bronze statue of Pratap astride Chetak stands in Udaipur, as well as a memorial *chhatri* on the spot where the heroic horse died. A most unusual war it must have been, when the most courageous participant was a horse.

As we climbed out of Haldighati the roads took on the character of Kenya, but unlike Moffat barreling toward the Masai Mara, this driver slowed to a crawl, which gave us time to examine the clusters of stone and stucco houses along the way. They were like most of the simple rural homes in India, except that their roofs were made of a tight layer of sticks on which flat round stones, thicker than slate shingles, had been placed. On some the row of sticks was completely covered and on others it formed a fringe. This gave an uneven, wavy look to the roof. I could picture such a unique structure bringing big bucks in Martha's Vineyard.

The remains of old walls, indicative of bygone property boundaries, bisected the desolate countryside and snaked up the sides of the tufted mountains. Like the roofs, they were made of alternating layers of sticks and stones with no cement or mortar. How pleasing to the eye! Giant restless reptiles slithering out of sight, their scaly hides melding with the gray earth.

Children, naked and dark-skinned, waved at us from the fields. But in the villages they took on a different character. I saw a few neatly dressed boys walking hand-in-hand with their mothers, but the girls wandered alone. And did the begging. Dressed in long skirts and blouses, they looked like miniature adults. Their clothes, brown and torn, blended with their snarled black hair. They were barefoot and the skin on their legs and feet was cracked and hardened. I watched them run in and out of piles of debris, or stand forlornly on a pile of discarded stones with a thin arm outstretched. Why little girls? Perhaps because it was so wrenching to look into their large, sad eyes. And because they were expendable.

The bus climbed steadily up the ancient dirt roadway, the driver blowing its horn insistently until we arrived at Nathdwara. Along the way I saw teams of men and women engaged in road repair, the same slow, tedious process I'd seen on my first day in Bombay.

Nathdwara boasts one of the most revered temples, the Vaishnava shrine of Lord Krishna, built in the early 18th century. Thousands of pilgrims come every year to worship and pay homage, but its doors are not open to foreigners or non-Hindus. We rode to the temple in horse-drawn buggies just as swarms of uniformed children were coming from school. I stood outside, enthralled by the chiming of the temple bells, their rich sound echoing through the streets, drowning out the noise of daily life. Waiting for our guide, a devout Hindu, to return, I tried to digest what he had told us about the thirty-three million gods and goddesses, incarnations of the various aspects of the Hindu triad—Brahma, Vishnu, and Shiva. But it was, to me, unfathomable.

Walking back through the village I came upon a most unusual traffic jam. In a busy intersection lay a Brahman bull resting on his side and blinking his eyes sleepily, oblivious to the commotion he was causing. Several cows had gathered and were grooming him. Large trucks negotiated, with infinite care, around the animals. Smaller vehicles detoured onto the sidewalk. Pedestrians scooted out of the way. The bull never moved and nobody honked or shouted or prodded. I stared, unbelieving, trying to keep a straight, respectful face.

As I neared the bus I saw a young boy with a rough-hewn plow driving horses as he cultivated a puny square of land within the village. I waved. He waved back. Women passed me, balancing outsized bundles of sticks on their heads. Beggar girls scampered alongside.

Our final stop was the famed Ecklingji Temple, a complex of 108 temples enclosed by high walls, built in 734 A.D. The *gopuram*, a pyramidal tower above the gateway composed of hundreds of knots, reminded me of a multi-tiered wedding cake. But instead of a bride and groom on top stood brightly-painted carved gods and goddesses. After we'd removed our shoes the guide took us through the temple, placing a wreath of flowers in front of the inner, most sacred room. Only Brahmans—the holy men—and the Maharana of Mewar could enter this room. Very old men, hunched over in a squatting position, were polishing a four-headed cow of black ebony, a service they had performed for the Maharana since childhood. We all expected these men to look resigned, downtrodden. On the contrary, there was a beatific, joyful look on their faces.

When I returned to Udaipur I tried to relax over a tasty meal of *dal*, spiced baked beans, *puri*, a light fried wheat cake, tomato *raita*, and *lasei*, a sweet dish made of yogurt and sugar. But once the excitement of the tour had diminished, I became aware of the pain in my side. I knew I had to get to a doctor. The strain of the constant, gnawing pain was debilitating.

I counted the horses and camels as the cab driver honked his way to the hospital. I had never noticed, before, how many animals shared the streets in India, but today I was eager for any kind of diversion. I was scared. I'd heard so many awful things about medical care in the Third World. My children had admonished me not to enter a hospital under any circumstance. But what if the alternative was blood poisoning? The driver left me at the emergency entrance, where I joined a group of ladies sitting on hard wooden benches. There was an overflow crowd, so I found myself sitting outside. By the time I'd moved indoors the shadows were lengthening.

Slowly it dawned on me that all the women were pregnant. So that explained the quizzical glances. How could I have missed the sign, *Gynecology*, its bold, four-inch letters glaring at me?

"Where do I go for an abscess?" I asked.

"Casualty, Madam," replied a crisp nurse, and pointed the way.

I walked along the driveway and entered a barn-like room with a simple wooden table in the middle and a thin man in a brown suit sitting behind it. He stood up, scraping the chair against the floor as he did. The sound echoed in the hollow space.

Bowing, he thrust out his hand. "How do you do, Madam. Welcome to our country. I am Doctor Hari Patel."

The dusty smell in the air and the sight of an old man kneeling on a nearby bench, raising and lowering his outstretched arms in rhythmic supplication, unnerved me. There was nobody else around. No stretchers, no equipment, no nurses. Spooky. I mumbled something unintelligible about a chronic sore and could I buy some sterile bandages and some antiseptic, and, really, there was no serious problem, just get me the bandages and I'd be on my way….

"Certainly, Madam," interrupted the doctor, trying to hide his amusement. "Step over here and let me have a look at it. Remove your clothes and I'll be right back. No problem."

He ushered me into a treatment room hidden behind a frayed curtain. I looked around for a gown. There was none. Old boxes littered the floor. And I was sure I detected the heavy odor of embalming fluid. Then I caught sight of the examining table. Two distinct footprints were visible on the white cloth. Large ones. Like from an eight-foot ghost. Perhaps the unfortunate person who needed the embalming fluid?

The old man's mutterings became louder. He must be getting close. There was nowhere to sit, to hide. I panicked. Get me out of this creepy place! You've got to stop reading those Stephen King novels, I told myself, as I shot out of the room, still dressed, almost colliding with Dr. Patel who was on his way in, stethoscope in hand.

"All I want is the bandages," I said to the doctor breathlessly.

"Come, I will find some and dress your wound." he said with great formality.

He led me across the room and into a small alcove where bottles of brown fluid were lined up on a frail, dust-covered table. Their tops were askew, allowing pungent odors to escape. I scrutinized them for pickled frogs and fetuses, but all I saw were swollen cotton balls.

"Now, let me see this wound," he commanded gently.

I lifted my voluminous black skirt and pushed down my underpants, displaying my belly. The doctor peered at the oozing red abrasion near my right hip.

"Yes, it looks bad," he said and went for one of the glass jars on the table.

Suddenly I looked up and saw eight male faces staring at my abdomen. The men who couldn't fit into the cubicle were straining to get a view. One held a pail with a mop in it. Unshaven, hollow-eyed, he was a character straight out of the Bowery. Others were dressed in overalls and work clothes. All were grinning, displaying various stages of tooth decay.

"Are all these men doctors?" I asked, wondering how they could have materialized so quickly when moments earlier the room had been empty.

"Leave at once. This is a disgrace," barked the doctor, his embarrassment almost as acute as mine. He turned to me. "Madam, you must excuse…."

"Never mind," I said as the ragtag group dispersed, looking not the least bit chagrined. "The bandages…*please*."

Regaining his composure Dr. Patel reached his hand into one of the jars. "These are sterile, you see."

Not any more. Seemed that rubber gloves hadn't made their way to Udaipur. He wiped my sore with a sopping mass of cotton. I winced. He repeated the procedure several times.

"Do you have any peroxide?" he asked.

I reached into my camera bag and handed him all I had left—a tiny half-filled bottle—plus the ointment Hamal had prescribed. I wasn't sure whether this was an economy measure on the part of the hospital or they really didn't have these basic items in stock.

He applied the peroxide and cream, covering it with a thin gauze pad. "Don't you have a larger one?" I asked.

"No. Do you?" he countered.

I took out my last homemade pad. "This is all I have. That's why I came here."

The doctor smiled ruefully. The situation had become so ludicrous it was almost funny.

Once the wound was dressed he wrote a prescription that I was to take three times a day for three days. Why such a short time? I couldn't understand the name of the medicine, so I asked if there were any known side effects.

"Every medicine has side effects," said Dr. Patel, repeating the sentence for emphasis. This did little to comfort me.

Timorously I asked for sterile gauze pads from which to make bandages. An assistant was summoned and he carefully picked out a dozen unpackaged pads and put them on a square of brown paper. So much for sterile. He folded the ends clumsily. I found scotch tape in my bag and completed the package.

"One last thing, Doctor. The ladies' room?"

I was directed down a dreary hall through an empty ward filled with ancient, filthy-sheeted iron beds and into a room so smelly and wet with urine that I gagged. No way would I squat in there, even in the direst of emergencies. But how was I going to get out without insulting this nice, albeit inadequate, doctor?

"I've changed my mind," I said when I returned to the reception area. "If you'll just give me the bill...."

He smiled. "It is a pleasure to have you in my country. There is no charge. It is a service of the government." He bowed and disappeared down the hall.

Shaken, I sat down on a wooden bench and took out an orange. What would have happened had I *really* been sick? I decided to step up my do-it-yourself healing techniques, heavy on imaging and positive thinking. Maybe, if things got worse, I could find an American doctor at the embassy in New Delhi, or an Indian doctor like the ones I'd met in the emergency rooms back home. I fought against rising anxiety, while an inner argument raged between common sense and wishful thinking. I could hear my 90-year-old friend, Lisa, saying, "Be sensible, Meg. Be sensible!" She was a Christian Scientist and laid most of my ailments to a lack of good "sense." She and my grandmother would have gotten along famously.

As I ate my orange the barefooted old man continued his rhythmic motions, praying and chanting softly. For the first time I noticed that his clothes were hanging off of his skeleton-thin body. He was deep into his own world...and quite harmless.

When I got up to leave, I looked back. I had left my impression in the dust.

30

ORDEAL AT THE C.P.O.

At 5:45 the next afternoon Jason and Mary Paul hurried me onto the Chetak Express with the comment, "I hope it's faster than that poor dead, one-legged horse."

It had taken an hour to locate the person in charge of bedding. This time the form I filled out became the ticket. The Indians were very inventive. Each local bureau had its own system, each questionnaire its individual caveats. Even Egyptian bureaucracy paled in comparison.

I shared a small compartment with Faith, an English teacher from Edmonton, Alberta, and her companion, James, a corporate lawyer from Minneapolis. Fortunately, James had his head in a Paul Theroux book, so Faith and I moved to the window, where we could talk freely.

"This is the big year, Meg, the big 4-0. And I still haven't decided where I want to live or whether I want to marry James. There are so many places to explore, so much to do before I settle down." I saw myself as I might have been at forty without children.

"You make it sound so deadly," I said. "Settling down is a state of mind. I don't think you or I will ever be 'settled.' We're too restless. Nobody needs to settle down these days, anyway. Not with all the choices."

"Too many," interjected Faith.

"So I was spared?" I ventured, tentatively.

"Well, they don't seem to be making *me* happy."

There was a parallelism about our lives despite the age difference. We were both single, questioning our ability or will to sustain a long-term relationship. We were at a major crossroad in our lives, searching for the best road to take. For us. Weighing its long-term impact.

"And who would ever want to bring a baby into a world like this, anyway? Everywhere you look, it sucks." Faith threw up her hands.

So this was the real problem. I looked at her sympathetically. In her tight jeans and sleeveless Tee she seemed more like a vivacious teenager than a woman approaching middle age.

Just as we were preparing for bed a portly Indian gentleman swathed in layers of white cloth peered through the door. Seeing an empty lower bunk he plunked himself down. Without a word. A few minutes later a woman, who I assumed was his wife, slipped through the door carrying a small baby. Two more children clung to her skirt. Surely this couldn't be legal.

The baby started crying.

James climbed down from his upper bunk and, with great ceremony, chained his luggage to the bed. He had already closed all the windows—to keep the dust down—so there was no air. The children snuffled and sneezed. The baby was inconsolable. Faith, oblivious to it all, turned her face to the wall and went to sleep. I dived under the covers, trying to escape the germs and the noise.

The beleaguered parents decided that the only solution was to serve dinner. This was a noisy affair, and the odors, combined with the swaying of the train, made me queasy. By midnight I could stand the talking no longer and pleaded with them to let me sleep. They were most apologetic and rustled about for some time, arranging and rearranging themselves into a giant, lumpy jigsaw puzzle, arms and legs spilling over the sides of the narrow mattress.

Shooka chugga, shooka chugga whispered the train. The words of Robert Browning flashed through my mind: "God's in his heaven—all's right with the world." Then the snoring began. Within minutes it had reached a Wagnerian climax and threatened to remain there until dawn. It was not unlike the transcontinental journey I'd taken when my children were small. Seven people jammed into a seventeen-foot Yellowstone trailer and Glen holding forth with Olympian snoring. Each night the children would tumble out into the campsite, sleeping bags in tow. They preferred a chance meeting with a bear to suffering their father's rasping, volcanic eruptions. So did I.

But tonight there was no escape. I lay awake in the crowded compartment, listening to the intermittent cry of the train whistle. There was a romance to it, a plaintive optimism. And it helped drown out the open-mouthed rumble from the bunk below. It soothed me, made me feel safe. A shrill cry, a warning to the world to leave me alone, get out of my way, let me pass.

At 3 A.M., just as the flimsy ceiling fan—my only hope of survival—sputtered and died, a conductor barged into the compartment and confronted the unsuspecting, snoring Indian. He must have been searching for missing passengers.

Bedlam ensued. The family was bundled up and herded into the corridor. Shouts. Threats. Weeping. Ah, but a chance to sleep at last.

"Let me take you to a charming hotel. It is near the market. You will not be sorry." It was 6:20 A.M and we were on the station platform in Jaipur, being pursued by an enterprising young man in a large motorized rickshaw.

"We have to go through a bad part of town, but don't worry, there is no problem. The hotel is beautiful and cheap."

"I'm beat," I said. "Let's try it. We can always change our minds." James and Faith nodded. All we wanted was a shower and a quiet place to lie down.

We squeezed into the padded front seat and held our baggage on our laps. The driver gunned the motor at every turn, narrowly missing one of the ornate pink gates leading to the center of the old city. It was like riding atop an aggressive power mower.

We entered a section of town where dogs and goats stood on refuse piles devouring the entrails of dead animals. The stench of garbage was pervasive. Women sifted through tables of clothing and foodstuffs in makeshift stores. Little children peed by the side of the road. We clutched our luggage as the rickshaw labored in and out of deep ruts. At last an open-air market appeared and beyond the crowded square we could see the gates of a mini-castle.

"See, I told you the hotel was off one of the worst streets in Jaipur," the driver said, with a satisfied smile.

Our spirits soared as we rode through the filigreed gates into the courtyard of the Hotel Bissau. Wide stairs led from the garden into a spacious marble foyer. Down a hallway were small alcoves with tables and chairs and decorative reading lamps, two libraries with plush leather sofas, a parlor, and a sunny dining room. All around us was the unmistakable ambiance of old world India. This may have been a secondary *maharana's* home, but it was a castle to me!

The hotel was made of stucco and painted light yellow. Each room was entered through a scalloped archway, a trademark of Indian architecture. Mine, located next to the garden, cost 154 rupees, about $12.00, complete with a stone bath, mothballs in the drain, and two low beds lining the walls. Gilt-edged tapestries hanging from floor to ceiling gave me the feeling of being in an immense canopied bed in the center of an exotic harem.

After breakfast our energetic rickshaw driver returned to take us on a tour of the city. Along with the plethora of cars and bicycles, we shared the road with a number of camels and elephants—some with ceremonial beaded headdress and others carrying merchandise—loosely lumbering along on their stout, rubbery legs. The elephants always looked on the verge of stumbling, their saucepan feet fishing around for a secure foothold beneath the oversized body. I found out later, riding on the prickly head of one of the big beasts in the jungles of Thailand, that they did, indeed, stumble a lot.

Jaipur, the capitol of Rajasthan, abounds in artistic treasures, monuments, and palaces. But, unlike Udaipur, it is laid out in a geometric grill pattern with wide streets reminiscent of a pioneer cattle town in Wyoming, and is completely surrounded by a thick pale-pink cement wall. Each of the eight entrances is unique—pointed or rounded arches with Byzantine decorations, and a variety of turrets shaped like minarets. The walls, themselves, are wide sections of cement, rounded on the top, and bound together like a grand replica of the old stockade fence.

Gate to Jaipur, the pink city.

Never had I been in a place where one color was dominant in all the local buildings. An exciting aesthetic uniformity. The entire town was suffused with a warm salmon glow, which changed with the sun as the day progressed, to become a vivid pink at dusk.

"Yes, this is really an old city," intoned James. "At least eight hundred years, so I've read."

Our guide smiled apologetically. "Sir, this city is only two hundred and fifty years old. But our forts at Amber and Nahargath were built in the 11th century. Perhaps that is what you read."

Faith gave me a warning look.

The guide continued. "Jaipur's most famous ruler, Sawai Jai Singh II was a talented man—an astronomer, statesman, scholar, and soldier. When he died he left the city with an open air observatory and the largest, most accurate sundial in the world."

We visited this beautifully appointed observatory, its dial thrusting toward the heavens like a giant shark's fin. In the same complex were two round sunken half-spheres, one a horoscope with the signs of the zodiac and the other a map of the world fashioned in marble and inlaid stone.

James walked away from us and busied himself with picture taking. He was probably still smarting from the guide's correction. When Faith went over to him and put her hand on his shoulder, he wrenched free. She shrugged and left him alone.

"Will you get a load of that handsome grump," she whispered to me. "How long is he going to sulk? He can't stand to be wrong. Is that men, or just him? Pisses me."

"Not all men...but a fair number." We laughed.

For the next two hours we covered the main points of interest in Jaipur: the elaborate five-story Palace of Winds with its intricately wrought facade of case-ments tucked beneath arches and spires; the museum at Albert Hall with its paintings, tapestries, and sculptures; and the City Palace with its raised center square, its painted columns, its huge silver urns. The patterns carved into the walls, balconies, and graceful stone arches reminded me of the pristine lace doilies my grandmother used to crochet for the arms of worn chairs. Delicately config-ured. Perfectly balanced.

After an intolerably spicy lunch we meandered through the crowded bazaars, buying fresh vegetables, fruit, nuts, and second-hand books. If you looked long enough you could find anything.

"I can't believe these prices," said Faith ecstatically. "Even before bargaining they're phenomenal! And the handmade shawls. Wow!" She could barely contain her enthusiasm as she rummaged through woven scarves, painted cloth, and embroidered *saris*.

It was frustrating not to be able to buy anything. But I had no luggage space, so I amused myself watching a snake charmer try to mesmerize an intransigent cobra.

Jaipur street scene.

By mid-afternoon I'd had enough and was ready to crash. James and Faith were bargaining for some block prints when I grabbed a rickshaw and rode back to the Bissau through the elegant pink gate. I lay down in my resplendent cocoon and drifted into a deep sleep, lulled by the soft afternoon breezes that filtered through the screen door.

It was after eight when I awoke. Not enough time for dinner. I'd have to be satisfied with a late tea if I wanted to get to the Central Post Office in time to call Chris. It had been three weeks since we talked and, as usual, I was imagining all sorts of catastrophes.

I splashed cold water on my face and ran over to the main lobby. As I was relaxing in one of the reading alcoves and drinking a pungent tea served with soggy scones, the concierge appeared and stood looking down at me. He was roly-poly and dressed in a shiny striped western suit. He carried a large portfolio in his hand and placed it on the table. How nice, I thought, a companion for tea. I was brimming with questions and pounced on him.

"Perhaps you can help me," I said. "Nobody seems to know why all the female goats are wearing those bags over their udders. Is it to keep the milk warm?"

The man stifled a smile. "No. It is to keep the baby goats from drinking all the milk. Didn't you notice how they prod the mother with their heads? They don't like it, but we can't afford to give them all the milk."

I felt rather silly.

"Madam, you look like an art lover." He reached for his portfolio. Oh, oh. I could feel a pitch coming.

"And what does that look like?" I asked. "Disheveled hair, old black skirt, backpack, circles under the eyes?" I was going to make him work for this one.

"And I can tell a woman who likes sex," he continued. "It is in the eyes."

I pushed my chair back and started to get up.

He held up his hand to stop me. "Please, lovely Madam, you misunderstand me. Let me show you something. You are under no obligation. I just want you to see some original, hand-painted miniatures that you will find nowhere else in the world. And they will only cost you—as a guest of this hotel—one dollar each."

He opened the portfolio and out spilled gilded reproductions of men and women engaged in the most explicit sex imaginable—the kind I later found sculpted on some of the temples in Nepal. The male organs were awesome. The contortions were laudable. It tickled me to think of this man spreading such graphic pictures out on a table for all to see, as if he were displaying fine jewelry. This would never happen in a hotel in Maplewood, New Jersey.

"My, my, they *are* unique," I said. "And I will give thoughtful consideration to them. But, first, I must make a phone call home….No, not to get permission. Just to make contact with my family." I swept out of the lobby and hailed a bicycle rickshaw.

This was my first ride in one of these quaint contraptions and it was heavenly. So quiet. No smelly, noisy motor. I was a kid, again, riding to the movies on the back of my cousin's bike down a dark country road. Half the fun had been whizzing down hills and through wide-open spaces without any lights. Only now the situation was a little more scary, faced with oncoming traffic.

"Say, do you have any headlights?" I asked. "Uh, you know, *lumier?*"

"Oh, not necessary, Madam. This is my light," he said, pointing to his eyes. We laughed. I said a silent prayer to the god of perilous journeys.

All of a sudden we came upon a wedding procession unlike any I'd seen so far. There were elephants followed by a large square car with loudspeakers blaring. The music was Indian this time, but at rock concert decibels. At the tail end came an entourage of colorfully attired men and women balancing empty gas cans, red, green, and yellow, on their heads. At least I *hoped* they were empty. Six lights branched, tree-like, off a single pole that came out of the top of each can. They hovered above the crowd like flaming torches.

At center stage the groom—alabaster from head to toe—sat in solitary splendor on a painted elephant. His headband was made of strands of white flowers, which hung down over his face. He looked very uncomfortable in the glare of the lights. His friends danced along the street, teasing and mocking him. But where was the bride?

I leaned back and breathed the cool night air. It was so restful gliding along behind the bicyclist. And I was in such good spirits. That was before my ordeal at the C.P.O.

As I entered the post office I bumped into a tall blond man who was shaking his head and cursing. I soon found out that he was a Swede who'd been waiting two hours to make a collect call to Stockholm. I told him I hoped to make a collect call, myself…to the United States.

"I hope you brought a book," he said. "It will take a good three hours."

"That's ridiculous!"

"Sure it is, but look for yourself. There's only one clerk. All the trunk calls and telegrams have to be handled by him. And don't forget, the Indians won't see the money for a long time, so they don't encourage long distance collect calls. I suggest you make your call from New Delhi, unless it's an emergency."

I went outside where my driver was waiting.

"You'd better go. It'll be hours I'm told."

He assured me that he was willing to wait.

"No, no. I will see you another time. Thank you. Please go."

I felt bad. I knew I'd never see him again. And the poor fellow looked so scrawny, almost tubercular. I thrust eight rupees into his hand. He nodded, thanked me profusely, and disappeared.

The Swede was right. People were three-deep, pestering the lone clerk for their calls.

"Beirut!…." "London!…." "Madrid!" he would yell as the calls came in, and each time someone would jump up and run to the solitary phone booth. There was one other phone at the end of the counter, and now and then someone would get on it and start shouting as if to eradicate the miles by sheer volume. It was a madhouse. Disgruntled customers, a surly clerk, and thick cigarette smoke curling up to the ceiling.

As a result of the Swede's advice, I decided to make a person-to-person call and gave the clerk a 200 rupee advance…to speed things up. The initial exchange was cordial. My hopes were high. Several times he tried my call, but all the circuits were busy. I watched, fascinated. Calls would come in at the instant he was trying to call out. I could imagine the frustration on the part of foreign operators trying to get through to that one line.

An hour passed. "The United States," he announced triumphantly.

I leapt from my bench into the booth. But nobody was on the line. I ran back to the desk, then to the booth, then to the desk. The clerk kept shouting, "Stay on the phone, Madam. They'll come back on." Silence.

I was shaking. Then I heard a faraway voice say, "He's gone to the bank and will be back later this afternoon."

I sneaked in a remark. "Is everything all right?"

"Everything is fine. Call back at five."

"I can't. I'm in India!" The line went dead.

I returned to the desk. "I couldn't reach my party, so may I have my 200 rupees back?"

"Won't you have some tea, Madam?" said the clerk.

"No thank you. I need my money. I realize this is hard work, and you've been patient...."

He smiled appreciatively. "Yes, it has been a hard day. As you can see, everybody is shouting at me." This seemed the accepted method of communication at the C.P.O.

"Do you want to place the call, again?" he asked.

"No, thanks. My party is out of the office. He won't be back for several hours. So, if you could just give me back my money."

The clerk ignored me and went on with his dialing. I waited. I tried not to act annoyed, knowing what happens if bureaucrats think they have power over you. Half-an-hour went by.

"Sir, if I could just have my deposit back, I'd appreciate it." He waved me away, then took some bills from a desk drawer, counted them slowly in front of me, unlocked another drawer, and transferred them.

People standing around—we'd all become friends—rolled their eyes and shrugged. "What can you do?" one old man whispered to me.

I contemplated walking out and forgetting the money. It wasn't that much. Two nights in a cheap hotel. But my ire had been aroused. And by the time another hour had passed, I was livid. I wasn't going to budge, even if I had to sleep on the floor.

Finally, I decided to go directly to the cashier, a wisp of a man sitting in a small cubicle behind three crooked bars. I explained my problem and asked—as politely as I could through clenched teeth—why I couldn't have my money. The clerk watched me and smiled. Suddenly, he and the cashier ducked into another room. I could hear them laughing. By now hopelessly paranoid, I was sure they were enjoying my discomfort.

Moments later the clerk returned. "So you want to cancel your call?" he said.

"YES. About two hours ago!"

"You don't want me to try again?"

"NO!"

Slowly, the triumphant clerk opened his desk drawer. I sensed that he felt he'd toyed with me long enough and it was time to let me go. Not a word was spoken. He counted out 190 rupees, taking ten for the "service." Then came a low, obsequious bow.

I grabbed the bills, stormed out of the post office, and marched down the drive. For several minutes I walked back and forth on the sidewalk, trying to dissipate my anger before finding a rickshaw. One peddled up alongside me.

"How much to the Hotel Bissau?" I asked.

"Twenty rupees."

"No way," I said. I had paid five to come here. I stomped away, prepared to walk back to the hotel. Nobody else was going to mess with me tonight.

The driver countered. "Ten, Madam?"

I took a good look at him and softened. He was so skinny. So pale. And his deep-set eyes had that dark-rimmed, mascaraed look that makes the Indians so appealing. I really should have bought him a meal. After all, hadn't I just *earned* 190 rupees?

As I rode home I said a little prayer: Oh, God, please help me, your frail servant, find serenity and peace, and sustain it...for more than a few moments.

31

FAREWELL, PINK CITY

The sun beat down relentlessly. How I wish I'd worn my safari hat or applied sunscreen. There was no top on the rickshaw and I had no idea how long it would take to go across town.

My driver kept turning his head, grinning and pointing to himself, saying, "I—me, eight rupees—me. Thank you, Madam."

I thought he was asking for more money than we'd agreed upon, and I'd have been glad to oblige. It was going to be an arduous peddle from the Teej tourist bungalow to Rambagh Palace.

"No, Madam, no money. You—me, the Post yesterday night."

Could this be the driver who'd taken me to the Central Post Office? Impossible odds! The same driver on two consecutive days in such a large city?

"Ah, yes. *Lumier!*" I said, pointing to his eyes. He nearly fell off the bike in his excitement.

Still grinning, and with renewed vigor, he skillfully wound his way through the old city, a labyrinth of narrow streets and occasional circles, where all manner of vehicles vied for supremacy. By now I was used to the honking and the shouting, part of the drama of daily life in Jaipur. It was fun being on a bicycle rickshaw, because the driver cut through the center of town where I could observe life up close. Its motorized counterpart traveled, instead, on the wide streets outside the gates, where all you could see were suburban-type homes or squalid shacks.

"It is special day, Madam," said the driver. "The prime minister from Pakistan comes to the palace. Everywhere busy streets."

It was February 22nd, Washington's birthday. Yes, a very special day. On this day in 1951 Glen and I had blazed a trail over the Swiss Alps through a raging blizzard to visit the deBivorts, friends we had met on our honeymoon. We'd been hitchhiking to North Africa when they picked us up and took us to Geneva. They were so enjoyable that we stayed for two weeks before changing our itinerary and heading for Germany. Once there we landed jobs with the U.S. government fifty miles from the Russian border—an ongoing adventure. A year later found us struggling over a mountain pass, unaware that the road had been closed, making our presence not only illegal, but extremely dangerous. And a tribute to the fortitude of our little TD MG. Today, a lifetime later, and two continents away, the weather was blazing hot and the adversary was traffic, not snow.

By the time we reached the entrance to the palace-turned-luxury-hotel, all traffic had stopped. I took leave of my driver, who refused any tip, insisting that I had given him more than enough money the night before.

"No, not necessary," he said, shaking his head emphatically. "You—me, friends."

I took his skinny brown hand in mine. "You're a good man," I said, "and I like you."

He was still smiling when I turned the corner and walked between two pillars onto a boulevard of shade trees and sculpted hedges. It was slow going as I plowed through the crowded street to the south portico of Rambagh Palace. Police and army personnel were standing at ramrod attention along the way. Suddenly, sirens began to wail. Several motorcycle policemen rode by in close formation. Behind them the turbaned prime minister, rising from his open car, stood and waved to the cheering throng…like the Pope. I waved back, and continued through the gate, past gardens that had been designed years ago by the ruling British. Decorative statues and fountains reflected the morning sun. The glare softened as it reached the creamy stucco surface of the sprawling edifice, with its domes and columns and wide verandas. A soft coral trim accentuated the perfect symmetry of the arches and windows.

Inside the palazzo I tried to ignore the plethora of overstuffed, bespangled tourists. Perhaps I could grab a cup of coffee on the terrace. Closed. For the Prime Minister. So I sat at a small front table of the grand dining room and ordered the only thing I could afford—a toasted cheese sandwich and a cup of coffee. I needed something bland after all the spicy food.

Two musicians, dressed in the traditional turban and *dhoti*, entered and sat cross-legged on a semicircular platform. One placed a multi-stringed bowed instrument between his legs, holding it like a cello although it was the size of a skinny violin. The other squatted next to two drums, which had been tied together at intervals with leather thongs. I scrambled for my tape recorder. Just what I wanted—authentic Indian music.

The first time the man pulled his bow over the strings the instrument gave a painful yowl. The "tune" was played briefly, followed by a scale going up and down the strings five times. It was not a traditional scale, but more of a *glissando*.

The tones all ran together. Then the tune was repeated. The rhythm was anybody's guess. This went on and on, played in a wavy, nervous vibrato that made me feel as if I were hanging over the side of a fishing schooner in a stormy sea. The drummer was a little more imaginative and tried, valiantly, to adjust to the erratic rhythm of the string player. At times he would go off on his own, beating wildly with the palm and heel of either hand, leaving his partner behind. Once I detected the beginnings of an Indian *raga*, tenuous and out-of-tune, which was interrupted by the drummer who, perhaps, felt it his duty to save the day.

My ears were ringing by the time the waiter brought my sandwich. I looked down at two limp, crustless pieces of white bread with a sliver of processed cheese between them.

"This is toasted cheese?" I asked. The words slipped out before I could stop them.

He looked apologetic. "This is India, Madam. Not our food."

I was immediately sorry I'd spoken like a spoiled tourist. "It's O.K., really. I mean, how can I complain? All this free entertainment...." I ventured a timid smile, but he didn't get it.

I left the dining room before the final scale had been executed, or should I say annihilated. If I hurried I might catch the last tour of the day to Amber Fort. As I left the palace grounds I passed another snake charmer. Nervously, I skirted the weaving cobra, giving him a wide berth.

I reached the bus. Breathless. Smoke was billowing from its belly. Young boys, who had been squatting at the curb waiting to pounce on any unsuspecting tourist, followed me to my seat. Kids are really enterprising in India. Seasoned merchants at eight years old. As I waited for the bus to leave they thrust packets of postcards into my lap and started bargaining. I played dumb.

"Oh, is this for me?" I asked. "A gift. How nice."

They pretended not to understand, and never quit pushing. When the bus started to pull away, they grabbed the cards and raced for the door, reaching it just before it clanged shut.

The bus jiggled along the rugged route to the bare hills ten miles out of town. On the way it passed an imposing palace built right into a lake, its ornate windows at water level and its towers faultlessly reflected in the still water. It looked like a Disney creation about to rise from the deep.

As we approached the mountains Amber Fort came into view—a complex of towers, walls, and ramparts. Built in 1592, this was the ancient capital of Jaipur State. It was mainly a residential fort as compared to Jaigarh, considered a defensive fort. Here had lived the *maharaja's* twelve wives and 350 concubines. A busy man.

We reached the entrance and raced up 260 stone steps into a spacious courtyard. More stairs led to the palaces of Sawai Jai Singh, the inventive ruler whose observatory I'd admired on my first day in Jaipur. The palace was a perfect synthesis of Moghul and Hindu styles—columns of carved elephants adorned with fancy cornices, intricately painted ceilings, and an ingenious set of arcades.

Large black-faced velvet monkeys roamed in the formal gardens, scampered up and down the terraces, and hopped among the branches of the leafless trees, while goats chewed the evergreens. The monkeys walked right up to me and begged for food, with frightening boldness.

This rich complex held several more palaces, but the most fascinating to me was the Hall of Mirrors (*Sheesh Mahal*), the *maharaja's* bedroom, used in the winter because the glass retained heat. We craned our necks to see the tiny beads of curved mirror set in elaborate patterns high above us. They were designed to twinkle like stars when the oil lamps were lit. As the guide moved two candles up and down, the beads seemed to travel back and forth across the vaulted ceiling.

Close by was a separate summer area with filigreed marble ducts, behind which scented water circulated, forming natural air conditioning. The water continued to flow down a series of chutes into the garden, where it provided needed irrigation.

I looked out the window at the remains of the deeply scalloped outer wall, built 350 years ago to make Amber Fort impenetrable. It ran up and over distant hills until it reached another monument to the Moghul emperors, Jaigarh Fort, reflected in the tranquil waters of Amber Lake.

The sun was setting when I arrived back at the Teej tourist bungalow and transferred to a bicycle rickshaw. At the fruit market I stocked up on apples and oranges, then walked the rest of the way to the Bissau. The air was still. The day was winding down. I was aware of the smell of cooking. The muted sounds of radio music. I let my fingers trail along the textured murals on construction walls, and I peeked into stairwells where I saw the same bold art crying out against everyday drabness. More proof that in every aspect of its life India was passionately artistic.

At one of the tiny stores opposite the Bissau's main gate I bought a beer and some bottled water. The illusive cluster of black, long-haired pigs, which I had been trying, unsuccessfully, to photograph, grunted and nosed around in the dirt at my feet. Several enterprising rickshaw drivers swarmed around me—smiling, cajoling, trying to sell me trinkets—as they did every time I came in or out of the gate. I was getting to know them. And I looked forward to their greetings.

A little boy I'd seen several times, barefoot with dark penetrating eyes, came up to me. "Are you leaving, Madam?" he asked, his head moving amiably from side to side.

"Yes, day after tomorrow. And I shall miss you. But we'll talk before then."

He smiled and bowed his head, hands in the traditional prayer position. I returned the gesture, then walked slowly through the archway to my cozy room.

No sooner had I settled down for an evening of letter writing than the wind began to blow. Tapestries lifted off the walls. Papers took flight. Torrents of rain—the first in about a week of perfect weather—descended, accompanied by ear-splitting thunder. The lights died. I lay on my bed, listening to the staccato play of rain on the clay roof and enjoying the coolness of the intermittent drops splashing in through the window.

After an hour I raced to the main building, which was all aglow with candles, and ordered dinner. The coconut chicken and fried rice were pleasant enough, but I still had letters to answer. And I was dreadfully behind in my journal. The lights came back on just as I returned to my room. Hooray! I didn't have to write by flashlight. I reread the beginning of Martha's letter.

Dear Mom,

I'm only three months pregnant and I feel big as a house. I'll barely make the fashion shoot in New York next month, but I have to do it. We need the money for Baby and for law school. Yesterday I heard the heartbeat. It was incredible! He/she kicked three times in 20 seconds, then swam and swooshed away. It was like a communication from deep within my body. I can't explain the feeling, but I <u>know</u> you know what I'm talking about. Russell put his ear to my belly and flipped. "It sounds like the ocean. Like an aquarium," he said. We're both so excited!

Your trip sounds marvelous. But what is this nonsense you wrote from South Africa? "I'll get used to living alone." Give me a break, Mom. Stop sounding like a martyr. Remember, it was <u>your</u> choice to go it alone. And a good one for both you and Dad. You have enormous energy and chutzpah. Look what you're doing right now. Create that kind of adventure here at home. Alone or not.

We're crazy about San Francisco and can't wait to show you our new apartment come June.

Dear Martha,

Thanks for the letter and the fight talk. Yes, I do get lonely, sometimes, when I think of the future, but there's too much distraction in my life right now to "dwell on it," to quote your Grandmother Noble. Sorry I sounded so gloomy. South Africa was pretty intense, but the "down" mood was short lived. After all, isn't one of the reasons for this trip to face the world as a whole person, not half a couple? So why am I in a panic about being alone? And why am I making predictions about the rest of my life? Good questions. Tune in next week to find out if....

Seriously, thanks for your faith in me. It's almost as if the tables are turned and you're my parent telling me to buck up. Your sister is doing the same thing. Is this what dotage is all about?

I just got a letter and a crazy poem from Robert. Seems to have settled into his Brooklyn apartment. He's quite a writer, and quite a photographer. But I wonder how long he'll be able to stand location scouting. It sounds exhausting. I must say that I'm happy with my children. See what you have to look forward to…in twenty, thirty years. In the meantime, you'll love the process. It's a fascinating journey. Enjoy every minute as it unfolds. I certainly did.

India takes a lot of getting used to. At first all you see is poverty and misery side-by-side with opulence and privilege. Although there's plenty of that in our country as well, it's somewhat hidden, more separate. But in India the contrast is all around you. I try not to let these depressing aspects spoil my appreciation of the overall beauty and uniqueness of the culture. Walking the streets, I feel the way I did when you and I were in Florence. Surrounded by history. Captivated. Entranced.

The religion, on the other hand, is more difficult for me to fathom—all those gods, all those reincarnations of the Hindu trilogy. And so is the caste system. There's a search for identity with the universe, and a rigid social order which is sacred. Therefore, a Hindu's acceptance of his place in society is essential in this quest for Cosmic oneness. But that idea is anathema to most Westerners. And it's also receiving some flack here, especially among those younger people who abhor the system.

In two days I go to New Delhi, then Agra and Varanasi (the sacred city, formerly Benares). Funny how much I miss Africa, especially Kenya and its wide open spaces, its relaxed pace. The days in India have been such a contrast. An intense, convoluted tapestry of people, sights, and sounds.

I think I'm toured and templed out for the moment. I've seen enough cows in the streets, and stepped over enough elephant dung, and been traumatized by enough sickly waifs to last a lifetime. I'm in need of quiet, pastoral beauty—that balm to the soul that Cary talks about. I can't wait to get to the mountains.

Keep writing with news of my developing grandchild. I treasure every tidbit.

Love to the "growing" Bixlers, Mom

As I drifted off to sleep I could feel the warm wind blowing the curled up dried leaves that had escaped the deluge. They circled about my window, gently slapping at the bars. Their smell filled me with memories of autumn and childhood.

32

DISCOVERING DELHI

A persistent knock on the door shattered my sleep. "Madam, I have your ticket for the super deluxe video bus to New Delhi." It was the voice of the concierge.

I sat up. "What time is it? When does it leave?"

"It is nearly seven. The bus leaves in two hours. You must hurry. You must not be late."

How pleasant to wake up to the gentle rolling r's of this congenial little man. I thanked him and lay back, watching a shaft of yellow sun stream into my room and dance, for an instant, on the golden threads of a tapestry. I took a deep breath. The heavy rains of two nights ago had wiped away all mugginess, leaving only the subtle fragrance of wild orchid. Another perfect day.

Faith and James would be well on their way to Kashmir by now. We had spent the previous day roaming around town, writing in our journals, talking. Most of the time without James, who was deep into a Michener novel. I saw very little future in their relationship, and it made me sad. It was obvious that they were in love, but the barriers to a lasting marriage seemed insurmountable. And it was certainly better to confront reality early on and not wake up twenty years later, as I had, to face the incompatibilities that were there from the very beginning. Glen believed in open marriage. I didn't. I loved classical music. He put up with it. I was a minister's daughter who cared little for money. He felt that I was totally unrealistic and lived in a dream world.

Faith finally admitted that she was afraid to have children—afraid of the physical pain and the responsibility—though she longed for them in the abstract. And James wanted a family. Maybe she'd adopt a ten-year-old or find somebody with a ready-made family. I didn't tell her how much easier babies were than ten-year-olds. She wouldn't have believed me, and she really didn't know *what* she wanted. Faith had no practical plan. She was all emotion. The epitome of a free spirit.

"Besides, James is too possessive. I feel stifled," she said, looking slightly ferocious. I related to this. I didn't want anybody ordering my life or planning my future, either.

"Could you love two people at the same time, Meg?"

"I can love many people at the same time, but two men, two lovers? No." I had been badly burned by infidelity. I was no longer trying to be broadminded in that area.

"For me there has to be trust. Commitment. Or nothing," I said.

In the late afternoon we stood at the station watching a couple of pigs wander on and off the tracks. It was an upbeat farewell, for we planned to meet, again, in Kathmandu. On the way back to the Bissau I wrapped myself in the fragile pink glow that filled the town. I felt rested, revived by the unhurried day.

"You must go quickly, Madam. The bus will not wait." The concierge had returned and was hovering over me at breakfast like a mother hen. Tucked between the pages of my journal were several of his outrageous, "reasonably priced" erotic prints. Before leaving I handed him fifty rupees, about $3.80, the cost of the bus ticket for the 350-mile trip from Jaipur to New Delhi. He bowed graciously and hurried me out the door. I walked slowly down the driveway past velvet lawns and flowering bushes. At the gate one of the drivers lifted my pack into his rickshaw. I turned toward the concierge and waved. He waved back nervously. So what if I missed the bus? I'd get to spend another night in the beautiful Hotel Bissau.

The stench in the streets leading to the station was augmented by an overflowing sewer. People stood around while a young man poked with a stick, trying to unplug it. Children played in the brown mess. All part of the morning activities.

I took in my last views of Jaipur. Women sat cross-legged in a circle, sorting stones. Artisans designed and polished the completed jewelry. Old men hovered over coal fires in their rag-covered cubicles, preparing food, forging metal. Some sat outside in front of treadle sewing machines, staring passively at the beehive of activity all around them.

Once at the station I engaged a red-turbaned porter for two rupees. There were just too many steps leading to platform 3. How different from my experience on the local bus in Zimbabwe. Prompt boarding, wide seats, *on time* departure. The concierge had been right. I barely made it.

I wanted the experience of an Indian movie—something the guidebooks said was a must—and I got it, at high decibel, for the next three hours. It wasn't as bad as the canned music going down the coast of South Africa, because I could laugh at the ridiculous antics on the screen. But it was bad enough. Loud singing, stylized dancing, broad acting. Drama at its most melodramatic.

We drove, steadily, for four hours. When a respite finally came I was so hungry that I bought a harmless-looking vegetable *samoa,* which set my throat on fire and cleared my sinuses. How I longed for some nice bland, swallowable food. Thank heaven I had a few pecans and a large red carrot stashed in my pack.

I settled back to read my guidebook. How could I absorb the 3,000 years of history surrounding Delhi? The rise and fall of Moghul shahs. Battles, counter-battles, invasions, massacres. And to think how I struggled with a few hundred years of American history. After awhile I contented myself with watching the changing panorama. Women squatting by the roadside stringing flowers. Stone quarries looming like mountains sliced in half. Shacks with roofs of red thatch. Palm trees, thorny *babool,* and *casuarina* with its whorls of scale-like leaves.

The arid landscape became flat and crisscrossed with farms as we approached Delhi. The remaining hilly spurs signaled the end of the Aravalli mountain range seen in Udaipur and Jaipur. Groups of sacred rhesus monkeys, multi-colored parakeets, and cackling myna birds perched on ridges and trees along the road, as if to spur us on.

All of this changed, abruptly, at 6 P.M. when we arrived at New Delhi's modern terminal. I stepped from the bus into a noisy gaggle of auto-rickshaw drivers.

"I want to go to the YMCA…or the YWCA," I shouted, waving my arms.

"No problem, Madam," said a large man, muscling his way through the crowd. In no time we were skimming along the grand boulevards of India's capitol and third largest city. Sprawling, modern, western in flavor, it had wide avenues, numerous parks, and seven million people.

Alas! Both "Y's" were filled, with long waiting lists. Now began a discouraging search for a "tourist rest house." But each place was worse than the previous one. The Bissau had spoiled me.

My rickshaw bill had reached 60 rupees by the time we entered a hole in the wall just off Connaught Place, the central, horseshoe-shaped hub of New Delhi from which all main streets radiated. At the top of a marble staircase was a spacious room with a picture window and bath—for 330 rupees ($25). Not in my budget. But for one night…why not?

That evening I turned into an unapologetic Westerner. My guidebook suggested Nirula's Potpourri for those who needed relief from the heat of Indian food. This was a Baskin Robbins-type ice cream parlor with a brightly-lit restaurant on the second floor. In the center was a salad bar. On each table were paper place mats with a menu and a map of the city. At last a dinner that didn't bring tears to my eyes. With Sangria, breads, and all the fruit and chocolate mousse I could eat—for $5. This was heaven!

After dinner I decided to continue my search for the greatest chocolate ice cream on earth, and planted myself in front of the display case lining one wall of the downstairs parlor. I sampled ten flavors, relishing each tiny spoonful, before deciding on a large chocolate almond fudge cone.

"This is the best ice cream I've ever tasted," I announced. "And to think it's *Indian!*"

"Oh no, it isn't, Madam," said a young man in white cap and uniform, one of six who stood behind the counter waiting to serve the customers. "It's made here in Delhi by an American."

There was such a warm feeling among all of us standing around the counter that I wasn't prepared for the stark reality waiting just outside the door. As I entered the street a wretched-looking woman and her two little girls accosted me, holding out their hands, pulling on my skirt. I was high on good food and good fellowship. And still clutching the cone. It was 11 P.M.

I took off down the street, through dark arcades lined with sleeping bodies. But there was no escape. The mother followed me and the little girls fluttered by, pushing their dirt-stained hands into my face. They were like mosquitoes buzzing around. I couldn't stand it, and finally handed them the ice cream cone, which is not what the mother wanted. I'd been told many times never to pay attention to beggars. They could find enough to live on if they only stayed in their own villages. But they hadn't. They were here. And they were hungry.

I reached Connaught Place. A car full of young men rode by. They began to follow me, slowing down, speeding away, returning.

"Lady—want to have a good time? Want to be happy? *Really* happy?" they shouted, as if repeating a well-worn mantra.

I ignored them and walked faster. This phrase, and variations thereof, would follow me throughout India. I'd already had a taste of the "pleasure" line in the Pune railroad station. Maybe, as Sham had said, it was my fuchsia shirt, the symbol of the *Rajneesh*. Or maybe these were just guys driving around, looking for a little action.

I ducked into my hotel. Their boldness hadn't scared me, but it was a nuisance. And it was becoming more and more evident that a woman traveling alone in the Third World was thought to be sending an unequivocal message: I'm available. That's why I'm here.

The next morning I strolled down to the American Express to collect my mail. Bunches of it, for I was about one month behind schedule. While standing in line

I was "chatted up" by an English gentleman who ran educational tours in India and was staying at the YMCA. Even before he told me, I had him pegged as a professor. For one thing he was smoking a pipe.

"Lucky you," I said. "I tried to get a room last night. There are no openings until April."

"By Jove, what a coincidence," he said, bubbling with good cheer. "I'm leaving today. Why not put your name down for my room? It's worth a try. That's the only way to do it, you know, if you don't have a reservation."

I flew back through town, dodging a wall of protesters marching in front of Parliament. I turned the corner onto Jai Singh Road and raced to the reception desk at one end of the lobby.

"Dr. Bruce Harcourt's room, please. We're friends and he said he's leaving and I could have it...I can move in right away." I'd have gotten down on my knees, if necessary.

"All right, Madam. We'll put you on the list." He tried to hide his amusement.

I sat in the lobby, breathless and sweating, and looked out at the garden. I was reminded of the time my children and I hitchhiked through Europe and stayed at the Studentenheim in Innsbruck, Austria. It was our fanciest hostel—a large, open building with lots of windows and a friendly, breezy atmosphere. The "Y" had the same ambiance, that of a busy college dormitory.

For half-an-hour I watched the faces of the world go by. And to add to the home away from home atmosphere, what should be hanging at one end of the lobby but the benign, beatific painting of the bearded Jesus—the one that hung in every Methodist Sunday school in North America in the 40's...and probably still does. So familiar, so comforting.

An hour later I stepped onto my private balcony and gazed into the garden five floors below. The perfume of bougainvillea floated past me and entered the cheery room through high casement windows. A fan cooled me. Such luxury! And for only $7, breakfast included. I lay down on the bed, hands propped behind my head, and pondered my good fortune. My eyes wandered to the opposite wall where a large religious calendar fluttered in the breeze. This month Jonah was pictured, swimming frantically, the whale in hot pursuit. Under the picture in large letters were these comforting words: HE WILL NOT FORSAKE YOU! GOD IS MERCIFUL. I smiled.

Now that the excitement of finding a room at the "Y" was over, I had to deal with the ever-worsening problem of my infected abdomen. I decided to go to the

American Embassy and find a doctor. And, if possible, get my visa for Nepal at the same time.

The long ride to the embassy gave me my first overview of Delhi. I had read that even before the British came it had acquired a synthesis of Hindu and Moslem traditions—a distinct Indo-Islamic culture. And that it was a city of a thousand monuments, reflecting its powerful pageant of rulers. Everywhere I looked I was intrigued by the mixture of old and new. Ancient *tongas* (horse carriages) and streamlined limousines shared the boulevards with scores of putt-putting motorized rickshaws like mine. Street acrobats, dancing bears, and monkeys entertained small groups of onlookers along the way. *Purdah*-clad women, with their faces veiled, walked two steps behind their husbands. Obediently, with heads slightly bowed. Jean-clad students, men and women in smart western attire, ladies elegantly wrapped in *saris*, old men in turbans and billowing *dhotis*, all strolled alongside one another.

I was in great spirits when I arrived at the embassy. Excited to be on a bit of legal U.S. "soil," again. Upon entering the building I immediately spotted an inviting water fountain—the hallmark of every U.S. facility I'd ever visited—and made a beeline toward it. A guard stopped me.

"Your passport," he barked. I fished into my camera case.

With cold efficiency he searched me, impounded my camera, Swiss army knife, and tape recorder, then motioned me to a holding room, where I sat on a hard bench for an interminable time, like an illegal immigrant. This is not the way I had expected to be greeted as a fellow citizen. Except for showing my passport every time I got up to go anywhere, including the bathroom, I felt invisible. I understood the need for security, but did this preclude a little chitchat to pass the time?

Finally, an officious lady called me to a barred window and stated that the medical services of the embassy were not open to me. And they could not issue a visa to Nepal. How could I not have known this, she asked, underscoring my stupidity. I was given a list of "acceptable" Indian doctors and the address of the Nepalese embassy. Dismissed. Next?

I grabbed a cab and went to the first address on the list. The residence, with attached office, looked like one of the '30's houses in upstate New York where I had lived as a child—wide porch, stubby pillars, ivy creeping up the lattice—except that it had a white painted metal gate guarding the yard, a bright-orange, tiled roof, and a new Mercedes parked at the curb.

Dr. N. P. S. Chawla was tall and aloof. He wore the traditional turban of a *Sikh*, and an immaculate white suit. Standing next to him I felt grungy and unkempt. His beard was meticulously groomed with a part down the jaw line, continuing up the middle of the chin. Elastics were training the bushy mass to grow in the right direction.

The treatment room was spotless. Shiny instruments lay all in a row on a clean towel. No footprints on the examining table.

"Why have you let this infection go for so long?" he asked, gruffly, looking at my stomach with disgust. I found my eyes filling with tears. Not waiting for an answer, he continued. "How very foolish to think it could be healed topically. You need to take a strong antibiotic by mouth."

Some bedside manner!

"You should not embark on such a journey without proper protection. You are in the Third World. What did you expect? I thought Americans had more sense. Yes, you are a foolish woman." My God, he sounded like Glen. Perhaps I should introduce them.

"But I did go to the hospital in Udaipur…." I began, weakly.

"I don't want to hear excuses…what you did or didn't do. Just take these pills four times a day for ten days. You can get them at any pharmacy." He scribbled a prescription and tore off the sheet. "Come back in a week if it is not completely healed."

Was he like this with everyone, or just women? A little devil deep inside told me to click my heels and salute. I resisted the urge, but I was angry. Come back in a week? Not on your life!

On the way out I paid the bill, $5.40. The pharmacy charge was $6.80. A little sweetener to make up for the doctor.

I met Katie Stillwell the next morning on a tour of Old Delhi. She was a thirty-six year old housewife from Australia. Perky, robust, determined. Still smarting from my encounter with Dr. Chawla, I told her about my experience with infection in India. She told me about her father, a pharmacist in the Outback who used natural, herbal medicines long before they were popular, and long before the introduction of synthetic, chemically produced drugs.

"You have to get an infection early, Meg, and it doesn't sound like you kept yours very clean. How come it got so out of hand?"

"It's quite a story," I said. "How many days do we have?" She laughed.

I could relate to this a woman. A direct, say-it-like-it-is, practical person, she also possessed a sparkling sense of humor that burst from her like buckshot, just when things seemed darkest.

Katie and her husband, Derek, ran a farm in eastern Australia, and she was here to pick up a second child—a five-month-old boy—from an orphanage outside Delhi. She already had a four-year-old Indian girl, but at the time of that adoption, she had been denied access to the orphanage. The baby had been delivered to her by a surrogate. This time she wanted to see conditions first hand, but was being given the runaround by the wealthy matron and her husband, who, until yesterday, had not allowed her to visit.

"I'm in a real snit," she said, her eyes flashing. "I wouldn't be on this bus if I could get my hands on my son. But it's better to be busy than sitting at the "Y" agonizing. You can't imagine what I've gone through. And this place calls itself a religious orphanage? Their religion is money. They don't care what happens to the babies. I saw them, myself, lying passively in their cribs. Never touched or hugged. What a sterile, deadening environment. And I'm certain they're being drugged to keep them quiet. It took three weeks for my daughter to come out of her lethargy once I got her home. It's scandalous! Criminal! These so-called service agencies do everything to stand in the way of giving children a real home. It could put you off adopting, now couldn't it?"

I didn't know what to say as the words came tumbling out.

"I'm going to write to the adoption bureau just as soon as I get my child out of there. Deliberate harassment of adoptive parents...that's what's going on. They think that if they put a sign on the wall that says "God is Love" they can do anything. The matron even suggested that it might speed up the adoption process if I made a contribution. And all the while she's using the older orphans to do her housework. I saw it! Downright slavery. Puts me in mind of 'Nicolas Nickleby.'"

As angry as Katie was, there was a bit of humor in that last remark. But she soon gathered a new head of steam.

"People here are blind to the misery of these orphans. Hindus think it's an inevitable stage in human evolution. You know, one of the million lives we're supposed to go through to reach perfection, or whatever it is that allows us *not* to be born again. So what if innocent babies suffer. It's their lot. Bull is what I say!"

There was no sense trying to calm Katie down. Who cared if people were staring. I agreed with her. This was just another example of the pervasive acceptance of the caste system, that stultifying societal and religious division of labor. And I didn't buy it. How can you accept misery? The longer I stayed in India the more I realized that many Indians felt the same way.

We reached our first stop, *Rajghat*, on the banks of the Yamuna River. The site of Ghandi's cremation on January 30, 1948. There was a hush as we entered the park. We removed our shoes and proceeded down a wide footpath to the memorial, which was a simple *samadhi*, a raised platform of black marble, six by nine feet. On this were inscribed the last words Ghandi uttered before his assassination: *He Ram* (Hail God). At one end was a large copper urn in which burned an eternal flame. Wreaths adorned the four corners, with a fresh spray of flowers in the center. Katie and I wanted to stand and be quiet, think about this man and his non-violent struggle for India's independence. But the tourists had picture taking in mind. They posed in front of the sleek marble, smiling and hugging, as if they were standing before the lions in Trafalgar Square.

As we walked back to the bus, past humble artisans demonstrating age-old crafts like spinning and weaving, two large *Sikhs* muscled their way in front of us and onto the bus.

"Blimey," spouted Katie loudly. "You blokes nearly knocked us over." She turned to me. "Did you ever meet such rude men? Hey fellas, ever hear of chivalry...or good manners?"

The men ignored her.

"I feel like the flea who annoyed the elephant," I whispered to Katie. This started us giggling until, like kids, we were doubled over in our seats. The two men turned and gave us withering glances worthy of their perceived status.

Our next stop was the Red Fort, or *Lal Qila*, built during the peak of Moghul power and considered one of the finest achievements of Indo-Islamic architecture. Construction was started in 1639 and completed in 1848. Its walls encircled the entire area for over a mile and rose to 100 feet on the city side.

Our driver squeezed the bus off the road near the crowded west end of Chandni Chowk, the main street of the historic city of Shahjahanabad, now the popular shopping bazaar of Old Delhi, specializing in ivory carving and silver and gold embroidery. Both the city and the fort were built by Emperor Shah Jahan of Taj Mahal fame, just after he transferred his capitol from Agra to Delhi. The slender streets and alleys were hopelessly congested. What a contrast from the spacious boulevards of New Delhi.

We entered the fort by the Lahori gate, which faces toward Lahore, now in Pakistan, and made our way through vaulted arcades into capacious galleries and marble halls. The *Diwan-i-Am* (Hall of Public Audience), with its rows of columns, was at the center of the fort on a raised plinth, three of its sides open for ceremonial events. It was originally ornamented with gold and precious stones and hung with brocaded velvet from Turkey and silk from China.

"Hey, Meg, take a look...there, behind you," said Katie, pointing to several men bent over an elaborate, fluted fountain. "I do believe they're scrubbing it with toothbrushes.

She was right. Down on their hands and knees, these men attacked the marble with vigor. It was a job that would certainly take days to finish. "Good thing the water is turned off," I said.

What a shame that so many of the marble halls had fallen prey to robbers and greedy rulers, men who absconded with gold ornaments, rubies, and sapphires, leaving gaping holes where the treasures had once been. Even the famous bejeweled Peacock Throne had been carried off to Persia by Nadir Shah in 1739. But, despite the plundering, what remained was superb.

Just before we left, I came upon an ancient Persian couplet inscribed on the marble alcove of the Hall of Justice. It said what all of us were feeling.

> If there is a paradise on earth
> It is this, it is this, it is this

Our last stop was *Jami Masjid*, the largest mosque in India and the last architectural extravaganza of Shah Jahan. It took 5,000 workers fourteen years to complete, and could fit 25,000 people into its central courtyard, which measured 4000 square ft. This vast expanse was enclosed by pillared corridors with domed pavilions at each corner. In the main prayer hall stood an arched facade and a pulpit carved from a single block of marble.

I counted three giant gateways, four towers, and two minarets, which stood 120 feet high and were constructed of alternating vertical stripes of red sandstone and white marble. Broad flights of stairs led to the imposing gateways and their heavy doors. Katie and I climbed up to the great raised central plinth. Straight ahead, through one of the archways, we caught a striking view of Red Fort. All around us people were bowing and praying. Birds were squawking as they swooped low over the crowds. Everything seemed to blend together. Onion-shaped domes, lotus leaf cornices, the calling of the faithful. It was a madhouse!

I decided to leave the confusion and wait in the bus below. Halfway down the bank of stone steps I stopped and leaned over to tie my shoe. A grimy brown hand thrust itself in front of my face. "Chocolate, Madam, pen, Madam, rupees. Two rupees, Madam. *Please?*"

The supplications continued. I didn't look up. Two more hands nearly touched my face. I turned to move away, and, in my haste, stepped on one of the thin, waxy laces. It snapped. Damn! My only laces. I'd never find another such pair in India. I moved over to the side to try to repair it. I was hot. Dusty. And there were those hands. I said nothing and kept my head down. As the children moved in on me I became acutely aware of the tiny feet attached to the bodies I couldn't see. The nails were chipped, the skin like leather. Those baby feet. It's not fair. It's not right. I stood up at last. The look that met my eyes had been perfected—wide-eyed, pleading. Next to me stood a well-dressed, pot-bellied *Sikh*, pearl-white turban, dark eyes staring straight ahead. I was angry…angry for all the times this had happened to me and for all the suffering and because my shoelace was ruined. I felt miserable. And I lost my cool.

"*He's* rich," I shouted, pointing to the well dressed, indifferent man. "Leave me alone and go bother *him* for a change!"

I turned my fury on the man. "How can you stand there oblivious to this suffering? These are *your* people. You have *some* responsibility. For heaven's sake, don't just stand there!"

He looked down at me disdainfully and moved a few paces away.

By now the crowd of waifs nearly surrounded me, some of them hardly bigger than the babies they held. Their noses ran, and I found myself thinking, how disgusting. More guilt. The hair stood in coarse clumps out from their faces and brown rags hung from the tiny bodies. Blending in with the skin. They were miniature women. Not little girls. I've had little girls.

Tears of frustration and despair erupted as I fled, almost falling over the clinging children. "Chocolate, Madam, rupees…."

Katie caught up with me and the children immediately turned to her, repeating their mantra.

"Chocolate?" she queried. "Heavens, no. I wouldn't even give chocolate to my own daughter. Now scat. Away. Be gone." In a dramatic gesture she dismissed them and turned to me.

"Don't feel bad, Meg. You were magnificent. Blowing off steam never hurt anybody, and may have done that bloke some good."

She grabbed my arm and walked me the rest of the way down.

That night it was my turn to minister to Katie. I could hear her in the hall, shouting through the phone to her husband.

"Just wire the money. We have to get him out right away….I don't care, dammit. We'll earn it some way. Derek, these people are evil, and I want our baby out of there! Please…send the money. Now." She slammed down the phone. It echoed in the corridor.

Tears were streaming down her cheeks when she came into my room. I held her in my arms, like a little girl.

"Sometimes men can be maddeningly practical," she said, unable to choke back the sobs. "I know Derek cares as much as I do and feels just as helpless. But he has no idea what it's like at that place. He can't imagine. Most people can't."

There, there, I thought, you'll get your little boy. I won't leave until you do.

33

MADAM, HAVE YOU EVER REALLY BEEN HAPPY?

"Even the stones here whisper to our ears of the ages of long ago, and the air we breathe is full of the dust and fragrance of the past."

—*Prime Minister Jawaharial Nehru*

It was a beautiful lazy morning. I decided to relax, alone. Yesterday had been exhausting, physically and emotionally. I really liked Delhi, but preferred to take it slowly. Roam around the streets on my own. Give the tours a rest. Besides, Katie had gone to the orphanage with fire in her eyes and I wanted to be here to pick up the pieces when she returned…if the news was bad.

I moved onto the terrace and began reading my mail. I hadn't realized how low I'd been that last week in Cape Town. But it must have come through in my letters. Martha had picked up on it and now my sister, Cary, was responding. I'm sure all the discussions with Jenny and Matilda about marriage had contributed to my mood. And I couldn't hide it. Every now and then I would panic. Feel so alone. Unreasonable, my head would say, but my head wasn't always in charge.

Dear Miggie,

I can understand your pangs of loneliness only too well. When I visited John to get my books, I looked at the beautiful, spacious parsonage and wondered if living in such a situation, instead of my cramped two rooms, would be worth the compromise. Then I reminded myself of the loneliness and disappointment I'd experienced in just such comfortable surroundings, and realized that I'm now free to be me with no limitations. It's scary. But I won't find out who I really am by living the old role. I've never had a chance to be spontaneous or even a little bit outrageous. You know, I rather identify with the youngest daughter in <u>Crimes of the Heart</u>. The one who tried to kill her husband. Does that shock you? Well, let me tell you, Sweetie, not all my thoughts are pure.

Whenever I get feeling low, which is usually about once a week, I think of Aunt Ditty. Remember how she'd say, "Maybe I'll just take the gas pipe," when her pain got really bad? Then she'd look at us mischievously and assure us that "it's not the end of the world, girls, so stop looking so glum." She was right, Miggie. It's not.

It was noon, and I was still reading my mail when Katie appeared. She was ecstatic. "I won! Can you believe it? In two hours I pick up my baby. And they didn't say a word about money. I'm sure the matron is afraid I'll make such a fuss—and believe me, I'm going to—that they want to get rid of me as soon as possible. And that suits me just fine!" She danced a little jig, then threw her arms around me.

"Thanks for sticking with me, Meg. I'll miss you. You *will* visit us, won't you? We're not far from Sydney."

After lunch I put Katie in a cab. She carried her baby pack around her neck and it hung limp on her chest. Soon it would hold her new son. And she would take him directly to the airport.

"I can't thank you…." she began.

"Hush," I said. "Nor I you. One doesn't find a new friend like you every day."

No tears. I would see her in Australia. No doubt about it.

That evening I attended a classical concert. It was a long way from the "Y" but the night was balmy and I was in good spirits. I'd spent the afternoon writing letters and drinking tea, which was served by creaky old men who tapped on my door, hoping to earn a few rupees for their service. They were bent, courteous, and sycophantic. And none of them wanted to make me happy.

After a ride through the plush part of town, past the estates of the super rich, we reached the pillared concert hall. I had commented to the driver, several times, on the beauty of the area and how different it was from anything I'd seen these past weeks.

"Why are you so surprised?" he said. "This is part of India, too. Just because all Americans are rich…." He stated this as a fact, with a slight lifting of the eyebrow as if to see my reaction.

"I'm not," I said as I handed him ten rupees.

He chuckled. "Then how did you get here?"

"By rickshaw," I said. His chuckle turned into a guffaw.

I entered the packed auditorium and found a seat on the floor in one of the side aisles. It was a program of traditional music played by an ensemble using guitar, lute-like instruments, bells, triangles, a xylophone, and a drum. A solitary man sat on his haunches near the front of the stage and clapped the rhythms softly, first striking his palms together, then, turning his hand over and hitting the back of one into the palm of the other. It gave an alternately sharp and muted timbre to the accompaniment. The music moved from lugubrious to sparkling, combining syncopated rhythms and traditional Indian scales. How unlike the poor imitation of Indian music I'd suffered through at the Rambaugh Palace in Jaipur. This was exciting. This was *real* music.

After the intermission, a plump dark-haired beauty with ample hips and buttocks entered from the wings. Hoots and hollers. She was a well-known dancer in the *Kathak* tradition of Jaipur. The crowd went wild as she began to move arms, feet, hands, and head in a slow, stylized manner. Her gilded clothing sparkled, twisted, and flowed. As the tempo increased so did the intricate footwork and frenetic arm waving. She was accompanied by voice, percussion, and one wailing violin. It was the most unusual Indian music I'd ever heard. I was enchanted.

The theater was off the beaten track, so rickshaws were scarce. I started walking. It was a long way to the first traffic circle, where I hoped to find a ride. The roads were deserted, the silence eerie, the sky a swirl of dark clouds. A canopy of trees hung over the lonely sidewalks. Leaf patterns made by the glow of modern streetlights played at my feet. As I was crossing from one traffic island to the next a bicycle rickshaw stopped. An enormous man stepped from the carriage.

"Please let me give you a ride," he said, in a thick accent. "You will not find another one at this time of night in this part of Delhi." I hesitated, looking at the small carriage and the even smaller driver.

The tall blond stranger continued in somewhat formal English, talking fast as if to convince me that he was a good person. "I come from Krakow. My name is Leszek Rafolski. I am sports announcer and I will cover the international table tennis tournament in New Delhi. I am going to hotel where the Polish team is staying. You would like to meet them, maybe?"

He said nothing about making me happy, so I stepped into the rickshaw, grateful to give my feet a rest.

"I am really here on my own," announced Leszek as we squashed ourselves into the tiny carriage. "Because I want an excuse to go to Kathmandu. That is my life's dream."

"How marvelous!" I said. "I have the same dream. When will you go? Perhaps we can meet." We nearly jumped from the carriage in our enthusiasm. The driver kept turning around and grinning. He seemed to be enjoying our spirited conversation, although we were two awfully big people to be pulling around.

By the time we reached the "Y" we'd made plans to leave messages at the American Express when we arrived in Kathmandu, and, perhaps, set up a trek on our own.

I handed the driver an extra ten rupees, which he gave to Leszek, who returned it to him. Back and forth the money went. "I cannot charge for the lady," the driver explained, "but perhaps she will need a ride to the train.".

Out came a piece of paper. He scribbled a phone number on it and handed it to me. I slipped it into my bag and thanked him.

Leszek bowed, took my hand, and kissed it. Wow! That would be some party in Kathmandu, especially if we connected with Faith and James.

I was so energized by the evening's events that I decided to try, once again, to reach Chris by phone. I'd been unsuccessful for the last two evenings, but hadn't endured the frustration of my lengthy episode at the C.P.O. in Jaipur. Busy circuits. That was all.

It was 1 AM. when I walked away from the desk and hurried toward the elevator. All of a sudden I became aware of quickening steps behind me and turned to see two men approaching.

"Madam, madam, please wait," they called in unison. Then the predictable, "Are you married? How old are you?"

I didn't wait for the rest. I was running by the time I reached the elevator. "But, Madam, you don't understand," they pleaded as the door closed.

Oh, don't I? I had never experienced such brazen harassment in all my travels. Of course I tended to be friendly, to ask a lot of questions and not hide the fact that I was alone. I even told my age upon request. Why not? It was fun to be honest now that I was out of the United States and in a part of the world where older was better. But perhaps I'd be a little more cautious in the future.

I reached my room and slipped inside. Where were all these unattached men back home, I thought, chuckling to myself.

I awoke feeling wonderful. It was my last full day in Delhi and I was determined to absorb every possible sight and sound. The weather was perfect and my painful infection was gone. The miracle of antibiotics. Why had I waited so long?

Delhi was like the heart of a gigantic artichoke whose leaves could be peeled off layer-by-layer exposing the relics of the seven medieval cities that had come and gone over the last 3,000 years. It was awash in monuments and shrines. And rich in stories. I shuddered at the gruesome tales of Moslem invaders, like the one where huge elephants ground every fort and Hindu temple to powder under their heels. They didn't fool around, those conquerors. But for all their ruthlessness they could never completely blot out the tenacious Indian culture.

The day began at the 16th century tomb of the second Moghul emperor, Humayun. It was here that the last Moghul emperor, his two sons and grandson, had taken refuge during the 1857 uprising. They were captured by the British and the sons and grandson sent to the gallows. Afterwards, their dead bodies were exposed to the people for twenty-four hours outside the Chandni Chowk police station. A grizzly episode from the days of Indian resistance to British rule.

The tomb, a precursor of the Taj Mahal, stands on an elevated arcaded sandstone platform. The arches are echoed on a larger scale inside the tomb, which consists of a number of rooms, instead of the usual single chamber. These smaller rooms contain the remains of 170 Moghul princes, many of whom met violent deaths. I felt as if I were back in Egypt as I stooped to make my way through the moldy, dank passageways and up the wide stone stairways.

Our guide took us out onto the spacious grounds so we could view the mausoleum from every angle. "This is the original example of the 'tomb-in-a-garden' complex," he intoned. "All perfectly symmetrical from every angle, and fashioned from red sandstone. Notice the delicate white marble detail, the fanciful cupolas. Clearly Indian in origin. But the large dome—a double shell surrounded by a planned square garden—is the first of its kind outside of Persia."

I moved away from the group and stood at the far end of the garden. As I stared at the crumbling edifice I wondered about the woman who had built such a noble memorial to her husband. The story of her devotion had not gripped the world's imagination as had that of Shah Jahan, the grieving husband who created the Taj Mahal. But the similarity was evident.

In an adjacent field a single peasant plowed behind his slow-moving ox. Everyday life went on in striking contrast to the grandeur of the past. Two black birds circled high, gliding and swooping, willing captives of the illusive thermals. I walked back to the bus, savoring the stillness.

Our next stop was the *Lakshmi Narayan* Hindu temple dedicated to Lord Vishnu, one of the Hindu trinity—*Brahma*, the creator; *Vishnu*, the preserver; *Shiva*, the destroyer. Within the sprawling complex were ornamented domes, columns of all shapes and sizes, and marble courtyards with inlaid sandstone borders. Every inch was highly decorated in pink, white, and light yellow. Idols resided in hidden alcoves. And a gold-clad figure of *Hari Krishna*, one of the reincarnations of Lord Vishnu, sat amidst burning incense. I was astonished to see swastikas carved into the stone. This hateful symbol of the Nazis had been a symbol of peace and good will for the ancient *Aryans*. A large plaque mounted on the marble wall states:

> This (Swastika) symbol is most sacred and ancient. At least for more than the last 8,000 years it has been the mark of Aryan (Hindu) civilization and culture. This symbol signified an implied prayer for success, accomplishment and perfection in every walk of life.

"There are four classes in India, and I am in the warrior class," our guide announced as we left the temple.

"How do you know?" I asked.

"It's my name...Singh," he replied. "It's a compulsory name for Warriors. There are Brahmans, Warriors, Business class, and Untouchables...those who do the lowly jobs."

A groan went up. "But you don't understand," he continued, anxious to clear up any misconceptions. "Things are changing. These Untouchables are getting more power, and they can make a lot of money these days, especially in the cities. Of course, in the villages it's more rigid. But the government has decreed against any discrimination because of caste."

"Yes," said a German tourist, "but you are still born into it and *that* cannot change." The guide shrugged and smiled wryly.

The tour ended ten miles south of New Delhi at the *Qutb* Complex, which surrounds the *Qutb Minar*, an impressive five-storied victory tower built in the 12th century. The first three stories are made of red sandstone and the other two of marble and sandstone, each one clearly distinguished from the outside by its uniquely-carved balcony.

Our guide, dwarfed by a filigreed obelisk that tapered upward to the sky, announced proudly: "This minaret is the largest in the world. And right here at its foot is the first mosque in India, *Quwwat-ul-Islam* (The Might of Islam), built on the ruins of twenty-seven Hindu temples."

I gazed at the remnants of columns that stretched ahead of me on the ground. They were smaller, more accessible, than those at the temple of Queen Hatshepsut in Egypt, and each had its own shape and design. I ran my fingers over some of the patterns. As I did, I felt an immediate connection with the stone and the earth and the creator of such beauty. I imagined that each column had just been completed and was waiting to be assembled, not part of a neglected graveyard.

It was early afternoon when I returned to the "Y". The doorman greeted me as "the girl in the safari hat." (I never went out bareheaded after baking in the midday sun of Jaipur.) I smiled and headed for the restaurant, where my reputation for having a sensitive palate preceded me.

"I can assure you, Madam," said one friendly waiter, as I sat down for lunch, "that if you will try this *raiki* made with fried rice and mutton it will be better this time. There will be absolutely no spices. I will personally tell the cook." Hope springs eternal.

My nose started running after the first bite. My mouth was an inferno. Tears streamed.

"Oh, my dear Madam," said the waiter, mortified. "I am so very sorry. Let me make you a sandwich. It will cost you nothing." He scurried to his sideboard and hunted for two *chapatties* and something to put on them. He returned, triumphant, with a concoction that looked like apple butter, apple slices, and hard cheese. Plus a full bowl of yogurt.

Now I fought back tears of a different kind. "How generous you are," I said, touching his arm. "This is one Indian meal I will remember happily."

I spent the rest of the afternoon at the nearest bazaar. The hours alone in Delhi were so enjoyable that I decided, impulsively, to stay another night and leave for Agra on the morning train. But I'd forgotten how tightly the "Y" was booked. And I'd forgotten that desk clerks, in my experience, were a special breed.

"Just one more night, sir," I pleaded. "I would be awfully grateful…."

For several minutes the clerk fingered his file cards and engaged in some serious rearranging. I wondered if he'd heard me.

Finally he turned and faced me with a fawning smile. "You are lucky. The "Y" is a very popular place, but I can make an exception just this once." I nodded happily. Then, as if to announce some earth-shaking news, he said, "Madam, tomorrow is my day off."

"That's nice," I mumbled.

"I will meet you in your room at 10 o'clock."

"What for?"

"Madam, I am single. You are single. I *must* see you."

"You're looking right at me now," I said.

"You do not understand, Madam. Have you ever *really* been happy?"

Not again! With all this happiness I would surely never get out of India. Without missing a beat, I answered. "Sir, I have, indeed, been truly happy many, many times. But thanks, anyway."

34

THE MIGHTY TAJ

With a furtive backward glance, half expecting to see the desk clerk leap out from behind a curtain, I made my early morning escape from the "Y", enjoying a hearty send-off from the turbaned doorman. A red sash and polished leather boots added a mischievous flair to his drab khaki uniform.

"Happy travels, girl in the hat," he said, bowing with exaggerated gallantry. Waiting at the curb was the beaming rickshaw driver who had given me his number after the concert. I'd called him the night before, hoping to repay him for his generosity.

What a relief to find myself booked into a first class coach all the way to Agra. I worked my way down a narrow corridor through a crowd of passengers who stood at the windows hoping to get some fresh air, but finding smoke and cinders instead. As I passed the toilet on whose door hung a large sign, INDIAN STYLE LATRINE, I smiled. Forewarned is forearmed.

My compartment was airy and clean. A retired couple, the Drs. Patel, were already seated by the window. Both were professors of psychology with doctorates from Columbia, and both had taught at the University of Oregon in Eugene before returning to India to enter government service. The coauthor of my first classroom music book was a professor from the University of Oregon, so we immediately connected. From then on conversation flowed freely, culminating in a discussion of the diverse religions practiced in India.

"Our prophet is Zoroaster," said Mrs. Patel. She sat ramrod straight and pressed her large hands into her lap, smoothing the folds of a modest blue cotton skirt. "He taught the worship of *Ahura Mazda*—the source of all good—who requires the practice of righteous thoughts, words, and deeds and the renunciation of evil."

This was the first time I'd met adherents of Zoroastrianism, and I was fascinated.

Mrs. Patel's dark eyes glowed. The silver hair fastened in a bun, and the gentleness of speech, gave me the feeling of being in the presence of a genuine ascetic. "The movement started north of the Himalayas and split, sending some of its members to Iran and some south to India. We who practice here are called *Parsis*."

"But we are fast disappearing as a religion," Dr. Patel said, rubbing his bony hands together and hunching lower into his seat. His lined face smoothed at the temples, where wisps of thin white hair poked through the olive skin. "You wouldn't believe the rules about intermarriage. They're totally unreasonable. For example, if a woman is not a Zoroastrian, but her husband is, the children can be. But if a man is not, even though his wife is, the children cannot be. Does that make sense to you?" I shook my head.

"We have only two children," interjected his wife, "and that's true of most of our people...another reason our numbers are dwindling. But we're determined to see that each child is well educated and can live a full life, materially and spiritually. And, of course, is a good person."

The hours flew by and we went on to other topics—government, food, social change, and, inevitably, the caste system.

"Our maid is Brahman," said Mrs. Patel. "Since this is the top of the religious hierarchy, she refuses to do certain lowly tasks, like sweeping and cleaning up. For such work we have to hire Untouchables. It's dreadfully sad. We pay more than most, but they hardly earn enough to eat."

I pictured the ragged, emaciated men and women I'd seen sweeping the streets and picking up litter, dust swirling around their heads and into their eyes. I could never get used to this abject poverty. It filled me with rage. It was so unfair. But to devout Hindus this is just one of the numberless sides of *Shiva*, who is manifested in every aspect of his creatures' life, humble or lofty, not a divine being standing outside of his creation like the God of the West.

We ordered tea and sat quietly for awhile. The terrain along the tracks was much flatter than in the south and dominated by puffy trees, irrigation canals, and round thatched huts. A more prosperous ambiance pervaded the small stations where we stopped. The people seemed better dressed and the children were in school uniforms. And there was no begging.

As I was preparing to leave, another couple barged into the compartment and demanded that the Patels vacate their seats. Their behavior was shocking, and put a damper on our farewells. The Patels, somewhat distracted, but calm, were still standing their ground when I left.

Two young men in a motorized rickshaw cornered me the minute I disembarked. Muhammad was a gnomish preppy type and Salim was an adonis with a black moustache and long sideburns. He was the driver—a gentle, friendly fellow who gave beggars a rupee without being gruff or disdainful. The three of us bonded at once.

I asked to stop at the Air India office on the way to my hotel, for I wanted to be in Varanasi in two days. An apologetic agent informed me that there were no seats available for the entire week, but recommended a new airline, Vayudoot, which flew eighteen-seat Dormiers—just the kind of planes that terrified me. "Their office is opposite the telegraph building. Easy to find," they said.

Off we sped over roads that scrambled my insides. My new friends insisted that this was false information, since they couldn't find any airline office near the telegraph building. So back we went to the train station, where I discovered that there were no seats on the train, either. I was actually relieved. It would have been a slow fourteen-hour trip.

There was no alternative but to go to my hotel, the Mayur Tourist Complex on the outskirts of Agra. It had been recommended by an acquaintance in New Delhi, and turned out to be an excellent choice. I was given a large, clean room…with a broken toilet and a dysfunctional bathtub. But the price was right.

"No problem, Madam. We'll fix it right away," said the scruffy, middle-aged desk clerk. He also offered to help me obtain a ticket to Varanasi, but held out little hope. "Just in case I fail," he added, "there's a small travel agency opposite the telegraph office. I don't remember its name."

Reluctantly, we returned to the dusty side street and looked more carefully. Sure enough, there stood one lowly storefront with a faded sign in Hindi. I could barely discern Vayudoot. No wonder we'd missed it. It was a veritable hole in the wall attended by an elderly, shuffling four-toothed agent wrapped in yards of white muslin. He looked like a cross between Alec Guinness and Indira Ghandi. His large feet were encased in sandals. His smile was crooked, fatherly. But he seemed to know nothing about planes or schedules. And he had no phone number. The more agitated I became the sadder he looked. The driver interpreted for me.

"He says he's sorry he can't help, but will take your name and put it on a reservation list."

He wrote laboriously on the back of an envelope. When I said I was afraid he might lose the envelope, he slowly transferred my name to an outdated desk calendar, then suggested that I return at 5…no 6…no, better make that 6:45 to catch the man from the airport, who would be stopping by at that time. Not very promising.

It was mid-afternoon before we left Vayudoot for the Taj Mahal. The ride through town was relaxing. I leaned back, watched the cloudless sky, and waited with anticipation for the first glimpse of the white spires. I had perused its alabaster face in storybooks and dreamed of seeing it since childhood. So I was not surprised at the depth of my emotional reaction.

We stopped at an outdoor bazaar, where Muhammad said goodbye. Salim stayed behind to wait for me. I entered the main courtyard and stopped, transfixed, upon seeing the gleaming monument framed in the large scalloped archway. Here was perfection! The ultimate blending of taste and simplicity.

I slowly walked inside, descended a bank of steps leading to a reflecting pool, and stood to one side in front of one of the rust-colored colonnades. Tears came to my eyes. A lump formed in my throat. Why was this affecting me so? Was it the thought of a profound love, which ended in a loss that transcended all the worldly needs and ambition of the bereaved? His beloved Mumtaz Mahal was the one thing money and power could not bring back to the great Moghul emperor, Shah Jahan. She was his confidante, his joy, and his constant companion, even during military campaigns. In 1631, in a tent near Burkenpur during the Deccan wars, she died giving birth to their fourteenth child. Shah Jahan's grief was so intense that he vowed to create the world's greatest monument to love. To me this had become a symbol of the ideal love that every man and every woman yearns for.

The sadness and disappointment that I'd experienced in my marriage came back to me at that moment. And, simultaneously, rushing to counteract the negative, came those special memories of young love, of family, of giving birth...those mountaintop experiences that fill the heart to overflowing.

"Meg. Hey, is that you?" shouted a voice. The spell was shattered. Damn.

A blonde woman waving a palate ran toward me—Barbara Wells, a school teacher I'd had tea with at the Lake Palace Hotel in Udaipur. She stopped short when she noticed the tears streaking my cheeks.

"Awfully sorry. Not a good time, eh? I understand. It's pretty awesome, isn't it?"

There was an uncomfortable pause. I had never expected to meet anybody who knew me. Not here.

"How did you recognize me from such a distance?" I asked.

"Are you kidding? That floppy safari hat and humongous telephoto lens and bright fuchsia T-shirt. You don't exactly fade into the crowd." I smiled.

We walked over to where Barbara had set up an easel. "I didn't know you were an artist," I said, looking at her rather primitive sketches.

"Oh, you don't need to be kind," she said, laughing gaily. "I'm not an artist. But I meet a lot of people this way. The Indians love to watch me work—you know, a dab here, a smudge there. They probably think I'm on the cutting edge. Try it sometime. It's a great ice breaker."

We agreed to meet in town for dinner at eight. After we parted I walked completely around the monument, which was perfectly symmetrical from every angle, and up onto the vast marble platform on which the main building rested. At each corner of the platform rose a slender minaret, 131 feet high, crowned by an open octagonal pavilion and built with a slight outward tilt, so that it would fall away from the Taj if it ever collapsed.

A quavering, eerie sound reached me as I entered the octagonal burial chamber, which was enclosed in a filigreed screen carved out of a single block of marble. Someone had sung a note, immediately followed by another at a different pitch. I sang a higher note and the sounds blended into a haunting cacophony. Koranic inscriptions carved in black marble adorned the arches, walls, cornices, and domes. The only asymmetrical element in the whole complex was Shah Jahan's cenotaph. His stingy eldest son had refused to finish the black marble replica of the Taj, which his father had started building on the other side of the river. Instead, he interred the dead emperor to the left of Mumtaz, upsetting the perfect balance of the original single cenotaph placed directly under the central dome. The actual graves are in a crypt below and are closed to the public.

Outside, the sun was blinding. I could see why they called this most famous mausoleum the shimmering white jewel, its inlaid flowers and precious stones catching and reflecting the sun.

I walked to the banks of the Yamuna River and watched the peasants carry on their chores in the shadow of the marble wonder. Many see it as a symbol of oppression, of the exploitation of lowly workers for twenty-two long years to satisfy the romantic whims of a powerful leader. On one level this is true. But now, after 350 years have passed, it has found its place in history as a testament to love, and an unsurpassed work of architectural beauty.

I watched the sun disappear and the red glow tint the dome and its reflection in the solemn pool. I was alone. This time there was no interruption. No sound. Not even the wind.

"Madam, it is time to return to the airline office...." Salim stepped in front of me as I was leaving the deserted grounds. Night was falling. The tables at the bazaar were emptying. Old men swept the pathways with their long straw brooms.

Salim took me back to Vayudoot airlines. With an exultant smile the white-robed agent handed me a ticket.

"He says this is 99% sure for tomorrow's flight," interpreted Salim. "If you will just pay thirty-nine dollars."

I was elated! And profuse in my thanks. How could a day be so perfect, I thought, as we drove up to the Fatehabad Restaurant, tiny lights outlining its modest front porch. Barbara sat nursing a drink at one of the small round tables.

Salim bowed as he dropped me off. "I shall meet you at 5:45 tomorrow morning in front of your hotel." I was determined to see the Taj at sunrise.

After dinner, Barbara and I took separate rickshaws, riding, slowly at first, side-by-side, chatting, and enjoying the shadowy surroundings by moonlight. The bicycles had no lights, but this no longer worried me. Suddenly, the two drivers started laughing and picked up speed. Their skinny legs pumped harder and harder until we were in a dead heat. A chariot race by rickshaw.

"Whoa, fellas," shouted Barbara. "Slow down a bit." She sounded genuinely scared.

"Sure, why not?" answered one of the drivers. This was an expression right up there with "no problem" and "don't worry." But they didn't slow down.

"Bet you fifty we win. Go for it!" I yelled. Barbara started screaming. I quickly changed my mind. "O.K. guys. That's enough," I said. "This lady is really scared."

Exhausted and sweaty, the two men careened around a corner and into the driveway of the Hotel Agra where Barbara was staying. She smiled wanly as she disembarked, but I had the feeling she was as annoyed with me as with our drivers.

"When you recover," I said, "think of the picture you can paint!" My attempt at humor failed. Subdued, my driver pedaled the last few miles to my hotel at a leisurely pace.

It was 11 P.M. when I turned the key in the door of my room. I was exhausted. God, I hoped the plumber had fixed the leaky pipes in the bathroom. All I wanted was to soak in a hot tub and wind down from the last seventeen hours.

Upon entering, I spotted a man lying on his back on my bed. My first impulse was to laugh—his presence was so unexpected—and my second was to call the police. Then he raised his head and I recognized him as the scruffy desk clerk I'd met in the afternoon.

"What the hell are you doing here?" I demanded.

He sat up, stretched, and yawned, displaying a mouthful of grimy, uneven teeth. Black stubble covered his chin and neck, and disappeared into a rumpled gray collar poking out of a threadbare argyle sweater. His head bobbled loosely from side to side as he peered at me out of hooded eyes, like an overgrown painted turtle.

"Where have you been?" he asked, nonchalantly. "I've been waiting for you since five o'clock."

"What on earth for?" I asked incredulously.

The eyes widened. "You asked me to get you a plane ticket, and I looked into it."

"You said you doubted you'd be successful, so I bought my own, and believe me, it wasn't easy." I'd never forget the long search around town for Vayudoot Airlines.

"O.K.," I said, facing the clerk. "Show me the ticket."

"Let me see yours first," he countered like a spoiled child.

I rummaged in my bag and found the ticket. Before I could stop him, he grabbed it and held it up to the light.

"Wait a minute," I said. "Just what do you think you're doing?" I took the ticket back.

"You asked me to help you and I tried," he whined. "I wanted to make sure it was in order."

"It's in order, all right. But you're not. Now please leave. I'm going to bed."

He didn't budge. "Madam, I am single and I live in this hotel."

"Great, then you won't have far to go."

Undaunted, he continued. "You don't understand. I am single, you are single, and I am lonely."

"Well, I'm not," I responded. "Just leave. Can't you see I'm tired?" I doubted that he'd even tried to get me a ticket.

"Madam, have you ever *really* been happy?" he asked.

"That does it! Get out of here," I shouted. "Now!"

Slowly the man stood up. "Please, Madam, let me give you a massage. I am very good."

He was also very large, and came toward me with outstretched arms and a self-satisfied leer that seemed to say, "How can you resist me? After all, I only want to make you happy." One whiff of his outstretched arms was enough to make me immediately *unhappy*.

I ducked behind a chair as he lunged, then ran for the door, opened it, and nearly fell over a figure crouching by the keyhole. The eavesdropper jumped up, colliding with the desk clerk, who murmured apologies and rapidly disappeared down the hall, shaking his head and sputtering about my lost chance for happiness.

"You called for a plumber, Madam?" the man asked, bowing ceremoniously in a vain attempt to regain his dignity.

"Good grief, that was twelve hours ago," I said. "And since when do plumbers enter a room through the keyhole?"

What had taken him so long? Busy making someone happy?

He said nothing as he slipped past me into the bathroom. I went outside to cool down, leaving the door open while he worked. The air was sweet with smells of an early spring, and the full moon cast a ghostly glow over the silent complex of rooms. I walked across a small wooden bridge which curved up over a muddy brook. The sky was so bright that I could see the dark circles of moist earth around each newly planted flower lining the walk. One bicycle rickshaw stood in the unpaved parking lot nearby, its driver wrapped in a blanket, fast asleep.

Fortunately, the plumber only specialized in plumbing. When he left I took one look at the color of the hot water that flowed into the tub and decided to forget the bath. But I found it difficult to sleep. After all, I had watched the sun set that evening behind the Taj Mahal, a symbol of one man's love for his wife. How I wished that someone loved me enough after fourteen children—231 concubines notwithstanding—to bankrupt a country to build such a memorial to me. And to think that after years of imprisonment by an ambitious son, this same man had only one wish—to die looking from his mirrored bedchamber in Agra Fort across no-man's-land to the domed splendor of the Taj, where his beloved lay entombed. How romantic. How sad. And what a letdown to return to my room and find a lecherous desk clerk on my bed.

35

SHANKER AND THE HOLY CITY

It was still dark when I reached the gravel courtyard of the hotel's entrance where Salim was waiting. I hugged myself against the bitter cold. Shadowy figures, engaged in morning ablutions, lined the dirt road that led to the Taj. Those still sleeping lay in beds next to the ditch or on front stoops. My brain, cloudy with fatigue, could not control the shiver of excitement that coursed through my body when we approached the main gate.

I was the first person to enter the grounds. A tentative blush was creeping behind the buildings, freeing them from the cloak of early morning mist. As I stood there an unearthly beauty unfolded. Like the flames of a giant furnace being released from the depths of the earth, great tongues of color outlined the minarets, the onion-shaped domes, and the octagonal tomb. The mist slowly disappeared and the two tiers of carved marble archways began to fill with dark red shadows, giving the illusion of half-seeing eyes. I stopped beside the *Al-Kawthar*, the Celestial Pool of Abundance, and watched its captured image turn pink.

The burial chamber was empty when I entered, but I heard what seemed like gentle sighing filtering through the jeweled screens. I remembered the words engraved on the cenotaph of Mumtaz. The anguished plea of a stricken husband. *Help Us, Oh Lord, To Bear What We Cannot Bear.* It resonated in any language. Slowly I left the chamber and traced the watercourse that ran through the gardens. Then circled the monument. Two soldiers were sitting on the main platform, laughing and smoking. They waved as I passed.

By eight o'clock the sun was yellow and the buildings had returned to their white, almost translucent purity. The morning rush had begun. I made my way back to the hotel under a bright, cloudless sky, and arrived just as breakfast was being served.

Imagine my surprise to find the television on in the dining room and the guests glued to the Indian version of the "Today" show. This was immediately followed by a workout session led by a man stripped to the waist chanting instructions in Hindi. The accompaniment was a jarring potpourri of sitar music. A far cry from the sun casting its early morning glow over the Taj.

After a tasty cheese omelet served with *chapatties,* South Indian brewed coffee, and lots of conviviality, I left for Agra Fort. Built in 1574 by the Moghul emperor, Akbar, it was the most exciting combination of Hindu and Moslem architecture I'd seen—an elaborately carved facade of red sandstone, a moat, and four gates. Although two-thirds of the structure was a working army base, a large horseshoe-shaped area of well-preserved ruins lay within the sixty-foot-high masonry walls. A guide—both knowledgeable and witty—took me through the complex of sixteen palaces.

"Notice the advanced water and bathing systems," he said proudly. A maze of ducts and drains fed the large baths, adorned with reflecting glass. "These are for the Moslem ladies. The Hindu women had to bathe in the river." His voice turned apologetic. "They were the servants. But there was air conditioning for everybody—see these hollow walls—and a separate system of pipes providing water for the many elegant fountains."

I looked up at the slender columns spaced geometrically around the decorative pools. How wonderful to have such grandeur right in your own living room. We wandered on, our footsteps echoing on the marble floor.

"Here is where 300 concubines lived. There is also a ladies prison close by for those who got into quarrels." The guide smiled. He was clearly enjoying his trip into the ancient fantasy-world of Moghul magnificence.

"Shah Jahan drastically altered these quarters," he continued, "and after his wife's death, built an underground tunnel leading to the Taj Mahal, so he could visit it alone in all kinds of weather." He paused. "Jahan was good, as Moghuls go. But his eldest son was bad. Very bad."

The complex stonework on the ground floor was reminiscent of the Taj, but the upper floors were covered with patterned green and blue tiles. We passed through private chapels and cathedral-sized ballrooms decorated with inlaid jewels, gold paintings, and silver ceilings. Everywhere was the unmistakable aura of sumptuous living. And each room had its story, embroidered by the guide to extract the full measure of passion. The elaborate quarters of Mumtaz and her children. The tower room where Emperor Jahan was imprisoned. The bed on which he had died, his eyes staring into the mirror at the reflected image of his beloved's tomb.

We reached the third floor and looked down from the great stone balcony. "See those large pits, Madam? That is where the famous elephant fights took place." And, as a whimsical afterthought, he added, "They had no television in those days."

I left with visions of beautiful silk-clad concubines and bloody contests between gray, heavy-tusked behemoths.

At noon I checked out of the Mayur Tourist Complex and drove with Salim to the airport. It was a solemn trip. Two friends for twenty-four hours, who would probably never see each other again. It was nice to have found a driver who knew so much history, and with whom I could talk so freely, and who never once urged me to buy carpets or souvenirs. I would miss him.

I was surprised at the extensive security check required at the tiny terminal, but overjoyed to get a seat on the plane. In one hour and forty minutes I would be in Varanasi, formerly Benares, the holiest city in India, with a stop in Khajuraho, famous for its temples and, especially, its erotica.

During the flight my fear completely vanished, as the small, but sturdy, aircraft skimmed low above the earth. Lulled by its roar, I felt secure in my own little bubble, circumscribed by the peaks and valleys below and the cottony clouds above. While I was luxuriating in this comfortable state, came the first news of the West I'd been exposed to in weeks. Suddenly I realized how out of the loop I was. But hadn't this been one of the reasons for the trip? For years a news junky, addicted to daily feedings of the NY Times and PBS, I needed a rest. I had to get away from the sameness of this daily ritual and the importance placed on analyzing world events…events that just kept coming, relentlessly. Here, I dealt with a completely different set of problems and priorities. How do I get from one place to the next? Where do I stay when I get there? What's the best way to meet people and learn about their country? And how does this affect my life in the process? Back to the simple basics, you might say. One did not invalidate the other. But it was a salutary change.

Upon arriving in Varanasi, I stopped at the office of Indian Air. Paint was peeling off the cream-colored walls. Two simple fans, suspended from a high ceiling, whirred constantly, confounding flies and fluttering papers piled high on a solitary desk. A skinny man pushed a long straw broom back and forth aimlessly. He swept with his right hand and couched a lighted cigarette behind his back with his left. I wondered how he kept from burning the palm of his hand.

An affable clerk booked me on a flight to Kathmandu, leaving in two days. No problem, I thought, as I stepped from the building and was caught up in a maelstrom of shouting, competing cab drivers. They leapt on me like a lion on a

Thompson gazelle. A stooped, bewhiskered old man offered me a fare of twenty rupees ($1.80) instead of the legal eighty-five for the fifteen-mile ride to town, and immediately became the object of loud denunciations. I entered his cab, judiciously rolling up the windows until we were clear of the airport.

The traffic came as no surprise. Trucks plastered with garish designs hogged the road and made passing perilous. HORN BLOW was printed in large letters on the back. The deep ruts combined with the lack of springs in the cab forced me to hold myself slightly above the seat, resting on my hands—a strain on my wrists, but better than putting my back out of alignment.

The scene was different from Agra. There was frenetic activity everywhere you looked. In the makeshift markets along the way I noticed several new varieties of green vegetables, giant pyramids of red peppers, and flat patties of dried cow dung neatly arranged inside large woven baskets. Women bargained for this cheap local fuel, then carried the overflowing baskets away, expertly balanced on their head. Crowds of people bought dishes of steaming food. Mechanics fixed machines and bicycles with primitive tools. Bright-eyed youngsters stood in clusters, their arms around each other. And naked babies lay on slatted beds beside the road.

For the first time I saw immense sheds loaded with sticks of wood to be used for funeral pyres on the banks of the Ganges. We passed a dead body wrapped in bright-colored shiny cloth—signifying a man—layered over the basic white. It was tied to a woven stretcher and pulled by a horse. A young man in somber robes, head shaven, walked alongside leading the horse. We passed slowly enough for me to get a good look at the man. I didn't know that I would witness the cremation of that very body later in the afternoon.

Donkeys with hobbles joined the usual assortment of cows and bulls that snarled traffic. "The cow, Madam, is a symbolic mother, and is determined holy by the priest, who then makes a cut in her ear and throws the piece into the Ganges." This was my driver's explanation for the lofty position of these animals. It was the first time I'd heard that particular theory.

We passed several decorated halls. "This is the season for weddings," he said, "It is very expensive…a good reason to have boys." Music blared at ear-splitting level. Golden yellow tinsel and shimmery paper streamers of electric blue and red hung down at the entrance, forming a door. Round bulbs all aglow had been hung wherever a hook or a pole could be found.

Just before we reached town the driver pointed out the house of the famed sitarist Ravi Shanker. The old fellow regaled me with many such tidbits, hoping I'd hire him as a tour guide. I explained that I preferred to see the city on foot or in a bicycle rickshaw. But I let him know how grateful I was for finding me a hotel, where I booked a deluxe room for 110 rupees ($9.50) a night.

The proprietor of The Hotel India was handsome, gray-complected, with full lips, black moustache, impeccable clothes, and a distinctly aloof manner. This was a relief compared to most of the men I'd encountered behind hotel desks. At first I was intimidated by his brusqueness, until he flashed a smile that could have melted a glacier. It wasn't until the next evening that I got a glimpse of why he was so controlled.

An open marble stairway led to my ample third floor room. Like so many middle class Indian hotels it had the look of tired elegance, as if nobody had bothered to put on the finishing touches. Crisp marble moldings around a beautiful stone floor contrasted with unfinished plastering and holes where a picture had once hung. Faded velvet curtains tried without success to hide cracks in the wall. Mothballs filled the drains in the bathroom, just like the Hotel Bissau in Jaipur.

I opened the French doors and walked onto the balcony, which looked over an expanse of walled-in lawn with an old mansion at the far end. A sign read: YMCA Educational Center. Outside the gate longhaired pigs roamed free, mixing with the bicycle rickshaws that hung around a small unpaved parking area. I liked the scene.

After washing up I decided to take a look around town. Ten drivers swarmed around me at the gate. Shouting. Gesticulating. As I was trying to extricate myself, I caught sight of a lone man on the periphery, a homely soul with protruding teeth and an emaciated body. He was just standing there, staring at me. He wore a drab tunic partially covering a calf-length *dhoti*. Why was I drawn to him? Physically, he was the ugliest man I'd ever seen.

"Dear lady," he said, moving toward me. "Do not think me bold, but I know we have met in another life. We are not strangers…."

The oldest line in the book. But I stood there, intrigued by someone who wasn't even interested in bargaining.

He took my hands in his. I didn't pull away, enjoying the feel of his warm skin. He looked into my eyes steadily. There wasn't a hint of insincerity. And no mention of happiness or pleasure.

"I am Shanker," he said, keeping his eyes fixed on mine. "Do you wish to see our holy city? I can take you wherever you want to go. You pay me whatever you wish. It will be my privilege."

"I want to go to the Ganges. I want to see a cremation ceremony," I said, like a child asking permission. Silently he retrieved his decrepit rickshaw with its frayed black top hanging at half-mast, and motioned for me to step in.

I sat back, drinking in this holiest of Hindu cities. Varanasi defined antiquity. It had survived three thousand years of history—Muslim invasions, the wrath of rival kingdoms, daily pilgrimages of the faithful. And the signs were everywhere.

Even the sacred cows were more visible. I had to laugh at the way they stood dumbly in the middle of town, straddling the cement center strips, blinking and chewing. One enormous brown and white bull caught my eye. He looked like an oversized statue, quite a contrast from the usual all-white or all-black brahman with its irregular hump and massive shoulders.

As we rode toward the river I was struck, once again, by how acutely conscious I was of my surroundings. My radar was operating at all times. I wondered what I'd write if I drank in the atmosphere at home with the same intensity, the same critical eye. I might learn a lot about what's right under my nose.

Shanker kept up a steady stream of conversation. "I'm from Nepal, and I haven't met any real friends since I came to India. They are not as friendly as the Nepalese." He paused before continuing. "I am also a holy man. You can tell by my hair."

He freed a cascade of thick knotted hair, which he kept wrapped in a plaid, coarsely woven scarf, the long end becoming a banner in the wind as he pedaled. When he tried to secure the black mass with one hand, the bike swerved. I gasped. He turned around to reassure me. "Have no fear my friend. I have never had an accident in seventeen years. I am now thirty-two and…." He narrowly missed a curb, a couple of animals, and a neighboring vehicle.

The route to the Ganges was rife with Shanker's close calls. I clutched the worn seat of the rickshaw. Whenever I admonished him to be careful he'd turn halfway around to tell me he'd never had an accident. And swerve. I finally kept my mouth shut. After all, it wasn't as bad as the motorcycle ride in Pune.

We decided to stop for tea and left the rickshaw in an alley. "Nobody will steal it," Shanker assured me. And nobody did. I marveled at the honesty of the Indian people. I concluded that it must be their religion. Not once did I have a problem with theft. And I never wore my money belt.

As we sat with a pot of boiling tea, Shanker pulled out a dog-eared journal that he kept hidden under the seat of the rickshaw. It was a cherished record of friends he'd met from around the world. And how proud he was of it! He pushed the pages toward me, urging me to read the comments, many of them difficult to decipher. As I read, he sat watching me. Intense. Eager. He possessed so little by western standards, but these pages told of instances when he'd taken people in after they had lost their belongings or had gotten into some kind of trouble with the bureaucracy. There were glowing testimonies from Germans, English, French, Scandinavians. It was clear to me that his job, no matter how lowly it appeared, provided a vital link to the outside world and he loved it. These associations made him feel special. And it didn't take me long to see that he was.

Shanker.

After tea we walked down a side street to the riverbank. One body was burning and another was being removed from its bamboo stretcher and set on a low pyre. I recognized the face of the young man I had passed on my way from the airport. I assumed that he was the son and this was his father's body. Shanker and

I stood on a grassy bank a few yards from the pyre. A young student joined us. He wanted to talk. I listened. And watched.

"See that gash in the ground over there with a tangle of cables," he said, pointing to a rectangular hole in the soil not far from where we were standing. "That's the beginnings of the new electric crematorium being built by the government to help save firewood. The high cost of wood has forced many families to throw their dead into the river before the bodies have completely burned." He paused for effect. "The government hopes to prevent this practice by installing twenty-nine electric crematoria on the banks of the river. This is a river used for washing, drinking, and bathing, and must be kept free of contamination." The student looked pleased with his assessment of the situation.

Shanker was skeptical. "That won't be easy," he said. "There are plenty of people who still believe the Ganges stops at midnight for several moments of peace and solitude, and cleanses itself before flowing again. So what harm can a few dead bodies do to this great and powerful river?"

The son had just walked over to a tall cement building open on all sides. Wood was piled high next to it. A man tended a fire that, according to folklore, had been burning on that spot for 2500 years. He also sold wood to the male relative in charge of each cremation, settling for a price the family could afford. We watched as the son bargained with the elderly fire keeper. They dickered for quite some time before the wood was brought out and piled under and on top of the body. The young man then washed in the river and changed into a white linen wrap. Barefoot and clean-shaven out of respect, he was now ready to perform his duties.

Slowly, relatives began to gather. The son disappeared, once more, into the building, and returned carrying a large bunch of smoldering straw. He touched the smoking grass to the dead man's lips to purify him, and circled the body five times before waving his arm swiftly, causing the straw to break into flames. Next, he ignited the wood. As the fire spread, a holy man read scripture.

Each relative participated in a ceremonious sprinkling of perfumed holy water over the corpse. Resins and *ghee* (clarified butter) were added to enhance the burning. Incense was scattered to minimize the odor. I watched in fascination as the outer garments burned off and the skin began to shrivel, causing the body to sink in the middle. The head and feet stuck out prominently, although the son did his best to keep the body covered. This family needed more wood.

I wanted, desperately, to take some photographs, but there was a sign warning against it. And a policeman keeping strict watch.

The body on the adjacent pyre had just about burned away, and a young man, also with shaved head, was poking the embers with a long pole. How personal this death seemed to be. And how natural. It was an accepted part of life, not like our sanitized western burials carried out without offending anyone. But this would be difficult for me to observe if it were my loved one.

"Cremation is done as soon after death as possible," said the young student. "It releases the spirit and sends it heavenward."

"But many bodies are not burned," interjected Shanker. "If the dead person had an infection like smallpox, or was pregnant, or died from cobra venom, the relatives believe there's the chance for a miraculous cure from the holy water of the Ganges. They feel it's worth a try. And if the fish eat the bodies, nobody is the wiser."

We stood for an hour watching the son shuffle back and forth on the packed earth, prodding the ashes and bone. I looked beyond, to the enigmatic Ganges, mother of rivers. Muddy, lethargic, adored.

"Let's go for a boat ride, Shanker. It's almost sunset."

The pyre was still aflame when we left.

At a nearby dock we bargained with the owner of a sizable dory. For twenty rupees he agreed to take us out. We were joined by an Indian woman, her son, and a bouncy Egyptian couple with two children. The diminutive oarsman rowed with crudely-fashioned oars, sweating copiously as he struggled with the fully loaded boat.

In front of us was the legendary Golden Temple of *Shri Vishwanath* (Lord of All) peeking out from behind an old building. It is said to contain the *Vishweshwar linga*, the first one on earth, which shot up from the ground as a shaft of light. All Varanasi is measured in circles around this temple. It's the city's most important pilgrimage site, open only to Hindus. The setting sun splashed against the dome, which is encrusted with 280 kg of gold, and came to rest on a lesser temple, gray-streaked and half-submerged in the Ganges.

"This is a sad story," began Shanker, and described the wrath of the gods who sank the temple. "This sunken temple is a lesson to arrogant sons who show disrespect for their mothers." As he talked, Shanker sat cross-legged on the floor of the boat, pensive, serious.

We passed honeymoon couples draped with garlands of flowers, young children enjoying a swimming party from the back of a barge, and old folks drifting in small boats down the river. And in the background, as if to remind us of our mortality, continuous strands of smoke arose from a large raised cement platform on the shore, where bodies burned for the requisite three-and-a-half hours. Occasional licks of orange were caught by the diminishing light.

"There you will see a burning pyre at all times," announced Shanker, somberly.

I looked at the series of *ghats* rising from the banks of the river. These multi-layered steps formed solid embankments where pilgrims gathered. People were bathing, and nearly naked men were engaged in ritual exercises. Large umbrellas, many torn with age, shielded those who had already gathered for the night. Shanker pointed out the white-cloaked Brahman ladies peering from windows high above the *ghats*. "After their husbands die they cannot remarry. They come to Varanesi to wait for death."

The small Indian boy pulled impatiently on his mother's sleeve. "I'm thirsty," he whined.

To my surprise, his mother dipped her cupped hands into the river and gave him a drink—and another. I gagged. Just then a young girl came alongside in a flimsy boat full of small lacy paper cups in which a flower rested next to a burning candle. She was selling them for one rupee. I bought one. She motioned toward the river, so I threw the cup overboard. Everyone laughed. The girl clapped her hands with glee.

"Oh, no," said Shanker. "Set the cup gently on the water. Then it will burn for a long time."

I bought another and handed it to one of the Egyptian youngsters. With great care he placed it in the river and watched in silence as it bobbed away, a pinprick of light in the approaching darkness.

The body was still smoldering when we returned, and two other ceremonies were in progress. We walked back down the side street and picked up the rickshaw. Shanker stopped at a vegetable stand and I bought several long red carrots and a small bunch of green bananas.

"I want you to meet my *guru*," he said matter-of-factly. "He is a fine man and a famous sitar player." I nodded. We worked our way through town, dodging wedding processions, animals, and partygoers, until we came to an alley sandwiched between two crooked houses. Shanker led me up a flight of decaying wooden stairs into a room completely insulated from the outside world. The floor was covered with mattresses. Silk cloth hung on every wall and billowed from the ceiling. It was like being in a huge cocoon.

"My friend, Meg Peterson, I want you to meet Mani lal Hasra." I gazed on a serene old man all in white—hair, beard, clothes—sitting yoga-style and holding an impressive eighteen-string sitar. The polished inlaid wood designs on the instrument seemed to dance as he played.

I leaned back on a mountain of pillows and drank in the intricate melodies and skillful runs. Here was a man who had performed all over the world and was giving me a private concert. Two boys with flat drums joined in, adding their rhythms to the mixture. I smiled at Shanker. He seemed the dearest, most sensitive man in the world. I was full to bursting. Thank you, thank you.

After Mani played, we talked. I took out the bananas and carrots and shared them. It made me feel good to be a part of the celebration. More people gathered, and someone brought out a pot of tea. As we were drinking, a well-dressed man came in and pulled back a panel of silk from one wall to expose cubbyholes full of material. He slid out a bolt and started to unfold it in front of me. I was stunned. Mani looked stricken. Shanker had disappeared.

The man had barely started his pitch, aimed directly at me, when I interrupted. "I must ask you to stop," I said, amazed at how much I feared this confrontation. "I may be the only Westerner you've met who is a non-materialist, but, you see, I'm getting *rid* of my possessions, not buying more." I looked at Mani, who nodded his approval. "I've traveled for four months and only bought a few small hand-painted miniatures. I have no space in my backpack for your lovely silks. There's been a dreadful misunderstanding."

An uncomfortable pause followed. Slowly, the man started to fold up the material. I was angry. And embarrassed. In a fury I grabbed my shoes and left the room. I bumped into Shanker outside.

"How *could* you have done this to me?" I said, trying to keep my voice in check. "I was having a wonderful time, and all the while it was a trap to get me to buy."

"No. No. It wasn't. I was as surprised as you, Meg. Forget this. Tomorrow we can return to Mani's private home, not the silk factory. Just you and me." Shanker looked distraught.

"But you *knew* it was a silk factory when you brought me here, didn't you?" I asked, still furious.

"That is where Mani plays. I did not know they would try to sell you...unless you asked." He was on weak ground. His worried glance begged forgiveness. We walked to the rickshaw in silence. I was not going to let this unfortunate incident ruin our day together.

As we approached the dark lonely road leading to my hotel, a bike sidled up next to us and a young man turned several times to look at me. "How old are you?" he asked.

"What difference does it make?" I countered.

"Are you married?" I didn't answer.

"Do you like sex?"

"Bug off!" I screamed. "Shanker, did you hear what this man said?"

"I'm peddling as fast as I can."

"Madam, have you ever *really* been happy?"

"Shanker....*Do* something. Get rid of him!"

My admirer was so engrossed in his fantasies that he didn't see the lone car parked on the side of the road. Deftly, Shanker swerved left, passing the car with only inches to spare.

"Madam, one moment. Let me tell you how beautiful...oooooh."

I heard the crash of wheel against metal. I felt awful. But Shanker didn't stop. He kept pedaling as if nothing had happened.

"Oh, Shanker," I wailed. "I hadn't meant to hurt him."

"Don't you worry," he replied. "This is not a good man. He did not pay attention to riding. He only saw you. It is *his* problem."

Before parting, we sat on a carved wooden bench outside the hotel and talked. All animosity had vanished. Shanker took the weather-beaten journal from the rickshaw and without a word handed it to me. I settled down to write.

◆　　　◆　　　◆

I awoke early. Two rickshaw drivers were huddled around small fires in the parking lot below. The glow played off the walls of my room. It was spooky. I stood and watched as the flames died down.

How quickly I got dressed these days. No make-up. No hair dryer. No fuss. And very little choice of clothes. A pair of long pants, a T-shirt, and a thin jacket. A safari hat to cover my head. The voluminous black skirt was buried at the bottom of my pack with the fuchsia shirt. Vanity had taken a back seat.

It was 5:45 A.M. when I reached the lobby. Shanker, who had urged me to take the morning tour on the Ganges, was waiting impatiently. "You will be late for the sunrise," he scolded, but delivered me to the tourist office just as the bus was leaving. "I will see you before dinner," he said, and pedaled away.

Our guide for the day, Mr. Prasad, was superb. The best since the Nile trip. He showed a profound understanding of the city and a reverence for the spiritual qualities of Hinduism and Buddhism. He had a sweet smile, light complexion, wavy gray hair, and a square-shaped face. He could have been mistaken for an Italian.

"Varanasi is situated on the western banks of the Ganges," he began, "between the two rivers Varuna and Assi, from which it derives its name. These rivers meet the Ganges at the northern and southern tips of the city." We reached a more populous section of the river than I had visited yesterday, and boarded a large boat. The heavy oars were wielded, again, by a thin, fragile-looking man.

The sun was coming up, bathing the earth in a dusty glow. Mr. Prasad stood on the hood across the bow of the boat, pointing out the sights. "Those steps," he said, indicating the embankment of *ghats,* "are visited by millions of devout Hindus every year. Notice that many people are already in the water. That's because early morning baths are sacred." He hesitated a moment. "In fact, every day during college I was one of the bathers. But the river was cleaner in those days." He smiled wistfully.

My eyes moved from the awakening humanity to the river. I half-expected to see a body float by. A boatload of lepers with sores and amputated limbs passed us. I returned my gaze to the shore where garbage and mud were collecting at the edges, and water was rushing into the all-consuming river from the streets and houses.

As the sun rose higher we could see donkeys laden with bundles of laundry, inching their way down the slope to the river, where wiry men stood knee-deep in water, waiting to wash the clothes in the natural clay. After slapping them against the flat rocks that jutted out of the bank they would place them on the ground to dry. How could these little men do such strenuous work? And how could the clothes be clean when clay and mud were used for soap?

"This city is older than Jerusalem," said Mr. Prasad. "It is called a living city because it retains its ancient rituals…phallic worship, worship of the sun, of the river, of Buddha, of Lord Shiva. It is truly a spiritual city." He was eager to share his love of Indian history with us.

"What are those fires on that high platform above the wall?" I asked. "They seem separate from the other fires."

"They *are* separate," he replied. "That space is reserved for the wealthy people. But all ashes are thrown into the Ganges, and they mix together, so what difference does it make where you are burned? People come from far away to deliver the ashes of family members to the Holy River. It's the great equalizer. Like death."

Funeral pyre on the bank of the Ganges River.

At that moment a small dory collided with our bow, upsetting Mr. Prasad. We gasped. He grabbed onto a gunwale as he went over the side, and held on, his feet dangling in the water. Nobody dared laugh, though he did look very funny hanging there, an astonished expression on his face. Suddenly he yelled, "Hey, Miss, you have a camera. Aren't you going to take a picture?" I grabbed my camera and snapped him being pulled aboard and clowning around, dancing a jig as he shook each pant leg dry. Now we could all laugh.

As we started back to the dock I took a closer look at the *ghats*. People were huddled asleep under blankets, but a few arose from their pallets and stretched as we passed. A dark-cloaked young man sat under one of the umbrellas and played a wooden flute. It was like the mellow trills of a song sparrow greeting the day. Underneath a colonnade a plump old man, dressed in a skimpy G-string, was doing his setting up exercises. Others were meditating or bathing. Performing lengthy ablutions or salutations to the sun.

By the time we reached the shore the city was awake. We started through the streets, looking at small temples and observing early morning activities. Each person was tending to business, operating within a narrow, rigidly circumscribed orbit. We walked back to the bus through the filthy, oppressively smelly side streets. A young boy was kneeling at prayer in a tiny stone alcove. Next to him lay an old lady half-hidden under a blanket. A badly stooped, toothless woman, wiry white hairs escaping from under a red scarf, was sweeping a small section of the alley. She hardly noticed us as we stepped around her. A well-dressed man was sitting at the entrance of his small souvenir shop. People were cooking over open fires in the semi-dark. A young boy was anointing *Hanuman*, the monkey god, with bright orange paint. His demeanor was caring, reverent. A second boy was washing the marble steps with river water. Each was concentrating on the task at hand. A swarm of individuals engaged in a mutable pattern of constant activity that gave meaning to their lives.

Cows pushed past me. Children scampered barefoot in and out of my path. Unparalleled history all around me. Stark contrasts. Beggars and *rajahs*. This mixture of humanity blended together in a jumble of color and sound. And if you didn't accept it as it was, you'd be miserable.

Early morning in the ghats on the Ganges.

These thoughts were with me throughout the day, many of them voiced by Mr. Prasad. "I denounce the caste system," he said. "It is inhuman and not good for our society. We should be judged by our deeds. Not all Brahmans are enlightened and not all Untouchables ignorant. I cannot understand the mentality that believes destiny has decreed the suffering of millions of unborn children." How many more times I would hear the same lament.

I sat quietly as we bumped along the rutted roads, passing farmers in the fields and horse-drawn carts bursting with people. In one ditch starving dogs were eating human excrement. In another, men urinated without even turning their backs. Later on we came upon women walking arm-in-arm, dressed fashionably in cotton wraps and bloomers, a modern version of the *sari*. Nothing surprised me.

The afternoon was full of temples and archaeological museums, but the most exciting was *Sarnath*, where Buddha preached his first sermon after enlightenment. Close by were several famous *stupas* where relics were entombed. Mr. Prasad, although a Hindu, had a great deal of respect for Buddha. "Buddha had courage," he said with a faint smile. "He allowed females in his monastic system."

When I arrived back at my hotel Shanker was waiting. "It was a lovely day, no?" he asked.

"It was a lovely day, yes," I replied.

"A farewell gift for you," he said and handed me a bag of fruits and vegetables. Deeply touched, I said, "You *must* have dinner with me."

There was an awkward pause. "No, let me say goodbye here."

"Oh, please, Shanker. At least have a cup of tea and some biscuits." He relented and we walked toward the terrace.

I noticed that the hotel guard was looking askance at me. And a few guests moved away when we sat down. Of course. Nobody entertains a lowly rickshaw driver at The Hotel India. Well, we'll see about that! The Nepalese waiter was enjoying the scene. He smiled graciously at me and whispered a few words to Shanker.

"I am breaking the social rules sitting here," he said.

"I know, and isn't it wonderful? I dare them to say something. Then I'll tell them who's special." Shanker smiled.

I felt an indefinable sadness when we said goodbye. As when we first met, he took my hands in his. "I will be here when you return," he said. "I will find you."

I turned and walked back into the hotel lobby, wondering what kind of life was in store for both of us. I knew that Shanker—his simplicity, honesty, and empathy—had touched my life in a profound way. He transcended the superficial outward trappings by which so many are judged. He embodied, for me, the true spirit of India.

An elderly Brahman, swathed in white, sat in the upholstered chair opposite the television. His hair and beard were long and silky. His thin brown feet bare. A sage with a walking stick at his side. A king surveying his kingdom from a throne. It was obvious that he was respected by the management as the height of gentility.

He nodded to me cordially, and lifted a hand in benediction. A symbol of Varanasi, the epitome of the hallowed past. I had no doubt that little would change over the next hundred years.

"I'll be leaving tomorrow," I announced to the proprietor.

"Do you have anything to dispose of, Madam?" he asked.

"Do you mean throw away?"

"No, I mean to trade." He saw my perplexed look. "I have fifteen children and three wives. And we can always use clothes. Is there anything you might want to trade for post cards, or these valuables that I'm selling?" He pointed to a collection of vases and jewelry locked in a glass case.

I looked at this seemingly proper man and at his wildly erotic post cards. "I would give you some clothing, but I'm carrying only the bare minimum. Let me take another look at these cards."

All at once his aloofness evaporated and he began to speak frankly about his view of life. "You wonder about my wives and children, don't you?"

"I wonder why you had so many, and how you can support them."

"I do not believe in birth control, because it detracts from a woman's sexual pleasure. Sex should be totally uninhibited. It is a man's duty to provide happiness and fulfillment to a woman."

Where had I heard *that* before?

He continued. "I support my family, but now I have renounced the temptations of the flesh and am concentrating on my soul."

Perhaps this accounted for the control I noticed when we first met.

"How do the ladies feel about that?" I asked. The desk clerk grinned. The proprietor wasn't listening.

"Hindus believe you must go through every emotion, every excess, every form of debauchery and perversion before you're able to give it all up and reach personal Nirvana. Sex is for procreation, and now that I have done that, it is finished."

"You mean you never made love to your wives when they were pregnant?"

"That's a good question," the desk clerk interjected. He was ignored.

The proprietor's rationalizations sounded like the perfect prescription for a man's world. I assumed that the comparable opportunity of finding the path to divine bliss was not given to women, although they certainly were a necessary accoutrement along the way. My heart went out to them.

Despite our differences, I had enjoyed the frank conversation. And it was nice to spend the evening with a man who didn't want to make me *happy.*

36

SHANGRI-LA

The small kingdom of Nepal is sandwiched between the two giants, India and China, and dominated by the highest mountain range on earth. No wonder it's called "The Roof of the World." But like Varanasi, Nepal is in no danger of joining the 21st century. It hasn't reached the 20th yet.

I stepped off the plane and breathed the clean mountain air. It was heaven! But I never expected it to be so warm. I'd forgotten that Kathmandu, despite its mile high altitude, was also in the heart of the Terai, a lowland jungle, an extension of the great Ganges valley of India. Before long I'd be yearning for a little of that warmth against the snow and wind of the Himalayas.

A cab driver delivered me to Thamel, the busy student section of the Old City, where cheap guesthouses abounded and a carnival atmosphere prevailed.

"This is where the action is," he said to my surprise, adding a wink.

Nepal—isolated from the west until 1950—had become a notorious "hippie" hangout in the 1960's and 70's. Its reputation flourished among the disenchanted of every nationality as one of the few places where smoking hashish and dropping acid were legal. You could get stoned and live comfortably for a pittance.

In 1975, after the coronation of King Mehindra, drugs were officially prohibited. The days of wild abandon were over, although you could still see a few flower children floating about. Thamel had now become the "trippie" center, full of eager trekkers poking around the crowded shops and preparing for extended expeditions into the mountains. And tourists who wanted to experience a living medieval town full of authentic architecture, religious festivals, wooden temples, and tons of trash.

"Tiger balm, Madam…cigarettes…T-shirts…?"

Already I was being besieged by pitchmen.

"American Express?" I asked. To my amazement, I was given good directions in English.

The American Express office was a short walk from Thamel, through a tangle of narrow alleys and decorative squares. The streets were not made for vehicles. Even the bicycle rickshaws, tooting impatiently with their bulbous rubber horns, had trouble getting through the throng of shoppers. People clustered on ornately carved balconies that jut out from the second stories of the crooked Newari houses. These ancient dwellings, closing in on either side of the cramped walkways, lean against one another, stacked so tightly that one roof can sweep, like a graceful drape, over several houses. A woman thrust her head out of an overhanging window and called to her friend across the street. This must have been what England was like in Elizabethan times. I fully expected a pail of water to be thrown on me as I walked under the eaves.

American Express operated from a dingy office not far from Durbar Marg and New Street, where trekking and tourist agencies flourished. I presented my card and passport, and a friendly clerk handed me a packet of mail.

"Good thing you came today," he said, tilting his head to one side. "I've held these letters for two months. That's our limit."

How far behind schedule I'd gotten.

I flipped through the pile, grateful to hear from my family, but hoping for news of Faith, James, and Leszek. There was a hurried note from Faith saying that she and James had decided to stay in Kashmir instead of going to Nepal, but hoped I wouldn't lose touch. And nothing from Leszek. He'd probably been to Everest and back while I was floating on the Ganges.

Disappointed, I went outside and joined the choking mass of people threading their way through town. In one of the small squares I collapsed like a rag doll onto a dirty stone plinth, resting my pack on the attached *stupa*. I knew I had to get away from the confusion—the traffic, the squawking vendors. I took a handwritten map from my camera bag. A big red arrow pointed to the bus station with the notation: "Here is where you get the bus for Dhulikhel. If you're looking for Shangri-la, this is it!"

The map had been written by AmyNoel Wyman, the daughter of my old friend and mountain climbing buddy, Sylvia, who had died the previous year, and whose memory had helped sustain me on the terrifying climb up Table Mountain in January. AmyNoel's enthusiasm about the time she'd spent working with the Newars, the original inhabitants of the Kathmandu Valley, had heightened my resolve to visit Nepal. She'd given me $500.00 to deliver to her friend, B.P. Shresta, toward the building of elementary schools in remote hill communities. This was a godsend for parents who were too poor to send their children to town schools. B.P., as he was affectionately called, owned a guesthouse and a fancy new resort hotel in Dhulikhel, a tiny farming village a few miles outside of Kathmandu, with one of the best views of the Himalayas.

At the station I boarded a dilapidated bus. Not even its Egyptian counterpart in the Sinai could compete. Seat covers were torn, a large metal box covered the motor—located up front next to the driver—and the windows were cracked and stuck open. The fringed windshield was plastered with pictures of *Shiva* and ropes of tinsel. There was only a small patch of unadorned glass through which the driver could see. In half-an-hour he arrived, lifted the box off the engine, and thumped it several times to get it started.

I was squeezed between two men, my pack on my lap. The overflow passengers sat on the box over the engine, until it became too hot. Then they moved to the door well. But despite the discomfort everyone seemed to be in a jovial mood, especially those who rode outside, hanging onto the bus. One man appeared to be the driver's helper. He banged on the back door and whistled, intermittently—the shrill, insistent warble of a frightened bird—which signaled just about everything. When to start, when to stop, and when to hurry up. I never did figure out the system.

The driver couldn't seem to control the bus, which careened wildly over the winding roads, narrowly missing oncoming vehicles. The passengers erupted in laughter, adding a chorus of "oh's" and "ah's" each time there was a close call. We labored this way for an hour. Sometimes the lights went out as the driver turned the wheel madly left and right to keep the old crate going straight. And with each turn came a high-pitched, tooth-shattering screech.

Shaken, I stepped off the bus in the town square in front of B.P.'s guesthouse, Dhulikhel Lodge. A flowery photograph of the king and queen perched above its modest sign. I entered through a brick hallway, which led into a stone courtyard. A young man, Mahandra, greeted me. He looked uneasy as he showed me the communal wash area and the elemental pit toilets, and offered an arm as we started up the three flights of stairs to my room.

At the top of the stairs was a hallway strewn with thick straw mats. We walked into the front room. Coarsely woven tan blankets covered the floor, colorful hangings lined the walls, and thin, filmy material drooped from the ceiling like clouds. A double bed, smothered under heavy comforters, stood beside a bank of small-paned windows that overlooked the main square. One bare bulb hung over the bed.

"Are you sure you don't want to go to the new hotel?" Mahandra asked. He looked worried. "I could take you there. It has a magnificent view of the mountains...."

"Are you telling me I can't stay here?" I interrupted.

"Oh, no, Madam. I'm thinking of your comfort."

"You're thinking of my age. You're thinking I'm too old."

His face turned scarlet. He lowered his head.

"Well, I'm staying," I announced. "The room is perfect."

We went back downstairs and I lingered in the garden, enjoying the aroma of flowers. Square brick planters choked with blossoms lined the walkways and two rustic benches nestled under a thick canopy of trees. At the far edge, where the hill dropped away, a ribbon of rice fields spiraled down to the river, dimly illuminated by a sliver of moon. Night birds and insects were tuning up. I inhaled the sweet mountain air. Again and again.

B.P. Shresta was sitting cross-legged behind a low table when I entered the dining room. He looked in his mid-forties. Slender, muscular, with penetrating eyes and graying hair. I introduced myself. His dark face crinkled into a full smile.

"Ah, AmyNoel's friend. I've been expecting you. Sit down."

I moved across the blanketed floor in my bare feet and sat on a mattress opposite him. Small tables and cushions framed the room. Decorative bamboo latticework partially covered the roughhewn windows. Straw lamps hung from the ceiling.

"I have a surprise for you," I said and handed him AmyNoel's crisp hundred dollar bills. He slowly ran them through his fingers as if caressing priceless silk. His look was one of absolute joy.

"Do you know what this means, Meg?" he asked.

"I have some idea, since AmyNoel told me how much you did with her first donation of twenty-five dollars."

"She is a lovely woman. An angel. With this money we can buy a new floor for one of our schools. And books. And paper and pens for writing. I can now go to the parents and tell them to start clearing land for another school. We can buy struts and cement. Of course, the labor they do themselves...." B.P.'s eyes were moist, but his face was glowing with excitement. This would be the sixth school he had started for elementary age children.

"Meg," he said, "tomorrow we'll go to the hills and I'll show you. These are simple farmers struggling to make a living. They can't afford to have their children gone all day. They need their help. But the government doesn't provide schools in the hills."

He paused, rubbing his hands together, leaning toward me as he spoke. "Most of the adults are illiterate, or have learned a bit of scripture by rote. Stories are passed down by word of mouth from one generation to the next. But they want something better for their children."

While we talked we ate. Mahandra was one of several young men who served us a choice of simple western or Nepali food. Dinner never cost more than $2.00. And every evening there was a Nepalese dish for seventy-five cents.

I sat in the comfortable dining room conversing with B.P.'s friends from around the world—students, teachers, and backpackers like me. In the next five days I would meet dozens of people eager to share their experiences. Full of advice on where to go, what to avoid, which routes to take.

It was difficult to get to sleep after so much stimulating conversation. And nobody had warned me about Friday night band practice in the town square. I love bands, but not when the clarinets and trumpets seem to be playing different compositions simultaneously. And the drummer hesitates just long enough to miss the beat. I sank deeper under the covers, but it was no use. Not even my ear-plugs could drown out the cacophony. I was marching to a different drummer, when I didn't want to be marching at all.

After finally dozing off, my sleep was shattered by the sound of pounding feet on the stairs. And shouts. Suddenly, Mahandra burst into my room.

"Madam, are you all right?" he asked, breathless.

I shot bolt upright, shaking from the intrusion. "What…what are you doing here at this hour?" I asked.

"Someone fell down the stairs, and I thought…."

"You thought it was me. Right? Because you think I'm too old to be here. Now confess, or I won't forgive you for waking me up."

"Then who was it?" he said, looking crestfallen.

"Probably some twenty-year-old student, drunk," I said.

That was the last time Mahandra patronized me.

I slept until the roosters and barking dogs made it impossible. When I walked down to breakfast I found B.P. sitting with some of his cronies, smoking unfiltered cigarettes and drinking coffee. It was a diverse group, some wearing work clothes, some draped in the traditional *galluka* with the cone-shaped, brimless *fez,* and others in western shirts and slacks.

"We're planning my campaign for mayor of the village," B.P. announced when I arrived. "I'm not sure I want to run, but my friends here are very persuasive."

"I'll vote for you," I said, "but only after a cup of coffee. Or don't you let the ladies vote?"

"We have a lot of reforming to do," he answered wryly.

A long pause. "I have a good life, Meg. I love people and I work hard. But I worry about all the details of being a mayor. I hate administration. And I don't want to lose my freedom."

"Let Kirin do it," said one of the men. Kirin was B.P.'s eldest son, who had just returned from two years in Salzburg, where he received a degree in hotel management.

"Yeah. A young man who is thinking about girls is going to run my office and manage the new resort at the same time?" He laughed, and we joined him. "Then I'll *really* have to spend all my free time being a trouble shooter."

Politics was the same the world over.

That afternoon B.P. took me to visit one of his schools. The walk along the hilly road was leisurely, the sun warm and soothing. Two little boys played, naked, in a mountain stream. Friends passed by. A few stopped to talk. A little girl about eight years old, with deep black eyes and lustrous hair, joined us as we walked. She was carrying a heavy milk can on her back.

Dhulikhel child.

After she left, B.P. said, "I asked her why she wasn't in school. She said that her mother needs her to sell the milk in the village." His tone was full of sadness.

Suddenly, we ducked up a steep path and waded through brambles and tall grass until we came to a neat white L-shaped building. You could hear the steady hum of children's voices in recitation. B.P.'s mood changed. He beamed with pride.

"We've been able to hire three teachers—a man for the 5th and 6th grade and two women for the other combined grades."

I stood outside the window and recorded an English lesson. It made me think of the dialogues I'd had to learn in German class in college. Rote repetition. Over and over. When they were finished the children giggled and clapped. One of them caught sight of me and a torrent of eager, squealing children poured into the yard.

They clustered around and ushered me into the school, showing me rows of simple desks and a blackboard with numbers. One of the children took my hand and pulled me to her desk. She thrust a note pad in front of me. On it were several English sentences.

"Please, Madam, read to us," she said haltingly.

I read the sentences, then a small book. The children watched in awe, some sidling up and touching me. I shall never forget the rapture on their faces. Had I been a performer on the grandest stage in the world, I could not have found greater satisfaction.

Elementary school in the hills above Dhulikhel.

On the way home B.P. showed me a partially constructed building. "Here's how it's done," he said. "First they put up wooden struts and fill the spaces with straw. Then they plaster it with cow dung, smooth it out, and paint it white."

But doesn't it stink?" I asked, feeling immediately foolish.

"I know this will surprise you," he said, "but once it's dry and painted there's no odor at all. Don't forget, we're a poor country and have to use our ingenuity. Cow and yak dung are very useful products here in Nepal."

We walked along in silence.

"You know, dear Meg," said B.P. at last. "There's therapy in doing everything yourself, even the simplest task. These people take great pride in their homes and their farms. They're building a future stone by stone, brick by brick, row by row."

At breakfast the next morning I met Terri, a young woman from Yosemite, who was staying at the guesthouse on a self-imposed six-month retreat.

"I had to get away from my frantic life," she said, skillfully twirling thin noodles around enamel chopsticks. "My parents thought I was crazy to go to Nepal, but that's how far I had to go before my motor stopped racing."

I sympathized. I was still plagued with self-inflicted pressures that refused to go away. The *shoulds* and *oughts* of everyday life.

"But I wonder how long a peaceful place like Dhulikhel will survive," she added. "The influence of the West is disturbing."

This didn't surprise me. I'd already seen the effect of creeping westernization in Africa. Window dressing with little or no respect for the indigenous culture.

"For example, the Nepalese smoke American cigarettes for their prestige value. And don't think the good old U.S. tobacco companies aren't pushing that. In fact, there's a terrific demand for both cigarettes *and* liquor. Most of it comes from the airport duty free shops, and is sold by Westerners for a huge profit. Now this may sound superficial, but it goes a lot deeper...."

I'd heard this discussion so many times, and it always made me feel powerless—the hapless observer of an inevitable, depressing trend. The next thing she'd mention was arms sales. I changed the subject. "What do you say we take a walk in the countryside? Get a glimpse of Shangri-la before McDonald's discovers it."

"You're right," Terri agreed. "I came here to let go and I'm still wound up like a bedspring."

We found a path leading away from town and winding through heavily terraced fields. The symmetrical bands followed the contour of the land—vivid green where the new wheat was growing and rich brown where the corn would soon be planted. Yellow mustard was everywhere in bloom.

In the distance women in flowing dresses and *saris* carried towering bundles of laundry down to a rock ledge at the bank of the river and placed them in large metal pans heaped with suds. Later, the women skipped along the banks, rinsing the clothes in the bubbling water. We inched closer and watched. It was definitely a social occasion. Talking and laughing accompanied the scrubbing. Soon, a patchwork of dazzling color began to emerge as more and more squares of cloth were draped over the supple branches near the river's edge to dry.

When we returned, a noisy market was in full swing in the town square. Swarms of school children in neat blue and white uniforms were heading home. With my camera hanging from my neck I was a sitting duck, a chance for the bravest to practice English. The children grabbed both of my hands and escorted me to their school. After I'd taken several group pictures in front of the building, I asked them to show me where the post office was.

No answer. Only puzzled expressions. I drew a letter from my bag and slowly repeated, "Air mail stamps." Then I put out my arms and swooped like a plane, making loud motor sounds. That did it! Off we went in a flurry of excitement. After I'd bought my stamps and mailed the letter, one little boy put out his hand for money.

I shook my head and said, "Oh, no, we're friends."

To my surprise and chagrin he was severely chided by the other children.

In early evening Terri and I climbed up to B.P.'s luxurious mountain resort two miles from the center of town on the road leading to the Chinese/Tibetan border. This was no ordinary hotel. It had been put together lovingly, with authentic touches from the past incorporated into the clean lines of a modern Buddhist retreat. Carved wooden windows salvaged from ancient buildings looked out on a spacious stone patio. From the patio we watched the sun set behind the Himalayas. When the last bits of color had receded, we treated ourselves to dinner, sitting behind those splendid windows and watching the valley fill with mist.

Two hours later we walked back down the hill to the lodge. How clear the sky was, drenched with stars, the only light a crescent moon lying on its back. It was like those heavenly summer evenings when I was a teenager walking down the camp road to my parents' cottage, breathing the clear air and hearing only the night sounds. I needed no flashlight. I had the moon.

"Look, Meg," exclaimed Terri. "That's a *shiva* moon. There must be a festival going on right now. I've never seen it like that."

The night before I left, a group of us were sitting in the dining room after dinner and B.P. was telling stories about his experiences twenty years ago as an exchange teacher at the University of California in Davis. I got the impression that the most difficult part of adjusting to American society was the toilets. He'd never used a seat before—a rather ironic twist.

"I hate to interrupt this fascinating discussion, B.P., but I wonder if you could put through a call to my son, Chris, in New Jersey. I haven't talked to him in weeks." I gave him the number and sat, nervously tapping my foot, giving suggestions as he talked to the operator.

He put down the phone and patted my knee. "Please, Meg, I've done this before. Slow down. Don't talk so fast."

No sooner had B.P. put the call through than the phone rang and he began to chat with one of his friends. I tried to relax, to be patient. I breathed deeply. Stared out the window. Why didn't he get off the phone so my call could come through? He saw my annoyance and cupped his hand over the receiver.

"Stop worrying. The operator will interrupt me for an overseas trunk call."

I waited an hour, but there was no call. B.P. looked at me and smiled sympathetically. "Meg, you're in Nepal now. There's no hurry. There's tomorrow."

Early the next morning B.P. walked me to the bus. I looked at this modest man as we stood together in front of the old brick dwellings in the village square. He was a genuinely good person, a doer, not a talker. His life embraced the highest values of this little country. He and his village would always mean Nepal to me.

As the bus was pulling up I moved to hug him. He stepped back. "Meg, it isn't the custom in Nepal to show affection between a man and a woman in public. It would be misunderstood. Please don't be offended."

I realized that I'd seldom seen men and women together in public and, if I did, they were never holding hands or hugging. Men, however, were allowed to be affectionate toward one another.

"Maybe things will have changed before I return," I said as we shook hands. "After all, B.P., there's *always* tomorrow!"

37

MATHIAS

The words of my friend, Carol, popped into my head. "Don't pay any attention to men in Africa or India," she'd said at my farewell party four months earlier, "because I know in my bones that you're going to meet a fascinating scientist in Kathmandu, and, wonder of wonders, he'll be single. A little eccentric, but single."

Ever since my divorce Carol had been trying to fix me up. It was inconceivable to her that I should be without a man. I knew she was a romantic, so I promptly forgot her prediction…until the day I walked into Himalayan Excursions, a tourist agency in Kathmandu.

"I can give you a very good deal," said Pushkar, the handsome young Nepalese who headed the agency. "I've organized a special three week trek to Everest base camp for an Austrian scientist. I'm sure I can get you included. We use the same number of Sherpas for one person as for two, so I'll just add another guide—in case either you or Dr. Bauer gets sick and has to return."

He quoted me 7,980 rupees—380 dollars—one fourth the price of a comparable trek from most other agencies. And that included round trip airfare to Lukla, our starting point in the Himalayas.

"How old is this Austrian scientist…and what does he look like?" I asked Pushkar.

"Oh, sort of middle-aged. Very attractive," he said, smiling. "Looks a little like your movie star—Matthau, is it?" My God, could Carol's prediction possibly be right?

"Sounds good to me," I said, trying to hide my excitement. "But I'll need a couple of hours to think it over. I'm used to traveling alone and don't know if I want to tie myself down."

I went outside into Durbar Marg and walked back to another agency I'd noticed earlier that morning. Colorful pictures of Everest, Annapurna, and the Chitwan wild animal habitat filled the front window. They offered me the

Instant Everest trek—eight grueling days from Lukla (10,000 ft.) to Kala Pattar (18,000 ft.). I'd been told to stay away from this unless I wanted altitude sickness. They also promoted a longer climb, starting closer to Kathmandu—in Jiri—and lasting four weeks. Tents, portable toilets, wine with the meals. First class all the way. And a price tag to match.

I knew nothing about trekking in this part of the world. I hadn't even had time to read the book given to me by my son-in-law, spelling out the perils of high altitude climbing. Perhaps I hadn't wanted to know. Like most everything else on my trip, I figured I'd find out as I went along.

My mind kept returning to Carol and the mysterious scientist. She had certainly been right so far. No males had captured my imagination in Africa or India. Plenty had crossed my path—helpful, interesting, intelligent—but not fascinating.

An hour later I returned to Pushkar and, feeling like a silly schoolgirl, announced: "I'll take a chance on your scientist, but you'd better check with him first."

On my way back to the Stupa Guest House in Thamel, where I'd been staying while researching my trek, I decided to duck into the luxurious Annapurna Hotel for a visit to their fancy Ladies' Room. All the trekkers came to use the modern facilities, wash their hands in warm water, and "borrow" a wad of pink toilet paper to introduce a bit of luxury into their spartan lives. I was no exception. We all tried to look as nonchalant as possible, walking across the marble lobby in our heavy boots.

As I was leaving the hotel I bumped into Moses, an Israeli with whom I'd argued politics at B.P's. When he spotted me, we fell into each other's arms.

"Hey, Meg. What are you doing in this high class neighborhood?" he asked.

"To be honest, Moses, I was running out of soft toilet paper."

"You Americans. Always looking for a bargain!" He laughed.

"Where better to replenish my stock? And what about you?"

"Slumming," he said. "I've been looking everywhere for the greatest *thangka* [Tibetan scroll painting] in the world. My mother collects them. You know, the Kathmandu Valley is like a giant museum. More shrines and temples per square mile than anywhere else on earth. And if you're looking for Buddhist and Hindu art...."

"Oh, Moses, I can't absorb one more temple or look at one more *stupa*. Not today, anyway. And as for art, how would I carry it? I just signed up for a trek to Everest base camp and what I *really* need is to rent a sleeping bag and a warm jacket in a hurry. Couldn't you just come down to my level and help me. Puleeeze?"

"Actually, I was thinking of buying a pair of those baggy cotton pants tied at the ankles. A Nepalese original. And how about a handmade wool sweater? You can get one for eight dollars."

That did it! We scooted past the king's palace toward *Asan Tol,* one of the busiest markets in Kathmandu. Bombarded by a mixture of sounds, colors, and textures, we worked our way through a warren of narrow alleys. All around us was the babble of myriad languages joined by the ringing of bells and the chanting of prayers. Dogs quarreled, babies cried. Candle makers crowded in on butchers and rug merchants. Pushcart salesmen accosted us at every corner. Open stalls displaying bolts of color-saturated cloth held the promise of custom-made shirts and suits. The shops in the old market lured us on. Like a couple of kids we had to sample everything, and ended up with the baggy pants and collarless shirts—our fashion statement of the day—for four dollars.

After pawing through more bookstores and second hand shops I grabbed Moses by the arm. "Hey, don't forget my sleeping bag."

"Then it's back to Thamel," he said, and we braced ourselves for the long walk home. Five o'clock traffic was building up, making crossing the street more dangerous than ever. Neither police nor traffic lights are heeded in Kathmandu. As in Cairo, you just put out your hand, stare the cars down, and walk.

In no time I'd rented a sleeping bag, a down jacket, and a small duffle. For fifty cents a day.

It was late when we arrived at Narayan's, my favorite restaurant, where the spice content of the food is tailored to Westerners.

"I read that Kathmandu is the best place to eat east of Istanbul," said Moses, "and we're going to this tourist trap?"

"Please, Moses. Have pity on me. Just one meal without tears."

We walked in, surveyed the crowd, and realized that almost everyone was wearing identical baggy pants and collarless shirts, just like us. And we thought we were being so imaginative.

I awoke early the next morning to the sound of yelping dogs, mingled with the curses of those whose sleep they'd shattered. I dressed and walked out into the empty courtyard. Within the hour I'd be picked up by Norbu, Pushkar's assistant, and taken to the airport, along with the unknown Dr. Bauer. I couldn't have slept—even without the noisy dogs. I was too excited.

I lugged my heavy pack to the storeroom behind the registration desk. "Enjoy comfortable homely staying," said the sign on the wall. And I had. For sixty rupees ($3) I'd rented a simple room with two beds, one hanging light bulb, a table, a chair, and paper-thin walls, behind which several Germans had partied all night. The shower and toilet were just down the hall. And the toilet had a seat!

As I crossed the courtyard the first rays of light played on an old-fashioned hand pump that stood in one corner in front of a row of orange flowers. Resting next to it was a sizable metal pan. How patiently I'd waited to use it the day I'd arrived. Laboriously I'd scrubbed one T-shirt, my tired red sweater, and grimy jeans in the cold pump water. I reached my room, picked up my camera bag, day-pack, and small duffle, and walked to the street.

Minutes later an old car screeched to a halt, and Norbu jumped out to load my bags. In ten more minutes we picked up Dr. Bauer at the Tibetan Hotel—a far cry from the Stupa Guest House. I could feel his energy as he strode toward the car and stretched out a large hand to greet me. Yes, he *was* attractive—tall, lanky, with thick black hair that refused to lie flat, a weather-beaten face, and deep-set brown eyes almost hidden under heavy eyebrows. His mouth was ample and his smile made me think of my father's. It started slowly, with the lips at a slight angle, then burst into every corner of his face. It took my breath away.

"I've been dreadfully sick for two days," he said to Norbu as he helped load the car. "Even went to the hospital. They gave me pills for *giardia*." He slid into the back seat next to me and continued, apologetically. "I was up most of the night. Don't be surprised if I can't make the trip."

He seemed embarrassed by this frank admission at our first meeting. I chuckled to myself, wondering what Carol would say, and knowing that I was being scrutinized as carefully as I was scrutinizing. Nobody could be *that* nervous over a case of *giardia*.

An hour after arriving at the airport I began to understand why the price had been so right. Norbu found no tickets waiting for us at the counter. One guide had failed to show up, and the other was late. When we found him he was frantically piling sacks of food and kitchen utensils near the runway as if his excessive activity would make up for his lack of punctuality.

He was introduced to us as Ram, Dr. Bauer's guide. I'd never seen a skinnier man. He was about thirty, half-Indian and half-Nepalese, with a large Adam's apple, protruding teeth—which showed a touch of gold when he smiled—an unkempt mat of dark hair, and a long wispy moustache. He kept his hands in his jacket pockets, hugging his elbows to his body and hunching his shoulders as if against the wind, all the time shifting from one foot to the other. I soon discovered that this was his normal stance, wind or no wind. And what he was wearing when we met was what he wore for as long as we knew him—skintight khaki pants, an old waist-length leather jacket, a faded flannel shirt, and battered shoes. No climbing boots. No hat or gloves. Just looking at him made me shiver.

But there was a more serious problem: overbooking. Even if our ticket reservation *had* been located, there were too many people for the three available planes. The first plane had not even taken off when the fog began rolling in, obliterating the white peaks which had been so dramatic in the early morning sun.

Dr. Bauer and I climbed to the balcony restaurant and sat at a table overlooking the crowd of frustrated travelers. Pushkar had instructed Norbu to treat us to a large western breakfast. Dr. Bauer approached it cautiously. "This will be a test," he said, as the waiter placed a platter of bacon and eggs in front of him. "I'm really very healthy, you know. I never get sick. I have a wonderful doctor who gave me all the right pills and instructions about what not to eat and how to purify water. So what did I do wrong?"

"You came to Nepal, and you breathed the air, and maybe you ate food at restaurants that were too high class. You should have come to my hangout in Thamel," I said. "Nobody ever gets sick eating at the Narayan."

"Perhaps you're right," he said. "Those of us who are too careful and think they have all the answers get caught. Keeps us humble." There was a pause. "And by the way, as long as we're going to brave the Himalayas together, I think we can stop being so formal. Please call me Mathias. Or Matthew, if you prefer.

"No, I like the German. And I'm Meg, short for Margaret."

I finally mustered the courage to ask him if he was married.

"My wife died almost four months ago," he said. "This was to be our thirtieth wedding anniversary trip."

Now I felt like an interloper.

"She'd been sick five years," he continued, sadness muting his voice. "It's been a terrible time for me and my family. I almost cancelled this trip, but the Nepalese government needed my help, and I guess I needed the change. I love mountain climbing and I love Nepal. And my dream is to reach Everest base camp."

Not knowing what to say, and feeling uncomfortable, I asked, "What will you be doing for the Nepalese government?"

"I'm a seismologist," he answered. "Northern India and Nepal are sites of a great deal of earthquake activity, and will continue to be." He pulled a pen from his pocket and began drawing on the paper placemat. He drew the Indian Ocean and showed India pushing up the Himalayas from the continental shelf. His mood changed. He became very excited. "When India crashed into Asia, the Himalayas were created. India is now pushing underneath Tibet. It's as if Asia is gulping India. I have a grant from the Austrian government to study evidence of recent displacement along the faults. I love photography, so I'll drive you crazy taking pictures of everything in sight, mostly rock formations." The more I listened the more I thought Carol was right. This could be the guy.

"How wonderful to be so enthusiastic about your work," I said. "And how wonderful to be able to explain it to me. I can't even understand running water."

We laughed. This trip was beginning to look good—if it ever got off the ground.

It didn't—at least not that day. On the surface it looked as if Nepal were trying to keep down the tourist traffic and make access to its mountains as difficult as possible. Later that morning in his office Pushkar shared our frustration: not enough planes, poor runways, and the unsavory practice of paying *baksheesh* (bribes) to the pilots to get return flights to Kathmandu.

"My people are not willing to do the hard work needed to improve our economy, educate our people, and attract tourists," he said. "It's discouraging. All we talk about is western aid, but what good is it if we won't help ourselves?" He threw up his hands. "Do you know that right this minute I have twenty trekkers stranded in Lukla, and don't know when they'll get out?"

Pushkar tried to talk us into other more reliable treks—Annapurna, or the hills around Pokara—but Mathias's enthusiasm for the Everest region was infectious. We decided to wait a few more days. Neither of us would settle for less.

At ten the next morning Mathias appeared at my door. He was smiling. "You see, I am healthy once again. And there is much to see around Kathmandu. I thought you might like to visit the small town of Patan with me. It's not so crowded and has some interesting temples. I have this guide book and I just thought, maybe...." His voice was a question. He tried to be casual, but there was something very formal in his invitation.

"That would be lovely," I said, trying to hide my amusement. "Just let me finish this letter. It's to my sister. My mother took a dreadful fall and we're all worried about her. She broke her shoulder and she's not doing well. And Anne—she's my older sister—has taken on her care." I looked up at him, as if for reassurance.

"And you feel a little guilty not being there to help?"

I nodded gratefully.

"I know what it is to care for somebody you love. To worry about her. It's natural. It's also part of life for all of us. And there'll be plenty of time for you to do your share. Your sister knows that, but it's important that you know it. I think your mother would not like this to ruin your trip. I'll sit here in the courtyard and let you finish."

His words were comforting. But seeing Mathias made it difficult to concentrate. I put the letter aside. I'd mail it tomorrow. I felt upbeat when we left the guesthouse and made our way to the bus station.

The bus was pulling out just as we arrived. Mathias ran, shouting at the driver to stop. He grabbed my hand and lifted me onto the bus. His grip was strong, solid.

Patan prefers its old name, *Lalitpur*, which means "city of art." It considers itself the focal point for Nepal's artisans—wood-carvers, bronze-casters, painters—whose skills are reputed to be the finest in all of Asia. We walked toward Durbar Square in the center of town. Suddenly, colored water rained from a window, landing on both of us. I jumped out of the way with a squeal, thinking it was garbage, but Mathias reminded me that this marked the end of a religious festival. Which one? Who knows? There are dozens throughout the year.

The old square was paved with irregular stones and rimmed with temples. On one of the platforms were statues of pigs and other domestic animals, streaked and weathered with age. As I photographed them a real pig came ambling toward me, stopping to fill up on garbage.

"Meg. Look. He wants you to capture him as he enjoys his banquet," teased Mathias. I stopped to take a picture of the real pig next to the stone facsimile, and a group of barefoot children caught up. Hands thrust out, engaging smiles on their faces, they surrounded me.

"Now look what you've done," I scolded. "From now on *you* handle the fans." He chuckled and dropped a small bill into each outstretched hand.

We hurried up the stairs of *Krishna Mandir*, a seventeenth century temple constructed of stone and girdled with three levels of verandas, each with countless columns. It was quite different from the other temples on the square, which had pagoda-type tiered roofs. This one adhered to the Moghul tradition. The mythical man-bird, *Garuda*, sat with folded hands on top of a pillar, since *Garuda* was *Vishnu's* animal, and *Krishna* is *Vishnu's* incarnation. All around the temple—carved in stone—were detailed scenes from the great Hindu epics, *Mahabharat* and *Ramayan*.

Opposite the temple, in a sunken courtyard smooth from centuries of use, women washed their clothes and hair in water that poured continuously from large iron spigots.

"Look at this, Mathias. I bet they've been doing the same thing in exactly the same place for hundreds of years." How seamlessly the past blended with the present.

I was not prepared for what I saw when we stepped into the next temple, named after *Shiva*. On the roof struts were carved the most detailed erotic scenes imaginable. Penises were enormous and shaped like stylized swords. Gods possessed numerous arms. Sexual orgies were depicted in graphic detail.

"I think the Nepalese must be vying with the Indians to see who has the largest genitals," said Mathias.

I wasn't sure how to behave or what to say. I didn't want to gawk, for I was afraid Mathias would think me too curious. I tried to be casual, but could not hide my embarrassment.

"According to legend the Nepalese believed that the goddess of lightening was a prudish virgin," he added, "and if they covered their temples with erotic art she would be too shocked to strike. Have you ever heard a better rationalization for pornography?"

Northwest of the main square we ducked through a thin passage and emerged at the center of *Hiranyavarna Mahavihara*, the Golden Temple, the most opulent in Nepal. The roof was gold-plated, and a three-tiered pagoda stood in the courtyard. It had been a Buddhist monastery since the twelfth century and was surrounded by buildings made up of large prayer rooms. Inside the temple, itself, were carved prayer wheels and ornate scenes from the life of Buddha. Before entering, we removed our shoes and belts. Nothing made of leather was allowed into this holiest of places.

A group of women sat in a balcony overlooking the inner courtyard, learning to recite prayers, and gently ringing bells at specified intervals. The atmosphere was hushed, almost eerie. A monk passed by, his soft shoes soundless on the polished stones.

We walked southeast from Durbar Square along a brick-paved road to reach *Mahabauddha*, a rococo masterpiece in terra cotta, called the Temple of a Thousand Buddhas. Originally constructed in the fourteenth century, the conical, Indian-style temple was made entirely of bricks. Small carved Buddha images and floral designs appeared on each brick. Inside was a shrine dedicated to *Maya Devi*, the mother of Buddha.

Before we left we peeked into several smaller temples, where young women were washing the stones as an act of religious charity. Their toddlers, tethered in foot bracelets, played in the courtyard next to them. It was a tranquil scene, worthy of Vermeer.

When we returned to Kathmandu Mathias suggested that we stroll over to their Durbar Square, a complex of forty-eight temples. I had the feeling that he didn't want the day to end.

"I'm really sick of temples, Mathias. I hope you don't mind."

"No, no," he reassured me, "we'll just look around. No sightseeing. And we do have to eat dinner eventually." We continued through the old streets, traveling back in time with each step.

"Wait, Meg," said Mathias, stopping abruptly at a sturdy iron gate guarded by two large icons. "I think this is the famous *Kumari Chowk*, the home of the living goddess." He began rapidly thumbing through his guidebook. "Yes, there's the courtyard…and the balcony." I looked into a dark, forbidding space.

There are many versions of the living goddess story and Mathias insisted on reading them all. The legend began two hundred years ago when the last *Malla* king of Kathmandu was alleged to have had intercourse with a prepubescent girl, resulting in her death. The king, guilt-ridden, was told in a dream to start the institution of the *Kumari*—the worshipping of a young girl. The child would be chosen for her fearlessness and purity after a rigorous series of tests. For three days every September, during the festival of the God *Indra* which marks the end of the monsoon season, the *Kumari* is taken by chariot around Kathmandu as penance for the king's sins. She blesses the King of Nepal on this occasion, putting a red *tika* mark on his forehead and receiving a gold coin in return. The rest of the time she lives in the elaborate three-storied building, until pubescence.

I studied the ornamental woodcarving on the windows, pillars, and balcony. And I thought of the poor little captive goddess inside, whose feet were never allowed to touch the ground. What kind of life lay ahead after she left her cloistered existence? Grim, I'll wager, since the popular belief was that anyone who married her would die young.

As we turned to leave I pulled on Mathias's sleeve. "Look…up there on the balcony. There's a shadow behind the wooden latticework. It has to be the goddess!" I was sure that her eyes—with the exaggerated dark makeup—were looking directly at me.

Mathias, indefatigable, dragged me through another round of temples. So much for promises. But it wasn't as intense as Patan, since we spent most of our time taking pictures of the people, the brightly painted holy men, and each other—Mathias clowning or sitting on the steps of *Jagannath Mandir*, the location of even more shocking erotica, and me hugging a large replica of *Hanuman*, the monkey god, in front of the royal palace. During our day together I was finding myself more and more drawn to this man. To his energy and warmth. His enthusiasm and curiosity.

At dusk we left Durbar Square, only to be caught in an end-of-the-day crush of people. Unable to extricate ourselves, we were carried along, an inch at a time, in the relentless flow of bodies. A motorcycle, loaded with fresh produce, edged through the crowd, honking shrilly and barely able to squeeze past. A moment later a lone cow brushed against my leg. I turned to Mathias, perplexed....

He burst out laughing. "It's the cow, not me."

In an instant a path was cleared, and the cow made her way through, stopping long enough to eat several cabbages from the back of the motorcycle, while the driver looked on, helplessly.

"I think it's safe to say that it will be a long time before Nepal loses its charm," observed Mathias.

38

ON OUR WAY!

Mathias pounded on my door before dawn the very next morning.

"Wake up, Meg, Pushkar himself is outside. I think he paid somebody to get us tickets…just to be rid of us." Mathias was bubbling with excitement. "I'll wait for you in the car."

The lobby at the airport was overflowing when we arrived. Ram, unshaven and smelling unmistakably of rice wine, greeted us with a jubilant grin. "*Namaste*! [I greet the god within you]," he said, bowing to me, his palms pressed together as if in prayer. "This Dawa Dorje, your guide. Just say Dorje."

I returned the traditional greeting, and grasped the hand of a lean young man with a shiny square face, coal-black hair, Tibetan features, and sparkling eyes. He was as polished in dress and manner as Ram was shabby. He looked more like an office manager than a wilderness guide. Little did I know that Dorje had never been to Everest base camp nor climbed higher than 4,000 feet. Like me, this was his first trip. Pushkar was *really* economizing.

The sky began to cloud over as we walked toward the tiny plane with the grand letters—Royal Nepal Airlines—emblazoned on its fuselage. I expected to be turned back at any moment and could hardly contain my joy as I squeezed into the last seat behind a mountain of duffel bags. "Hurrah, we made it!" I shouted. Mathias, ecstatic, sat in the opposite corner of the overloaded plane, readying his cameras.

Tears of happiness spilled over as the propellers started churning, lifting us off and shaking the cabin violently. The motor's roar was high-pitched, deafening. As we climbed, the weather cleared. Snow-streaked mountains rose above the green, neatly terraced valleys. The valleys gave way to brown foothills, where small squares of wheat struggled to survive. A panorama of layered mountains stretched before me, reminiscent of the sunrise three months before on top of Mt. Moses in the Sinai.

The sky was icy blue, changing to ethereal green as it reached the highest peaks. I'd never seen such mountains! Saw-toothed, silent, untouched. And we flew down the valley between the ridges like a flea between two herds of elephants.

Forty minutes later an opening in the trees revealed the sloping rooftops of Lukla. We swooped down, sounding like an asthmatic bumble bee, and bounced the length of the narrow dirt runway, wings dipping from side to side. It was like negotiating a tight rope on a tricycle. There was no margin for error. A rocky cliff greeted us at the end of the runway.

Once unloaded, the pilot turned the plane around and headed back to Kathmandu, scheduled to return with another group of climbers before noon. I stood at a distance, alone, my daypack and camera bag on the ground next to me. What excitement as the plane took off! Shouting, waving, children running, dogs barking. I watched the small craft bump down the short runway and drop into a sea of thick vegetation. I watched until it became the size of a fly and I could hear the motor no more. Now I really felt isolated—by weather, by altitude, by language, by culture. I also felt light-headed and giddy. Here I was at 11,000 ft., on the spot where Sir Edmund Hillary started his conquest of Everest in 1953—this man so loved by the *Sherpa* people. I would soon walk the same path leading up to base camp, where his historic climb began.

When I turned I saw Ram standing in the middle of a group of *Sherpas,* talking rapidly and gesticulating—bargaining for our cook and our porters. Mathias had already started down the main street of Lukla—a narrow path of hard-packed dirt and stone—camera in hand. I hurried after him and we poked around the town together. Each house was built separately, but so close to its neighbor that it touched where it had sagged and buckled—like very old people supporting one another after years of living together. The shingled roofs were made of pieces of hand-hewn wood or slate. Large rocks held them in place and protected against heavy wind and storms. The windows—divided into four small panes—were outlined in bright colors, mostly red and royal blue, and several of the buildings had flower designs painted on the cement sides.

But it was the *Sherpas* who were the main attraction. The people the British trained as high-altitude porters for the first expeditions on Everest. These rugged mountain people live in the Khumbu, the complex of valleys south of Everest in the Nepalese Himalayas. They barely eke out a living making handicrafts, tending their grazing yaks, selling the milk, wool, and cheese, and working their small gardens of potatoes, wheat, and hardy greens. For me they had stepped right out of The National Geographic—young women with broad faces and shy smiles, and old women with weathered skin and deeply lined faces—all with the high cheekbones and almond eyes of Mongolia and Tibet. But these women were not old by western standards. Most of them would not survive past fifty. Tuberculosis and pneumonia were implacable enemies. And missing teeth contributed to the appearance of age. If a tooth ached, you pulled it out. Simple as that.

And the clothes. I wondered where they found so many shades of gray, brown, and olive for the blouses, long skirts, and sweaters that they wore, layer upon layer. The blouses made of hand-woven cloth crisscrossed the bodice, and the woolen aprons of muted horizontal stripes were tied tightly around the waist for warmth. Sometimes a large ornamental silver belt buckle was displayed in front. It was a monochromatic uniform totally unlike anything I'd seen in Africa. Only the colored kerchiefs, used to tie back their straight, shiny hair, added a touch of brightness.

The young men were stunning—trim and muscular, like my guide, Dorje. They had quantities of ebony hair and luxuriant moustaches. But the old men I met along the way were dark and bent and sinewy, attesting to the fact that life in the mountains was strenuous.

Putti.

Ram caught up with us. He'd been giving instructions to our two porters—an exquisite fourteen-year-old *Sherpani* named Putti, and her diminutive friend, Tenza. They'd already loaded our gear onto their backs and secured it across the forehead with a wide leather band. No pack frames for them. They leaned into the weight and bounced along, chatting and laughing as if taking a Sunday stroll in the park. According to Ram, they were excited to have landed this job and planned to stay with us for at least a week. There would be other porters for the higher altitudes.

Putti carried a large woven basket full of kitchen utensils, reaching below her waist, and Tenza packed two heavy duffels roped together, reaching to her knees. The cook, sixteen-year-old Kumar, carried our tents, the stove, and a water jug. Far less than the girls. I was shocked to see that he wore nothing but rubber thongs on his bare feet. The girls wore thin canvas sneakers. Not a hiking boot in the lot. And they didn't bother with gloves or mittens, either. How I admired their fortitude. I felt like a coddled tourist next to them, with my high-tech down jacket and my Peter Limmer custom-made boots. I was a sissy. These were the *real* mountain people.

The porters went ahead while Ram led us to a simple lodge where an open fire burned in a stone hearth. A guitar stood in one corner and a baby crawled on the bare floor. He wore no diaper, just pants with a slit up the back requiring quick action on the part of the mother. The baby held a peeled potato and sucked on it. More potatoes were cooking on the grate. Ram offered us some—plain or fried—along with lemon tea. Thinking it was just a snack, I took only a few. I didn't want to load my stomach before starting. Unfortunately, for me, it turned out to be our lunch.

I also experienced my first hole-in-the-floor-with-sawdust-and-twigs-out-house. It was located in a field next to an old burned-out airplane fuselage. "TREKKES TOILET" was printed in large white letters on the side. Not bad, if you happened to be among the first hundred users and there was still an ample supply of sawdust or shavings. It could get pretty rank later on. But it was all we had on the trek, except at 18,000 feet, where we had nothing.

I soon realized why the *Sherpa* women wore skirts instead of jeans. All they had to do was squat, but we had to expose ourselves from the waist down to gale winds in the ice fields. That's why you paid so dearly for the portable toilets on the fancier treks.

Namaste! Children in the mountains of Nepal.

A gentle rain began as we started up the trail. Rock enclosures built to keep the animals from eating the wheat and vegetables, covered the steep, terraced slopes. Sturdily built stone houses seemed to be plunked in the middle of nowhere. The roofs were made of heavy burlap or straw matting—not wooden or stone shingles as in Lukla—and the usual rocks held them in place.

Mathias had an encyclopedic knowledge of Himalayan flora and pointed out each new discovery. "Meg, look! The first sign of spring, *primula denticulata*, Himalayan primrose." He photographed the tiny fluttering flower, paper-thin in delicate hues of violet and pink, and became ecstatic over the mountain rhododendron, its buds shyly peeking out of their green sheaths. "By the end of March, in just three weeks, we'll see them in bloom," he assured me. And we did. Tall bushes laden with fiery balls of crimson and deep purple.

For the next ten miles we worked our way uphill toward Phakding, passing through what was left of the once thick alpine forests, thinned by the continued cutting down of trees for fuel. Ram kept cautioning us. "Take it easy, please. It is first day over 10,000 feet." So we found lots of excuses to stop, most of them to examine the ubiquitous *mani* walls made of stone slabs on which religious inscriptions and prayers had been carved. (The gods smiled on you if you donated one of the heavy tablets.) The walls—erected along the route or right in the middle of it—were shaped like the prow of an ocean liner. Sometimes the vertical stones were mounted in tiers, held up by several layers of horizontal stones and stretching along the trail for many yards. We were cautioned to walk clockwise, around the left side, so as not to risk insulting the gods.

At each shrine white and blue prayer flags—triangular banners atop tall, skinny poles—snapped in the wind.

I couldn't stop taking pictures.

"That's enough, Meg. You've already used up three days of film," warned Mathias.

How could he know how much film I'd need? "You can boss me if you wish," I said good-naturedly. "But I'm not married to you, so I don't have to listen."

My remark took him by surprise. "You're right," he said. "My wife always said I was bossy. I can see that with you I'll have to be more careful." I was pleased that he had taken me seriously.

For the next hour we bombarded Ram with questions.

"Ram, are we getting close to Phakding?" I asked.

"Yes, Missus," he answered, smiling broadly—always smiling broadly.

"Ram, are we very far from Phakding?" Mathias asked, winking at me.

Mani wall.

"Yes, Mister," Ram answered. He moved his head slightly from side to side, as many Indians do. It reminded me of a doll I'd once played with as a child. Its head was attached to its body by a spring, and it wobbled when you picked it up.

Mathias leaned over and whispered to me, "It seems that you must pay more for a guide who speaks your language."

"Poor fellow," I said. "He's just trying to please. You might as well get out your maps. I have a feeling we're on our own."

From then on we tried never to ask questions that could be answered with a simple "yes" or "no." Ram, however, dug into his barrel of well-worn phrases and found ample ways to circumvent this. His favorites: "Is no problem." "Is O.K." "Not to worry." Whenever we heard any of these cliches, we started to worry.

Late in the afternoon Ram became very talkative and began thumping Mathias on the back and calling him "good fellow." Along with being overly ebullient, he was also a little unsteady on his feet. He even took his hands out of his pockets a couple of times to keep his balance. Mathias, also very talkative, was having a fine time, feeling that, despite the language barrier, things were looking up. They were going to be friends.

Suddenly it started to rain and Ram took off at a fast clip, leaving us far behind. Mathias was furious.

"What kind of guide is he? What right does he have to leave us like that? Suppose we lose our way? And suppose I need my wide-angle lens? He has my white leather bag. Damnation!"

"Mathias, it's raining. You won't be taking any pictures. And besides, couldn't you see that he was drunk?"

"Drunk?" he said, looking at me incredulously. "I don't believe it! When, how? He's been with us all the time."

I shook my head. "Are you kidding? All those flowers, all those *mani*, all those photographs? He's had plenty of opportunity to guzzle some of the rice wine he smelled of this morning."

"You're exaggerating, Meg. He's just a thoughtless, stupid man."

"Thoughtless, yes, but not stupid. I know an alcoholic when I see one. I spotted him immediately. I lived with one for years."

Mathias looked crestfallen—and embarrassed. "You never told me. I'm sorry."

We walked on in silence, until we came to the edge of town. We didn't know the name of our lodge, so stopped at several along the way. No Ram. We were getting panicky by the time we spotted a campground on the hill above the river. Mathias was fuming. I grabbed his arm.

"Take it easy," I said. "I'm sure that's our campground ahead. If not, they'll give us directions...and look how beautiful the mountains are in the setting sun...and how about that gorgeous new outhouse perched above the river and emptying right into the rapids." Words spilled out. Anything to change the mood.

"I can't believe that!" Mathias said, shaking his head in disgust. "Some system. No wonder they say in our country that the formula for water in Nepal is urine plus iodine tablets."

"That's gross," I said.

Cold, wet, and tired, we stumbled across a wobbly wooden bridge high above the river and climbed a steep hill to the lodge at the edge of the campground. We entered a small bunkroom and were delighted to see our duffels stacked against the wall. The room was cozy—rough wood panels and low ceilings. Mathias had to duck his head to go through the dining room to the kitchen, where a blazing fire burned in one corner. The heat felt wonderful.

Still no Ram. We had been expected, however, and were handed tea and cookies by Kumar, our cook, accompanied by gracious bowing. A bed stood near the fire, and several babies crawled or toddled about, barefoot and scantily dressed. A wrinkled old man in drab clothing sat watching. The women labored over the fire, made by placing an iron grating over a hole into which sticks of pine were inserted from every angle—like a three-sided wheel. As the wood burned, the sticks were shoved further under and new ones added. Conversation was low, almost murmured, and the faces were sad and careworn—a look that became all too familiar over the next weeks.

After a dinner of rice, potatoes, and canned tomato soup, we returned to the bunkroom to prepare for bed. And there was Ram, standing in the doorway. He staggered over to Mathias.

"Hello, you, my father, my friend, and you [pointing to me] my mother. You guide me, yes? Welcome and sleep good." Without waiting for an answer, and before Mathias could launch into a tirade, Ram was gone, weaving down the path into the darkness.

"Now I believe you, Meg. You were right. It looks as if we *are* going to be his parents." He shook his head wearily. "Thank God you're here. I couldn't cope with this maniac by myself."

Ram, we discovered, had a reputation for drinking. Several *Sherpas* said they felt his behavior was shocking, and promised to speak to him in the morning. Dorje was embarrassed and apologetic, but had little time for us. He was too busy impressing Putti—and any other females in the vicinity—with his beauty and strength. We huddled outside in our down jackets, watching the stars appear and listening to the music of the river while Dorje stripped to his underwear and washed his entire body, including his hair, using cold water from the pump. He carried an assortment of toiletries fit for a Parisian dandy. This grooming became a daily ritual.

Just before bed Kumar brought us tea, cookies, and two basins of hot water for washing. He did the same at about six each morning. He spoke almost no English, but communicated with his eyes and the graceful movement of his body. He exuded lighthearted boyishness. Whenever he misunderstood us, which was frequently, he would laugh nervously and run from the room, returning with several alternative items in the hope that one of them was correct. When we made our choice he would clamp his hands to the sides of his cheeks and move his head back and forth with unbridled glee. Kumar's smiling face was the perfect way to begin and end each day.

Grateful to be inside the lodge and not in a tent, we laid our sleeping bags out on wide wooden benches attached to the wall. I knew, when I saw Mathias's light bag, that it was much too thin. He groaned as he slipped into the cold envelope. I lay awake after he'd gone to sleep, listening to the wind rattling the windows and watching the even flow of my breath in the moonlight. I snuggled deeper into the down in an attempt to leave only my nose exposed to the intense cold. I could almost hear Mathias shivering.

The moon shone into the room and onto a pile of comforters stacked in the corner. I tiptoed across, unfolded one, and gently covered him. Then I returned to my bed. For a long time I watched the moon—encircled by the yellow glow of impending rain—as it crossed the sky, playing tag with wisps of trailing clouds.

39

NAMCHE BAZAR

"That was lovely—what you did last night," Mathias said as we drank our morning tea. "I didn't want you to know, but I was awake. Nobody has cared for me like that in a long time." He reached over and touched my hand. "I'm grateful to Pushkar for finding you."

I bowed my head, hoping he wouldn't notice the color rising in my cheeks.

The sun was shining when we began our climb out of Phakding, but it started to rain around noon, just before we reached a large rustic cabin a short distance from the trail. For the first time I realized that you could climb in these mountains without a guide, porter, or cook, and get lodging at intervals along the way—for about two rupees a night—if you bought their food. Mattresses lined the bunkrooms. All you needed was a sleeping bag.

The room was thick with wood smoke and crowded with hikers sitting at heavy wooden tables reading maps, swapping stories, and enjoying a meal. And the food looked great! *Sherpa* stew, made with quantities of potatoes and a spinach-like vegetable, bubbled in iron kettles over an open fire. Now and then bits of dried yak meat were added, but not often, since the Buddhists have very strict rules about the killing of animals. Spicy ginger or curried rice was served with fried *chapatties,* cooked to a golden brown. Steaming bowls of chicken soup sat at each place next to mounds of thin noodles mixed with chopped onions. Of course, the ever-present *dal bhat,* a thick Nepalese lentil soup, was always available, except at the higher altitudes, where the cook depended more on dehydrated soups and pastas. There was even a salad of shredded cabbage, and, as usual, hot lemon tea made from a powdered mix and kept in large thermos jugs. A hefty choice, especially since it had to be carried in on someone's back.

We dried ourselves at a pot-bellied stove, fed, like the one last night, by shoving wood into the bottom. We were soaking. Was it the rain, or was it sweat? Probably both, for the climbing had been strenuous and constant.

"Ram, let's eat here," I begged. "At least a bowl of soup."

"No, Missus. Lunch is not now. It is up the trail." He motioned, impatiently, toward the door. It was hard to leave such a congenial group. And what would lunch have cost...a few rupees?

Half-an-hour later I watched with great admiration as our porters dismantled their enormous packs and set up a kitchen on the hard dirt floor of a shed adjacent to the lodge where we were to eat. It took almost two hours for them to cook and serve a full meal of boiled potatoes, rice, greens fried in vegetable oil, and *chapatties*. Tea and plain English biscuits sufficed for dessert.

Putti was only a porter, not the cook, but she did most of the work. *Sherpa* women expected and received no favored treatment when it came to hard physical labor. In fact, the men did little more than sit around, joke with the girls, and serve the meal. And maybe scrub a pan or two.

Our drinking water was supposedly boiled, but we didn't trust it, knowing how long it takes to kill bacteria at high altitude. Kumar would bring us boiling water that we poured into our canteens. After it had cooled we added special tablets, which Mathias had brought, that gave the water a terrible, metallic taste. We both wondered whether this tedious process of purification did any good, since the dishes and eating utensils were washed in cold water right out of the river.

Mathias and I sat alone in a bare room on the second floor of the lodge, talking. "I find it amazing that you can be so optimistic and cheerful after what you've been through with your ex-husband," he said. I had told him about my husband's drinking, about our company going bankrupt, and about my decision to get a divorce after thirty-three years of marriage.

"Divorce is something I never envisioned for myself," I said. "It's a terrible failure. A part of you dies. But there's also a great feeling of relief and, yes, joy, when you finally face a problem and take steps to alter the old, destructive patterns. When you're dealing with alcoholism the whole family suffers. We become 'enablers,' whether we realize it or not. And that has to change."

Mathias sat very quietly with his chin resting on his hands.

"And what about you?" I said. "Your life hasn't been exactly easy these past few years. But I've never met a more positive person in my life. You're like a kid looking for a new challenge around every corner. I thought I'd die this morning when you climbed down that steep embankment just to photograph a flower. Maybe it was rare, but you took an awful chance. Did you happen to notice that Ram was sweating bullets?"

"It's being with you," he replied. "You make me live again. *You're* the adventurous one." He sighed and looked at me very seriously—a look I found both endearing and unnerving. "Meg, it would have been such a mistake to come alone. Can you imagine just sitting here staring at these four walls—no communication with Ram or the others? I would have gone crazy!"

Neither of us had realized what a separation there would be between the *Sherpas* and us. It reminded me of the camping safari in Africa, where Moffat had made two campfires—one for the guests and one for the crew. It hadn't been easy to persuade him and his men to eat with us and share their stories and songs. I still hoped for such a breakthrough with Ram.

In the afternoon we descended through the mud to the *Dudh Kosi* (Milk River)—turbulent and aqua-blue—only to climb back up the other side of the ravine and be met by a blizzard. When the snow subsided we found ourselves on the edge of a cliff, looking into a valley covered with tall pines. Each tree reached up, uninterrupted, from the floor of the valley—a forest of elongated Christmas trees. I was experiencing the winter I'd skipped this year, and I loved it. And I was especially glad for the polypropylene underwear and nylon ski pants I'd begrudgingly carried around on my back all these months.

The trail was steep and we had to stop often to catch our breath. I could see that Mathias was having a great deal of trouble controlling his emotions. When he finally spoke his voice was close to a sob. "My wife always loved to climb in the Alps in the winter. I keep thinking how much she would love this. I'm sorry. I'm just a very emotional person."

"Don't be sorry." I said. "If you *didn't* feel this way, you'd have reason to be sorry." How wonderful to find a man who wasn't afraid to show emotion. I had a tremendous urge to hug him, to comfort him, but knew he needed to be alone with his thoughts.

When we reached Jorsale we showed our trekking passes and entered *Sagarmatha National Park,* a 480-square-mile area established in 1976 to help preserve the natural beauty of the region around Mt. Everest. *Sagarmatha* means "sky head," the Nepalese name for Everest.

Population is spiraling in Nepal. So is tourism. And the impact on the forests of the great Khumbu is devastating. Now only the locals are allowed to cut down trees for firewood, and, by law, trekkers *must* use kerosene stoves for cooking. But even these measures are not enough to stop the erosion of valuable topsoil, which, once gone, can never be replaced.

It was dark when we reached Namche Bazar at 11,200 feet. The snow had melted and the streets were slippery with mud. Ram had stayed sober all day, and it was a good thing, because walking through town was life threatening. Huge potholes, once filled with ice and snow, were now ready to devour an unwary pedestrian or maybe just gobble up an ankle or two. Here and there someone had placed a rough plank or flat slate across the holes—a challenge to would-be gymnasts.

We stayed on the second floor of the Kallapattar Lodge, a modest house on the main drag, with a hazardous staircase, slanting floors, and dreadful iron beds. Our low-ceilinged room could accommodate six people. We were just getting acquainted with an assortment of roommates when a young woman came running in from the adjacent room, crying out: "There's a lady in my room who's moaning…do you hear her? She's been on her bed all day, hardly breathing. Can't stand or walk, and is very pale. Please, are any of you doctors? I'm afraid she's going to die."

A young man jumped up from a bed under the eaves where he'd been resting. "Sounds like altitude sickness to me. I'm not a doctor, but I've seen enough cases to recognize the symptoms." He and a companion hurried down the hall while the rest of us looked at each other helplessly.

Mathias had already given me a lengthy lecture on altitude sickness, and warned that we might have to stay at each camp longer than planned, to get used to the thinner air, especially if we developed symptoms like dizziness, nausea, edema, lack of coordination or excruciating headaches.

"What's going to happen if she can't walk out?" I asked.

"They'll take her out by yak, or if she's really bad they'll radio for a helicopter," said an American public relations executive, who, moments before, had introduced himself to us. "And that's a bitch. Even if you can locate one in time, when she gets the bill she'll wish they'd let her die. I just hiked down from 14,000 feet, accompanying one of our party who was so sick he had to be sent out by yak-back." He smiled wryly. "What a bummer."

No wonder he was upset. He'd flown from New York to Kathmandu with an expensive tour made up of young men who thought they were super fit. They'd raced ahead, refusing to heed the warnings to stay at least two nights at each camp and climb in increments of 1,000 feet a day until they'd become acclimated. They paid dearly for their bravado by not reaching base camp.

"I couldn't let him die, you know. Everyone was feeling pretty bad, including me, and the guides had their hands full." He shrugged. "But we got as far as the monastery at Thyangboche. It was glorious while it lasted, and I'll be back another time—with my own *Sherpa* at my own pace."

Just before Kumar brought our dinner we were assured that the lady next door would survive. A doctor had been summoned and she was being given oxygen. It was amazing how concerned everyone was. It didn't take long to become a family in these mountains.

One of our roommates—a schoolteacher from Australia—had hired her own porter/guide, a weathered old man who seemed to adore her. While we were talking, he curled up in a blanket on the bed next to hers and went to sleep. No cold shed and dirt floor for him.

"We've been friends for years," she said, adjusting her long khaki skirt and preparing to eat a steaming bowl of vegetable stew. "He's not like other porters. He's independent and he's crusty, and nobody pushes him around. We've been all over Nepal—Annapurna, Pokhara, Langtang, Kangchenjunga—and now Everest base camp. He takes good care of me."

She looked about my age, and we hit it off immediately. "One thing wonderful about these mountain people," she continued, gesturing toward the sleeping man. "They respect age. They call me the venerable old Mama. I'm revered because I've lived so long. Past fifty, imagine! They're sure that God has smiled on me. So am I."

Ram was in rare form—although not as rare as the previous night—and eager to exonerate himself. He made meat crepes for dinner, and announced that the tea and special dessert biscuits were "real from English."

After dinner I took out my tape recorder. "Let's have a song, Ram…like the ones you and Dorje were singing as we climbed." Dorje beamed. He loved to be in the limelight, but made sure Putti and Tenza were on hand before he agreed.

Ram started off with a Hindi *raga* to which he did a wild dance, with arms and legs flying at every angle. He had lived in Calcutta for eleven years and knew the music well. The tune was high, nasal, and repetitive, and we all encouraged him by clapping the rhythm and shouting at specified moments. Dorje was next with a Nepalese love song a la Sinatra. I played each selection back, much to the delight of the performers, which encouraged them to share an hour of songs you'd never find in any record store—certainly not with such enthusiastic audience participation.

Putti, who stood most of the time with her hands folded in front of her and her eyes lowered, became beet-red when asked to perform. She and Tenza finally agreed, and giggled their way through three high-pitched ballads. The last one was in two-part harmony, and so moving that nobody spoke for several seconds. Dorje cleared his throat self-consciously and haltingly translated the lyrics—a tale of two lovers who were lost in the mountains and died in each other's arms. After a long pause the girls rushed from the room followed by Ram and Dorje, who turned at the door and bowed deeply from the waist. I felt exhilarated. Mathias was visibly moved. What a jolly evening. This was the breakthrough I'd hoped for, and all because of one little tape recorder.

The next day, Friday the 13th, we awoke early. It had snowed in the night and the whole town was white. We scraped the frost from the windows and watched the solid silhouette of the mountains soften to reveal individual alabaster peaks unfolding as the sky lightened. The whitewashed stone houses with their decorative windows rested silently on the terraced slopes of the horseshoe-shaped valley. Each one of us stood for a long time, wrapped in our own thoughts as we looked at the mountains surrounding the sleeping town.

Kumar interrupted us. It had been a very cold night so we dived at the hot water he brought to our room—especially Mathias, who was eager to shave off two days of heavy growth.

Before breakfast I slid around the corner of the lodge and through the campground, where another trek was packing up. I headed for the outhouse, which was perched on a platform three rickety stairs above the ground. Directly in front of me was the lady with altitude sickness. She was mumbling incoherently while two men tried to hold her upright. The sight of her head lolling from side to side as she made uncoordinated attempts to walk was sobering. To add to this I nearly vomited when I stepped into the outhouse. Too many campers. Too much curried rice. Too few cedar chips. I fled.

After last night's freeze, Mathias and I decided to rent two more sleeping bags from the man who ran a small supply store on the ground floor of the lodge. Ram offered to get them for us—"No trouble, Missus"—for twenty rupees a day. But we could get them ourselves for ten (50 cents). Drunk or sober, Ram was an operator. But I was beginning to soften. He had so little. Why not let him make a few rupees on us. Mathias agreed.

Today was our first acclimatization day, so we explored Namche, often referred to as the *Sherpa* capital. It had once been a trading post on the route to Tibet via the Nangpa Pass, but in 1958, when the Dalai Lama fled Tibet, the border was closed and the lucrative trade came to an abrupt end. The village, famous as the staging point for Everest expeditions, was now enjoying a dubious comeback: renewed prosperity—and pollution—caused by the influx of trekkers.

We poked around the shops, slipping and sliding on the steep snow-covered streets where the low buildings were nestled. We sampled yak cheese and a variety of dried fruits, and bought extra mittens, hats, and scarves made of hand-spun yak wool in natural-colored tans, browns, and creamy whites. One dollar would buy a pair of handmade patterned mittens. We also found some thin cotton gloves to wear inside the heavy wool mittens so we could handle our cameras with ease. The bargaining was reminiscent of Egypt—all part of the game—and the crafts were superb. But so was our sales resistance. We had no way to carry out souvenirs.

Late in the morning we reached the Visitor's Center high above town. Paintings, photographs, books, and information about the culture and religion of the *Sherpa* people were artistically displayed within its walls, as well as an extensive pictorial history of climbing expeditions in the Himalayas.

In the distance, moving in and out of the clouds, we caught our first glimpse of Everest (29,028 ft.) flanked by the jagged face of Lhotse and the fluted edge of the Nuptse ridge. I was wearing special glasses to protect my eyes from the high altitude ultraviolet rays, but even so I found myself squinting against the powerful light as I looked at this dramatic scene.

Everest, Lhotse, and Nuptse.

Much closer on our right loomed the formidable Ama Dablam (22,494 ft.) whose double peak looked like a gigantic white camel and whose changing presence was to dazzle us for the next two weeks. It was the most beautiful mountain of all. Its name means "mother's charm box," for the ornament the *Sherpa* women wear around their necks, but the lower peak (the "charm box") is really a snowy bulge formed by a hanging glacier just below the summit.

"Hey, that's the mountain on the one rupee note," exclaimed Mathias. He reached for his wallet. "Sure enough, here it is, testimony to Nepal's good taste in mountains." He pulled out the small rectangular bill with the engraving of Ama Dablam on its face and two spotted fawns leaping over a chasm in the foreground. "How about that? The perfect gift. And the price is right!"

By afternoon the snow had melted and the village streets were a river of water, used to advantage by the many old wooden mills we saw as we explored the lower valley. We bumped into a young Irish couple, Peggy and Sean Fitzpatrick, who would figure prominently in the final days of our journey. They were on their honeymoon and had packed in alone from Jiri. Together we continued our exploration, stopping to read the inscriptions on the *mani* stones at the base of a large *stupa*. Sean translated several of the texts, reading from a book about *chortens*, *mani*, and *stupas*, important physical symbols of Mahayana Buddhism, the religion of the majority of *Sherpas*. *Om Mani Padme Hum*, the Buddhist *mantra* of compassion, appeared over and over again.

This *stupa* had a small pagoda-like house, with a peaked roof and a gilded spire, and sat on top of several layers of rock and grass. Each layer, or platform, was graduated, reminding me of an outsized wedding cake. Tattered prayer flags flapped from heavy string connected to skinny poles a few feet from each corner. A pair of almond-shaped eyes under ferocious black eyebrows peered at us from all four walls—eyes that had been painted white and outlined in red, with a round blue iris in the middle. A cloth fringe attached to the base of the roof almost obliterated the eyebrows.

Toward evening the Fitzpatricks returned to their lodge, but we stayed to watch the sunset. I ran ahead, jumping over rivulets and stopping to examine the remains of burial *chartens* piled in clusters on the hillside.

"You're not a cat, but you're certainly curious like one," said Mathias when I stuck my head into one of the old shacks housing a whirling millwheel.

"Don't be a stuffy European," I said, laughing. "I just want to see how these things work."

I stepped inside. The boards were slippery and old and my next words were shouted: "Jesus, I'm falling!" Buddha would have been more appropriate, but I had no time to think. I grabbed the side of the wooden crib and could feel the whir of the wheel close to my face. One leg went straight through the rotten boards and into the cold water, while the other crashed onto the floor and held me up by the knee. Water sprayed over me. I hate to think what would have happened had my body lurched forward into the wheel.

Mathias came flying across the rocks. "Hang on. Don't move."

The look on his face scared me. It had happened so fast that I didn't have time for fear or pain. But there I was, suspended, immobile, and feeling very foolish.

He placed his hands under my arms and slowly helped me out, one leg braced on the crib and the other behind a large flat rock. I was more embarrassed than hurt. And I was very cold.

Once he'd established that I was all right, Mathias became angry. "You're a silly woman," he said. "How *dare* you scare me like that?" His eyes were wet and they pierced me with a look I would not soon forget. It was the Indian doctor all over again. I turned away to hide my feelings at being spoken to so harshly. I knew he cared or he wouldn't have reacted so strongly. He was right, of course, but that didn't help. I said nothing, and we walked back in silence.

The narrow road in front of our lodge was a muddy stream by the time I took my water bottle and toothbrush downstairs and started my evening ablutions. Can you imagine brushing your teeth in the street in front of your house? But I was not alone.

How beautiful everything had looked that morning, covered with snow, but now you could see the gutters full of cans and garbage, old rags and paper, bottles and plastic. It was Kathmandu in the mountains. I was ready to move on.

We never took off all our clothes at night—it was too cold—so there was no problem of modesty. The bunkhouse was just one big locker room without the showers and lockers. I lived in my polypropylene undergarments and merely added extra clothing at bedtime when necessary. I suppose it was unhygienic, but it sure beat freezing.

Tonight I felt at peace, and more than a little grateful. It had turned out to be a lucky Friday the 13th. Though a little sore, the "curious cat" was still functioning. Mathias had put up a makeshift clothesline in the corner of the room for my wet jeans and socks, and filled my boots with dry rags. What better way to apologize for his gruff words at the old mill?

As I was slipping my mummy case into the heavy down bag and putting on my hat, gloves, and scarf, Mathias very cautiously asked if he could move his bed closer to mine, so we could talk quietly without disturbing the others.

"Well, it can't be very dangerous," I said, considering the layers of clothing between me and the world. "As Ram would say, 'Is no problem.'" I tried to sound flip, but inside I was churning.

40

THE LURE OF THE MOUNTAINS

Getting out of Namche Bazar was like swimming upstream in the Colorado River. It was market day and the slippery streets were crowded with merchants from the surrounding area. Vendors hawked their wares, bombarding us with a chorus of discordant chants. Ram, eager to get an early start, had sent us on with Dorje and the porters while he stayed to buy fresh vegetables and yak meat. He had told Mathias that we would go directly to Thyangboche, but had told Dorje he would meet us in the small village of Khumjung below the precipices of Khumbila, the sacred mountain of the *Sherpas*. This was near Khunde, where Sir Edmund Hillary had established a hospital. Mathias consulted his maps and it was clear that we were *not* going directly to Thyangboche, but taking the long way around. Considering the strenuousness of the climb, we did not relish a lengthy detour, especially uphill.

"Dorje, go back and get Ram," ordered Mathias, after all attempts at friendly persuasion had failed. "Meg and I will wait right here until you return." It was obvious that Dorje was no guide, but an office boy who wanted a vacation in the mountains. He huffed and puffed up the trails worse than we did, and refused to carry the smallest pack. I felt sorry for Ram, because the extra weight was picked up by him.

I finally figured out what Dorje is doing on this trek," said Mathias, grinning mischievously. "He's combing his hair and letting the girls wait on him." For some reason this struck us both as very funny, and we leaned against the *mani* wall at the fork in the trail and roared.

The sun was extremely bright and penetrating. Despite the protective glasses I still had to squint. And my face was getting burned. I carried an old tube of sunscreen, which I hesitated to use since it made me look as if I'd been dead a year.

But I finally broke down and applied a thin coating. I'd waited far too long. This exercise in vanity was to cost me dearly.

Ram came steaming toward us, his arms waving, Dorje close behind. "Mister, the porters go to Khumjung for lunch," he shouted. He did a double take when he saw me. Probably figured I had some rare skin disease.

"Then run after them and stop them," said Mathias. "You promised we'd go directly to Thyangboche, and Khumjung is definitely out of the way."

The two men glowered at each other. Ram frantically consulted with Dorje in Nepali, then hurried on up the trail.

"Whose trek is this, anyway?" grumbled Mathias as we started off, again. "This is not a reliable person. This Ram is a madman."

At the moment they seemed an even match, but I decided to let things cool down before saying anything.

I spoke at last. "Mathias, I hope you two don't come to blows. Please talk things over and reach some understanding because it isn't any fun for me like this—all the tension, all the fighting."

"You're right, Meg. Forgive me. I have a temper, and sometimes it gets the better of me. Perhaps you could help me control it. I'd appreciate that."

"I'm not a lion tamer and I'm through looking after other people. I have enough trouble keeping my own life on an even keel. I'm not responsible for anybody else anymore—and I'm glad of it." My tone surprised me. Why had his remark upset me so?

"I guess I really struck a nerve, didn't I?" Mathias said, looking very serious. "I didn't mean for you to be my conscience, but I guess I like the idea that someone as sensible as you might take an interest in me." He raised his heavy eyebrows, tilted his head, and smiled apologetically.

I suddenly regretted my outburst. "I've been called a lot of things," I replied, "but 'sensible' is not one of them, and I'm not sure I want it to be. Hey, let's continue this tonight. It does bring up a lot of old stuff, but I can't talk and climb at the same time. In fact, it's all I can do to breathe."

We finally left the brawling *Dudh Kosi* behind us—that milky glacial stream which foams from one rocky gorge to another, and which we'd been crossing and re-crossing since our first day—and began climbing on slowly ascending footpaths, which hugged the mountain on one side and dropped into a deep ravine on the other. I dared not look down. This is referred to as "exposure," and provides the sort of danger that tantalizes many climbers. I'm not one of them. My palms were sweating and my heart was doing cartwheels. One misstep and they'd still be looking for me.

As if this weren't bad enough, we frequently had to negotiate the trail when a caravan of yaks was coming toward us from the opposite direction. Lean wiry herders grunted, whistled, and shouted sing-songy commands, prodding the poor creatures with sticks as they labored over the narrow, rocky path. Tiny bells attached to the ears and around the necks of the animals announced their presence on the trail long before they appeared. I taped the sweet music. It became as familiar to me as the temple gongs.

Just before noon we experienced a yak traffic jam and had to wait in the bushes while the shaggy animals lumbered past us with their top-heavy loads. Everything from machinery and tools to planks of wood were strapped to their backs. A steady stream of *Sherpas*, mostly women carrying unwieldy bundles of wheat and brush, followed behind the yaks. For the first time I saw *Sherpani* wearing jewelry in their noses. They refused to allow pictures, however, and turned their backs to the camera. This was an invasion of privacy they would not allow, and we respected it.

It was becoming increasingly difficult to breathe, so we took the trails at yak speed. The day was clear and a new configuration of mountains appeared around every turn. Ama Dablam followed us on the right and was joined by the fluted ice walls of Thamaserku and Kangtega (22,370 ft). These two giants kept unfolding like a stegosaurus carved in ice, rising and falling.

We stopped for lunch at a small village in a wooded area—superb fried onions in noodles, potatoes, and lemon tea. It was freezing, so we sat close to the fire watching Putti prepare the meal. She worked in the cold, without a sweater or gloves. The skin on her hands was tough and she picked up the hot kettles without protection. As I watched I vowed to buy her gloves and a sweater at the next opportunity. The food was served so lovingly that it brought tears to our eyes. We noticed this sudden, inexplicable reaction in each other, but said nothing. We just watched the serene face, delicate as porcelain—one moment pensive, the next moment creased with laughter.

"Putti makes me think of my own daughter," Mathias said. "But what's in store for her? Will she have any chance at all?"

"I wonder about that, too, and it makes me sad. But please, tell me about your daughter."

"She's married and had her first baby a month ago. A handsome boy. But it's heartbreaking to see how much she misses her mother. They were very close. My wife was a child psychologist and my daughter is a specialist in early childhood education. How they were looking forward to this baby! They could have shared so much." He was silent for several moments before going on.

"My son's in college. I'm not as close to him. He seems angry about his mother's death and doesn't want to talk about it. He studies very hard and keeps to himself. I've left him alone until he's ready to open up to me—if ever."

"Still, they must be a comfort to you at this time," I said, knowing that there was little I could say to alleviate his pain.

"Yes, of course," he agreed, "but I can't live through them. They have their own lives. Children and grandchildren, wonderful as they are, are no substitute for a loving relationship."

"Try not to analyze too much, Mathias," I said, rather tenuously. "Right now all you can do is live each day as it comes."

He gave me a weak smile. "And I can drink some more of this lemon tea and explode."

"We'll both explode," I said.

When our meal was over the *Sherpas* began theirs. Now I realized why they'd giggled when we ate our boiled potatoes. We kept the skins on so they wouldn't think us finicky or snobbish. But to them this was ill-mannered and unsanitary. Nobody in the mountains ate the skins. They also ended each meal by lifting the bowl to their mouths and meticulously licking from center to rim, until it glistened. So much for Emily Post and Letitia Baldrige.

By mid-afternoon I was dragging. My hips ached. Blisters had formed on my feet and I stopped to apply quantities of soothing moleskin. How on earth did these little *Sherpanis* with their thin canvas shoes swing along with such a heavy burden and not collapse?

I put my body on automatic pilot and let my mind wander. Inevitably, when I returned home, I'd be asked why I put up with such discomfort. Did I like to suffer? Was I masochistic? Why had I picked this God-forsaken wilderness? And why did I want to climb in the first place, especially at my age?

It would never be enough to say that I simply liked it, as someone might say if you asked her why she liked tennis or golf, dancing or swimming. Being in the woods or in the mountains has been the closest I've come to real spiritual awareness. Here there is a stripping away of excess baggage. I have to face myself alone, look inside, and wrestle with questions that have perplexed me all my life—questions about purpose, about values—questions, perhaps, that have no answers for a limited, earth-bound mind, but lead, simply, to acceptance. And, ultimately, serenity.

But my love affair with nature started long before my ability to analyze and define. The tall pine trees protected me as a child. I looked up at them at night—a continuous path to the sky and whatever mysteries lay beyond—from my pine needle bed in the New Hampshire woods. I splashed and played all morning long in the clear lake, running from the beach into the water, arms flailing, diving for fresh water mussels, fishing for sunnies, hunting for crayfish. I played in the woods on fallen trees, in hidden glades, exploring the underbrush, its wild flowers, toadstools, and ferns. I felt free and self reliant. I was immersed in a kind of pantheism, embraced by my parents, who shared a love of the sun, the wind, the thunderstorms that swept across the lake, and the wooded trails of the Great Gulf, deep in the White Mountains. It was the natural backdrop for my father's belief, as a Protestant minister, that the joy of life was in the struggle. And the most meaningful truths could be found in a simple life lived as close to nature as possible. This was home to me. This was where I felt safe. This was where the answers lay.

I used to say that I climbed so my body would take my mind—my conscious essence—where it wanted to go. At such times I felt that I left my aching body behind while the real me soared ahead. Fanciful? Maybe, but the more I talk with people who push themselves to the limit of their physical endurance, the more I know that I'm not alone in feeling euphoria when the physical is transcended...when life is lived to the hilt, and beyond.

I wondered if the *Sherpas* felt this same closeness to nature, or were just doing a backbreaking job while we, the outsiders, romanticized it. Perhaps they felt it, but didn't think about it. Nature was just a part of them as they were a part of it—the mountains, the valleys, the changing seasons.

I walked on slowly, listening to the rhythmic crunch of my feet on the loose stones. I was acutely aware of each breath—the air being sucked in and released, sucked in and released. I became transparent—a part of all the sounds and smells; the tiny flowers, the towering hills; the quivering leaves, the wild junipers. I was everywhere, in everything. And everything was in me.

The ruts grew deeper as the trail turned sharply upward through the forest. The rays of the sun, weak in the late afternoon, left me suddenly cold. A new sound entered my consciousness—the low throbbing of a gong, which became one deep, continuous vibration by the time it reached me. Mathias pressed my arm. "Meg, the bells. Listen, it must be the monastery at Thyangboche."

The mountains had darkened against the sky and patches of new snow lay in the open clearing that greeted us as we slogged up the last few hundred feet. We had walked ten miles and reached 12,761 feet...and we felt it!

Exhausted, I stopped to catch my breath, only to have it taken away again when I caught sight of the monastery. Nestled into the side of a hill was this venerable treasure I had so often seen in photographs—the two-story building with its whitewashed walls, its oriental roof turned up at the corners, its carved wooden windows set back in cut-outs wider at the bottom than at the top, and its small spire perched on the peak of the bell tower. A crudely printed sign in red paint was tacked to a beam over the entrance: WELCOME TO TANGBOCHE MONASTRY.

The steady throbbing of the great gong in the belfry, mixed with the desultory clanging of the yak bells as the animals stood restlessly in the yard, were the only sounds breaking the stillness. Mathias and I moved to the middle of the clearing where the flags of a large *stupa* fluttered in the breeze. The fog was moving in, covering some of the highest peaks. I stood listening to the gongs—a mountain Evensong.

"Do you know, Mathias, that it's exactly four months today since I arrived in Cairo to begin my world trip?" I whooped, threw my head back, stretched my arms to the sky, twirled around a couple of times, and breathed deeply—taking in the gongs, the bells, and the cold, lung-searing air.

"I probably shouldn't mention it, because you're so happy, but this is also an anniversary for me. My wife died exactly four months ago today."

How helpless and foolish I felt. And deflated.

"If you had seen me then, you would not have thought I could live another four months," he said, talking very slowly as if to himself. "Now I feel that I can pick up the threads of my life and start over. Just before my wife died she told me that I, too, would want to die, but that after a period of time my eyes would be open again, and this was what she wanted for me. She knew me better than I knew myself. So, dear Meg, we can celebrate how wonderful it is to be alive and to be in this beautiful place." He put his arm around me and together we walked up the steps to the monastery.

The steps were wide and made of flat rocks piled haphazardly on top of each other. Round bundles of sticks and branches—the kind we'd seen being carried on the backs of the *Sherpani*—were stacked on either side. Wood used to fuel the small stoves of the living quarters reached twice as high as the tightly built stone wall, which wrapped part-way around the compound.

We climbed to the main building, which was considered the spiritual center of the *Sherpa* people and the home of the reincarnate lama. It had been built seventy years ago by an old hermit from Khumjung, Gulu Lama, with money and labor donated by all the villages of the Khumbu. It was now being refurbished. I stuck my head into a large hall and inhaled the smell of fresh wood shavings left by the workmen. I walked outside in the gathering dusk and ran my fingers over the cylindrical prayer wheels recessed waist-high in the wall and decorated with pale designs. I spun the wheels and listened to their hum.

As we started back down the path Ram came running toward us. "I look for you all over," he said. "No tent tonight. Your room private. Very nice. Come."

He led us to a small stone guesthouse and up some wooden steps onto the front porch. Our room was large, with windows across the front, a pot-bellied stove in one corner, and two iron beds under the eaves. A small wobbly table stood between the beds, and rough beams crisscrossed the ceiling. The toilet was outside under the porch.

I had just collapsed on one of the beds and Mathias was eyeing the few scraps of wood next to the stove, wondering if he dared start a fire, when three large Italian climbers strode through our room, followed by two *Sherpani* porters.

"We sleep on the sun porch," they explained. "Come, we're having a party."

Why not? We followed them out a glass door at the far end of the room and enjoyed a little mountain *antipasto*—wheat crackers and yak cheese—along with Italian wine. It was my first drink in weeks and left me glowing. Mathias was also thoroughly enjoying himself. He'd forgotten all about the fire and was concentrating on communicating in broken Italian. The result was hilarious, but I was no one to throw stones. My knowledge of the language consisted of *forte, pianissimo, largo, andante non troppo,* and any words I'd gleaned from reading a musical score. Not much help in a social situation.

The party ended with a clear message in English. "We won't bother you, only to go to toilet. *Salute!*" And with a wave of the wine bottle they closed the door.

"Some private room," I said, laughing. "Thank God there's a moon tonight. Maybe they can make it to the toilet without destroying the furniture."

Mathias started unpacking while I went outside and sat on the back steps in the bitter cold, listening to Putti and Tenza sing as they prepared dinner in the space directly under our room. It was a dark, windowless hovel with dirt floors and a low, wide ledge all the way around for sleeping, cooking, and storing supplies. They didn't have fancy sleeping bags. They just wrapped themselves in a blanket and curled up on the ledge.

"Come on out, Mathias," I called. "You have to hear this singing." We huddled close, shivering, as we listened to the high, clear voices, mixed with the sounds of banging pots and the insistent hissing of the kerosene stove. We felt very naughty eavesdropping, but the blending of the voices was almost ethereal, and much more spontaneous than the command performance I'd taped in Namche Bazar. Between songs there were bursts of giggling and bits of conversation with Ram, Dorje, and Kumar. Then someone would start to hum and be joined by the others in a new song.

We sneaked back to our room just before Kumar arrived with dinner.

After the meal we walked down to the clearing. Not a sound. Even the yaks were asleep. The mountains were almost completely covered with clouds, but we could still feel their solemn presence. An explosion of stars filled the sky each time the moon broke through. We stood in silence, holding hands and watching the changing heavens, then slowly started back up the stairs.

Halfway to the top an enormous figure stepped out of the shadows and blocked our way. I let out a cry. In the dim light stood a character right out of a Chinese horror movie—seven feet tall, long robe, fur collar, shaved head, Mongolian features, and mammoth teeth that looked as if they'd forgotten to stop growing. His smile was cavernous.

"Sorry to have frightened you," he said in perfect English, tilting his head quizzically. "Won't you come in and join me for tea?" He folded his arms across his chest and bowed.

Mathias and I looked at each other as we stepped into an unlit hall...surely a dungeon. "Do you think this is wise?" he whispered. Before I could answer, our host returned with a large candle and motioned us to follow him. He placed the candle in a wall holder and proceeded to light several others until we could see our way to a corner table with built-in benches. We sat down while he went to get a thermos of hot water for tea.

The room was cozy—hand-carved furniture, plates hung in wooden racks, simple paintings, and one small, clouded window.

"You must be an artist, by the looks of your home," said Mathias.

"Yes, I am an artist, but I'm first a Buddhist monk. My home is in Tibet, my work is in Nepal." He poured steaming water over the tea, and placed some biscuits on a metal plate.

Questions tumbled out. All the things we always wanted to know about Buddhism but never dared ask. Can monks marry? Is it true that many monks are offended if a woman looks at them? What has happened to Buddhism in Tibet now that the Chinese have come? Has it changed radically, or just gone underground?

The monk listened, then smiled, revealing those endless teeth. "I cannot answer for all Buddhists," he said. "We are different in every country. We are not as strict here as, for example, India and Thailand. Come, would you like to see my private chapel?" We got the message. No more questions.

He led us through a nearby door. The chapel was a miniature of others I'd seen in India. Small candles, small dishes of water and food, statues and pictures of the seated Buddha, and lots of bright-colored decorations and carvings filled the small room. There were no windows and very little air. The smell of incense was strong.

After a second cup of tea we realized why we'd been invited. "Let me show you my art work," said the monk. "It's Tibetan—very special. You won't find it anywhere but in these mountains."

He left the room and returned with an armload of copper and brass bowls, rice paper prints, and carved rectangular pastry molds to be used with rice dough to make imprints of religious symbols and native scenes. The only thing I wanted was a prayer wheel, but that seemed to be the only thing he didn't have.

Mathias was enthralled with the wooden molds, but not so enthralled with the price. After a long bargaining session it had gotten down to $10, but he wondered if we had enough money between us to spend so much on one item. This wouldn't be the last time we regretted heeding Pushkar's advice to carry a small amount of cash.

"We're coming back in two weeks," said Mathias. "Perhaps we'll buy it then." We not only ran out of money before the two weeks were up, but we found the identical molds for half the price in a small village north of Lukla.

It was late when we returned to our room, and the temperature was below zero. One of the Italians was making his way back to the porch and raised an arm in greeting. Then all was quiet.

I made a speedy visit to the outhouse, donned an extra layer of clothing, and slid the lower part of my body into my double sleeping bag. Still wearing my down jacket, I pulled out my journal and started writing. Even with woolen gloves my fingers were like ice, and writing was slow and uneven.

Mathias was sorting, rearranging, and taking another sweater out of its plastic sheath. For a large man he moved quickly. I loved watching him, his bubbling vitality and energy. He was meticulous in his packing and unpacking. It amused me to see him sort his vitamins and film and clothing. Were all scientists like this? He caught my eye and winked. "You think I'm fussy? Are you laughing at me?" he asked. I shook my head, but I didn't answer. Oh, no, I don't think you're fussy. I think you're sexy, but you'll never get me to say it.

I closed my journal. It was much too cold to write.

Mathias had taken off his jeans and was putting on another pair of long underwear. His legs were muscular and his body lean. He'd given up slicking his hair down, and random curls brushed his forehead.

"You look like Sir Lawrence Olivier playing Hamlet," I said.

"You have deeply insulted me," he retorted, lowering his head and dramatically pressing one arm to his chest. He wheeled around, attempted a pirouette, and, as if on cue, fell over the pile of wood next to the stove. He landed on one knee, arms outstretched.

"Thank you, Sir Lawrence," I said. "That was magnificent!"

"That was an Austrian bow, my dear Ophelia. *Verflügte* logs!" he muttered as he kicked the wood aside. "I should have made a fire with them."

Mathias recovered his dignity, walked across the room, removed the small table from between the beds, and pushed his bed close to mine. It was narrow and old, and two limp mattresses hung precariously over the sides of the metal springs.

"It's very cold tonight and, besides, we don't want to wake the Italians with our talk," he said. With a grand gesture he flung himself onto the mattress, misjudging the width of the bed and rolling off, backside first, onto the hard wood floor.

Humiliated, he picked himself up, and in his haste, rammed his head into one of the overhanging beams. He crumpled to the floor and sat there, rubbing the back of his head.

"Are you O.K., Mathias?" I asked, scrambling out of bed. "For heaven's sake, are you trying to kill yourself and leave me all alone with Ram and Dorje?"

"I seem to be very clumsy tonight," he said. "I'm going to the outhouse now. I hope I don't meet with another disaster. If so, call out the Italians." He smiled halfheartedly and left the room, still rubbing his head. It was only then that I allowed myself to laugh. He had looked so funny, so bewildered sitting on the floor. But I found myself very relieved that he wasn't hurt.

It suddenly dawned on me what was happening. I stayed awake, waiting for him to return. This time he lowered himself very carefully onto the bed, slipped into his bag, and lay there for a long time without speaking.

"Are you all right, Mathias? Truly?" I asked tentatively.

"Yes, I'm fine," he answered. "But I know I'm behaving like a silly fool, and I also know why. It's because I'm becoming very fond of you, Meg. And this scares me. It's been a long time since I've had these feelings, so please be patient with me." He reached over and laid his hand on my arm.

I took his hand and pressed it to my cheek. "It's been a long time for me, too," I said.

41

THE TRAIL TO PHERICHE

The rhythmic striking of the temple gong woke me early in the morning. Eager to explore the monastery grounds before breakfast, Mathias and I raced outside and into a world covered with fresh snow. The clouds had disappeared, allowing the sun to play on the distant trio: Everest, Nuptse, and Lhotse. Ama Dablam hovered close to Thamaserku, Kantega Kwandge, and Khumbila, each one changing its countenance with the movement of the light. These giants blended with lesser peaks—too many for us to count—forming the jagged edges of a great crystal bowl in which we were willing captives.

I raced to the prayer wheels and gave them the first spin of the day, spraying fine snow into the air. Slender icicles had formed on the eaves and were beginning to melt, now and then clinking to the ground like glass chimes. I leapt through the drifts in the courtyard and up to the edge of the ravine beside the monastery.

"Come over here, Meg," shouted Mathias. "I'll show you the world's most dangerous outhouse."

I looked to the right about a hundred yards. A slab of rock jutted out from the cliff. In a clump of gnarled trees, which were growing out of the fissures of the rock, was the entrance to a skinny wooden shack, which hung, in its entirety, over the ravine. Two flimsy planks were nailed to the bottom at an angle and jammed into the side of the cliff. I could hear them creak and feel the house "give" as I started to step inside. Peering over the edge, I saw a drop of several hundred feet.

"No way will I enter without a full compliment of rappelling equipment," I said. "I prefer the outhouse further down, with a scenic view of Everest and a yak guarding the door."

"I think you're called a chicken in your country," said Mathias, who insisted that I take his picture emerging from the precarious perch. His horsing around scared me. I loved his spontaneity and fearlessness, but I didn't want him to get hurt.

By the time we left Thyangboche the clearing beneath the monastery was free of the tents that had dotted its surface during the night—orange igloos, leaving round brown patches in the snow like a great Swiss cheese soon to be eaten by the morning sun.

The trail led into a forest of cedar and birch. Lichen clung to the rocks and trees, and light green moss hung in lacy patterns from the branches. The ice-hardened snow was dangerous. We never knew where our feet would come to rest once they had penetrated the glittering crust, so we plowed ahead with extreme caution.

We descended sharply into a valley and found ourselves in the middle of a thick river of melting snow and mud. To work our way down the trail and negotiate the slippery turns we had to grab each tree in ape-like fashion. No photos were possible, but I did manage to tape the sounds of our feet slurping and sliding through the mud.

I remember, warmly, how concerned Ram was for our safety. He would stand where the trail bent and grab us as we went by, to slow our descent.

"Today Ram is being a gentleman," said Mathias during one of our breaks. "I'm grateful to him. I'm not used to skiing on mud."

The mountains shone through the trees on all sides, their whiteness almost blinding whenever we left the woods and entered an alpine meadow. Scrub grass and open fields greeted us. The snow was gone, and in its place was rust-colored flora just waiting to burst into bloom. We had moved from winter to spring in one hour.

Mani walls were everywhere, and *chortens*—stark, upright slabs of stone in memory of the dead—peppered the sides of the hills.

"I can never enjoy coming down when I know I have to go back up," I told Mathias. "But this will probably be the last warm spot for quite some time, so I won't complain."

Nor did I have the breath to complain. We wound in an upward spiral along footpaths so narrow—inches away from rocky ravines—that it took every ounce of energy just to control my mounting panic. I knew my fears were irrational, just as they were when, as a child, I tried to climb a fire tower and became dizzy halfway up, or when, as an adult, I inched my way around the outside of the roof of Salisbury Cathedral, protected only by an ancient stone barrier reaching to my shins, and nothing but air between me and the tiny figures walking on the grass hundreds of feet below.

Before long the trail descended, again, and we were at the Sherpa Lodge in Pangboche (13,150 ft.), a bustling village situated on the north side of *Imja Khola*, and site of a well-known temple, or *gompa*. Before lunch we strolled through a grove of cedar trees. Little children played on the rocky paths and women went about their work, greeting us with a friendly *Namaste* as we passed. Tall feathery fir trees mixed with the sweet-smelling cedars to provide a woodland paradise that, for the moment, had escaped the woodchopper's ax.

While Kumar prepared food on the kerosene stove in an adjacent shed we warmed ourselves in front of a blazing fire tended by a handsome young mother. Her year-old baby crawled on the blanket-covered floor and gnawed on a peeled potato. The lodge was rimmed with shelves on which tins, dishes, and pots had been carefully arranged. Kitchen utensils hung from the beams and the walls were covered with loosely woven straw mats.

The baby crawled under our feet, gurgling and squashing the potato as he went. Seeing our interest in her child, the mother, unlike most of the *Sherpani* we'd come across, pointed to our cameras and pulled the baby onto her lap. Her smile was contagious and the pose worthy of Raphael. Just as I snapped the picture, however, the baby did what all babies do. But there was no diaper. I treasure this picture of the beatific mother, the gurgling infant, and the big wet spot right in the middle.

Pangboche is very proud of its Buddhist monastery that houses the supposedly authentic skull and skeletal hand of a *Yeti*—the hairy, manlike creature of Himalayan folklore known as the *Abominable Snowman*. After lunch we were escorted to the monastery and greeted by a wizened old lady who ceremoniously unlocked the heavy door leading to the inner temple. With a dramatic flourish she kneeled down and went through a number of religious procedures before removing the relics from their glass case.

The room was musty and filled with colored streamers and paintings of Buddha. This added to the mystery as we gazed at the old bones. The skull was a metallic gray, with miniscule holes in the top and red hair on the sides. It was oblong, like a football, and reminded me of a Prussian army helmet belonging to my great Uncle Oscar. The hand was huge and discolored, and the long fingers had enormous joints.

"Looks pretty phony to me," I whispered to Mathias, who was taking flash pictures from every angle. (This cost him another ten rupees over the twenty-rupee admission price.)

"I wonder where they got the red hair—if it *is* hair," I continued. I couldn't believe that he was taken in by this. He was acting like a little kid.

"Come on, Meg, have you no romance? No imagination? Why do you think I watch my feet when I climb? I'm looking for those big footprints in the snow."

"You're *making* those big footprints," I said. "But maybe you're right. If I survive this trip we'll come back and search for your illusive creature. It may take the rest of our life, but I can't think of a more beautiful place to die."

"Nor can I," he said, looking at me intently. There was that feeling churning around in me again. I turned away, embarrassed.

Now the climbing began in earnest. Up we went, then down into a valley only to climb back out again. I had to be very careful of my footing, because views of the mountains—through the trees or on either side of the river—were not only distracting, but bewitching. And I couldn't bear to miss a single scene. Now and then we'd catch a glimpse of Everest way in the distance peering over the top of the massive 25,000-foot mountain wall joining Lhotse and Nuptse.

Mathias went wild taking pictures of the streams and the frozen waterfalls, the strata and the gorges. We walked high above the turbulent waters on two-planked wooden bridges, which were suspended by ropes, and swung and rippled to our gait like indolent serpents.

Just before Pheriche we crossed an especially rickety footbridge behind a convoy of shaggy yaks loaded with wooden planks. I held onto the rope railings and found myself almost crouching so my legs, slightly apart, would respond to the movement of the boards and I could keep my balance. Mathias walked behind me, laughing at my anxiety and calling me a bowlegged cowgirl.

When I reached the other side I happened to notice the metal rings that were imbedded in the rock and attached to the bridge. Like the links in an old necklace, they had pulled apart, almost to the breaking point. One more inch and the bridge would plummet into the ravine.

"Mathias, get Ram! Look at this! We all could have been killed." I pointed to the rings.

"Dear God, you're right," he said, and ran ahead to get Ram.

Ram must have thought I'd fallen off the bridge, because he came tearing down the hill, hair flying, eyes wide.

"Missus, you are fine, *no*?" he asked.

"Ram, I am fine, *yes*, but look at these rings. Someone could be killed one day, so we must report this immediately. Understand?"

"Oh, Missus, is no problem. Very strong. Guaranteed."

I stood there in disbelief. "I will *not* go back over that bridge under any circumstance, and I think it's criminal that such a condition is allowed, and if you won't report it, *I* will...."

"Is not problem," he interrupted. "We go back a different way. And I report."

The clouds were rolling over the highest peaks when we reached the wide path leading into Pheriche (14,058 ft.). A somber headstone in memory of a climber who had perished from altitude sickness cast its shadow beside a benign stream. The terrain was flat and we could see in the distance the stone walls of the village and a few modest one-story dwellings sprinkled along the rocky lane that went through town.

Kumar and the girls had already begun the evening meal when we arrived. The main bunkhouse was filled to capacity, so we dropped our gear in a dreary back room. One large wooden platform, piled with mattresses, was against the wall, and a potbellied stove stood in one corner. We were the only occupants.

Right outside the bunkhouse door was what came to be known to us as "the black hole of Pheriche," a cave-like room with a rounded ceiling and rough stone walls blackened by years of wood smoke. The cracks were stuffed with dry yak dung for insulation and the floor was made of packed dirt, so trampled that it shone. There was one small soot-covered window next to a door made of planks that reached all the way to the roof. It looked as if someone had thrown large woven mats over the top of the shack, holding them down with rocks and heavy sacks, and causing the roof to dip and ripple like a Walt Disney creation. Thick stone ledges came out from the wall in front of a mammoth fireplace where the cook had put his supplies. What a contrast between this dreary space and the clean white mountains in the background.

A huge pot of water was boiling on the stove as we entered the room. Everyone was hovering around it, except Dorje, who was reclining dramatically on one of the ledges. He had forgone his nightly wash. It was even too cold for *him*. That morning I had loaned my thin windbreaker to Kumar, who had grinned and bowed as if I'd presented him with the Hope diamond. It was already covered with grease and dirt, but at least he wasn't shivering anymore.

Ram was surprised when we appeared, and a little uncomfortable. We were supposed to eat in our room, not invade the inner sanctum. "Let's all eat together tonight," I announced. "We made it through the snow and mud, and that's cause for celebration."

"I think you're too bold for them, Meg," whispered Mathias, "but I like it. Why not be one family? Besides, it's too cramped in that back room."

The girls giggled as Ram motioned for me to sit on the ledge. He handed me a worn blanket. Gratefully, I wrapped it around my shoulders.

Mathias looked at me paternally. "My poor little Indian squaw. Do you think you will survive this weather, or this food?"

"The food is great—it's warm," I said. Unconsciously, we moved closer together until we were sharing the blanket. Our eyes smarted from the smoke. Putti and Tenza were humming as they worked, and soon the activity around us blended into a slowly moving haze. I sat as if in a dream, wrapped, now, in the even warmer blanket of camaraderie.

As we left the "cave" I almost stumbled over a sleeping yak in the courtyard. There was no moon, so we rummaged for our flashlights, then slowly made our way to the outhouse, being careful to avoid the piles of dung—a formidable obstacle along the way. The small shack was located on a mound in the field out back, its contents so frozen that there was no odor.

"At least the cold is good for something," said Mathias. "But don't get your hopes up. Tomorrow it may thaw."

We were both so keyed up that sleep was impossible. "I think the altitude is getting to me," I said. "Have you noticed that my breathing is shallow? And I'm still frozen under all this down. And, well, I just can't absorb all these new sensations so quickly."

"I wouldn't blame everything on the altitude," he said. "Your breathing sounds fine to me. As for being frozen, it's probably twenty below right now. And the new sensations....Which ones are you talking about?"

Before I could answer Mathias reached over and touched my cheek. Slowly he removed my wool cap and ran his hand through my hair, behind my neck, and down my shoulder. Gently, very gently, he stroked me, slipping his other hand under the covers. Oh, my God, this man is crazy! My heart was thumping wildly as I started to move with his touch. How could anyone make love in this weather—through all this clothing? His arms surrounded me, and there were no more thoughts. And no more cold. I was caught in the path of a tornado, unable to resist, unable to stop.

42

A DAY OF REST

When I awoke Mathias was propped up on one elbow looking at me. Without a word he leaned down and took me in his arms. The tumult and ecstasy of the night before returned. We were kissing when Kumar barged in, teakettle in one hand, cups and biscuits in the other. He uttered a strangled gasp and ran back out.

"I'm afraid we've traumatized Kumar," said Mathias. "But he'll get over it. And I'm sure if he knew how happy I am at this moment he would be glad."

Small children, scantily dressed, were playing in the dirt courtyard when we emerged from the bunkhouse. They had no toys. Instead, they'd locked their legs together to form a train, scooting along the ground on their bottoms. As they bent their knees, alternately, to help wiggle their bodies forward, they made chugging and whistling noises. When I returned from the outhouse they had changed "conductors" and were having a spat about whose turn it was—not unlike children everywhere, except that their little hands and faces were red with the cold.

"Today is rest day," announced Ram, giving us a conspiratorial grin. "We go to Chhukung."

Some rest! The climb to 15,600 ft. was strenuous, through brown meadows, over rushing streams, and along rocky ridges that looked down on small villages. In one village, Dingboche, we stopped for tea at a friend of Ram's, and had our first inside view of a *Sherpa* home. Ram said it was grand for these parts—two stories with a gabled roof made of overlapping slabs of pine, held down by the usual logs and rocks. The ground floor room was a vast windowless cavern set on a foundation of pounded earth. This was where the farm implements, firewood, and fodder were stored. Animals shuffled in and out at will. They were allowed to sleep inside—to contribute their body heat. We walked upstairs to where the family lived. In one corner of the largest room was an open hearth around which several family members sat. The walls were made of rock cemented together with mud, and the wooden floor was covered with an assortment of mats and furs. There was a simple kitchen on one side of the main living area and a large bedroom on the other. We huddled, gratefully, around the crackling fire.

After tea and biscuits we were offered a small glass of *chang*, a light, bubbly rice wine. We took a few sips, and although the alcoholic content was low, it went straight to our heads. Mathias blamed the altitude, but we both knew that there was an unmistakable glow from last night that enhanced the good feeling—an electricity we felt as we sat together, shoulders touching.

Ram, however, did not limit himself to a few sips. Mathias pulled at my arm. "Let's get him out of here," he said in hushed tones, "before we have to carry him."

We bowed our goodbyes and hurried down the stairs and out through the basement room. The early afternoon sun, reflected off the snow, was intense. I was slathered with sunscreen, but it was useless against the powerful ultaviolet rays. My lips swelled and my cheeks throbbed.

Tension began to mount once more between Mathias and Ram, who kept racing ahead while we slogged our way over the icy trails. We stopped, frequently, to photograph the mountains, gigantic striated patterns etched on their faces by the ice and snow.

"Let him go, Mathias," I said. "He must be half-frozen, and we *are* taking a lot of time for pictures. He'll wait for us at the next ice cave." I walked ahead. Let Mathias freeze his fingers taking movies. I was content to wander alone in one of the high silent places of the world.

The ridge soon widened into a valley covered with scrub grass and boulders. Yaks grazed through a thin layer of snow. Ram warned us not to get too close to the herds, because some were ferocious, while others were the docile *zums*—a cross between the hairy yak and the Indian cow—bred to be a good milk-producer and a tough high-altitude animal. I couldn't tell the difference. They were all gentle, soulful creatures to me. But I kept my distance.

The sun disappeared by mid-afternoon, and with the clouds came the wind. It sliced through our down jackets and dusted our faces with spirals of fine snow. I caught the flakes on my tongue. Let them cool my cheeks. Took great gulps of the clean, moist air. We finally ducked under an overhanging ledge and ate cold *chapatties* and jam—Kumar's idea of a sandwich. We sipped lemon tea as we peered out at the darkening sky. I leaned against Mathias, deriving pleasure from his warmth.

Yaks along the way.

By the time we reached Chhukung we could barely see the lodge directly in front of us, and the mountains were totally obliterated. I liked the feeling. The isolation. The quiet of the fog closing in. The contrasting heat of the cabin.

Ram was in a bad mood. "I tell you 'hurry.' Now Everest gone."

"It's O.K., Ram," I said. "This *also* is part of the mountains. It's beautiful. I like it."

We stayed close together on the way back, listening to each other's footsteps through the heavy mist. I felt wrapped in the atmosphere, protected by the unseen mountains, and insulated from Ram's negative attitude. Nothing could spoil this day.

That night we slept in one of the igloo tents—a challenge at this altitude, but our only chance to be alone, since the back room had two additional occupants.

Mathias, in his systematic way, tried to make a double sleeping arrangement out of our disparate bags. But it didn't work, and all night long the freezing wind shook the tent. No amount of cuddling could warm me or stop my teeth from chattering like a mechanical wind-up doll. How I yearned for the pot-bellied stove, despite its stinky, burning yak chips.

Cold night tenting in Pheriche.

Waking early I poked my head out of the tent. The mountains, viewed from ground level in the first glow of morning, seemed much closer and more over-powering than the night before, when their dark blues and purples blended into the evening sky. No clouds remained, only air so fresh it cut at my lungs. In my haste I stepped from the tent into a mound of steaming yak shit, and slid all the way to the nearest pile of snow. In front of me was a *Sherpa* girl squatting in the path, her skirt fanned out as she relieved herself. Oh, for such a skirt!

When I returned from the outhouse Mathias was sipping tea, which the cook had brought. "You should have seen Kumar's face," he said, while I gingerly removed my soiled boot and looked around for some Kleenex. "He could hardly get out *Nameste* for all the giggling. I guess we've completely shocked the crew."

"I dare say we've completely shocked each other, too," I added. I reached around and put my hand on his neck. How much I liked his raw strength, the thick, wild hair, the muscular body.

In the recesses of my mind I heard Ram announce breakfast. We crawled out of the tent. The day had become brilliant.

"I see spots on your skin, Mister," Ram said as he watched us eat. "You feel O.K., no?"

Mathias rubbed his cheeks. They *were* slightly swollen. "Well, to tell the truth, I do have a slight headache, but it's really nothing," he answered.

"Is not nothing, is from high altitude, and is dangerous."

Right after breakfast we walked down the main street—a narrow, rocky path—to a small building housing the well-known Pheriche hospital. Supported by the *Nepal Rescue Association*, it was run by two Australian doctors, a husband and wife team, whose duties were to pull teeth and study altitude sickness—the latter still very much a medical mystery.

The doctors examined Mathias and advised him to go no farther than Thugla, a one-thousand-foot climb, returning to Pheriche for another night. Ram stood by with a self-satisfied grin on his face, as if glad to see Mathias slowed down. I learned more about altitude sickness than I wanted to know, but remember only that the doctor warned against taking any kind of diuretic for edema, and told us to rest if we became nauseated. All these caveats left Mathias greatly subdued.

"Let's get going," I said. "It's a great day for pictures."

Ram objected. "Be careful, Missus. Must rest today. Climb tomorrow. Old Father [his favorite name for Mathias] much sick."

What was Ram up to? Perhaps he just wanted a day off.

Mathias and I returned to the bunkhouse. We knew we needed plenty of sleep while adjusting to the thin air. But just as we were settling in the door opened and Ram threw my windbreaker on the bunk. "Cook thanks you, Missus," he said.

"That's O.K., Ram. He can keep it until we return," I said.

"He and Putti and Tenza gone down. I pay them. They gone."

Mathias looked shattered. "Where did they go?" he asked.

"No more need them, Old Father. You sick and can't climb. We save money. I cook. Dorje cook."

Mathias flew off the bunk and out the door, hoping to stop them. But no one was in sight. He came back, shaking his head incredulously. "What have you done, Ram? These were our friends. You had no right to dismiss them without our permission."

"No money. Only for one day more."

"What are you talking about?" said Mathias, moving toward Ram. "We paid for three weeks, and promised to pay for an extra few days if we needed them for acclimatization."

I put my hand on his arm to restrain him.

"Fresh vegetables and yak meat much money," said Ram. "And extra guide. Already 8,000 rupees gone. Only 500 left. Must pay for bunkhouse. You and Missus no use tents." He drew back. His eyes were wild. He was clearly afraid of Mathias, who towered over him.

"Rice wine is expensive, too!" Mathias turned to me. "He's a liar! You've already paid for your guide, and I can't believe Pushkar sent us out with only 8,500 rupees. Ram is a madman...."

"Enough, Mathias. Let's all simmer down. I'm as upset as you are, but what good is shouting?" I spoke to Ram. "We'll talk at dinner, but don't forget, we are *not* going down. *We are going to Everest Base Camp.*" Ram departed for the kitchen...rather unsteadily.

Mathias was crestfallen. He sat on the bed resting his elbows on his knees. How sweet and boyish he looked.

"I can't believe Putti would leave without even saying goodbye," he said. "I know she liked us. She gave us special things, and I thought we meant more than just a paying job. And remember how she loved those tapes you made? They all did. I feel sad, Meg. And disillusioned. I think my skin is not tough enough."

"It's no crime to have feelings." I went over and put my arms around him. "I'm pretty furious myself, but in my bones I feel real adventure ahead. I don't know what's going to happen, Mathias, but it's going to happen soon, and I'm sure glad we're in it together. If you don't have a heart attack everything will be fine." We kissed, and in that moment all our problems vanished.

In the afternoon we went to a lecture at the hospital and learned more gruesome facts about illness in the Himalayas. It did nothing for my spirits, so I left early and poked around the hills, taking pictures until the sun set, and enjoying camaraderie with climbers who stayed at other lodges in the village. Mathias was so upset with Ram that he forgot all about his headache and spent the evening talking German with some Austrian hikers. Ram stayed out of our way, except to serve dinner. At nine o'clock the lanterns were turned off and the candles blown out. All was quiet.

During the night I kept waking up, trying to get a deep breath. I didn't have a headache, so I chalked it up to the excitement of the past few days and the newness of my feelings for Mathias. But by early morning I was definitely having problems. My breathing was shallow, and when I tried to inflate my lungs fully, I couldn't. My heart was racing and I felt dizzy.

I sneaked out of bed and walked down the path through the sleeping village. The simple stone houses, and their isolating rock walls, were far apart. There was no sound, except the crunch of my boots. The mountains that had been my friends yesterday looked ominous, their snowy peaks cutting into the orange sky. I walked briskly from one end of town to the other, talking to myself.

"I won't do it. My fingers are tingling. I can hardly breathe. I feel as if I'm drowning. I may die. Mathias, I can't do it. I'm sorry." I repeated this over and over like a *mantra*. Disappointment overwhelmed me. Then, suddenly, I felt better. The panic was gone, and I breathed normally.

Mathias was sitting up in his bunk when I returned. "I'm worried," he said. "My neck and head ache—this time, badly."

"Move around and it'll get better," I said, walking over and putting my hand on his forehead. "Didn't you tell me that altitude always affects you more at night when respiration is at its lowest? I felt terrible an hour ago, and was going to tell you that I couldn't possibly go on. But I walked around and now I'm O.K...I think. Had a devil of a time breathing in the middle of the night, though. I'd rather go back with Dorje than have that happen again."

Mathias reached out and pulled me to him. "You should have wakened me. I might have been able to help. Tell you what," he said, holding both my hands. "We'll wait one more day, and if either of us isn't one hundred percent, I promise you we'll go back."

"You don't have to go with me. That's why we have Dorje."

Mathias laughed. "Meg, while you were gone Ram asked me if I had any pills for altitude sickness. Why? Because Dorje is throwing up and has a splitting headache. Some guide! No. If you go, I go. You mean more to me than Everest Base Camp—or didn't you know?"

"Let's go walk you around," I said, flushing. "I predict that neither of us will be returning to Kathmandu for at least two more weeks."

After breakfast Mathias insisted on heading for Thugla (15,246 ft.) despite Ram's continued insinuations that we couldn't possibly make it. By now I was sure that Ram wanted us to feel like invalids. It was part of his plan to abort the trek.

We walked up a broad valley that turned steep as it approached the tiny village. From a ridge high above a glacial stream we crossed over a flimsy footbridge into Thugla. This bridge looked worse than the one leading into Pheriche, but I didn't examine it. I said my prayers and walked across. Very carefully. Directly on the other side was a rustic cabin.

"Look over there, Mathias. Just coming out the door." I ran ahead, shouting, "Hey Sean...Peggy. It's us." The Fitzpatricks waved back enthusiastically.

Mathias caught up and whispered furtively, "Don't tell them about my headache."

Just like a man! Heaven help him if he should appear vulnerable. "I'll just tell them you beat up the guide and fired the crew," I retorted. "Is that permitted?" Mathias smiled wanly.

The Fitzpatricks had stayed in Thugla overnight and were heading for Lobouche. While Mathias chatted I played with a lively three-year-old boy, who was fascinated by my tape recorder. He was wearing pants with the slit up the back, like the baby in Pangboche, and every time he leaned over, he exposed his buttocks to the cold. No wonder these kids were hardy.

I pulled out my steel mirror and handed it to him. His eyes widened and he started to laugh. On his face played a full range of emotions, from quizzical to unbelieving to mirth. He ran in circles around the courtyard, showing the mirror to everybody.

"You'll never get it back," said Sean. "I don't think they have mirrors in these mountains."

Just then a dog ran by and the boy dropped the mirror to join his siblings in the chase. I'd already concluded that the Nepalese keep dogs just so they can throw stones at something. The poor mangy creatures all seem to have sprung from the same mongrel hound. They spend their lives outside, sleeping in holes and ducking the sticks and stones and insults of angry men and bored children.

"Let's go to Lobouche with the Fitzpatricks," said Mathias after we'd eaten our lunch of boiled potatoes and dehydrated chicken soup. "I feel great. Must be the thin air!"

Ram wagged his finger imperiously. "Lobouche very far—six hours, maybe. Is getting cold. Much danger on rocks and ice."

"He's crazy," Sean said when Ram was out of earshot. "It's three hours at the most. That guy is an incompetent drunk. Get rid of him and join us. We'll be waiting for you tomorrow night."

We waved them on and started back over the bridge just as the wind picked up in earnest.

By the end of the day my lips had developed cracks. The sunscreen was useless. Peggy was having the same problem and had given me some new salve, which didn't help, only smarted. It hurt to talk and it hurt to smile. And to kiss.

Ram served us a terrific dinner—stuffed *momos* with a sweet *chapatty* for dessert. I'd taped his singing in the afternoon and was sure the crisis was over. But all during dinner he stood stiffly in the corner with his arms folded across his chest. He cleared the plates and returned an hour later while we were preparing for bed. He'd been drinking and was almost incoherent. Dorje, still suffering from altitude sickness, was at his side. Ram chose to confront us in the presence of other climbers, thinking, perhaps, that this would keep the lid on Mathias's anger. We discovered later that this was a favorite Nepalese trick—discussing business in front of others to gain possible allies.

"Mister and Missus," he began. "We must be in Lukla six days from now—twenty-four March—or we lose plane tickets."

We knew the chances of getting a seat on a specified day were slim, so the date didn't matter. And Ram knew it, too.

"I have only money for six more days, and nothing for porters," he continued.

"Wait a minute," interrupted Mathias. "This morning you said you had only money for one day. Did you rob a bank in the interim?"

Ram looked confused and turned to Dorje, who was at least sober.

"I am from the company, and we must protect your health. We cannot let you go on," he said, as if reading from a script.

"Seems to me that *your* health is the problem," said Mathias.

Dorje then brought up the real issue: *money.*

"If you ask me," said Mathias, shaking a finger close to Dorje's nose, "someone has been doing some heavy pilfering since we arrived in Lukla. How much money *have* you two stolen?"

Dorje threw up his hands and stalked out. This left Ram and Mathias and some very silent, bewildered climbers who did not wish to become involved. I tried to mediate, but there was no reasoning with either of the men. They went round and round, and when the shouting was over, nothing had been settled.

The final blow-up came at ten the next morning. We cornered Dorje, after calculating what had been spent on porters and accommodations over the past nine days. He admitted that Ram had been given 11,500 rupees and he 2,000, and he couldn't account for the shortage of money. He said he would give us 1,000 because of our predicament, and promised not to tell Ram of our deal.

But Dorje lied. Fifteen minutes later Ram emerged from his quarters followed by a porter, who was carrying our food, our tent, and the kitchen supplies. The porter scurried down the road.

"I go home," Ram shouted. "I have wife. I have child. I have money for two days more."

"First it's one, then it's six, and now it's two," shouted Mathias. "If I kill you, you won't need any money at all."

Ram's arms were flailing as he paced the courtyard, adding gestures of despair to the drama. Mathias was matching Ram gesture for gesture. I found myself, again, in the role of mediator, although referee might be a better description. I feared the two of them would have simultaneous heart attacks.

A lone *Sherpani* was sitting on the stone wall. She lowered her head shyly and looked as if she wanted to melt into the ground until the explosion was over.

"Dorje and I go now to Lukla," he announced finally. "You are fools to stay." He refused us any money, saying we had gotten enough from Dorje. It was settled. Ram had known all along what he planned to do.

Mathias stood in the courtyard, fist raised. "So we are being abandoned in this treacherous weather, with no knowledge of the trails or the mountains," he shouted. "This may kill me, you bastard, but you'll pay. Do you hear me? You'll pay!"

Ram hunched his back against the verbal blows, and without a backward glance, he strode out of Pheriche.

43

PASSANG LEADS THE WAY

Mathias walked back and forth like an angry lion whose prey had escaped. With each thundering step a puff of fine snow spurted into the air. His breath came in huge sighs, as if to extinguish the fire within. What was I doing here? It was cold. It was dangerous. We had no guide, no cook, and very little money.

The figure sitting on the wall stood up. She was much larger than Putti or Tenza, and her black hair, parted in the middle and knotted tightly under a blue kerchief, was tinged with gray. The smooth fold of skin above each eye and the high cheekbones declared her Mongolian background.

"Not to worry, Madam," she said as if reading my thoughts. "I know Ram. He many trouble. He ask me be your porter. I...me...Passang. These my mountains." She stretched her arms wide and moved her head slowly from side to side. "Please, not to worry."

Mathias stopped pacing and looked at her. A smile, somewhere between amusement and relief, began to form. "She's right, Meg. We're finished with Ram and his craziness. Hooray!"

He swooped me up in his arms and whirled me around the courtyard. Passang put her hand over her mouth in an effort to stifle the giggles.

"Alone at last," he shouted. "Absolutely *not to worry!*"

Exhilarated by the absence of tension, we made the return trip to Thugla over a higher route, and on to Lobouche (16,269 ft.) in record time—four hours. A layer of fresh snow made the trails and frozen rivers perilous. Just as I stepped onto the Khumbu Glacier, my legs flew out from under me and I landed on sheer ice, lying on my pack like a helpless turtle. Thank God for the heavy wool cap that shielded my head from the blow. Moments later Mathias, running over to help, followed me to the ground, fooled by the deceptive covering of light snow.

Passang turned and smiled at our clumsiness. Her round cheeks were flushed and snow clung to her hair. "Walk slow," she said, standing with her hands on her waist, and leaning forward to support the heavy duffels hanging on her back.

"Make feet wide like snowshoes—like the *Yeti*—and you no fall." She plodded on, while we picked up our bruised egos and followed.

We climbed slowly, for breathing was becoming more and more difficult. After the final ascent we came to a level area. In the middle stood a simple *chorten* dedicated to all the *Sherpas* who had met with disaster on Everest. Moments later we walked into a noisy, smoke-filled cabin, or *kharka*, in Lobouche.

"We've been expecting you," said Sean Fitzpatrick. He and Peggy were sitting at a long wooden table with assorted climbers. "I knew you'd shake that bastard. Now you're one of us!" He cut a huge slice of homemade bread, slathered it with yak cheese, and handed it to me. Then he cut another piece for Mathias. How wonderful to hear his lilting Irish accent once more.

"I'm afraid this lodge is full, but there's a smaller one higher up," he said after we'd had our fill of noodles and lemon tea. "We'll join you in the morning. You'll sleep well tonight—without Ram to disturb you."

There was one cluttered storeroom left by the time we arrived at the small cabin, and it was littered with dried yak dung. We watched as an old woman laboriously swept the floor and dragged two heavy mattresses from a loft, placing them on the narrow benches that hugged the wall. We protested, but she refused any help. Instead, she went to the kitchen, returning with two basins of steaming hot water. Next, she located an old cardboard box, which she placed by the door.

"Throw paper outside or in box only," she admonished us with two wags of her index finger. She stooped over and picked up a scrap of paper. "And not in fire. It bring snow."

"There must have been a lot of paper throwing yesterday," whispered Mathias. "Can you imagine…she's worried about one piece of paper, but lives with yak shit all over the place."

Orange tents filled the clearing out front. We had just arranged our sleeping bags on the mattresses when a group of Minnesotans flooded in to warm themselves by the fire and socialize with the owner, a very cultured, full-bodied lady from Kathmandu, whose husband was their guide. Without consulting us they invaded our room, set up a table, covered it with a checkered cloth and silver candlesticks, and started playing cards. Wine was uncorked, followed by the click of glasses. Between the flickering candlelight and the loud talking, sleep was impossible. Mathias and I fled.

"Why do these people spend thousands of dollars to come to the Himalayas," I fumed, "then isolate themselves from the land and the people? They run up and they run down. They eat their own kind of food and stay in a tight little group.

It's as if they never leave home. They bring Minneapolis to the mountains. A great way to get to know Nepal."

Mathias listened patiently. "As I see it, the one good thing about a luxury trek is the portable toilets. Don't forget, we're the ones adding to pollution. Did you know that over 6,000 pounds of human waste get deposited in these mountains every year?"

"I wonder who came up with *that* statistic," I said. "Must have done some interesting research."

"Well, there has to be some truth to it. Why do you think the *Sherpas* call toilet paper left along the trail the Westerner's prayer flags?"

I had to agree with Mathias from a sanitation point of view. There were only two outhouses in Lobouche, and they were so full you had to kick off the top layer before using them. We elected, instead, to squat behind a rock or in a hidden gully. This was extremely uncomfortable in subzero weather, and you had to be careful not to get too close to the cliffs. But it sure beat outhouses.

Bright sun greeted us on our expedition into the rocks the next morning. Sean was right—we did sleep well, free of Ram.

The Minnesotans had departed early, leaving us alone with our hostess. I finally realized why she seemed so different from the other *Sherpanis*. She wore glasses. She also had a distinctly cosmopolitan air, perhaps because she spent part of the year in Kathmandu, where her four children lived, and journeyed to the city twice a month—from March to November—with time out for the monsoon season. While she was gone, the old woman ran the cabin.

After enjoying a breakfast of fried buckwheat *chapattis* and milk tea, Mathias posed the question of how much to pay Passang. "We have no idea, and she seems too shy to ask," he said.

"Passang is excellent," replied our hostess. "Did you know that she was visiting a sister in Pheriche when Ram asked her to be your porter? She felt very sorry for you, all alone in the mountains."

"Not as sorry as we felt for ourselves," I said. So that's why she was without the usual *Sherpa* "uniform"—the long skirt, the crisscrossed blouse, the striped woolen apron. Poor thing. She looked frozen, with her flimsy shoes and thin jacket.

The answer came. "Eighty rupees a day. Yes, that's fair for the higher, colder altitudes."

"Ridiculous," Mathias interjected. "That's nothing…it's not even four dollars."

"For her it's not 'nothing.' She'll be very happy. Most porters at lower altitudes are paid twenty-four rupees a day and have to provide their own food. Eighty rupees and food is most generous."

Before we left Lobouche I gave Passang my extra windbreaker, wool socks, a pair of mittens, and some money for new sneakers "Oh, Madam, you are good woman," she said, smiling radiantly. Who could ask for more?

The Fitzpatricks joined us for the six-mile trek to Gorak Shep (17,107 ft.), the most northern outpost before base camp. In front of us was another wide valley rimmed with boulders. Rising in the distance was Pumo Ri (23,631 ft.), so dramatic that we thought it must be Everest, and snapped pictures feverishly. Passang—in the laughing way she had of dealing with our foolishness—informed us of our mistake. But it was exciting, anyway, realizing that in two days we'd be at the foot of the snow-covered cone.

As the sun became brighter the burning and stinging moved from my lips to my face. Nothing would help. Peggy had warned me against using vasoline—my last resort. She said it would act as a magnet, attracting the ultraviolet rays and intensifying the sun's heat. Frying me like a steak on a hot griddle. But it seemed soothing at first, and I was desperate. Now an angry cold sore had formed on my upper lip, making it impossible to smile...or kiss. Mathias and I had to be satisfied with hugging, or holding hands, until my hands began to swell and display broken, splotchy, blood vessels, making them, also, too painful to touch. For the first time in my life, I felt like a complete physical wreck.

But Mathias's ardor was unquenchable. He kept reassuring me that I was beautiful no matter what, and would be better soon. I was annoyed at this, because I was sure I'd never look normal again, and I didn't want my suffering minimized.

The climb up to the ridge overlooking the Khumbu and Changri Glaciers was steep and slippery. Swiftly flowing streams ran under the icy path and my feet were constantly cold. I wore a wool scarf over most of my face, but this didn't stop the fierce wind and unrelenting sun from burning my skin.

We crossed the Changri Glacier, scrambling up the lateral moraine to the opposite bank. Directly ahead was Kala Pattar (18,298 ft.) and below were two stone *kharkas*, our final campsite. We raced diagonally down into the small level area of Gorak Shep, whooping and shouting for joy, and entered the first hut, its ceiling so low that the men were in danger of decapitating themselves. There we were welcomed by a jolly lady and her eight-year-old son, who immediately took my cold hands in his rough little palms and began to rub them gently. What a greeting!

"Come, have tea, Madam," he said, in English better than his mother's. "It will heat you. You be better soon."

I couldn't believe the amount of tea we consumed at every stop. We either had iron stomachs or the iodine pills were working. Most hikers weren't so lucky. *Giardia* was rampant.

There were two sleeping areas in the hut. In one, a slight woman—rather weather-beaten, but pretty—was reading a paperback. She was dressed in shades of tan, and, with her dull blonde hair, seemed to blend into the monochromatic surroundings.

In the other were four men, sound asleep.

"Have you heard of the rabbit lady?" asked Sean in a low voice.

"Yes," I answered. "Kind of weird, they say. Didn't she save a rabbit from a stew in Kathmandu, and leave it with those doctors in Pheriche, because she was afraid it would suffer from altitude sickness? And somebody made fun of her climbing with the rabbit, so she pulled a knife and threatened to stab him…."

"That's the one. And she's right down the hall, where we're going to sleep."

Sean tiptoed into the room and put his pack down on the platform. Instantly, the woman leapt up and shouted, "This section is for women alone as God would have wanted it."

"Sorry, but I'm married and I've gotten used to sleeping with my wife," retorted Sean.

"Well, you can't do it in this section. It's for women only."

"That's strange," he said. "I don't see any signs. We'll have to see about this."

We looked around for the owner of the hut. She had vanished. Mathias and I tried to squeeze in among the young men and find an extra spot for the Fitz-patricks, who were not prepared to go to war with the rabbit lady.

Just then a young German came through the door and plunked his sleeping bag down next to the woman.

"And you…you get out of here, too," she yelled.

He ignored her—pretending not to understand English—and proceeded to unpack. In the middle of her long harangue, the German turned to her and announced, loudly: "I'm tired of this. I am a free man, and I will sleep wherever I wish. *Sie sind verrückt!* [You are crazy!]"

"God will punish you, you Nazi bastard pig," she screamed as she flew at his neck.

"Leave him alone," Mathias said, grabbing her arms. "And you apologize for your nasty language. Now! He's not responsible for something that happened before he was born."

The woman wrenched away from Mathias, snatched three packages of spaghetti from the kitchen shelf, ripped them apart, and threw them at him. He ducked, as dry pasta flew everywhere.

"Men are bad," she shouted. "God has told me so. He'll protect me in my righteousness. No German pig will sleep in *my* room."

I put my arm around the fuming young man and hurried him outside, trying to get him as far away from the cabin as possible, all the time expressing my disgust at the woman's behavior.

"But did you hear what she called me?" he asked.

"Yes, I did, but I also know that she's crazy, so you mustn't even listen."

He began to calm down just as the owner of the cabin returned. "Get out," she thundered at the rabbit lady, when she heard what had happened. "This my house. Nobody does my guests bad."

The pitiful, disheveled creature scurried out, clutching her balled-up sleeping bag and paperback. I turned away and didn't go back inside until her receding steps had faded completely. We heard that she survived the night, alone on the trail with no men to bother her. But this was not the last we were to see of her.

Greatly subdued, we helped clean up the spaghetti. For dinner we enjoyed a meal of Sherpa stew, made with large amounts of potatoes, small amounts of yak meat, onions, and ground red peppers. The temperature inside the cabin was five above zero. It was too cold to write and too dark to read. I wondered what it was like outside on the trail. No mention was made of the rabbit lady.

Our hostess's good humor and hearty laugh had returned and she sat with the women, grinding dried red peppers and talking excitedly in Nepali. Just before we went to bed I saw her reach up and offer a steaming glass of tea to a tiny shrine high on a shelf in the kitchen. Then she wrapped herself and her little boy in a coarse blanket and curled up alongside the porters, who lay like one long braided knot on the large bench next to the fire, and slept.

44

SNOW BIRDS ON KALA PATTAR

"Morning time, Meg," shouted Lhakpa, the owner's little boy. He stood next to my sleeping bag and tugged at my woolen cap. I opened one eye to a grin that lit up the darkest corner of the cabin, and closed it, immediately, to escape the sting of heavy smoke still hanging in the air from the smoldering fire.

Mathias turned over and reached for me. His patterned ski cap, which came to a point on which was perched a saucy pom-pom, was pulled down over his hair and forehead, obliterating his thick eyebrows. I started to laugh, but stopped abruptly. The pain in my lips and face was too excruciating.

"How could we sleep so long?" I asked, trying to ignore my discomfort. "Come on. We have seven hours of strenuous hiking ahead. I'm not wasting another minute."

I slipped away from Mathias and stood in the doorway for a few moments, breathing deeply to get my respiration going after the long sleep. Insulated in my down jacket, I stepped out into the sub-zero weather. Tiny Gorak Shep was completely surrounded by mountains, which illumined a landscape that had seemed desolate the night before. Not any more. It was bold and at the same time inviting—a gossamer vision dressed all in white. Someone must have been throwing a lot of paper into the fire during the night.

Mathias came looking for me, but I had ducked behind some boulders for privacy and didn't hear his call. I decided to explore the rocky field behind the hut, unaware that he had become alarmed and enlisted Lhakpa in his search. When I returned I was greeted with joyful shouts from the boy. "Meg is not finished. Look. She is good!"

Mathias explained: "When you didn't come back, the little fellow ran around frantically. Finally he gave up and returned to face me. 'Meg is finished,' he said mournfully. 'No more Meg.' I had to laugh in spite of my apprehension. And now, my dear one, I can see that you're definitely not finished...and how glad I am."

Slowly, he unzipped the top of my jacket and kissed my neck. He caressed my cheeks, being careful not to touch my swollen lips. It was wonderful to feel his strong arms around me, to be fussed over while I was feeling so bad. I liked being taken care of, so long as he didn't boss me.

It was ten o'clock by the time the four of us had climbed up the moraine outside Gorak Shep and were traversing the glacial zone of ablation, where the ice had melted enough to form a small lake. After walking a short distance along a rocky area we reached the right bank of the Khumbu Glacier and followed footpaths and cairns to the center of the enormous ice mass. We proceeded with great caution in order to avoid large clefts in the surface, where the ice had separated, forming deep, angry-looking chasms, their fluted sides resembling the meat of freshly-cracked coconuts.

Traversing the Khumbu Glacier.

I walked along the glacier—a great white way between the lofty peaks—grabbing hold of the protruding sharp fingers of ice that covered the surface like three-foot spikes of transparent grass. The ice formed exotic figures—a group of dancers in flowing cloaks, a leaping frog, a crooked skeleton. It was like bush-whacking through a forest of ghostly, misshapen trees. Mathias lagged behind, taking photos of glistening Pumo Ri on the left and the saw-toothed Nuptse ridge on the right. He was making me nervous. What if the sheets of ice split apart and swallowed him up?

"Look over here," shouted Sean, as he rounded a bend and discovered a cave at the bottom of an incline just off the trail. He slid down the embankment and reached the yawning, jagged entrance. At his feet a shallow stream flowed into the opening, forming a clear glacial pool. He leaned down and filled his cupped hands with the blue-green water, and drank.

"Peggy, m'love, let me give you pure water from the depths of the earth," he shouted, filling his hands, again, and letting the cold liquid run through his fingers. "Meg, Mathias…." His voice echoed eerily from the depths of the cave. He leaned his head farther into the gaping tunnel and howled. "Ooeeee, owwwww, ayoooo." He was smiling with glee as the sound echoed back. "Eeeooo, ayaaaa…."

"Get out of there, Sean. Fast," shouted Mathias, responding to the shouts. "Any sudden noise could cause a…."

The rumble began deep down. Peggy screamed and Sean flew out of the cave, clawing his way up the white walls of the incline until he was back on the main trail. Mathias grabbed my hand and pulled me along the slippery path as the thundering sound increased and the earth shook beneath us. There was a mighty crack and the sound of ice and rock breaking up. Terrified, we stumbled up onto a narrow plateau above the trail. We ran for another five minutes, and then, suddenly, all was quiet. We looked around. Where the cave had been was a dome-shaped wall of snow. The old trail had been swallowed up, cairns and all. Wisps of snow still circled and danced gracefully in the air above where we'd been.

Beads of sweat shone on Sean's forehead. His cap was askew. Snow caked his beard. "Dreadfully sorry, folks," he said, his voice wavering. "Damned stupid of me. I almost ruined the day…to say nothing of our lives. I'm truly sorry, and grateful to you, old chap, for the warning." He nodded to Mathias, who put his arm on Sean's shoulder, giving it a reassuring squeeze.

"I must say…I never saw anyone climb the underbelly of a glacier so fast," he retorted. "You looked as if the devil, himself, was chasing you. It was funny…like a circus clown with a lion in hot pursuit. But I was in no mood to laugh then. Would you excuse me if I did now?"

Without waiting for an answer Mathias started to laugh, slowly at first, then with such intensity that tears rolled down his cheeks. It was a kind of hysteria, a shedding of tension. One by one we joined in, hanging onto the columns of ice to steady ourselves, grateful to be alive.

When we reached Everest Base Camp the trail ended abruptly, blocked by the famous Khumbu Ice Fall—the biggest wall of ice I'd ever seen. It looked like a cascade of water frozen in slow motion, a sculpted mountain of glass sparkling in the sun. I stood at the edge of the glacier in front of the chasm that separated us from the wall. How tiny I felt. How mortal. So this barren no-man's-land was Everest Base Camp. I had imagined a village of tents filled with eager climbers, but at this time of year it was a wilderness of ice and snow, gurgling water, and *seracs*, those pinnacle-like masses formed by the melting of the ice. Their thickness and depth were impossible for me to calculate...or capture on film. Envision whole cities of stark white church steeples or upside down icicles, some conical and some cylindrical, like the varied spires of Bryce Canyon, Utah—blue-white ice instead of red rock.

Khumbu ice fields.

"Let's see the rest of the camp," yelled Sean, who was about to cross a flimsy sheet of ice, which lay across a glacial stream tumbling out of the fall. Beyond this was another wide expanse—a continuation of base camp.

Peggy flew at him. "Get back here, or the honeymoon's over! That ice will never hold you and there are crevasses all around." She held up both arms and gestured frantically. "Have you gone mad, Sean?"

I looked beyond the stream, seeing another great fissure filled with what looked like tons of whipped cream, or giant peaks of meringue. The glacier dropped off haphazardly all around us. It was impossible to tell which was solid ground and which wasn't.

"I came all the way from Jiri for this, and I intend to explore every inch," he said. "And I'm as sane as any Irishman you'll ever meet!" With arms akimbo, he started across the stream.

"Come back, Sean," Mathias interceded sternly. "If you go across there you'll not only be a crazy Irishman, but a dead one. Heaven knows where that stream would carry you. We've had one close call today…that's enough. It's just too dangerous."

Sean looked devastated. It was one thing to be harangued by a nervous wife, but Mathias was a seasoned climber and couldn't be discounted. Poor Sean. As far back as he could remember he had wanted to be in the place where the big adventure began. I was sure he possessed the same enthusiasm and courage as the hundreds of climbers who had started the ascent up Everest from this very spot. How many had tried and how many had failed. But right now the place looked far more scary than in any photograph. The terrain was as haunting as the moon, and as forbidding.

We ate our lunch of cold pancakes, cookies, and water—which was fast becoming solid ice in our canteens—while sitting on the edge of the glacier. All around we could hear the rumble of small landslides changing the shape of the ice field. On the way back the results were evident. We scrambled up the newly arranged rocks and snow, carefully negotiating each move. The ghostly presence of Pumo Ri hovered in the background. "Just you wait," it seemed to be saying. "It's my turn tomorrow. You think you're cold *now*?"

It was twilight when we arrived back in Gorak Shep, and a pink blush had settled on the mountains. Mathias and I sat outside on a rock wall until it was dark. We were still full of energy, euphoric at having reached base camp and survived the dangerous trek.

Mathias put his arm around me. I rested my head on his shoulder. "You know, Meg," he said after several minutes of silence. "There are simple, seemingly unimportant events in everyone's life that leave a big impression, a warmth far beyond the event itself. And it usually involves love of the deepest kind. This day with you was one of those events."

I sat quietly in the glow of his love.

Stars covered every inch of sky by the time we left the clearing and entered the cabin. "I have the strongest heart muscle in Nepal," I announced, impulsively, pounding my chest. "No breathing problems. No headache."

Peggy started to giggle. Six men—four Germans and two Swedes—looked up, curiously, from the table. They were eating the usual soup, rice, and potatoes, known to us as the hiker's carbo-load.

"They probably think you're as nutty as the rabbit lady," whispered Mathias.

"Is it for sale?" asked Roger, a Swedish engineer, who was in Nepal with a Christian mission. "My friend Lars, here, could use it, although he'd prefer a new stomach."

Lars looked up weakly. "Do strong hearts cure *giardia*?"

Now I was embarrassed by my bragging, and slid onto a bench to await my soup. The Fitzpatricks tried to be jolly, but were unable to shake off the memory of Sean's near accident and his disappointment at cutting short his explorations. They went to bed early while we stayed up talking with the Swedes.

How we all wished there were more light in the cabin. The kitchen had one candle and there were no windows near the sleeping platforms. During the day an occasional ray of sun filtered through the cracks, where yak dung had fallen out of the holes, but at night it was dark and oppressive. I shuddered to think of what happened during the rainy season. The flat roof—paper and burlap held down by heavy rocks—must have been as reliable as a sieve.

The attraction between Mathias and me was becoming stronger with each night of separation. "We have to get away alone," he said, "or I'll go crazy. Don't you find the frustration maddening?"

My answer was a silent caress. My mouth still felt so bad that I couldn't even think of kissing. Instead, I put my head on his chest and snuggled as close as separate sleeping bags would allow. If only we were alone in the bunkroom.

Long after the kitchen candle was out and the *Sherpas* were huddled by the fire, we lay awake, talking. We had tried to keep our feelings from Sean and Peggy, but they were no fools. We were acting like a couple of teenagers, goofy in love. Glen no longer haunted me. I wasn't thinking of anything beyond the next breathless step, and the next warm embrace.

Damn…today was the day to get up early, but the cook overslept and the Fitzpatricks announced that they needed some "marital time" together. I'd never heard love-making expressed that way, but there was no point in being envious of people who'd had the foresight to bring a double sleeping bag.

Passang looked worried. "We must leave soon," she warned. "Everest gone by noontime."

I had heard this prediction numerous times, which is why I became irritated with Mathias and the Fitzpatricks for their slow, meticulous packing. If they didn't hurry, we'd miss the most anticipated view of the trip.

I played with Lhakpa while I waited. He took me to his corner of the kitchen. There were no games—dolls or trucks or crayons—the sort of toys we assume are part of every child's life. He put his index finger to his lips, as if to indicate a secret, and slowly withdrew a book from under the folded blankets. Its cover was torn, the pages faded. He proudly thrust it toward me. I turned the pages with him, making up a story about the pictures as I went along. He squealed with delight.

"Oh, Meg, again, please," he begged. As I spun my tales I thought about my own children with their bookshelves full of colorful volumes overflowing with stories and fantasies. But this child's days were spent socializing with the hikers, following along with them for fifteen minutes or so—as he did with us—then running back and helping his mother with chores. No carefree childhood play. No playmates. No school.

As we left, Lhakpa said goodbye by taking both my hands in his as he had at our first meeting. How I yearned to give him a book, a piece of candy, some small 'thank-you.' When I returned home I would send him the most beautiful book I could find. That was a promise.

We crossed a patch of the Khumbu and started up the brown-tufted trail to Kala Pattar (18,298 ft.). The frozen rocks crumbled and slid under my feet, pushing me backward as I struggled to climb the steep slope. I'd take two steps, then stop to breathe. Then two more steps. I was sure my heart would burst from the exertion. How on earth had Reinhold Messner climbed Everest twice without oxygen?

I fumbled with my tape recorder. I wanted to record the ascent—the sluggish rhythm of our footsteps and our laborious breathing. Even the young Germans behind us were walking like men on the moon. Their slow, exaggerated steps—arms dangling loosely and head thrust forward—looked like simulations of weightlessness.

I thought of my son, Tom. Today was March 23rd, his birthday. He was born 29 years ago in Miami, Florida, when I was 29 years old. I wondered, fleetingly, if he'd received my letter. He was a mountain climber and would have loved this trip. Disconnected thoughts flooded my mind. A perfect delivery it had been, with no drugs, and a doctor who sat on the end of my bed and read *The New Yorker* while waiting for me to dilate. Birthdays were important in our family. Big celebrations. And I always wrote a poem a la Ogden Nash. Humorous couplets for a good family laugh. I tried my hand at a few. It kept my mind off my pain.

> When Tom lost his temper, we stayed far away,
> And waited until a more sunshiny day
> When he'd sit by his plants cogitating ethereal,
> Or whistling the Beach Boys while eating his cereal.

Yes, Tom would be disappointed. No poem this year. Maybe when I get back to Kathmandu....

"Look, Meg." Mathias jolted me back to the cold present. "The great Khumbu. Our nemesis...almost." He was looking down at the cities and mountains of ice we had traversed yesterday. The gigantic spires had become diminutive tepees, the glacier a dirty blue sea.

Passang trudged ahead, singing to herself, oblivious to our misery. It was a plaintive tune, "Resham Firiri," I'd heard Putti sing many times and would never forget. I watched her move up ahead of me, and concentrated on the steady crunch of her feet on the frozen scree. I marveled at her stamina.

A sudden idea hit me. "Stop, Passang!" I said, forcing myself to run to catch up. "I must record your voice." I was holding the tape recorder toward her and taking deep breaths to steady myself.

She turned around, blushing crimson, and laughed, shaking her head so fiercely that her entire upper body moved. "No, no, Madam."

O.K., I thought. I'll do it without her knowledge. I dragged myself over the never-ending pile of rocks as if in a dream, holding out the recorder to capture the singing, accompanied by the crunch, slide, crunch of our steps. Her clear high tones never wavered.

It was bitter cold by the time we arrived at the top. My lips were bleeding and my fingers and toes were numb. If only the brilliant sun had been warm. Passang stopped and pointed across the ravine. "Look, Madam, there my mountains...Lhotse, Everest, Nuptse."

We had made it just in time! I looked at Everest's long plume and knew the winds were strong and cruel. The chilling view made my freezing toes and fingers feel instantly better in comparison.

On top of Kala Pattar.

Puffy clouds began to move over the famous trio. They were no longer those faraway humps on the horizon. They had taken command. I reached out in my fatigue and light-headedness, as if to touch them. Then, gasping for breath, I lowered myself onto one of the wide flat granite rocks of the Kala Pattar ridge. Through the penumbra of consciousness I could see the Fitzpatrick's making their way up the side of Pumo Ri. They walked slowly, jerkily, like wind-up toys. I could go no further. I had seen the view. That was all I wanted.

As I lay on the rock, my eyes squinting out from under a heavy scarf, I became aware that Mathias was leaning over me.

"Beautiful lady," he said, the glow of accomplishment on his wind-burned face, "come and see what I've found for you...a snowbird out of the frozen sky, a little white and black bird sitting on a point of rock waiting to greet you."

"Oh, Mathias," I said, "Thank you, but Meg is finished. This time Meg is definitely finished."

45

THE LONG WAY BACK

The Fitzpatricks had returned and were regaling Mathias about the hazards of Pumo Ri. I opened my eyes just as a cluster of tiny birds swooped down out of the frozen sky to feast on Sean's ample supply of English biscuits. They would dive down, grab a morsel, and disappear, returning a moment later for more. How did these little beggars survive in this desolate terrain? There couldn't be enough biscuits to go around. In my stupor I wrestled with the incongruity. Just then a raven appeared, driving the smaller birds away. I sat up as Sean held out a biscuit and the sleek black creature landed on his outstretched hand. More incongruity.

Revived, I felt a rush of joy, and hurriedly picked my way over the icy boulders, eager to view the dazzling panorama from every angle. Only the tip of Everest was still visible through the clouds, but that didn't matter. Dozens of lesser peaks surrounded us, dwarfing our 18,000 foot perch. Getting here had been a monumental accomplishment. Nothing could dampen our spirits.

Mathias and I were silent as we retraced our steps down the trail. We were conserving our strength, for it was a long way back to Lobouche. I vowed not to complain, but my lips were bleeding, and the cold sore had grown to considerable proportions. I tried to dwell on the positive feelings of the last hour—as my mother would have instructed me—but the colder I became the more miserable and ugly I felt. Not even Mathias's reassurance helped.

By the time we reached the stone hut in Lobouche a rosy alpenglow had settled over the mountains that rimmed the Khumbu Valley. It was impossible not to be affected by their silent beauty. And it was like coming home to be met at the door by the smiling, bespectacled *Sherpani*. She epitomized the warmth and hospitality of the *Sherpa* people—their openness, their intelligence.

The two Swedish engineers were sitting gloomily in one corner. Their porter and guide had abandoned them that morning. Roger had already located another porter, but Lars was still furious.

"It's not fair! After all we've done for these people…how could they treat us this way?" he said, still looking weak and gray from his bout with *giardia*. Such remarks distressed me, but I said nothing. Tourists from the West often arrived with a full complement of arrogance, something they would deny vehemently, and something I'd been guilty of myself, but which I was now working hard to mitigate. Just getting to know these people better, trying to understand their culture, and discarding any judgments can bring about a remarkable transformation. I would still fall short, but I was making progress.

"Fairness is not something I've come to expect in this life," Mathias said, pompously. How philosophical he'd become, the further he distanced himself from those first stormy days with Ram.

Passang and friend on the trail.

Early the next morning the Fitzpatricks departed, promising to wait for us in Thyangboche. We took the longer route through Thugla and Pheriche. On a narrow path above a deep ravine we overtook a friend of Passang's, who was carrying a towering basket of hay reaching from her head to her ankles. From behind she looked like a walking haystack. The two of them strolled together, talking excitedly, then breaking into song. This time Passang allowed me to tape the singing. As I was playing back the recording a young mother and her baby came along the trail. They stopped, curious to see where the singing was coming from. The baby squealed and clapped his hands to the rhythm of the singing.

"Look at that baby, Meg. He loves the music," said Mathias, ecstatically. Out came the movie camera to capture the wonder and glee of the little child.

At Pheriche Passang left us to go to her home for additional clothes. Mathias and I were to take a more direct route and join her in Thyangboche. We were thrilled to be on our own for the rest of the afternoon.

We stepped into the cabin where one week ago we'd first made love. It looked bleak and uninviting in the daylight, and the stove gave off an unpleasant odor. But we were alone, connected to each other in a very special way. For the moment all my pain and discomfort disappeared.

We circumvented the rickety bridge outside Pheriche and entered a heavily wooded area. How soothing to breathe the perfume of pine and cedar once more. Down the winding paths we went, crisscrossing the glacial valleys and passing through a cluster of small villages along the *Imja Khola*. I rushed ahead while Mathias photographed every stone house and now and then a schoolyard with children at play. So eager was he to explore the terraced fields and examine the budding flora that he led us off the main trail, until we were hopelessly lost. At first it was funny, but as the afternoon shadows lengthened, I began to worry.

"Mathias, I have only one small flashlight, and we haven't come to Pangboche, yet." I was frightened, and despaired of ever reaching the monastery. I couldn't imagine roaming these hills in the dark. "Honestly, sometimes I want to take your cameras and throw them all over a cliff!"

"When you come to Austria and I show you these pictures you won't feel that way," he said, looking at me with somber eyes. That was the first time he'd talked about the future and it gave me a pleasant, but unsettled feeling. Was he ready so soon to dive into a relationship, or was this his way of healing after his wife's death? I wasn't sure I was ready for a serious commitment. So why didn't I say so? Because I never was good at confronting, especially if I thought someone's feelings might be hurt. And this was all so new, so unexpected. Why couldn't I just enjoy the moment?

After another hour of wandering we stumbled into the forests above Thyangboche. A miracle! The melting snow had turned the trail to mud. Balancing ourselves with arms outstretched we labored through the muck in the waning light and into the path of the imposing monk who had tried to sell us his artwork. He thundered by with a show of long teeth and a jolly wave…leaning heavily on a wooden staff to keep himself aloft. The smell of *chang* was unmistakable.

Looming just ahead was the bell tower of the monastery and three figures standing at the top of the trail. "Hooray!" I shouted, greatly relieved. "Hey Fitzpatricks, we made it."

They started running toward us, followed by Passang.

"Where the hell have you two been?" asked Sean, annoyed. "Passang has been frantic with worry. We were about to send out a search party with a stretcher…and some brandy." Seeing how tired and muddy we were his manner softened. "Can't leave you kids alone a minute, can we?"

"We have a friend waiting to see you," chimed in Peggy. "The rabbit lady *and* her rabbit!"

"Just what we need," I said. "A little turmoil to go with our fatigue!"

This time we stayed at the Tashidhyleck Lodge, a new building smelling of freshly cut pine. As we entered the airy dining room the rabbit lady was being escorted out the door. I lowered my head, afraid of being recognized, but not before I saw her defiant look and the pink eyes of the rabbit peering out of her jacket.

"She's been haranguing the owner about the immorality of Gorak Shep and Lobouche," said Peggy. "They're finding a special place for her to sleep. Alone. Hope it's not the *loo*!" We all laughed, but it was more nervous than hearty.

Mathias groaned when he saw the large bunkhouse. "More communal living," he whispered. "But at least it's democratic." This was the first time we'd seen Nepalese and Westerners sleeping side by side—we in our down bags and they wrapped in thin, patched blankets. But I missed the old monastery. No rowdy Italian climbers with a giggling *Sherpa* entourage, and no Kumar to bring us hot water in the morning and wobble his head amiably from side to side.

I awoke early to the stares of a very old man in the bunk next to me. It was unnerving. He was sitting bolt upright with his arms folded across his naked chest, yoga-style. I slipped out of bed without speaking and tiptoed out the door.

In one week spring had come to Thyangboche. What had been a field of snow was now a meadow. Early morning shadows played on the grass, the frosty dew highlighted in each sliver of sunlight. As I descended the great stone steps I could see the yaks scattered about the field, still lying down. Everest—so far away and bounded by Lhotse and Nuptse—was clearly visible from the small triangular window of the outhouse. But it was Ama Dablam—its "charm box" heavy-laden with snow—that dominated the landscape.

Ama Dablam.

I sat on the grass, drinking in the sounds and sights of the awakening day—the monks in their billowing orange robes scurrying to prayers, the tinkle of the yak bells as the animals rose and slowly moved around the meadow, and the deep, rhythmic throbbing of the temple gong.

After leaving Thyangboche the trail became more difficult. But I loved it! This was my kind of climbing, over rocks and high passes, where I had to concentrate on every step. It gave me a dual sense of lightness and power to be able to negotiate the steep turns and switchbacks. It seemed far more dangerous than before, because I was looking down into the ravines instead of climbing away from them. The occasional rumble of rock falls resounded through the valley while the river thundered in its gorge below. Ama Dablam moved around us, like an ever-watchful guardian, flanked by Khumbila and the bewitching white fan of Thamaserku.

By afternoon my face and lips were worse, and I begged to go to the hospital in Khunde. But Passang, who was carrying a heavy load, said it was too much of a trip for one day. We must go directly to Namche Bazar.

Gone was the snowy, muddy Namche of two weeks ago. It was even warm enough to return our extra sleeping bags and collect the $80 deposit. A godsend, for our treasury was empty.

"Meg, are you there?" shouted Mathias. "If you are, come to the window!" I couldn't believe that this conservative man was making so much noise. I was sitting in the second-floor dining room of the Nameste View Lodge and ran to look out the window. Mathias was standing by a latticed bamboo stall in the middle of the dirt courtyard, camera in hand.

"Come on down and take a look at this shower," he said.

"Madam wish shower?" asked the ample *Sherpani* in charge. "Is cheap. Fourteen rupees."

I rushed down the cellar stairs, through a dirt basement into a room where weaving and wool carding were taking place. A door opened into the backyard. There stood Mathias next to a small shack, a conspiratorial grin on his face.

"You go first," he said. "I don't want to miss this." He held the camera to his eye and clicked the shutter.

"Don't you dare stick that camera into this stall or I'll smash it to pieces," I said, playfully, as he handed me a towel.

"This is my surprise. Everything's ready to go. Just step in there, young lady, and undress, and see what happens." He made a flourish with his arm, like the master of ceremonies at a circus. The *Sherpani* was looking out the open window and holding a bucket. Before I could completely undress she poured its contents into a wooden trough that sloped from the kitchen down to the stall. A rusty showerhead had been wired to the end of the chute and steaming hot water came tumbling over me. I screamed, but the water kept coming. By the time I was fully undressed it had stopped, and I was doubled over with laughter.

"More water?" asked Mathias.

"Yes, only not so hot!" I replied. I fumbled around for some bar soap and lathered my hair, though I feared it might come out in big clumps—it was so dirty.

Before the next onslaught I handed Mathias as many items of clothing as possible, but my boots, socks, and jeans were soaked. All I had left was the small towel, which hardly passed the test of decency. Without warning, the water came, again, full force and steaming. How delicious to be getting clean! I would never take another shower without thinking of this one. Luckily, the sun was setting when I stepped out of the stall. Protected by the deepening shadows, I sneaked up the stairs to my room.

When I appeared at dinner nobody, including me, could believe the change. My hair, which had been matted under my hat for two weeks, was clean and fluffy. My lips were less swollen, although I'm sure it had nothing to do with the shower—more likely the lower altitude. And I wore the fuchsia shirt that had gotten me into so much trouble in Pune. Sean stood up impulsively and sang "My Wild Irish Rose." He was joined by Peggy and two Canadian climbers. Afterwards they presented me with the remainder of their lip salve in recognition of my stoicism.

Mathias thoroughly enjoyed the charade. "If I'd known you were so beautiful I would have fallen in love with you immediately," he said, kissing my hand. I thought my heart would explode.

At ten the next morning we met the Fitzpatricks at the modest Rastriya Banijya Bank. It was far less bureaucratic than the banks of India or Egypt. The foreign exchange officer was efficient and our transactions went rapidly. Mathias sold three rolls of film to Sean for English pounds, which we cashed, along with another forty dollars. We left with enough rupees to pay Passang and last another week in the mountains—a situation we never dreamed would materialize.

At 1 P.M. we said farewell to the Fitzpatricks and by late afternoon we had departed *Sagarmatha National Park*. Yak caravans lumbered past us—the poor animals grinding their teeth and grunting from exertion—retracing their steps because of washed out bridges. The spring thaw had done its damage. Several of the swinging bridges over the *Dudh Kosi* were gone, and their makeshift replacements were made of planks—many of them rotten—lashed together with branches. And there were no handrails at all. In contrast, the bridge at Pheriche looked like a super highway.

We had reached a small cabin in the woods when Passang turned to us. "We can no get to Phakding this day," she announced. "Here is Benkar. We stop for night. O.K?" She was sweating profusely. I couldn't imagine asking her to negotiate another cliff.

"This is fine, Passang." I said. Her face lit up with relief. "Look, Mathias, we have our own castle by the romantic *Dudh Kosi*!"

Our hostess was an elegant *Sherpani* who spoke English but took forever to cook dinner. She insisted on preparing her own noodles. I would have settled for dehydrated soup, box and all.

"She's making eyes at you, Mathias," I whispered, finally realizing why she seemed so distracted. "Maybe if I leave the room, it will hurry dinner...."

"If you leave the room I'm coming with you. She scares me. I've heard about the mating rituals of these people, and I'm too tired to even contemplate it. Besides, my eyes see only one woman." He put his arms around me and pulled me to him. The fire danced off the wall and the *Sherpani* smiled knowingly. Passang, who seemed to have given up, lay sleeping in one corner of the kitchen.

Dinner was worth the wait. Spicy sauce and cooked greens covered the heavy noodles. A dense, very sweet yellow cake was served with two small glasses of *rakshi* for dessert. I wondered if I'd ever walk again.

"Who's going to rebuild all those bridges?" Mathias asked as we sat watching the fire turn to glowing coals.

"It is serious matter," our hostess replied. "Many people will be hurt before it is done." She told us that only yesterday a young *Sherpani* had been crossing the bridge a mile above Benkar. When she moved aside to let a yak pass, she stepped on a loose plank and plummeted one hundred feet into the river below. By the time she was fished out her body was lifeless, smashed against the rocks by the churning waters. I remembered that bridge. It was barely three feet wide. My inclination had been to crawl across it on all fours.

Typical bridge over the Dudh Kosi.

All night long I tossed and turned, thinking of the young *Sherpani* struggling to live against impossible odds. This was raw, wild country. People accepted the impermanence of life and the inevitability of death as a matter of course...so unlike Westerners. It was this acceptance of existence as transient that seemed to give them peace of mind. I sensed it, and I admired it.

The moon was flooding into the room. From the window I could see a patch of sky crowded with stars. I lay for a long time listening to the river, feeling a part of it, and the trees, and the mountains. I reached over and touched Mathias.

"I'm so glad you're awake," he said, as he moved toward me. "I know why you're so restless. It's the young *Sherpani*, isn't it?"

I slid my hands around his neck and lay my head on his chest.

"That's one of the things I love about you," he said. "You take everyone's troubles as your own, even when there's nothing you can do about it. But now that I've found you, I have no troubles to give you. Will you love me, anyway?" He enveloped me in his arms, comforting me, caressing me.

In the morning we saw our first mountain rhododendron in bloom, its large, blood-red blossoms surrounded by delicate oblong leaves. Soon other varieties appeared—white and peach—their flowers, like bobbing lanterns, lighting up the forest. We stopped for lunch at a small lodge, the first one I'd seen with a veranda. As we entered, a large white rabbit ran between my legs, almost tripping me. I screamed and grabbed Mathias.

"Don't worry, he won't hurt you. Joe is gentle, like a baby."

Oh, my God, the rabbit lady! She was sitting all alone at a low wooden table eating a bowl of fried potatoes. Why was this frail woman so intimidating?

We talked for a long time. Fortunately, she didn't recognize either of us. She told us about the recent death of her parents in a car crash on the Santa Ana Freeway, and the loss of her only child. I began to see another side of this troubled, lonely woman.

As she was leaving Mathias asked to photograph her. The rabbit was hanging in a hand-woven pouch on the front of her jacket, its furry face peering out like a newborn baby in a snuggly. The rabbit lady was pleased.

On a hill outside the village, Tibetan monks were selling handcrafts—wooden bowls, pastry molds, parchment paintings. The goods were spread on blankets and the monks sat cross-legged next to them. Everything we had been offered in Thyangboche by the long-toothed monk was on display—at half the price.

This was the third time I had tried, unsuccessfully, to buy Glen a prayer wheel—a small copper cylinder mounted on a metal or wooden stick. Inside is a tightly wound roll of paper on which many *mantras* are printed. (These wheels are miniatures of the large metal drums seen in every Buddhist temple.) As you hold the handle and rotate your wrist clockwise, the wheel spins around. The faster it spins the more you pray. The wheel does the work much more quickly than the spoken word. You can pray while you talk, shop, or just walk around town. A pretty efficient system.

"I don't understand why you want to buy that man a gift," said Mathias. "He gave you so much grief. Forget him. Let him buy his own prayer wheel."

Mathias was tired of hearing about Glen. He had had time to come to terms with his wife's impending death, and had accepted it. His mourning had been deep, but finite. Now he was ready to begin a new life. My mourning was taking a lot longer. A divorce is a constant reminder of failure. It sits like a stone in the heart. In some ways it's worse than a death, as I had told Jerry. I found it difficult to verbalize these feelings to Mathias. I don't know whether it was his happy marriage or his years of looking into a microscope that gave him the idea that life's choices were clear and simple—black or white, right or wrong. That wasn't how my life had been. It was filled with shades of gray. There was no explaining to Mathias's rational mind my connection to Glen. But I tried, anyway.

"Mathias, Glen has always been fascinated by the religions of the East, and admires Tibet and the way its people have endured in spite of Chinese oppression. He's a beaten man. He'll never realize most of his dreams, and he'll never get here. Perhaps having a simple prayer wheel is his symbol of support."

I didn't expect Mathias to understand. But I wish he had been less impatient, less rigid in his opinions.

When we reached Lukla we stopped to eat at a small restaurant and struck up a conversation with one of the guests. He ran a travel office in town and told us that there had been no flights to Kathmandu for days due to the weather and poor runway conditions, and that there was a real battle among trekkers to get on the waiting list.

"I'm looking for a Dr. Mathias," he said, reaching into his pocket and coming out with a large envelope. "You see these tickets? They were left at my office by an agency guide on March 24, and I've been searching for this doctor ever since." What an amazing coincidence, I thought.

"I am Dr. Mathias Bauer," said Mathias, "and I think those are our tickets." So Ram hadn't used them after all. Now all we had to do was get a seat on the plane.

Overjoyed, we headed down the dirt pathway for the Royal Nepal Airlines office. The poverty and squalor that I had observed three weeks ago were still very much in evidence. Half-naked children running around. A woman sleeping in the doorway, her little boy picking lice from her hair. The child seemed strangely engrossed in the process. I didn't know if this was his duty, or he just found it fascinating. I tried to put it in perspective. But for me it was sad to see.

The airline office was a cubbyhole. As we stood in line we were filled in on the routine. A man arrived each morning with a list of passengers, and added the names of a few new people to assuage the anger of the crowd. Those who were put at the head of the list had paid the notorious *baksheesh*, unknown to the rest, who waited patiently in line. I spotted some of the people from the Minneapolis trek. They'd been waiting for three days, they said. We stood with them and finally, after an hour, made it onto the list. Reservation number 90 and 91. Would I *ever* get out of Lukla?

We left the travel office and walked toward the lodge on the other side of the runway, hoping to find a room for the night. Suddenly I stopped and drew in my breath, horrified. There, in the middle of the runway, was the body of a man, grossly bloated and covered with flies. He was lying spread-eagle on his back. People were walking by, paying no attention, as if he weren't there.

"Oh my God, what happened to that man? How long has he been there?" I cried, averting my eyes. "Somebody *do* something." I was no longer trying to understand. I had lost my cool.

Mathias looked around in disbelief. "Why don't they cover the body? Show a little respect for the dead…at least call the police.l" There was nobody to hear him.

"It's awful. No wonder the planes aren't running." My eyes filled. As damaged as he was, I could see that this was a young man. I would never forget the dark swollen face, the swarms of insects…

Just then I looked up to see Roger walking slowly toward us. I ran to meet him. "Roger, oh Roger, what's the meaning of this?" I sobbed, sick at heart.

46

WAITING

"There *is* no meaning," said Roger. "At least not from our point of view." He tried, awkwardly, to comfort me by reaching a large, mittened hand around my shoulder. "The only possible explanation is custom. I'm as horrified as you. But we have to wait for his family or for a Buddhist priest. Nobody dares cover him or touch him. It's against their religion."

"Is there no such thing as a sanitary code?" I asked.

"Meg, stop thinking like a Westerner. You're in Nepal. You have to respect their traditions."

"Letting a body rot in public is a tradition? Freezing at night and decomposing during the day? It's disgusting!" What happened to my resolution not to judge. I was out of control.

Roger went on. "In Nepal the local officials won't deal with a dead body. And in Lukla there are no police, no monasteries, and, of course, no monks. But what's *really* sad is that the man died at all. That's what makes *me* furious."

We must have seemed a curious, forlorn trio to the local residents, who carefully avoided us, going about their daily business without a sideways glance.

Roger told the chilling story. The young *Sherpa* had been hired by a group of Japanese tourists to take them to Kala Pattar. They refused to stop at the customary intervals for acclimatization, despite his constant warnings. The *Sherpa*—underdressed and carrying a heavy load—contracted pneumonia on the way, but his charges insisted that he continue without a rest.

"He begged to be relieved, but a contract is a contract," Roger said cynically. "After all, what's the life of a lowly *Sherpa* compared to setting a record for reaching Kala Pattar?"

By the time he had brought his party back to Lukla, the young man could hardly breathe and his cough had become more and more debilitating. He had a ticket on the plane, but was bumped to allow a western tourist to have his seat.

He pleaded, knowing he was desperately sick, and when the plane took off without him he just lay down and died…right there on the runway.

"This was like his last defiant gesture," said Roger angrily. "He's been lying there for three days. He might have been saved if he'd gotten to the hospital in Kathmandu."

"I'm here as a Christian missionary, not as an engineer," continued Roger, "and I'm beginning to conclude that it's the West that needs converting, not these humble, kind people. I think I'm learning more from them than they could ever learn from me."

We walked silently past the body to the recreation hall, a drab one-story building filled with waiting tourists, eager guides, and a smattering of British soldiers. People clustered around the bar or in wooden booths. Smoke swirled to the ceiling. The din was unbearable.

Mathias and I inquired about accommodations and were directed back across the runway to the Buddha Lodge, a ramshackle old house with two interconnecting bedrooms and a dining room. In order to get to our room we had to traipse through the bedroom of a couple sitting upright and stony-faced in bed, eyes closed.

"Sorry to intrude this way," I said, then stopped. Not a movement. They were meditating.

The outhouse in the back was new, and in my enthusiasm to be one of the "first" I sprinted around the corner of the lodge in the dark and headlong into an overhead timber that was dangling from the eaves. The blow just missed my eye. Now I had an angry goose egg on my forehead to counterbalance my swollen lips.

It was pitch black when we started for the recreation hall after dinner. Rain and fog had taken away the moonlight, and the runway was fast becoming a river of mud. We reached it and made a wide arc to avoid the body. In so doing I misjudged the height of the field and went sprawling face first in the mud, smacking my right arm on a jagged rock.

"What's going on, Meg?" asked Mathias. "One dead body in Lukla isn't enough?"

"Shhh…Mathias, look. Over there." In the light from the recreation hall I could see someone leaning over the body. As we watched, several men in long robes moved onto the field. They appeared to be wrapping the corpse. After a time they hoisted it onto their shoulders and headed slowly toward us. My head throbbed and my arm ached, but I stood mute. The entourage passed a few yards from us and headed into the darkness.

"I wonder where they're taking the poor fellow," said Mathias. "And I wonder where his family is. Do they know about him?"

We didn't have long to wait for the answers. Our host was full of the news. "How fortunate," he said, "that a group of monks is here. My friend, Tsering Phurba, is letting them use his house. They will tend the body until the family comes. Yes, it is most fortunate." He rubbed his hands together and smiled reverently.

The next morning my upper arm was extremely sore. Mathias kept teasing me about being accident prone, so I defiantly rolled up my sleeve to show him my bruises. There, imbedded in my flesh was a large tick, squirming in the middle of its swollen red chamber.

"Oh, Mathias, how revolting!" I cried. "What more can happen to me? I'm falling apart."

"Let's get over to the barracks," he said. "There must be an army doctor who can remove the tick. And I can give you my supply of penicillin, which you've been chiding me about for the last three weeks." I'd never had a tick bite before, so I was unaware of the possible complications.

As we approached the hall Roger and Lars were returning from the airfield, where they'd persuaded several *Sherpas* to help them repair the potholes in the runway. They'd rented tools and figured that in two days of hard work the planes could start flying again.

"Sometimes being a missionary means hard physical labor," Lars said. "The Nepalis are very casual about certain responsibilities—like getting people to and from their town. They don't see the connection between their wellbeing and keeping the tourists happy. You must put the spirit to work through the body, I tell them."

"Lars finds a sermon in everything," said Roger. "But he'll never make compulsive Swedes out of these folks. Already they've slowed *him* down to a crawl."

"What's the story on the young *Sherpa*?" I asked. "I thought there were no Buddhist priests or monks in town, but last night...."

"So you saw," he said. "I wondered what had happened to you."

"Actually, Meg fell onto the runway, and after she picked herself up we saw the monks carry the body away." said Mathias.

Roger filled in the story. In the early evening a group of monks came down from the mountains, having heard the rumor that the exiled Dalai-lama might be paying a visit to Nepal. They had walked for days from a monastery on the Tibetan border, and hoped to fly together to Kathmandu. Instead, they joined the throng of hikers stranded in the overcrowded village.

Just as we had seen, they wrapped the body in a makeshift shroud and took it to the home of a local resident. Once inside, they began the chanting and praying that would continue, unabated, for the next three days and nights.

"You don't need to tell us about that house," I told Roger. "It's about four doors from us. All night long the monks sang, chanted, and played strange musical instruments. I've never heard chanting like that. It had an almost supernatural quality."

"That's called cyclical breathing," said Roger. "It's amazing. Not only do they have the unusual ability to sing three notes at once, but the special kind of breathing makes the song sound continuous. It seems to have no beginning and no end."

"Mathias called it eerie," I said. "For me, it was soothing. It actually put me to sleep. If it hadn't been for the drums...."

"The drums didn't bother me," interrupted Mathias. "It was the weird instrument that sounded like a herd of yaks in heat."

"Oh, that's a horn made out of a human thigh bone," said Roger. "You'll see them at the cremation. The bone is hollow. At one end is an engraved silver cap and mouthpiece—like a clarinet—and at the other is a flared silver funnel—like a trumpet. The sound expands like nothing I've heard before. Penetrating. Melancholy. Very fitting for the occasion of a young man's death."

"Thigh bone? Good God!" said Mathias.

"The Tibetans are not at all averse to using certain parts of a dead body for instruments," explained Roger. "I've seen drums made out of two human skulls, joined crown to crown. The instrument is twirled, and a leather bead on a string beats out the rhythm on the surface of the skulls. There isn't the taboo about dead bodies that we find in the West. In fact, I'm fascinated by the sky burials that take place in the frozen areas of northern Tibet, where the bodies are ritually dismembered—presided over by a holy man—and flung off a cliff to the vultures. It seems a very sensible way to dispose of bodies in a climate where the ground is frozen. It also speaks for their belief that the soul is the essence of a person, not the earthly body. We Christians say we believe this, but the way we adorn our dead bodies....I often wonder."

"Well, someday I'm going to make it to Tibet, but that's not one of the sights I want to see," I said. "I also don't plan to be here for the cremation. I intend to be in Kathmandu the day after tomorrow. I'm getting worried about my family."

"Your family is fine," interjected Mathias. "Enjoy the peace of the mountains. Relax. What's the hurry?"

He turned to Roger and shrugged. "Meg is hopeless when it comes to relaxing. I tell her all the things we can do around here. All the places we can explore. It'll be wonderful!"

"Meg, Mathias is right. This is Nepal. There is no hurry for tomorrow."

Where had I heard *that* before? But relaxing was something I never did on command, and who was Mathias to tell me not to worry? And now Roger, with his unending philosophizing, was getting involved. I hadn't talked to Chris in over a month. Why was it so difficult for them to understand my nervousness at being stranded in Lukla? I knew Mathias was happy to be spending more time with me, but I was beginning to feel crowded. He wanted to plan *everything*—even telling me what I would enjoy and when. He was beginning to sound more like Glen every day.

In the afternoon the dead man's family arrived. Local police in Khunde had escorted them from a small town above Namche Bazar all the way to Lukla. They disappeared into the house and did not officially emerge until the morning of the third day. I caught a fleeting glimpse of them. Though they seemed sad, they didn't weep and wail as I'd expected. They maintained their dignity, perhaps out of respect for their dead relative.

Despite the milder weather we huddled every evening near a wood stove in the large kitchen of the recreation hall. There was always a group of Nepalese gathered around the fire to share bowls of *chang* and listen to the *dramyan*, a five-string Himalayan lute. I loved watching these people. They did everything with gusto. Singing, drinking, eating. And when they smiled, their whole face was transformed, their eyes closing as if in momentary rapture.

Nothing more was said about the body. It was taken for granted—a part of life in the mountains.

Every morning for the next three days we walked through the bedroom next to ours, where the young couple sat like zombies, transfixed. We speculated on the number of hours they spent in this position. We had yet to hear them speak, or see them ambulatory. They became our only source of comic relief during the long wait.

Every day by 7 A.M. we'd finished our porridge and were standing in line at the airline office to check on the status of "the list." The nights of drumming and chanting had left us in a constant state of somnambulism, which made the tedium of waiting more bearable. It began to look as if I'd be in Lukla for the funeral after all.

My arm was still red and swollen, but the army doctor who had examined it assured me that Mathias's penicillin would take care of the tick bite until we could get to the Canadian clinic in Kathmandu. I was glad he had brought a three-day supply.

In the afternoons Mathias and I roamed the hills outside the village, reveling in each new sign of awakening spring. Tender shoots—*primula*, bush honeysuckle, and *edelweiss*—poked their heads from under the dark layer of winter. Serrated outcroppings, their veins of quartz washed clean by melting snow, sparkled in the sun's rays. The lengthening days gave us time to climb and explore these manifold strata of rock and earth, which Mathias so lovingly explained. My anxiety about our delay was decreasing, and I was becoming more relaxed as my body mended from the rigors of the trek. Tensions eased. We were again lovers, companions, one with the all-encompassing beauty that surrounded us.

Dusk was heralded by the smell of wood smoke and cooking. Intense sunsets overflowed the valley, shutting down the village until dawn. And underlying it all, like a heavenly *mantra*, was the drumming and chanting of the monks.

The third day arrived, crisp and sunny. The mountains had shaken off their cloak of fog and stood individually carved against the horizon, as if ready to receive the spirit of the young *Sherpa*.

His family filed out of the house, followed by Buddhist monks and shaman priests in colorful robes. Together they bought wood and constructed a pyre such as the one I'd seen in Varanasi. They set up a tent next to the pyre. Inside they held a private ceremony.

Mathias and I waited at a distance.

The ceremony was conducted by the Buddhists and the Bon shamans. Bon is a sect of shaman, and was the major religion of Nepal 800 years ago, before Buddhism swept in from Tibet. It practiced divination and exorcism, allowed animal and human sacrifice, and, although supplanted by Buddhism, was still very much a part of the life and folklore of the people. One of the sources of Buddhist strength in Nepal has been its remarkable elasticity—its willingness to embrace many of the traditions and ceremonies of the old Bon shamanism, as it was doing this day.

The family was the first to leave the tent. I wondered if the old lady draped in black was the mother. She was probably not more than fifty, but already her body was frail and bent. Leaning forward and sobbing, she was held up and comforted by two young men, probably her sons. While the body was being burned the monks chanted from a book of scriptures. Several held bells in their hands and a lightning scepter that they shook to punctuate the chanting. Many of the onlookers gently whirled their copper prayer wheels. The low boom of drums rolled across the airfield, and the horns wailed. The drumming continued as the flames grew brighter.

We left quietly before it was over, and went to where the first plane from Kathmandu was landing, its grinding motors drowning out the last of the receding drums. A cheer went up from the crowd of waiting tourists. I looked back at the small group of mourners. The young *Sherpa*, like the dying flames, was gone.

47

A DIFFERENT PLACE

"How *could* you have given us such a terrible guide?" shouted Mathias, pounding the desk with his fist. All the rage he had felt toward Ram returned with a vengeance.

Pushkar sat behind his desk at Himalayan Excursions, pale and shaken as Mathias related our story. The ingratiating smile, which had seemed a permanent part of his face, disappeared.

"Ram and Dorje are both in the hospital," he said nervously. "They've been there for a week with AMS [Acute Mountain Sickness]. I had no idea they abandoned you. Ram said you chose to stay in the mountains alone. If what you say is true, Ram will never work in Nepal again."

"I don't believe any of it," Mathias said. "A guide with altitude sickness? Ridiculous! Ram is a liar and a thief…and so are you. I demand my money back!"

I touched Mathias's arm and gave him one of my mother's most compelling "high signs," hoping to lower the level of his fury. "I should ask for every penny of it, to make up for our mental suffering, but I'll only ask for one week." His voice softened. "It's not your fault about the three days in Lukla."

Pushkar seemed to relax a little. He looked at me beseechingly, perhaps hoping I'd intervene and save him. I lowered my eyes and said nothing.

"And this will be paid in dollars," Mathias continued, his voice rising once more. "None of your colored funny money this time. Your drunken friend tried to play tricks with that already."

I couldn't bear it. Where was the gentle Mathias I had fallen in love with?

Pushkar recoiled from the continuing barrage. Finally, he sighed heavily and reached into his desk drawer, lifting out a metal strong box. He pulled out a wad of dollar bills and slowly peeled off one hundred and fifty for Mathias and one hundred for me. Fortunately, Mathias was counting his money and didn't notice that I received less. I was worried that this would bring forth another outburst—if he knew that Pushkar's original "deal" with me had been better than his.

"I am sorry, Doctor," Pushkar said, his smile returning. "These things happen." He stood up and reached across the desk. Mathias reluctantly shook his hand.

After we left the office Mathias turned to me. "Why did you try to stop me? I was right. Everything I said was true, but I felt you weren't supporting me. I felt alone in my fight." His tone was angry, but controlled.

"Yes, you were right, Mathias, but I thought your attack on Pushkar was unnecessarily brutal. Couldn't you have been gentler, more reasonable? Did you have to crucify him? You were acting just like those Germans who pushed everybody around in the mountains. You remember how you hated their behavior?" I felt bad saying this, for I knew how sensitive he was about Germans. It would only make him feel worse. But he needed to know how I felt about his actions.

Mathias's whole body seemed to sag. He looked at me sadly. "Then there's no future for us. Is that what you're saying?"

I answered him, my own questions tumbling over his. "If I don't always agree with you…does that mean there's no future for us? If I think you treated someone badly in one instance does that mean that you will always do it? Is it possible for people to change their behavior? Is everything so simple, so cut and dried? If I'm honest and tell you what I don't like, does that mean that I don't like *you*?" I felt as if he wasn't even listening.

"I can't understand you, Meg. I don't see what I did wrong. That Pushkar is a devil and he deserved to be crucified. We could have died in those mountains—and you want me to be *nice*?" He spat out the words.

He was acting just like Glen. Overbearing, dictatorial. Was this what all men were like in a crisis? Or did I unconsciously attract this kind? I couldn't find the right words to express my revulsion, my disillusionment, and my surprise at the turn of events. We had awakened this morning happy and in love, and now I felt like fleeing, never seeing him again. I couldn't stand being spoken to sharply and I wasn't ready to change that. I had so looked forward to leaving Lukla and spending a few romantic days in Kathmandu with Mathias, but now everything was crumbling.

It had been wonderful to talk with Chris last night and hear him say, "Mom, keep writing and enjoying yourself." Evidently he liked the stories I'd sent so far. This made me feel good, because I felt as if I were in a fallow period. I hadn't realized what an enormous letdown it would be—coming from the excitement of the mountains to the confusion of Kathmandu. The newness and charm of Nepal were fading. I didn't want that to happen. If only I could get back to the rural beauty of Dhulikhel—alone—for relief from the noisy city. How I wanted to see B. P. and the gang at the Dhulikhel Lodge. I missed the simple meals, the sliver of moon at the top of the hill with its promise of Shiva, and the roosters—those maddening messengers of dawn. I even missed the out-of-tune band that played its heart out in the town square on Friday nights.

And now, damn it, in a moment of impulsiveness—of honesty—I had blown it with Mathias. Was it really my business what he said to Pushkar? After all, Pushkar *did* try to cheat us. I was so conflicted. I always seemed to be conflicted where men were concerned. I had trouble trusting my perceptions—my gut feelings. And I just wanted to be left alone when the going got tough.

We walked on. The silence was tense, uncomfortable.

Mathias spoke first. "Please don't pull away from me, Meg." It was as if he could read my mind. "This is all so new to me. You won't believe it, but I never had even one fight with my wife. Maybe that's not good. I'll admit I've had my way most of the time. But never before did I see my actions the way I do now...as you described them. And I think you're right. I have to find a better way to express anger. Will you give me another chance?"

I couldn't believe it! A man who listened to me and actually heard what I said. A man who admitted that he'd been wrong. I was right to be honest after all. "Hell, Mathias. I was angry, too. And pretty blunt. But I'm a great believer in chances. And a great believer in talking things out."

He turned and gleefully grabbed both my hands.

"Suppose we start by going to *Swayambunath*," he said. "You know, the monkey temple. If we hurry we'll get there before dusk. You might even find Glen a prayer wheel. Now, is that a change?"

I could have cried for joy! We walked hand-in-hand through the middle of town, over the river, and into the country. And all the time we talked. About everything: his family, mine, the war, the Nazis, dreams, plans. In no time we had walked the three miles to the foot of the 365 stone steps that led to the gold-domed temple.

As we started up the centuries-smoothed steps little gray monkeys scampered around us playing leapfrog, sliding down the railings, showing off just like kids. At first their begging was cute, but when added to that of the women and children, it soon dampened our spirits.

"Have you noticed how it's always women and little girls who do the begging, Meg?" asked Mathias. I nodded.

"Males are too important to waste on such things," I said. "It's the same in India. Makes me furious. And sad. I want to throttle the men."

We stopped to rest at the second landing. How could I be so out of shape after having just trekked to 18,000 feet? "This is Kala Pattar all over again," Mathias said, puffing.

I looked up. How far away the temple seemed. All I could see was its golden spire and a pair of curious painted eyes staring down at me from the top of the *stupa*. Prayer flags fluttered from long strings, which fanned out like ribbons on a giant Maypole. A rotund Buddha—each one representing a different aspect of the Buddha—greeted us at every level. And spurred us on.

Swayambunath Temple, Kathmandu.

We reached the top and found ourselves in a spacious stone courtyard—a temple complex inhabited by monks of every shape and age. Some were making a *kora,* walking around the grounds clockwise. Some sat in clusters playing a game with coins. Some knelt in prayer, chanting softly. And some hawked trinkets and crafts to the passersby. We stood by a stone railing, looking down. Below us lay the Kathmandu valley—patchwork farms, modest temples, crooked streets—a miniature etched in the shadow and light of the late afternoon sun. It had been worth the climb.

Four shrines, connected by a line of prayer wheels, stood at the base of the main *stupa.* Every time a monk walked by he'd give the wheels a spin, like a kid clicking a stick along an iron fence. How different these colorful wheels were from the faded wooden drums in the Thyangboche monastery, or the water-driven barrels that hummed beside a mountain hut along the trail.

A large replica of *Ganesh* the elephant god, painted bright orange, stood at the entrance to the temple. This was only one of the many Hindu gods that adorned the courtyard, a testimony to the harmonious blending of the Hindu and Buddhist religions in Nepal. Inside was the usual plethora of dishes containing water, food, and small candles. The decorations were simple, executed in bright primary colors.

Mathias spent most of his time photographing the mischievous antics of a family of monkeys, whose mother was trying to round them up before settling down for the night. Finally, they all fell asleep sitting up, holding onto each other like a monkey train, heads resting on the shoulder of the monkey in front of them.

I watched for a while, then wandered from table to craft-laden table, until I found the perfect prayer wheel for Glen. By then the sun was hanging at the edge of the horizon, an orange globe that turned the dome of the *gompa* a luminous golden-red.

It was dark when we mounted the marble steps of our hotel, the Vajra, with its luxuriantly carved wooden interior and individual balconies looking out at the mountains. We were both exhilarated by the afternoon's walk and by our intense conversation after the blow-up at Pushkar's. Mathias was certain that our differences were reconcilable. I was not as optimistic. In spite of his promise to go slowly, he had already begun to pressure me anew. It was as if the imminence of my departure had triggered a kind of panic. No amount of reassuring from me helped.

"If you love me, you will come visit. You will not hesitate," he insisted. He wanted to know, immediately, when we'd meet again and how soon I could come to Austria…or he to the United States. Unpleasant feelings began to well up in me. Feelings about being pushed and dominated and suffocated.

"Let me catch my breath, Mathias," I pleaded. "You're in a different place from me. I can't make any big decisions now, so please stop asking me to. You're pushing too hard."

"When you want something bad enough, you push—or you don't get it," was his answer.

"Not always," I countered. "Sometimes you only manage to push away what you want the most."

His mood changed abruptly. He became despondent, which made me feel guilty. Was I unsympathetic…too hard on him?

I reached over and gently touched his face. "Oh, Mathias. If only you would let things develop naturally."

Early the next morning I went to the American Express Office. It was an hour before opening, but the line was already long. I stood there, enjoying the warm weather, looking at the mix of nationalities, and trying to ignore the fumes spewed forth by the old buses and broken-down vehicles that drove inches from the curb where I was standing. I concentrated on just being in the present—something I'd always had trouble doing. I thought about the affirmation I'd made so often before the trip, and chuckled to myself as I repeated it several times: "I, Meg Peterson, am looking forward to an exciting trip and a new life. I accept and do not fear the unknown. I am optimistic about the future."

For the most part it had been true. My life had certainly changed, as had my attitudes these past four months in Africa and Asia, and I was optimistic about what lay ahead. But the "unknown" part still gave me trouble. It was much easier to face a new culture and the unknown customs of a foreign land than walk into the unknown recesses of my inner world and change some of the old patterns that ruled my personal life—namely, the ones that hadn't worked. My unconscious subservience to men; trying to please; putting my own needs last; and being unrealistic in the face of disaster. But I was finding, even as I became more involved with Mathias, that a familiar rut is sometimes more comfortable than the risk of a journey into the unknown. And that worried me.

I handed the man at the desk my card and he gave me a pile of letters that had arrived during the trek. The one on top was from Glen. Enclosed was a letter he'd sent to his old friend, Leon Weill, the ambassador to Nepal, asking him to give me the royal treatment when I came through town. He wrote that I was a "remarkable woman," even though he couldn't live with me, and that he always encouraged me in all my endeavors, the latest one being a round-the-world backpacking trip. He went on to tell my life story in three paragraphs, and asked the ambassador to give me whatever advice and assistance I might need. He suggested that I get in touch with the embassy, immediately, upon my arrival in Nepal.

I don't think Glen realized how patronizing and embarrassing the letter was. As in our life together, he couldn't resist the urge to point out what was best for me. He ended his letter by asking me to pick up a small prayer wheel for him. "There are times in my life when I'd like to have one and give it a spin," he said.

I felt a sadness when I finished the letter. Glen wanted so much to be a part of my experience, to help run my life. But I had no more emotional energy left for him.

Leon Weill's answer was in the pile. The letter was cordial, but informed me that Ambassador Weill would be leaving his post on January 25, almost two months before my arrival.

When I returned to the hotel Mathias had begun the task of washing all our dirty clothes by hand. We made a game of it, seeing who could come up with the blackest water. It was a tie. The room looked like a laundry by the time we took off for dinner at K.C.'s, the western tourist's favorite hangout in Thamel. I agreed to go so Mathias could have his favorite dish—pan pizza. I settled for vegetarian lasagna, an interesting combination of East and West.

Late into the night we listened to my tapes of the trip—the singing of Putti, Tenza, and Passang, and the sound of all of us struggling up Kala Pattar, gasping for air. Now that my tick bite had almost healed and my lips were once again kissable, it was hard to remember how miserable I'd been such a short time ago.

On the day before my departure we went for one last look around Kathmandu. It was early morning, but the market was in full swing. Women peered out of second story windows, their elbows resting on the carved window frames. Flute sellers strutted about playing wild tunes on their bamboo flutes and pestering us to buy. They carried a long pole over their shoulder with dozens of the slender instruments tied in a bundle at the top, sticking out at every angle like a bunch of thick porcupine quills. I never saw this anywhere but in Nepal.

The narrow streets were jammed. Bicycle rickshaws wove in and out and cars came careening around corners. People scattered good-naturedly like balls of mercury, to flow together after the danger passed. Curd sellers squatted on the pavement next to earthenware bowls full of the white, creamy substance. Boxes of spices, bags of rice, and baskets of fruits and vegetables overflowed onto the ground. And, as always, there were the ubiquitous piles of garbage that we had learned to step around—garbage that would be shoveled into open trucks at dawn once a week.

Flute sellers in the Kathmandu market.

I stopped at a candle-lit alcove next to a wall in which hundreds of nails had been hammered by people suffering from toothaches. If no relief was forthcoming, there just happened to be a dentist's office nearby, advertised discreetly near the wall.

Everywhere were small elephant shrines, with children placing garlands of fresh flowers on them or plucking the blooms and putting them in their hair. I watched a believer take a pinch of orange powder between her fingers and smear it on her forehead. Like Varanasi, many rituals were going on simultaneously, each group functioning independently, in its own little world.

As we walked out of town we saw men and women performing morning ablutions by the side of the road. Little children were defecating in the gutter, their tiny bottoms turned toward the street, a thin yellow ribbon of excrement curling on the ground behind them.

I shuddered every time someone passed close to me, if he was coughing, spitting, or blowing his nose with his fingers. I never knew what might hit me.

"Haven't you gotten used to the sounds by now, Meg?" Mathias asked jovially.

"The sounds, yes, but the actual act, no." How I wished someone would introduce Kleenex into Nepal!

In the afternoon we went to make our airline reservations. I could tell that Mathias was trying to give me space, but he wasn't succeeding.

"Why can't we leave for Bangkok on the same day?" he asked for the third time. "Why must you go a day earlier? What's one day in a year's journey?"

"I'll see what's available," I said as I was called to the agent's desk.

Why did it irritate me the way Mathias sat—with his arms folded imperiously across his chest—as if judging me, telling me what I should do? Suddenly I knew I had to get out of this place, get away from Mathias. I was losing my momentum.

"I'll take one ticket for tomorrow's flight to Bangkok," I said without hesitation.

"Yes, Madam. Your flight leaves at noon. Will that be all?"

Mathias said nothing about my decision. He left the next morning to work in Patan.

As I was leaving our room I turned back and, impulsively, scribbled a note and placed it on his pillow.

Dear Big-Footed Abominable Snowman,

My capricious heart almost persuaded me to change my flight, but my logical mind won out. I know if I don't leave now I may never. Last night was wonderful. I shall treasure it always. With abiding love,

Your crazy Meg.

Then I grabbed a cab and headed out of town.

Sitting in the airport I was filled with the excitement of a new adventure. But I couldn't help thinking of all the things I hadn't done in Nepal, the many places I hadn't seen. I knew I'd come back soon. I had to. I'd roam around ancient Bhaktapur and visit its temples. I'd stand silently at the cremations on the bank of the sacred Bagmati River that flows through the heart of Kathmandu. I'd gaze on the renowned Buddhist *stupa* at Bodhnath, with its four pairs of eyes looking at the four corners of the world. And, finally, I'd trek to Annapurna, walking all the way from the tropical valley to the cold, snowy slopes.

And who knows, Mathias just might go with me. Suddenly, I missed him with all my heart.

EPILOGUE

The final four months of my journey started on April first when I arrived in Bangkok. I stepped off the plane and was blasted by a heat wave reminiscent of New Jersey in July. Relief was nowhere to be found, even in the darkest recesses of the elaborate Thai temples. Hoping to escape the sweltering city, I took a bus to Chiang Mai in northern Thailand, where I found even more heat in the sweltering jungle. For $57 I purchased a four-day wilderness trip from a small trekking company in the middle of town. At last I'd get to walk through the jungle, luxuriate in its many hot springs, ride on an elephant, and visit the opium-smoking *Akha* and *Karen* hill tribes. But I had no idea how primitive the conditions were in both tribal communities. We lived in thatched huts and slept on grass mats. Toilet facilities were non-existent.

Akha hill tribe village at dawn.

Top picture: Rafting in northern Thailand.
Bottom picture: Thai children watching the building of the rafts.

On the last day, after watching two handmade bamboo rafts sink to the bottom of the river, our party of four bravely piled into a third. We'd finally found a way to beat the heat! While two of us stood with long heavy poles and maneuvered the feeble craft around rocks and waterfalls, the other two enjoyed being drenched every time we'd shoot a rapid. Despite our efforts, however, the raft was totally destroyed by the end of the run. Luckily we survived, but not without several unexpected dunkings in the river.

I stayed in Chiang Mai during the spring water festival of *Songkran*, which celebrates the beginning of the lunar year. The custom encourages everybody to throw water on everybody else, after which the "victim's" face gets smeared with a white flour paste, a symbol of cleansing for the coming year. This happened to me many times and was a surefire way of getting acquainted. It was accompanied by a great deal of hugging and laughter. And since the weather was hot, nobody walked around wet for very long.

Four letters from Mathias were waiting for me when I arrived in Hong Kong. I called him, immediately, and the feeling of love and longing that I had felt at the Kathmandu airport came flooding back. It was as if we had never parted. I thought of him constantly as I toured China, which was just opening up twenty years after the Cultural Revolution and two years before the Tiananmen Square massacre. And I wrote him almost every day—long letters filled with my impressions of this sometimes sad, struggling, enigmatic country. What struck me about China was the sheer number of people. Near the Forbidden City in Beijing hundreds of bicycles moved down the road like a Roman phalanx. And in the countryside rice farmers still used water buffalo to pull handmade wooden cultivators in picture book pastoral settings. It was a time when a walk on the Great Wall or a boat ride down the Li River from Guilin were relatively free of tourists. Frequently a husband and wife would come up to me holding their baby, and ask me to take a family picture. You could see the pride they took in this treasured offspring, but, according to my guide, there was lots of grumbling about the one family/one child rule.

"One child will often be very spoiled," he said. "I hope when my son grows up he can have more than one."

During the next three months I continued to hear from Mathias. His letters became more passionate and more urgent. I wrote and phoned as much as I could. But no matter how often I communicated, it was never quite enough for him. He was in Austria thinking about me, expecting me to write every day, and I was on the road, eager to experience each new place to the fullest. I tried to explain this, but it only made him feel unimportant and neglected.

In Australia and New Zealand I got my fill of hitchhiking, although traffic along the coast was meager. Hostelling and trekking are favorite activities Down Under, and make it an hospitable, inexpensive haven for backpackers. I explored North Island with two New Zealanders I'd met in China, and spent two weeks at a sheep farm on South Island, acting as a shed hand for a rancher I'd met on the Wellington-Picton ferry. I was treated like a member of the family, and participated in the daily chores, which included sheep shearing, a skill that required great strength and a lot of fast action on the part of the hired hands. Visiting New Zealand was like entering a time warp. The pace of life, the manners, and the family cohesiveness reminded me of the United States in the 1950's.

Just before leaving Australia I stayed for several days at a charming convent in Sydney, while teaching Autoharp workshops for music teachers in the surrounding area. At the airport, moments before I was to board my plane for two weeks of snorkeling in Cairns on the Great Barrier Reef, I felt compelled to call my daughter, Martha. I had just spoken to her the night before, but suddenly I had the feeling that something was very wrong.

When I reached her she cried, "Oh, thank God you called. Cary and I have been concentrating on you all morning. We've been repeating over and over, 'Mother call home, Mother call home.' And you got the message."

"Yes, I got the message. Now I'm *really* scared."

"Oh, Mom, Dad has prostate cancer and must be operated on tomorrow. He may not live a week, the doctor said. We think you ought to come home."

"Martha, why wasn't I told?" I asked. "You talked to me last night."

"He didn't want you to know." By now she was sobbing. "He said it would ruin your trip. Cary's flying to New Jersey, today, to be with him."

Very much shaken up, I went to the gate and asked the airline representative to change my ticket. As I related my story, I, too, began to cry. I was divorced, yes, but there was no way I could erase thirty-three years of marriage and five children with a piece of paper. I had to get home.

Glen lived for two more pain-filled years and died at the age of sixty-seven. In his hand was the prayer wheel I had bought for him at Swyambunath temple in Kathmandu.

◆   ◆   ◆

Returning to the United States after such a long absence was wonderful and shattering. Wonderful to see my family, again. Wonderful to hold my first grandchild. Wonderful to return to the comfortable New Hampshire mountains of my childhood. But for the first weeks I felt as if I'd suddenly been thrown into overdrive, and no matter how much I put on the brakes I couldn't throttle down. I didn't want to get back into the old rat race, but I was bucking the odds. Computers, electronic communication, and the ever more invasive data banks frightened me. In just eight short months my typewriter had become obsolete. And I was computer-illiterate. I was overwhelmed by a glut of information. I walked around New York City in a daze. There were no more people than in India, certainly, but everyone was walking faster. Busyness was in the air like a fast-flowing river, and I knew I'd better start paddling or I'd be swept away by the current. It was all I could do to keep my head above water. I walked up Eighth Avenue past pawnshops, strip joints, and souvenir stores. The faces were as varied as in any Third World country. I reached into my pocket, finding a wad of toilet paper I'd automatically stuffed there in case of emergency. But I no longer needed to be self-sufficient in the same way. My survival kit was obsolete. Take heart, Meg. This is the United States of America. You'll get used to it.

It's been eighteen years since I completed this first round-the-world journey, and nine years ago I embarked on a similar adventure, this time traveling to Tibet, southern Thailand, Laos, Cambodia, Vietnam, Malaysia, Singapore, and Indonesia. I ended the eight-month trip by revisiting Australia, New Zealand, and Tasmania. Unfortunately, I had to cancel Papua/New Guinea because of political unrest, and Fiji because of hurricanes.

As I'd promised myself, I returned to Nepal and explored all the places I missed the first time. And for thirty glorious and strenuous days I trekked to Mt. Kangchenjunga base camp in eastern Nepal, the territory of the legendary snow leopard. I also spent time in Dhulikhel with B.P. Shresta, who had, indeed, become the mayor and transformed the little town. It now had a modern municipal building, a splendid hospital, and a first rate university. And, yes, this time he let me hug him goodbye. Things had *really* changed in Nepal!

Six years ago I returned, once more, and completed the Annapurna circuit, climbing over the Thorong la Pass (17,650 ft) to base camp. But Mathias did not go with me on these adventures. We had visited each other and corresponded for two years after the trek to Everest Base Camp. His letters were intense and beautiful. After awhile I began to think it was his letters I was in love with, not him. I needed more time to sort out my divorce and Glen's death, and Mathias wasn't willing to give me that time. The pressure from the beginning had been a warning signal. In the end, we recognized that our differences—geographically and emotionally—were just too great. But nothing can take away those perfect days we spent together in the Himalayas.

◆   ◆   ◆

What have I learned from these journeys into Africa and Asia, and what keeps calling me back? I've always been fascinated with cultures completely different from my own. I'm also driven to find new challenges that make me stretch. Risk is a factor as well. Not the risk of bodily danger, but the risk of approaching an unknown place, an alien experience. That, too, is part of the stretch.

And I exult in paring life down to the essentials and then paring it down some more.

I've learned that I'm never alone, even on a high mountain pass. I carry with me my loved ones, my friends, my past memories, and my dreams. And, of course, I come to terms with my limitations. I'm grateful for the freedom to travel—a luxury that many cannot afford, even on a simple scale—and the good health that carries me through the most difficult days.

My travels have strengthened my belief in the essential goodness and compassion of individuals. And I am convinced more than ever that the differences between peoples are greatly overshadowed by their similarities. This is what I've learned. This is why I keep going back.

POSTSCRIPT

There remain many places in Asia that I envision exploring. Four years ago, however, I found myself floundering as a result of the death of my eldest son, Christopher, who, after years of suffering, lost his battle with AIDS. You may remember that he became my connection with home during my journey. Chris, himself, traveled extensively. He visited more than twenty countries, and especially loved the islands of the pacific, Virgin Gorda, and the Galapagos. In fact, he so loved the Galapagos that he treated his entire extended family to a week of exploration in the protected sanctuary of these unique islands.

In 1996, on my second world trip, I met up with Chris in Australia and we flew by helicopter to Heron Island on the Great Barrier Reef to snorkel and, as he put it, "enjoy a little luxury before you die." (He was never fond of my "fly-by-the-seat-of-the-pants" mode of travel.) Four months before he died, he left the hospital and insisted on making one final trip to Paris.

The death of a child, one with whom I had such rapport and who brought so much joy into my life, is devastating. But Christopher was the sort of person—upbeat, funny, creative, adventurous—who would be disappointed in a mother who spent the rest of her life in mourning. During his illness I worried about being away in case there was an emergency, but Chris urged me to go. "Mom, as I see it you can stay home and feel sorry for yourself because your son is sick and might die, or you can go out and live your life. It's your choice. Be my guest...."

Last spring I returned to Tibet with my eldest daughter, Cary, and we circled sacred Mt. Kailash together, pausing at the Drölma La at 18,000 ft. to remember Chris. He who never blanched when faced with a challenge, no matter how difficult the odds or how high the stakes. He who climbed out of the abyss and reached a different plane, where his spirit can soar and where the view is infinite. The memory of his love and his life kept me warm and helped *me* soar as I climbed along the Roof of the World.

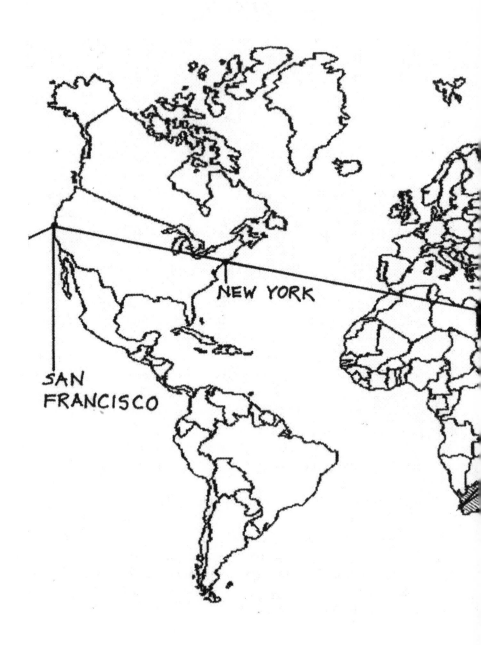

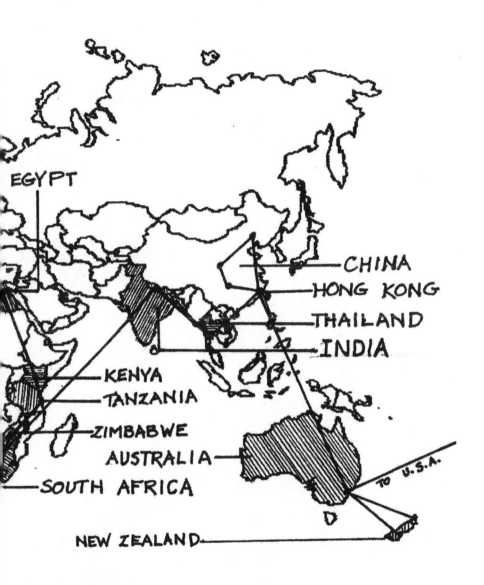

978-0-595-34601-1
0-595-34601-4

CPSIA information can be obtained
at www.ICGtesting.com
Printed in the USA
FSHW021214141019
63000FS